The Story of Julia

Kathleen Thompson Norris

Alpha Editions

This edition published in 2024

ISBN : 9789362924261

Design and Setting By
Alpha Editions
www.alphaedis.com
Email - info@alphaedis.com

As per information held with us this book is in Public Domain.
This book is a reproduction of an important historical work. Alpha Editions uses the best technology to reproduce historical work in the same manner it was first published to preserve its original nature. Any marks or number seen are left intentionally to preserve its true form.

Contents

PART I .... - 1 -

CHAPTER I .... - 3 -

CHAPTER II .... - 27 -

CHAPTER III .... - 47 -

CHAPTER IV .... - 61 -

CHAPTER V .... - 78 -

CHAPTER VI .... - 94 -

CHAPTER VII .... - 125 -

CHAPTER VIII .... - 137 -

PART TWO .... - 163 -

CHAPTER I .... - 165 -

CHAPTER II .... - 184 -

CHAPTER III .... - 197 -

CHAPTER IV .... - 211 -

CHAPTER V .... - 235 -

CHAPTER VI .... - 246 -

CHAPTER VII .... - 254 -

CHAPTER VIII .... - 284 -

CHAPTER IX .... - 317 -

PART I

CHAPTER I

To Emeline, wife of George Page, there came slowly, in her thirtieth year, a sullen conviction that life was monstrously unfair. From a resentful realization that she was not happy in her marriage, Emeline's mind went back to the days of her pert, precocious childhood and her restless and discontented girlhood, and she felt, with a sort of smouldering fury, that she had never been happy, had never had a fair chance, at all!

It took Mrs. Page some years to come to this conclusion, for, if she was shrewd and sharp among the women she knew, she was, in essential things, an unintelligent woman, and mental effort of any sort was strange to her. Throughout her entire life, her mind had never been truly awakened. She had scrambled through Grammar School, and had followed it with five years as saleswoman in a millinery store, in that district of San Francisco known as the Mission, marrying George Page at twenty-three, and up to that time well enough pleased with herself and her life.

But that was eight years ago. Now Emeline could see that she had reached—more, she had passed—her prime. She began to see that the moods of those early years, however violent and changing, had been fed upon secret springs of hope, hope vague and baseless enough, but strong to colour a girl's life with all the brightness of a thousand dawns. There had been rare potentialities in those days, anything might happen, something *would* happen. The little Emeline Cox, moving between the dreary discomfort of home and the hated routine of school, might surprise all these dull seniors and school-mates some day! She might become an actress, she might become a great singer, she might make a brilliant marriage.

As she grew older and grew prettier, these vague, bright dreams strengthened. Emeline's mother was an overworked and shrill-voiced woman, whose personality drove from the Shotwell Street house whatever small comfort poverty and overcrowding and dirt left in it. She had no personal message for Emeline. The older woman had never learned the care of herself, her children, her husband, or her house. She had naturally nothing to teach her daughter. Emeline's father occasionally thundered a furious warning to his daughters as to certain primitive moral laws. He did not tell Emeline and her sisters why they might some day consent to abandon the path of virtue, nor when, nor how. He never dreamed of winning their affection and confidence, or of selecting their friends, and making home a place to which these friends might occasionally come. But he was fond of shouting, when Emeline, May, or Stella pinned on their flimsy little hats for an evening walk, that if ever a girl of his made a fool of herself and got into trouble, she need never come near his door again! Perhaps Emeline and May and Stella felt that the virtuous course, as exemplified by their parents, was not all of roses, either, but they never said so, and always shuddered dutifully at the paternal warning.

School also failed with the education of the inner Emeline, although she moved successfully from a process known as "diagramming" sentences to a serious literary analysis of "Snow-Bound" and "Evangeline," and passed terrifying examinations in ancient history, geography, and advanced problems in arithmetic. By the time she left school she was a tall, giggling, black-eyed creature, to be found walking up and down Mission Street, and gossiping and chewing gum on almost any sunny afternoon. Between her mother's whining and her father's bullying, home life was not very pleasant, but at least there was nothing unusual in the situation; among all the girls that Emeline knew there was not one who could go back to a clean room, a hospitable dining-room, a well-cooked and nourishing meal. All her friends did as she did: wheedled money for new veils and new shoes from their fathers, helped their mothers reluctantly and scornfully when they must, slipped away to the street as often as possible, and when they were at home, added their complaints and protests to the general unpleasantness.

Had there been anything different before her eyes, who knows what plans for domestic reform might have taken shape in the girl's plastic brain? Emeline had never seen one example of real affection and cooperation between mother and daughters, of work quickly and skilfully done and forgotten, of a clean bright house and a blossoming garden; she had never heard a theory otherwise than that she was poor, her friends were poor, her parents were poor, and that born under the wheels of a monstrous social injustice, she might just as well be dirty and discouraged and discontented at once and have done with it, for in the end she must be so. Why should she question the abiding belief? Emeline knew that, with her father's good pay and the excellent salaries earned by her hard-handed, patient-eyed, stupid young brothers, the family income ran well up toward three hundred dollars a month: her father worked steadily at five dollars a day, George was a roofer's assistant and earned eighty dollars a month, and Chester worked in a plumber's shop, and at eighteen was paid sixty-five dollars. Emeline could only conclude that three hundred dollars a month was insufficient to prevent dirt, crowding, scolding, miserable meals, and an incessant atmosphere of warm soapsuds.

Presently she outraged her father by going into "Delphine's" millinery store. Delphine was really a stout, bleached woman named Lizzie Clarke, whose reputation was not quite good, although nobody knew anything definite against her. She had a double store on Market Street near Eleventh, a dreary place, with dusty models in the windows, torn Nottingham curtains draped behind them, and "Delphine" scrawled in gold across the dusty windows in front. Emeline used to wonder, in the days when she and her giggling associates passed "Delphine's" window, who ever bought the dreadful hats in the left-hand window, although they admitted a certain attraction on the right. Here would be a sign: "Any Hat in this Window, Two Dollars," surrounded by cheap, dust-grained felts, gaudily trimmed, or coarse straws wreathed with cotton flowers. Once or twice Emeline and her friends went in, and one day when a card in the window informed the passers-by that an experienced saleslady was wanted, the girl, sick of the situation at home and longing for novelty, boldly applied for the position. Miss Clarke engaged her at once.

Emeline met, as she had expected, a storm at home, but she weathered it, and kept her position. It was hard work, and poorly paid, but the girl's dreams gilded everything, and she loved the excitement of making sales, came eagerly to the gossip and joking of her fellow-workers every morning, and really felt herself to be in the current of life at last.

Miss Clarke was no better than her reputation, and would have willingly helped her young saleswoman into a different sort of life. But Emeline's little streak of shrewd selfishness saved her. Emeline indulged in a hundred little coarsenesses and indiscretions, but take the final step toward ruin she would not. Nobody was going to get the better of her, she boasted. She used rouge and lip red. She "met fellers" under flaming gas jets, and went to dance halls with them, and to the Sunday picnics that were her father's especial abomination; she shyly told vile stories and timidly used strong words, but there it ended. Perhaps some tattered remnant of the golden dream still hung before her eyes; perhaps she still clung to the hope of a dim, wonderful time to come.

More than that, the boys she knew were not a vicious lot; the Jimmies and Johnnies, the Dans and Eds, were for the most part neighbours, no more anxious to antagonize Emeline's father than she was. They might kiss her good-night at her door, they might deliberately try to get the girls to miss the last train home from the picnic, but their spirit was of idle mischief rather than malice, and a stinging slap from Emeline's hand afforded them, as it did her, a certain shamed satisfaction.

George Page came into "Delphine's" on a windy summer afternoon when Emeline had been there for nearly five years. He was a salesman for some lines of tailored hats, a San Franciscan, but employed by a New York wholesale house. Emeline chanced to be alone in the place, for Miss Clarke was sick in bed, and the other saleswoman away on her vacation. The trimmers, glancing out through a plush curtain at the rear, saw Miss Cox and the "drummer" absorbed in a three hours' conversation. From two to five o'clock they talked; the drummer watching her in obvious admiration when an occasional customer interrupted, and when Miss Cox went home the drummer escorted her. Emeline had left the parental roof some two years before; she was rooming, now, with a mild and virtuous girl named Regina Lynch, in Howard Street. Regina was the sort of girl frequently selected by a girl of Emeline's type for confidante and companion: timid, conventional, always ready to laugh and admire. Regina consented to go to dinner with Emeline and Mr. Page, and as she later refused to go to the theatre, Emeline would not go either; they all walked out Market Street from the restaurant, and reached the Howard Street house at about nine o'clock. Regina went straight upstairs, but Emeline and George Page sat on the steps an hour longer, under the bright summer moon, and when Emeline went upstairs she woke her roommate up, and announced her engagement.

George came into the store at nine o'clock the next morning, to radiantly confirm all that they had said the night before, and with great simplicity the two began to plan for their future; from that time they had breakfast, lunch, and dinner together every day; they were both utterly satisfied; they never questioned their fate. In October George had to go to San Diego, and a dozen little cities en route, for the firm, and Emeline went, too. They were married in the little church of Saint Charles in Eighteenth Street, only an hour or two before they started for San Jose, the first stop in George's itinerary. Emeline's mother and sisters came to her wedding, but the men of the family were working on this week-day afternoon. The bride looked excited and happy, colour burned scarlet in her cheeks, under her outrageous hat; she wore a brown travelling gown, and the lemon-coloured gloves that were popular in that day. Emeline felt that she was leaving everything unpleasant in life behind her. George was the husband of her dreams—or perhaps her dreams had temporarily adapted themselves to George.

But, indeed, he was an exceptionally good fellow. He was handsome, big, dashingly dressed. He was steady and successful in his work, domestic in his tastes, and tenderly—and perhaps to-day a little pityingly—devoted to this pretty, clever girl who loved him so, and had such faith in him. His life had kept him a good deal among men, and rather coarse men; he had had to do more drinking than he cared to do, to play a good deal of poker, to listen to a good deal of loose talk. Now, George felt a great relief that this was over; he wanted a home, a wife, children.

The bride and groom had a cloudless three weeks of honeymoon among a score of little Southern towns—and were scarcely less happy during the first months of settling down. Emeline was entirely ignorant of what was suitable or desirable in a home, and George had only the crude ideals of a travelling man to guide him. They enthusiastically selected a flat of four handsome, large, dark rooms, over a corner saloon, on O'Farrell Street. The building was new, the neighbourhood well built, and filled with stirring, interesting life. George said it was conveniently near the restaurant and theatre district, and to Emeline, after Mission Street, it seemed the very hub of the world. The suite consisted of a large front drawing-room, connected by enormous folding doors with a rear drawing-room, which the Pages would use as a bedroom, a large dining-room, and a dark kitchen, equipped with range and "water back." There were several enormous closets, and the stairs and hall, used by the several tenants of the house, were carpeted richly. The Pages also carpeted their own rooms, hung the stiff folds of Nottingham lace curtains at the high narrow windows, and selected a set of the heavily upholstered furniture of the period for their drawing-room. When Emeline's mother and sisters came to call, Emeline showed them her gold-framed pictures, her curly-maple bed and bureau, her glass closet in the dining-room, with its curved glass front and sides and its shining contents—berry saucers and almond dishes in pressed glass, and other luxuries to which the late Miss Cox had been entirely a stranger. Emeline was intoxicated with the freedom and the pleasures of her new life; George was out of town two or three nights a week, but when he was at home the two slept late of mornings, and loitered over their breakfast, Emeline in a loose wrapper, filling and refilling her coffee cup, while George rattled the paper and filled the room with the odour of cigarettes.

Then Emeline was left to put her house in order, and dress herself for the day—her corsets laced tight at the waist, her black hair crimped elaborately above her bang, her pleated skirts draped fashionably over her bustle. George would come back at one o'clock to take her to lunch, and after lunch they wandered up and down Kearney and Market streets, laughing and chatting, glad just to be alive and together. Sometimes they dined downtown, too, and afterward went to the "Tivoli" or "Morosco's," or even the Baldwin Theatre, and sometimes bought and carried home the materials for a dinner, and invited a few of George's men friends to enjoy it with them. These were happy times; Emeline, flushed and pretty in her improvised apron, queened it over the three or four adoring males, and wondered why other women fussed so long over cooking, when men so obviously enjoyed a steak, baked potatoes, canned vegetables, and a pie from Swain's. After dinner the men always played poker, a mild little game at first, with Emeline eagerly guarding a little pile of chips, and gasping over every hand like a happy child; but later more seriously, when Emeline, contrary to poker superstition, sat on the arm of her husband's chair, to bring him luck.

Luck she certainly seemed to bring him; the Pages would go yawning to bed, after one of these evenings, chuckling over the various hands.

"I couldn't see what you drew, George," Emeline would say, "but I could see that Mack had aces on the roof, and it made me crazy to have you go on raising that way! And then your three fish hooks!"

George would shout with pride at her use of poker terms—would laugh all the harder if she used them incorrectly. And sometimes, sinking luxuriously into the depths of the curly-maple bed, Emeline would think herself the luckiest woman in the world. No hurry about getting up in the morning; no one to please but herself; pretty gowns and an adoring husband and a home beyond her maddest hopes—the girl's dreams no longer followed her, happy reality had blotted out the dream.

She felt a little injured, a little frightened, when the day came on which she must tell George of some pretty well-founded suspicions of her own condition. George might be "mad," or he might laugh.

But George was wonderfully soothing and reassuring; more, was pathetically glad and proud. He petted Emeline into a sort of reluctant joy, and the attitude of her mother and sisters and the few women she knew was likewise flattering. Important, self-absorbed, she waited her appointed days, and in the early winter a wizened, mottled little daughter was born. Julia was the name Emeline had chosen for a girl, and Julia was the name duly given her by the radiant and ecstatic George in the very first hour of her life. Emeline had lost interest in the name—indeed, in the child and her father as well—just then; racked, bewildered, wholly spent, she lay back in the curly-maple bed, the first little seed of that general resentment against life that was eventually to envelop her, forming in her mind.

They had told her that because of this or that she would not have a "hard time," and she had had a very hard time. They had told her that she would forget the cruel pain the instant it was over, and she knew she never would forget it. It made her shudder weakly to think of all the babies in the world—of the schools packed with children—at what a cost!

Emeline recovered quickly, and shut her resentment into her own breast. Julie, as she was always called, was a cross baby, and nowadays the two front rooms were usually draped with her damp undergarments, and odorous of sour bottles and drying clothes. For the few months that Emeline nursed the child she wandered about until late in the day in a loose wrapper, a margin of draggled nightgown showing under it, her hair in a tumbled knot at the back of her head. If she had to run out for a loaf of bread or a pound of coffee, she slipped on a street skirt, and buttoned her long coat about her; her lean young throat would show, bare above the lapels of the coat, but even this costume was not conspicuous in that particular neighbourhood.

By the time Julia was weaned, Emeline had formed the wrapper habit; she had also slipped back to the old viewpoint: they were poor people, and the poor couldn't afford to do things decently, to live comfortably. Emeline scolded and snapped at George, shook and scolded the crying baby, and loitered in the hall for long, complaining gossips with the other women of the house.

Time extricated the young Pages from these troubled days. Julia grew into a handsome, precocious little girl of whom both parents could be proud. Emeline never quite recovered her girlish good looks, her face was thin now, with prominent cheek bones; there was a little frowning line drawn between her eyes, and her expression was sharp and anxious, but she became more fond of dress than ever.

George's absences were a little longer in these days; he had been given a larger territory to cover—and Emeline naturally turned for society toward her women neighbours. There were one or two very congenial married women of her own type in the same house, pleasure-loving, excitable young women; one, a Mrs. Carter, with two children in school, the other, Mrs. Palmer, triumphantly childless. These introduced her to others; sometimes half a dozen of them would go to a matinee together, a noisy, chattering group. During the matinee Julia would sit on her mother's lap, a small awed figure in a brief red silk dress and deep lace collar. Julia always had several chocolates from the boxes that circulated among her elders, and usually went to sleep during the last act, and was dragged home, blinking and whining and wretched, by one aching little arm.

George was passionately devoted to his little girl, and no toy was too expensive for Julia to demand. Emeline loved the baby, too, although she accepted as a martyrdom the responsibility of supplying Julia's needs. But the Pages themselves rather drifted apart with the years. Both were selfish, and each accused the other of selfishness, although, as Emeline said stormily, no one had ever called her that before she was married, and, as George sullenly claimed, he himself had always been popularity's self among the "fellows."

In all her life Emeline had never felt anything but a resentful impatience for whatever curtailed her liberty or disturbed her comfort in the slightest degree. She had never settled down to do cheerfully anything that she did not want to do. She had shaken off the claims of her own home as lightly as she had stepped from "Delphine's" to the more tempting position of George's wife. Now she could not believe that she was destined to live on with a man who was becoming a confirmed dyspeptic, who thought she was a poor housekeeper, an extravagant shopper, a wretched cook, and worse than all, a sloven about her personal appearance. Emeline really was all these things at times, and suspected it, but she had never been shown how to do anything else, and she denied all charges noisily.

One night when Julia was about four George stamped out of the house, after a tirade against the prevailing disorder and some insulting remarks about "delicatessen food." Emeline sent a few furious remarks after him, and then wept over the sliced ham, the potato salad, and the Saratoga chips, all of which she had brought home from a nearby delicacy shop in oily paper bags only an hour ago. She wandered disconsolately through the four rooms that had been her home for nearly six years. The dust lay thick on the polished wood and glass of the sideboard and glass closet in the dining-room; ashes and the ends of cigarettes filled half a dozen little receptacles here and there; a welter of newspapers had formed a great drift in a corner of the room, and the thick velour day cover of the table had been pushed back to make way for a doubled and spotted tablecloth and the despised meal. The kitchen was hideous with a confusion of souring bottles of milk, dirty dishes, hardened ends of loaves, and a sticky jam jar or two; Emeline's range was spotted and rusty, she never fired it now; a three-burner gas plate sufficed for the family's needs. In the bedroom a dozen garments were flung over the foot of the unmade bed, Julia's toys and clothing littered this and the sitting-room, the silk woof had been worn away on the heavily upholstered furniture, and the strands of the cotton warp separated to show the white lining beneath. On the mantel was a litter of medicine bottles and theatre programs, powder boxes, gloves and slippers, packages of gum and of cigarettes, and packs of cards, as well as more ornamental matters: china statuettes and glass cologne bottles, a palm-leaf fan with roses painted on it, a pincushion of redwood bark, and a plush rolling-pin with brass screws in it, hung by satin ribbons. Over all lay a thick coat of dust.

Emeline took Julia in her lap, and sat down in one of the patent rockers. She remained for a long time staring out of the front window. George's words burned angrily in her memory—she felt sick of life.

A spring twilight was closing down upon O'Farrell Street. In the row of houses opposite Emeline could see slits of gaslight behind lowered shades, and could look straight into the second floor of the establishment that flourished behind a large sign bearing the words, "O'Connor, Modes." This row of bay-windowed houses had been occupied as homes by very good families when the Pages first came to O'Farrell Street, but six years had seen great changes in the block. A grocery and bar now occupied the corner, facing the saloon above which the Pages lived, and the respectable middle-class families had moved away, one by one, giving place to all sorts of business enterprises. Milliners and dressmakers took the first floors, and rented the upper rooms; one window said "Mme. Claire, Palmist," and another "Violin Lessons"; one basement was occupied by a dealer in plaster statuary, and another by a little restaurant. Most interesting of all to the stageloving Emeline was the second floor, obliquely opposite her own, which bore an immense sign, "Gottoli, Wigs and Theatrical Supplies. Costumes of all sorts Designed and on Hand." Between Gottoli's windows were two painted panels representing respectively a very angular, moustached young man in a dress suit, and a girl in a Spanish dancer's costume, with a tambourine. Gottoli did not do a very flourishing business, but Emeline watched his doorway by the hour, and if ever her dreams came back now, it was at these times.

To-night Julia went to sleep in her arms; she was an unexacting little girl, accustomed to being ignored much of the time, and humoured, over-indulged, and laughed at at long intervals. Emeline sat on and on, crying now and then, and gradually reducing herself to a more softened mood, when she longed to be dear to George again, to please and content him. She had just made up her mind that this was no neighbourhood for ideal home life, when George, smelling strongly of whiskey, but affectionate and repentant, came in.

"What doing?" asked George, stumbling in the dark room.

"Just watching the cable cars go up and down," Emeline said, rousing. She set the dazed Julia on her feet, and groped for matches on the mantel. A second later the stifling odour of block matches drifted through the room, and Emeline lighted a gas jet.

"Had your supper?" said she, as George sat down and took the child into his arms.

"Nope," he answered, grinning ashamedly. "Thought maybe you and I'd go to dinner somewheres, Em."

Emeline was instantly her better self. While she flew into her best clothes she told George that she knew she was a rotten manager, but she was so darn sick of this darn flat—She had just been sitting there wondering if they hadn't better move into the country, say into Oakland. Her sister May lived there, they might get a house near May, with a garden for Julia, and a spare room where George could put up a friend.

George was clumsily enthusiastic. Gosh, if she would do that—if she could stand its being a little quiet—

"I'd get to know the neighbours, and we'd have real good times," said Emeline optimistically, "and it would be grand for Julie!"

Julia had by this time gone off to sleep in the centre of the large bed. Her mother removed the child's shoes and some of her clothing, without rousing her, loosened her garters, and unbuttoned whatever buttons she could reach.

"She'll be all right," she said confidently. "She never wakes."

George lowered the gas, and they tiptoed out. But Julie did waken half an hour later, as it happened, and screamed for company for ten hideous minutes. Then Miss Flossie Miniver, a young woman who had recently rented the top floor, and of whom Emeline and the other ladies of the house disapproved, came downstairs and softly entered the Page flat, and gathered the sobbing little girl to her warm, soft breast. Miss Miniver soothed her with a new stick of gum and a pincushion that looked like a fat little pink satin leg, with a smart boot at one end and a ruffle of lace at the other, and left Julia peacefully settled down to sleep. But Julia did not remember anything of this in the morning, and the pincushion had rolled under the bed, so Emeline never knew of it. She and George had a good dinner, and later went to the Orpheum, and were happier than they had been for a long time.

The next Sunday they went to Oakland to see Emeline's sister, and possibly to begin househunting. It was a cold, dark day, with a raw wind blowing. Gulls dipped and screamed over the wake of the ferryboat that carried the Pages to Oakland, and after the warm cabin and the heated train, they all shivered miserably as they got out at the appointed corner. Oakland looked bleak and dreary, the wind was blowing chaff and papers against fences and steps.

Emeline had rather lost sight of her sister for a year or two, and had last seen her in another and better house than the one which they presently identified by street and number. The sisters had married at about the same time, but Ed Torney was a shiftless and unfortunate man, never steadily at work, and always mildly surprised at the discomfort of life. May had four children, and was expecting a fifth. Two of the older children, stupid-looking little blondes, with colds in their noses, and dirt showing under the fair hair, were playing in the dooryard of the shabby cottage now. The gate hung loose, the ground was worn bare by children's feet and dug into holes where children had burrowed, and littered with cans and ropes and boxes.

Emeline was genuinely shocked by the evidences of actual want inside. May was a thin, bent, sickly looking woman now, her graying hair hanging in a loose coil over her cotton wrapper. Floors everywhere were bare, a few chairs were here and there, a few beds running over with thin bedding, a table in the kitchen was covered with scattered dishes, some dirty and some clean. Ashes drifted out of the kitchen stove, and in the sink was a great tin dish-pan full of cool, greasy water. The oldest child, a five-year-old girl, had followed these dazzling visitors in, and now mounted a box and attacked this dish-pan with pathetic energy. The two younger children sat on the floor, apathetically staring. May made only a few smiling apologies. They "could see how she was," she said, limping to a chair into which she dropped with a sigh of relief. They had had a "fierce" time since Ed—Ed was the husband and father—had lost his job a year ago. He had not been able to get anything permanent since. Ed had been there just a minute ago, she said—and indeed the odour of tobacco was still strong on the close air—but he had been having a good deal of stomach trouble of late, and the children made him nervous, and he had gone out for a walk. Poor May, smiling gallantly over the difficulties of her life, drew her firstborn to her knees, brushed back the child's silky, pale hair with bony, trembling fingers, and prophesied that things would be easier when mamma's girlies got to work: Evelyn was going to be a dressmaker, and Marguerite an actress.

"She can say a piece out of the Third Reader real cute—the children next door taught her," said May, but Marguerite would not be exploited; she dug her blonde head into her mother's shoulder in a panic of shyness; and shortly afterward the Pages went away. Uncle George gave each child a dime, Julia kissed her little cousins good-bye, and Emeline felt a sick spasm of pity and shame as May bade the children thank them, and thanked them herself. Emeline drew her sister to the door, and pressed two silver dollars, all she happened to have with her, into her hand.

"Aw, don't, Em, you oughtn't," May said, ashamed and turning crimson, but instantly she took the money. "We've had an awful hard time—or I wouldn't!" said she, tears coming to her eyes.

"Oh, that's all right!" Emeline said uncomfortably, as she ran down the steps. Her heart burned with sympathy for poor May, who had been so pretty and so clever! Emeline could not understand the change! May had graduated from High School with honours; she had held a good position as a bookkeeper in a grocery before her marriage, but, like Emeline, for the real business of life she had had no preparation at all. Her own oldest child could have managed the family finances and catered to sensitive stomachs with as much system and intelligence as May.

On the boat Emeline spoke of her little money gift to her sister, and George roused himself from a deep study to approve and to reimburse her. They did not speak again of moving to the country, and went straight from the boat to a French table d'hote dinner, where Julia, enchanted at finding herself warm and near food after the long cold adventures of the day, stuffed herself on sardines and sour bread, soup and salad, and shrimps and fried chicken, and drank tumblers of claret and sugar and ice water.

There were still poker parties occasionally in the Page flat; Emeline was quite familiar with poker phraseology now, and if George seemed less pleased than he had been when she rattled away about hands, the men who came were highly diverted by it. Two or three other wives generally joined the party now; there would be seven or eight players about the round table.

They all drank as they played, the room would get very warm, and reek of tobacco and of whiskey and beer. Sometimes Julia woke up with a terrified shout, and then, if Emeline were playing, she would get George, or one of the other men or women, to go in and quiet the little girl. These games would not break up until two or three o'clock. Emeline would be playing excitedly, her face flushed, her eyes shining, every fibre of her being alert, when suddenly the life would seem to fade out of the whole game. An overwhelming ennui would seize her, a cold, clear-eyed fatigue—the cards would seem meaningless, a chill would shake her, a need of yawning. The whole company would be suddenly likewise affected, the game would break up with a few brief words, and Emeline, going in with her guests to help them with hats and wraps, would find herself utterly silent, too cold and weary for even the most casual civilities. When the others had gone, she and George would turn the lights out on the wreckage of the dining-room, and stagger silently to bed.

Fatigue would follow Emeline well into the next day after one of these card parties. If George was going out of town, she would send Julia off to play with other children in the house, and lie in bed until noon, getting up now and then to hold a conversation with some tradesman through a crack in the door. At one she might sally forth in her favourite combination of wrapper and coat to buy cream and rolls, and Julia would be regaled on sausages, hot cakes, bakery cookies, and coffee, or come in to find no lunch at all, and that her mother had gone out for the afternoon.

Emeline had grown more and more infatuated with the theatre and all that pertained to it. She went to matinees twice a week, and she and her group of intimate friends also "went Dutch" to evening performances whenever it was possible. Their conversation was spattered with theatrical terms, and when, as occasionally happened, a real actress or even a chorus girl from the Tivoli joined their group, Emeline could hardly contain her eagerness and her admiration. She loved, when rare chance offered, to go behind the scenes; she frankly envied the egotistic, ambitious young theatrical beginners, so eager to talk of themselves and their talents, to discuss every detail from grease paint to management. To poor hungry Emeline it was like a revelation of another, brighter world.

She would loiter out from the brief enchantment of "Two True Hearts" into the foggy dampness of Market Street, at twilight, eagerly grasping the suggestion of ice-cream sodas, because it meant a few minutes more with her friends. Perhaps, sipping the frothy confection, Emeline would see some of the young actresses going by, just from the theatre, buttoned into long coats, their faces still rosy from cold cream; they must rush off for a light dinner, and be back at the theatre at seven. At the sight of them a pang always shot through Emeline, an exquisite agony of jealousy seized her. Oh, to be so busy, so full of affairs, to move constantly from one place to another—now dragging a spangled gown, now gay as a peasant, now gaudily dressed as a page!

Emeline would finish her soda in silence, lift the over-dressed Julia from her chair, and start soberly for home. Julia's short little legs ached from the quick walk, yet she hated as much as her mother the plunge from brightly lighted O'Farrell Street into their own hall, so large and damp and dark, so odorous of stale beer and rubber floor covering. A dim point of gas in a red shade covered with symmetrical glass blisters usually burned over the stairway, but the Pages' apartment was dark, except for a dull reflected light from the street. Perhaps Julia and her mother would find George there, with his coat and shoes off, and his big body flung down across the bed, asleep. George would wake up slowly, with much yawning and grumbling, Emeline would add her gloves and belt to the unspeakable confusion of the bureau, and Julia would flatten her tired little back against the curve of an armchair and follow with heavy, brilliant eyes the argument that always followed.

"Well, we could get some chops—chops and potatoes—and a can of corn," Emeline would grudgingly admit, as she tore off her tight corsets with a great gasp of relief, and slipped into her kimono, "or you could get some spaghetti and some mangoes at the delicatessen—"

"Oh, God, cut out the delicatessen stuff!" George invariably said; "me for the chops, huh, Julie?"

"Or—we could all go somewhere," Emeline might submit tentatively.

"*Nit*," George would answer. "Come on, Ju, we'll go buy a steak!"

But he was not very well pleased with his dinner, even when he had his own way. When he and Julia returned with their purchases Emeline invariably met them at the top of the stairs.

"We need butter, George, I forgot to tell you—you'll have to go back!" she would say. Julia, tired almost beyond endurance, still preferred to go with her father.

There was not enough gas heat under Emeline's frying pan to cook a steak well; George growled as he cut it. Emeline jumped up for forgotten table furnishings; grease splashed on the rumpled cloth. After the one course the head of the house would look about hungrily.

"No cheese in the house, I suppose?"

"No—I don't believe there is."

"What's the chances on a salad?"

"Oh, no, George—that takes lettuce, you know. My goodness!" And Emeline would put her elbows on the table and yawn, the rouge showing on her high cheek bones, her eyes glittering, her dark hair still pressed down where her hat had lain. "My goodness!" she would exclaim impatiently, "haven't you had enough, George? You had steak, and potatoes, and corn—why don't you eat your corn?"

"What's the chances on a cup of tea?" George might ask, seizing a half slice of bread, and doubling an ounce of butter into it, with his great thumb on the blade of his knife.

"You can have all the tea you want, but you'll have to use condensed milk!"

At this George would say "Damn!" and take himself and his evening paper to the armchair in the front window. When Emeline would go in, after a cursory disposition of the dishes, she would find Julia curled in his arms, and George sourly staring over the little silky head.

"It's up to you, and it's your job, and it makes me damn sick to come home to such a dirty pen as this!" George sometimes burst out. "Look at that—and look at that—look at that mantel!"

"Well—well—well!" Emeline would answer sharply, putting the mantel straight, or commencing to do so with a sort of lazy scorn. "I can't do everything!"

"Other men go home to decent dinners," George would pursue sullenly; "their wives aren't so darn lazy and selfish—"

Such a start as this always led to a bitter quarrel, after which Emeline, trembling with anger, would clear a corner of the cluttered drawing-room table and take out a shabby pack of cards for solitaire, and George would put Julia to bed. All her life Julia Page remembered these scenes and these bedtimes.

Her father sometimes tore the tumbled bed apart, and made it up again, smoothing the limp sheets with clumsy fingers, and talking to Julia, while he worked, of little girls who had brothers and sisters, and who lived in the country, and hung their stockings up on Christmas Eve. Emeline pretended not to notice either father or daughter at these times, although she could have whisked Julia into bed in half the time it took George to do it, and was really very kind to the child when George was not there.

When George asked the little girl to find her hairbrush, and blundered over the buttons of her nightgown, Emeline hummed a sprightly air. She never bore resentment long.

"What say we go out later and get something to eat, George?" she would ask, when George tiptoed out of the bedroom and shut the folding door behind him. But several hours of discomfort were not to be so lightly dismissed by George.

"Maybe," he would briefly answer. And invariably he presently muttered something about asking "Cass" for the time, and so went down to the saloon of "J. Cassidy," just underneath his own residence.

Emeline, alone, would brood resentfully over her cards. That was the way of it: men could run off to saloons, while she, pretty and young, and with the love of life still strong in her veins, might as well be dead and buried! Bored and lonely, she would creep into bed beside Julia, after turning the front-room light down to a bead, and flinging over the "bed lounge," upon which George spent the night, the musty sheets and blankets and the big soggy pillows.

But George, meanwhile, would have found warmth, brightness, companionship, and good food. The drink that was his passport to all these good things was the least of them in his eyes. George did not care particularly for drink, but he usually came home the worse for it on these occasions, and Emeline had a real foundation for her furious harangues in the morning. She would scold while she carried him in hot coffee or chopped ice, scold while she crimped her hair and covered her face with a liquid bleach, scold as she jerked Julia's little bonnet on the child's lovely mane, and depart, with a final burst of scolding and a bang of the door.

One day Emeline came in to find George at home, ill. She had said good-bye to him only the day before, for what was supposedly a week, and was really concerned to find him back so soon, shivering and mumbling, and apparently unable to get into bed. Emeline sent Julia flying to a neighbour, made George as comfortable as she could in the big bed, and listened, with a conviction as firm as his own, to what he believed to be parting instructions and messages.

"I'm going, Em," said George heavily. "I'm worse now than I was when I started for home. I wanted to see you again, baby girl, and Julia, too. I—I can't breathe——"

Julia presently came flying in with a doctor and with a neighbour, Mrs. Cotter, who had telephoned to him. The doctor said that George had a sharp touch of influenza, and Emeline settled down to nurse him.

George was a bad patient. He had a great many needs, and he mentioned one after another in the weighty, serious tone of a person imparting valuable information.

"Ice—ice," said George, moving hot eyes to meet his wife's glance as she came in. "And take that extra blanket off, Emeline, and—no hurry, but I'll try the soup again whenever you say—I seem to feel weak. I must have more air, dear. Help me sit up, Em, and you can shake these pillows up again. I think I'm a good deal sicker man than Allan has any idea——"

Emeline got very tired of it, especially as George was much better on the third day, and could sit up. He developed a stiff neck, which made him very irritable, and even Julia "got on his nerves" and was banished for the day to the company of the cheerful Jewish family who lived on an upper floor. He sat in an armchair, wrapped in blankets, his rigid gaze roving a pitifully restricted perspective of street outside the window, an elaborate cough occasionally racking him.

Emeline had gotten a fairly tempting dinner under way. She could cook some things well, and at five o'clock she came in from the kitchen with an appetizing tray.

"Gosh, is it dinner time?" asked George.

"After five," Emeline said, flitting about the bed-room. Julia had come home now, sweet and tired, and was silently eating slice after slice of bread and jelly. Emeline opened out the bed lounge, spread sheets and blankets smoothly, and flung a clean little nightgown for Julia across the foot. Darkness had fallen outside; she lighted the gas and drew the shades.

"This is comfortable!" said George. "I wouldn't mind being sick now and then at this rate! Come over here and undress near Pop, Julie. I'll tell you what, Em—you call down the air shaft to Cass, and tell him to send Henny up to make us a nice little coal fire here. I'll give Henny a quarter."

"She's gone into the bathroom to fix her hair and wash her face," Julia observed, as Emeline did not answer. A second later the child jumped up to answer a sharp knock on the door.

To George's disgust it was Emeline's friend, Mrs. Marvin Povey, who came in. Mrs. Povey was a tightly corseted, coarse-voiced, highly coloured little blonde, breathless now from running upstairs. Her sister, Myrtle Montague, was an ingenue in the little stock company at the Central Theatre, and Mrs. Povey kept house for her and Mr. Povey, who spent all his waking hours at the racetrack. The Poveys' flat was only a block away from the Pages'.

George was furious to have this woman, whom he particularly detested, come in upon him thus informally, and find him at so great a disadvantage. His neck was better, but he could not move it very easily still; he was trapped here in blankets like a baby; he was acutely conscious of his three days' beard, of Julia's bed made up in the middle of the drawing-room, and of Julia's self, partly disrobed, and running about in the general disorder.

"Well, how does the other feller look?" said Mrs. Povey, laughing good-naturedly. "You look like you'd broke out of San Quentin, George, with that face! Hello, darlin'," she added, waylaying Julia. "When are you going to come and be Aunt Mame's girl, huh? Going to come home with me to-night?"

"Em!" bellowed George, with only a sickly smile for the guest. "*Em*!"

"My God, what is it now?" said Emeline sweetly, popping in her head. "Oh, hello, Mame!" she added, coming in. "Where's the rest of the girls?"

"They've all blew up to the house with Myrt," said Mrs. Povey, staring blankly at Emeline. "But say, ain't you going, dear?"

"Wait till I get my dress on, and we'll talk it over while I hook up," Emeline said, disappearing again. She did not glance at George.

"Myrt's in a new show, and a few of us girls are going to see that she gets a hand," Mrs. Povey said. "We're going to have supper at my house. Mary will have some of the boys there."

"I guess Emeline will have to wait till the next time," George said coldly. "She wouldn't get much pleasure out of it, leaving me here as sick as I am!"

"Oh, I don't know!" Mrs. Povey half sang, half laughed. "Emeline likes a good time, like all the rest of us, George, and it don't do to keep a pretty girl shut up all the time!"

"Shut up? She's never here," George growled.

"Well, we'll see!" Mrs. Povey hummed contentedly. A moment later Emeline came in, wrenching the hooks of her best gown together. She had her hat on, and looked excited and resolute.

"I forgot I'd promised to go out with the girls, George," she began. "You don't care, do you? You've had your supper, and all Julia's got to do is get into bed."

George looked balefully from one to the other. Mrs. Povey chanced a quick little wink of approval and encouragement at Emeline, and he saw it.

"A lot you forgot!" he said harshly to his wife. "You've been getting ready for the last hour. Don't either of you think that you're fooling me—I see through it! I could lay here and die, and a lot you'd care! You forgot—ha!"

The blood rushed instantly to Emeline's face, she turned upon him her ugliest look, and the hand with which she was buttoning her glove trembled.

"Now, I'll tell you something, Mr. George Page!" said she, in an intense and passionate tone, "there *are* things I'd rather do than set around this house and hear you tell how sick you are! You think I'm a white chip in this family, but let me tell you something—there's plenty of lovely friends I got who think I'm a fool to keep it up! I had an offer to go on the stage, not a month ago, from a manager who didn't even know I was married; didn't I, Mame? And if it wasn't for Julie there——"

"You've not got anything on me, Em," George said, breathing hard, his face blood red with anger. "Do you think that if it wasn't for this kid, I'd——"

"Oh, folks—folks!" Mrs. Povey said, really concerned.

"Well, I don't care!" Emeline said, panting. She crossed the floor, still panting, kissed Julia, and swept from the room. Mrs. Povey, murmuring some confused farewell, followed her.

Julia climbed out of her big chair. Like all children, she was frightened by loud voices and domestic scenes; she was glad now that the quarrel was over, and anxious, in a small girl's fashion, to blot the recent unpleasantness from her father's mind.

She sat on his knee and talked to him, she sang, she patted his sore neck with sleek, dirty little fingers. And finally she won him. George laughed, and entered into her mood. He thought her a very smart little girl, as indeed she was. She had a precocious knowledge of the affairs of her mother's friends, sordid affairs enough, and more sordid than ever when retailed by a child's fresh mouth. Julia talked of money trouble, of divorce, of dressmaker's bills, of diseases; she repeated insolent things that had been said to her in the street, and her insolent replies; her rich, delicious laugh broke out over the memory of the "drunk" that had been thrown out of Cassidy's.

George laughed at it all; it sounded very funny to him, coming from this very small person, with her round, serious eyes, and her mop of gold. He asked her what she wanted him to bring her next time he came home, and Julia said black boots with white tops and tassels, and made him laugh again.

Thus early did Julia act as a mediator between her parents, but of this particular occasion she had no recollection, nor of much that followed it. Had she been a few years older she might really have affected a lasting reconciliation between them, for all that was best in George made him love his daughter, and Emeline was intensely proud of the child. As it was, Julia was too young. She might unconsciously be the means of reuniting them now and then, but she could not at all grasp the situation, and when she was not quite seven a decree of divorce, on the ground of desertion, set both Emeline and George free, after eight years of married life.

Emeline was too frightened at the enormity of the thing to be either glad or sorry. She had never meant to go so far. She had threatened George with divorce just as George had threatened her, in the heat of anger, practically since her wedding day. But the emotion that finally drove Emeline to a lawyer was not anger, it was just dull rebellion against the gray, monotonous level of her days. She was alone when George was away on trips; she was not less alone when he was in town. He had formed the habit of joining "the boys" in the evening; he was surly and noncommittal with his wife, but Julia, hanging about the lower hall door or playing with children in the street, always heard a burst of laughter as he joined his friends; everybody in the world—except Emeline—liked George!

Poor Emeline—she could easily have held him! A little tenderness toward him, a little interest in her home and her child, and George would have been won again. Had he but once come home to a contented wife and a clean house, George's wavering affection would have been regained. But Emeline was a loud-mouthed, assertive woman now, noisily set upon her own way, and filled with a sense of her own wrongs. She had discussed George too often with her friends to feel any possible interest in him except as a means of procuring sympathy. George bored her now; as a matter of fact, Emeline had almost decided that she would prefer alimony to George.

Goaded on by Mrs. Povey, and a young Mrs. Sunius, affectionately known as Maybelle, Emeline went to see a lawyer. The lawyer surprised her by his considerate brevity. Getting a divorce was a very simple affair, much better done than not. There were ways to make a man pay his alimony regularly, and the little girl would stay with her mother, of course; at her age no other solution was possible. Emeline felt that she must know how much expense she would be put to, and was gratified to find that it would cost her not more than fifty dollars. The lawyer asked her how soon she could get hold of her husband.

"Why, he'll let me know as soon as he's in town," Emeline said vaguely; "he'll come home."

"Come home, eh?" said the lawyer, with a shrewd look. "He knows your intentions, of course?"

"He ought to!" said Emeline with spirit, and she began again: "I don't think there's a person in the world could say that I'm not a good wife, Mr. Knowles! I never so much as looked at another man—I swear to God I never did! And there's no other man in the case. If I can have my dolling little girl, and just live quiet, with a few friends near me, that's all I ask! If Mr. Page had his way, I'd never put foot out of doors; but mind you, *he'd* be off with the boys every night. And that means drink, you know—"

"Well, well," the young lawyer said soothingly, "I guess you've been treated pretty mean, all right."

Emeline went home to find—somewhat to her embarrassment—that George had come in, and was in his happiest mood, and playing with Julia. Julia had somehow lost her babyish beauty now; she was thin and lanky, four teeth were missing, and even her glorious mop of hair seemed what her mother called "slinky."

"I landed the Fox order right over Colton's head!" said George.

Emeline said: "I wish to the Lord you'd quit opening that window, leaving the wind blow through here like a cave!"

"Well, the place smelled like a Jap's room!" George retorted, instantly aggressive.

"We're going to the Park!" Julia chanted.

"How d'ye mean you're going to the Park?" Emeline asked, as she slammed down the offending window.

"Well, I thought maybe I'd take her there; kinder fun walking round and seeing things, what?" George submitted.

Emeline shrugged. "I don't care what you do!"

She sat down before a dresser with a triple mirror, which had lately been added to the bedroom furniture, and began to ruffle the coarse puffs of her black hair with slim, ringed fingers.

"You've got something better to do, of course!" George said.

"Don't go to a matinee, Mother!" said Julia, coming to lean coaxingly against her mother's arm. Emeline looked down at the pale, intelligent little face, and gave the child a sudden kiss.

"Mama isn't going to a matinee, doll baby. But papa ain't as crazy for her to go to the Park as you are!" she said, with an oblique and challenging glance at George.

"Oh, come on!" George urged impatiently. "Only don't wear that rotten hat," he added. "It don't look like a respectable woman!"

Emeline's expression did not change, but fury seethed within her.

"Don't wait for me," she said levelly. "I'm not going."

"Well, put the kid's hat on then," George suggested, settling his own with some care at the mantel mirror.

"Get your hand-embroidered dress out of your drawer, Julia," said her mother, "and the hat Aunt Maybelle gave you!"

"I'm going to Cass's to telephone, and I need some cigarettes," George announced from the door. "I'll be back in five minutes for Julie."

"Don't forget to get a drink while you're in Cass's," Emeline reminded him, as she flung an embroidered dress over Julia's limp little draggled petticoats. George's answer was a violent slamming of the hall door.

Julia's little face was radiant as her mother tied on a soiled white straw bonnet covered with roses, and put a cologne-soaked handkerchief into the pocket of her blue velvet coat. The little girl did not have many pleasures; there were very few children in the neighbourhood, and Julia was not very strong; she easily caught colds in dark O'Farrell Street, or in the draughty hall. All winter long she had been hanging over the coal fire in the front room, or leaning against the window watching the busy street below—but today was spring! Sunlight glorified even the dreary aspect from the windows above "J. Cassidy's" saloon, and the glorious singing freshness of the breeze, the heavenly warmth of the blue air, had reached Julia's little heart.

When she was quite dressed, and was standing at the window patiently watching for her father, Emeline came and stood beside her.

"I'll tell you what!" said Emeline suddenly. "I'll go, too! It's too grand to be indoors today; we'll just go out to the Park and take in the whole show! And then perhaps papa'll take us somewhere to dinner!"

She began swiftly to dress, pinning on a hat that George liked, and working on long gray kid gloves as a complement to a gray gown. Then she came to stand behind Julia again, and both watched the street.

"I guess he's waiting for his change?" suggested Julia, and Emeline laughed.

"We'll walk over and take the Geary Street car," said she. "We'll go right to the fountain, and get dummy seats. And we could have dinner at the Poodle Dog—"

"Here he comes!" Julia cried. And indeed George was to be seen for a moment, between two friends, standing on the corner.

A long wait ensued. Then steps came up the stairs. Emeline, followed by Julia, went to the door. It was not George, but a note from George, delivered by Henny, of Cassidy's saloon.

"Dear Em," Emeline read, "a couple of the fellows want me to go to Emeryville, have dinner at Tony's, and sit in a little game afterward. Tell Julie I will take her to the Park to-morrow—and buy her anything she wants. George."

"Thanks, Henny," Emeline said, without visible emotion. But Julia's lip quivered, and she burst into bitter crying. Six-years-old knows no tomorrows, and Julia tasted the bitterness of despair. She cried quietly, her little body screwed into a big armchair, her face hidden in the crook of a thin little arm. Emeline stood it as long as she could, then she slapped and shook Julia to stop her, and Julia strangled and shrieked hysterically.

Peace was presently restored, and Julia was asked if she would like to go see her Auntie Mame, and assented with a hiccough. So her mottled little face was wiped with a soggy gray towel, and her bonnet straightened, and they set out.

Mrs. Povey was so sympathetic that Emeline stayed with her for dinner, a casual meal which Myrtle Montague and a sister actress came in to share. Julia sat with them at table, and stuffed solemnly on fresh bread and cheese, crab salad and smoked beef, hot tomato sauce and delicious coffee. The coffee came to table in a battered tin pot, and the cream was poured into the cups from the little dairy bottle, with its metal top, but Julia saw these things as little as any one else—as little as she saw the disorderly welter of theatrical effects in the Poveys' neglected rooms, the paint on the women's faces, the ugly violence and coarseness of their talk.

But she did see that they were an impulsive, warm-hearted, generous set. Nobody ever spoke crossly to her, she was given the freedom of their rooms, she listened to their chatter, she was often caught up for embraces heavy with cologne; they loved to dress her up in preposterous costumes, and shouted with laughter at the sight of her in Dolly Varden bonnets, Scotch kilts, or spectacles and wigs. "Baby doll," "Lovey," and "Honey Babe" were Julia's names here, and she was a child hungry for love and eager to earn it. To-night she ate her supper in that silence so grateful to grown people, and afterward found some stage jewellery and played with it until her head was too heavy to hold up any longer. Then she went to sleep upon an odorous couch piled deep with all sorts of odd garments, her feet thrust into a tangle of lifeless satin pillows, her head upon the fur lining of some old cape, a banjo prodding her uncomfortably whenever she stirred.

Julia—all pins and needles—was presently jerked up into a glare of lights, and tied into the rose-crowned bonnet, and buttoned into the velvet coat again. She had not been covered as she slept, and sneezed and shivered in the cold night air. Emeline walked along briskly, and Julia stumbled beside her. The child was in such an agony of fatigue and chill that every separate step toward bed was dreaded by this time. She fell against her mother, as Emeline tore off shoes and stockings, stretched blundering, blind little arms for her nightgown sleeves, and sank deliciously against her pillows, already more than half asleep.

But Emeline sat wide eyed, silent, waiting for George.

George did not come home at all that night. On the next afternoon—Sunday afternoon—Julia was playing in the street with two other small girls. Their game was simple. The three huddled into the deep doorway that led to Julia's home, clinging tight to each other, laughing and shouting. Then at a given signal they rushed screaming forth, charged across the street as if pursued by a thousand furies, and took shelter in a similar doorway, next to the saloon across the street. This performance had been repeated, back and forth, perhaps a dozen times, when Julia found her father waylaying her.

"Where y' going?" asked Julia, noticing that he carried a hand bag.

George sat down on the dirty cement steps that connected his dwelling with the sidewalk, and drew Julia between his knees.

"I've got to go away, baby," said he soberly.

"And ain't choo going to take me to the Park—*never?*" asked Julia, with a trembling lip.

George freed a lock of her hair that had gotten caught in her collar, with clumsy, gentle fingers.

"Mama's mad at me, and I'm going away for a while, Babe," said he, clearing his throat. "But you be a good girl, and I'll come take you to the Park some day."

Something in the gravity of his tone impressed Julia.

"But I don't want you to go away," she said tearfully. George got up hastily.

"Come on, walk with Pop to the car," he commanded, and Julia trotted contentedly beside him to Market Street. There she gave him a child's soft, impersonal kiss, staring up at the buildings opposite as she did so. George jumped on a cable car, wedged his bag under his knees as he took a seat on the dummy, and looked back at the little figure that was moving toward the dingy opening of O'Farrell Street, and at the spring sunshine, bright on the child's hair.

CHAPTER II

In summer the rear parlour that was Mrs. Page's bedroom was a rather dim and dreary place; such light as it had fell through one long, high window that gave only upon a narrow air shaft; it was only in mid-July that the actual sunlight—a bright and fleeting triangle—touched the worn red carpet and the curly-maple bed. In winter the window gave almost no light at all. Julia dressed by gaslight ten months out of the year, and had to sit up in her warm blankets and stare at the clock on a certain January morning in her fifteenth year, to make sure whether it said twenty minutes of eleven or five minutes of eight o'clock. It was five minutes of eight—no mistake about it—but eight o'clock was early for the Pages, mother and daughter. Julia sighed, and cautiously stretched forth an arm, a bare, shapely little arm, with bangles on the round wrist and rings on the smooth fingers, and picked a book from the floor. Cautiously settling herself on the pillows she plunged into her novel, now and then pushing back a loose strand of hair, or bringing her pretty fingernails close to her eyes for an admiring and critical scrutiny.

An hour passed—another hour. The clock in the front room struck a silvery ten. Then Julia slammed her book noisily together, and gave a sharp push to the recumbent form beside her.

"Ah—no—darling!" moaned Mrs. Page, tortured out of dreams. "Don't—Julie—"

"Aw, wake up, Mama!" the daughter urged. Whereupon the older woman rolled on her back, yawned luxuriously, and said, quite composedly:

"Hello, darling! What time is it?"

Emeline had aged in seven years; she looked hopelessly removed from youth and beauty now, but later in the day, when her hair would be taken out of its crimping kids, her sallow cheeks touched with rouge, and her veined neck covered by a high collar, a coral chain, and an ostrich-feather ruff, some traces of her former good looks might be visible. She still affected tight corsets, high heels, enormous hats. But Emeline's interest in her own appearance was secondary now to her fierce pride and faith in Julia's beauty. Drifting along the line of least resistance, asking only to be comfortable and to have a good time, Emeline had come to a bitter attitude of resentment toward George, toward the fate that had "forced" her to leave him. Now she began lazily to fasten upon Julia as the means of gratifying those hopes and ambitions that were vain for herself. Julia was beautiful, Julia would be a great success, and some day would repay her mother for the sacrifices she had made for her child.

Emeline dressed, went about, flirted, and gossiped still; she liked cocktails and cards and restaurant dinners; she was an authority on all things theatrical; her favourite pose was that of the martyred mother. "All I have left," Emeline would say, kissing her daughter effectively, before strangers. "And only God knows what it has cost me to keep my girlie with me!"

Julia would grin good-naturedly at this. She had no hallucinations about her mother. She knew her own value, knew she was pretty, and was glad with the simple and pathetic complacence of fourteen. Julia at eight had gone to dancing school, in the briefest skirts ever seen on a small girl, and the dirtiest white silk stockings. She had sung a shrill little song, and danced a little dance at a public benefit for the widows of three heroic firemen, when she was only nine. Her lovely mop had been crimped out of all natural wave; her youthful digestion menaced by candy and chewing gum; her naturally rather sober and pensive disposition completely altered, or at least eclipsed. Julia could chatter of the stage, could give a pert answer to whoever accosted her, could tell a dressmaker exactly how she wanted a gown made, at twelve. While her mother slept in the morning, before the girl learned to sleep late, too, the child would get up and slip out. Her playground was O'Farrell Street, dry and hot in summer, wrapped in soft fog four mornings a week the year round, reeking of stale beer, and echoing to the rattle of cable cars. The little Julia flitted about everywhere: watching janitors as they hosed down the sidewalks outside the saloons, or rinsed cuspidors; watching grocers set out their big signs for the day; watching little restaurants open, and first comers sit down to great cups of coffee and plates of hot cakes. Perhaps the sight of food would remind the little girl of her own empty stomach; she would straggle home just as the first sunshine was piercing the fog, and loiter upstairs, and peep into the bedroom to see what the chances of a meal might be.

Emeline usually rolled over to smile at her daughter when she heard the door open, and Julia would be sent to the delicatessen store for the component parts of a substantial meal. Julia loved the cramped, clean, odorous shop that smelled of wet wood and mixed mustard pickles and smoked fish. A little cream bottle would be filled from an immense can at her request, the shopkeeper's wife wiping it with a damp rag and a bony hand. And the pat of butter, and the rolls, and the sliced ham, and the cheese—Herr Bauer scratched their prices with a stubby pencil on an oily bit of paper, checked their number by the number of bundles, gave Julia the buttery change, and Julia hurried home for a delicious loitering breakfast with her mother. Emeline, still in her limp, lace-trimmed nightgown, with a spotted kimono hanging loosely over it, and her hair a wildly tousled mass at the top of her head, presided at a clear end of the kitchen table. She and Julia occupied only two rooms of the original apartment now; a young lawyer, with his wife and child, had the big front room, and the dining-room was occupied by two mysterious young men who came and went for years without ever betraying anything of their own lives to their neighbours. Julia only knew that they were young, quiet, hard working, and of irreproachable habits.

But she knew the people in the front room quite well. Mrs. Raymond Toomey was a neat, bright, hopeful little woman, passionately devoted to her husband and her spoiled, high-voiced little son. Raymond Toomey was a big, blustering fool of a man, handsome in a coarse sort of way, noisy, shallow, and opinionated. Whenever there were races, the Toomeys went to the races, taking the precocious "Lloydy," in his velvet Fauntleroy suit and tasselled shoes, and taking "Baby," a shivering little terrier with wet, terrified eyes. Sometimes Mrs. Toomey came out to the kitchen in the morning, to curl her ostrich feathers over the gas stove, or join Mrs. Page in a cup of coffee.

"God, girlie, that goes to the spot," she would yawn, stirring her cup, both elbows on the table. "We had a fierce day yesterday, and Ray took a little too much last night—you know how men are! He had a stable tip yesterday, and went the limit—like a fool! I play hunches—there's no such thing as a tip!"

And sometimes she would put a little printed list of entries before Julia and say:

"Pick me a winner, darling. Go on—just pick any one!"

Julia soon reached the age when she could get her own breakfast, and then, mingled with a growing appreciation of the girl's beauty, her mother felt that gratitude always paid by an indolent person to one of energy. She knew that her child was finer than she was, prettier, more clever, more refined. She herself had never had any reserves; she had always screamed or shouted or cried or run away when things crossed her, but she saw Julia daily displaying self-control and composure such as she had never known. There were subtleties in Julia: her sweet firm young mouth closed over the swift-coming words she would not say, her round, round blue eyes were wiser already than her mother's eyes.

The girl had grown very handsome. Her joyous, radiant colouring was contradicted by her serious expression, her proud, unsmiling mouth. Her eyes were dark, her colouring softly dark; she had the velvety, tawny skin that usually accompanies dark hair. Yet her hair was a pure and exquisite gold. She wore it fluffed over her ears, cut in a bang across her forehead, and "clubbed" on her neck, in a rather absurd and artificial fashion. But the effect of her grave little face and severe expression, with this opulent gold, and her red lips and round blue eyes, was very piquant. Even powder, earrings, and "clubbing" her hair did not rob Julia of the appearance of a sweet, wilful, and petulant child. Besides the powder and earrings, she indulged in cologne, in open-work silk stockings and high heels, in chains and rings and bracelets; she wore little corsets, at fourteen, and laced them tight.

Julia's mind, at this time, was a curious little whirlpool. She had the natural arrogance of her years; she felt that she had nothing to learn. She had an affectionate contempt for her mother, and gave advice more often than she accepted it from Emeline. Julia naturally loved order and cleanliness, but she never came in contact with them. Emeline sometimes did not air or make her bed for weeks at a time. She washed only such dishes as were absolutely necessary for the next meal. She never sent out a bundle to the laundry, but washed handkerchiefs and some underwear herself, at erratic intervals, drying them on windows, or the backs of various chairs. Emeline always had a pair or more of silk stockings soaking in a little bowl of cold suds in the bedroom, and occasionally carried a waist or a lace petticoat to the little French laundress on Powell Street, and drove a sharp bargain with her. Julia accepted the situation very cheerfully; she and her mother both enjoyed their lazy, aimless existence, and to Julia, at least, the future was full of hope. She could do any one of a dozen things that would lead to fame and fortune.

The particular day that opened for her with two hours of quiet reading progressed like any other day. The mother and daughter arose, got their breakfast in the kitchen, and sat long over it, sharing the papers, the hot coffee, the cream, and dividing evenly the little French loaf. Julia's nightgown was as limp as her mother's, her kimono as dirty, and her feet were thrust in fur slippers, originally white, now gray. But her fresh young colour, and the rich loops and waves of her golden hair, her firm young breasts under her thin wraps, and the brave blue of her eyes made her a very different picture from her mother, who sat opposite, a vision of disorder, feasting her eyes upon the girl.

There was a murder story, of which mother and daughter read every word, and a society wedding to discuss.

"The Chases went," said Julia, dipping her bread in her coffee, her eyes on the paper. "Isn't that the limit!"

"Why, Marian Chase was a bridesmaid, Julie!"

"Yes, I know. But I didn't think the Byron Chases would go to Maude Pennell's wedding! But of course she's marrying an Addison—that helps. 'Mrs. Byron Chase, lavender brocade and pearls,'" read Julia. "Well, Maude Pennell is getting in, all right!"

"What'd Mrs. Joe Coutts wear?" Emeline asked. Among the unknown members of the city's smartest set she had her favourites.

"'Mrs. Joseph Foulke Coutts,'" Julia read obligingly. "'Red velvet robe trimmed with fox.'"

"For heaven's sake, Julie—with that red face!"

"And Miss Victoria Coutts in pink silk—she's had that dress for a year now," Julia said. "Well, Lord!" She yawned luxuriously. "I wouldn't marry Roy Addison if he was made of money—the bum!" She pushed the paper carelessly aside. "What you going to do to-day, Ma?" she asked lazily.

"Oh, go out," Emeline answered vaguely, still reading a newspaper paragraph. "Gladys has had to pay over a quarter of a million for that feller's debts!" said she, awed.

"Well, that's what you get for marrying a duke," Julia answered scornfully. "Let's pile these, Ma, and get dressed."

They went into the bedroom, where the gas was lighted again, the bureau pushed out from the wall, that the mirror might catch the best light, and where, in unspeakable confusion, mother and daughter began to dress. Julia put on her smart little serge skirt, pushing it down over her hips with both hands. Then she fixed her hair carefully, adjusted her hat, tied on a spotted white veil, and finally slipped into a much-embroidered silk shirtwaist, which mother and daughter decided was dirty, but would "do." Rings, bangles, and chains followed, a pair of long limp gloves, a final powdering, and a ruff of pink feathers. Julia was not fifteen and looked fully seventeen, to her great delight. She gave herself a sober yet approving glance in the mirror; the corners of her firm yet babyish mouth twitched with pleasure.

She locked the doors, set an empty milk bottle out on the unspeakably dreary back stairway, and flung the soggy bedding over the foot of the bed. Then mother and daughter sauntered out into the noontime sunshine.

It was their happiest time, as free and as irresponsible as children they went forth to meet the day's adventures. Something was sure to happen, the "crowd" would have some plan; they rarely came home again before midnight. But this sunshiny start into the day Was most pleasant of all, its freshness, its potentialities, appealed to them both. It was a February day, warm and bright, yet with a delicious tingle in the air.

"Leave us go up to Min's, Julie; some of the girls are sure to be there. There's no mat. to-day."

"Well—" Julia was smiling aimlessly at the sunlight. Now she patted back a yawn. "Walk?"

"Oh, sure. It's lovely out."

It was tacitly understood that Julia was to be an actress some day, when she was older, and the boarding-house of Mrs. Minnie Tarbury, to which the Pages were idly sauntering, was inhabited almost entirely by theatrical folk. Emeline and Julia were quite at home in the shabby overcrowded house in Eddy Street, and to-day walked in at the basement door, under a flight of wooden stairs that led to the parlour floor, and surprised the household at lunch in the dark, bay-windowed front room.

Mrs. Tarbury, a large, uncorseted woman, presided. Her boarders, girls for the most part, were scattered down the long table. Luncheon was properly over, but the girls were still gossiping over their tea. Flies buzzed in the sunny window, and the rumpled tablecloth was covered with crumbs. Mrs. Tarbury kissed Mrs. Page, and Julia settled down between two affectionate chorus girls.

"You know you're getting to be the handsomest thing that ever lived, Ju!" said one of these. Julia smiled without raising her eyes from the knives and forks with which she was absently playing.

"She's got the blues to-day," said her mother. "Not a word out of her!"

"Is that right, Ju?" somebody asked solicitously.

"Just about as right as Mama ever gets it," the girl said, still with her indifferent smile. Because her mother was shallow and violent, she had learned to like a pose of silence, of absent-mindedness, and because of the small yet sufficient income afforded by the rented rooms and from alimony, Julia was removed from the necessity that drove these other girls to the hard and constant work of the stage, and could afford her favourite air of fastidious waiting. She was going to be an actress, yes, but not until some plum worthy of her beauty and youth was offered. Meanwhile she listened to the others, followed the history of the favourites of the stage eagerly, and never saw less than four shows a week. Julia, at Juliet's age, had her own ideas as to the interpretation of the Balcony Scene, and could tell why she thought the art of Miss Rehan less finished than that of Madame Modjeska. But personally she lacked ambition, in this direction at least.

However, she joined in the girls' talk with great zest; a manager was to be put in his place, and several theories were advanced as to his treatment.

"I swear to God if Max don't give me twenty lines in the next, I'll go on to New York," said a Miss Connie Girard dispassionately. "There's a party I know there rents a house that Frohman owns, and he'd give me a letter. What I want is a Broadway success."

"That time we played—you know, seven weeks running, in Portland," said a stout, aging actress, "the time my little dance made such a hit, you know—"

"Mind jer, Max never come near us this morning," interrupted a Miss Rose Ransome firmly. "Because he knew what he done, and he wasn't looking for trouble! He wrote a notice—"

"One of the Portland papers, in c'menting on the show—" the dancer resumed.

"Say, Julie, want to walk down to Kearney with me?" Miss Girard said, jumping up. "I want to get my corsets, and we might drop in and see if we can work Foster for some seats for to-night."

"I've got a date to-night," said Julia, with a glance at her mother.

"What's that?" Emeline said sharply.

"Why, Mama, I told you I was going to the Orpheum with the Rosenthals—"

"She's going with the whole bunch," Mrs. Page commented, with a shrug. "I can't stand them, but she can!"

"I think Mark Rosenthal's a darling," some girl said, "I want to tell you right now there's not anybody can play the piano as good as he can."

"That's right," Julia said, very low.

"Well, excuse me from the bunch!" Mrs. Page said lazily.

"But we've got a real pretty little blush, just the same!" Mrs. Tarbury said, smiling at Julia. The girls shouted, and Julia grew still more red. "Never mind, baby love!" said the older woman soothingly. "It's just Aunt Min's nonsense! Say, but listen, Julia!" Her tone grew suddenly intense. "I meant to ask you something—listen. Say, no fooling, Artheris wants to know if you would take a job."

"Twenty a week, and twenty towns a month," Julia said, still ruffled. "No, I would not!"

"No, this isn't anything like that, dearie," explained Mrs. Tarbury. "There's going to be a big amachure show for charity at the Grand next month, and they want a few professionals in it, to buck up the others. All the swells are going to be in it—it's going to be something elegant! Of course they'd pay something, and it'd be a lot of fun for you! Artheris wants you to do it, and it wouldn't hurt you none to have him on your side, Julia. I promised I'd talk to you."

"One performance?" Julia asked. "What play?"

"I'd do it in a minute," said the stout actress from Portland, whose dance had been so gratifying a success, "but I'm signed up."

"One night, dear," Mrs. Tarbury said. "I don't think they've decided on the play."

"I don't know," Julia hesitated. "What d'ye think, Mama?"

"I think he's got his gall along," Mrs. Page admitted. "One night!—and to learn the whole thing for that. I'll tell you what to tell him—you tell him this: you say that you can't do it for one cent less'n a hundred dollars!"

"Lay down, Towse!" said Connie Girard, and Mrs. Tarbury expressed the same incredulity as she said benevolently: "What a pipe dream, Em—she's lucky if she gets ten!"

"Ten!" squeaked Julia's mother, but Julia silenced her by saying carelessly:

"I'll tell you what, Aunt Min. If Con and I get through in time we'll go in and see Artheris to-day. I'd do it for twenty-five—"

"You would not!" said her mother.

"Well, you might get twenty-five," Mrs. Tarbury said, mollified, "if it's a long part."

"If it don't take a lot of dressing," Julia said thoughtfully, as she and Miss Girard powdered their noses at the dark mirror of the sideboard.

"Don't you be fool enough to do it for a cent under fifty," Emeline said.

Julia smiled at her vaguely, and added to her farewells a daughterly, "Your hat's all right, Mama, but your veil's sort of caught up over your ear. Fix it before you go out. We'll be back here at five—"

"Or we'll meet you at Monte's,'" said Connie.

The two girls walked briskly down Eddy Street, conscious of their own charms, and conscious of the world about them. Connie was nearly nineteen, a simple, happy little flirt, who had been in and out of love constantly for three or four years. Julia knew her very well, and admired her heartily. Connie had twice had a speaking part in the past year, and the younger girl felt her to be well on her way toward fame. Miss Girard's family of plain, respectable folk lived in Stockton, and were somewhat distressed by her choice of a vocation, but Connie was really a rather well-behaved girl,—and a safe adviser for Julia.

"Say, listen, Con," said Julia, presently, "you know Mark Rosenthal?"

"Sure," said Connie. "Look here, Ju!" She paused at a window. "Don't you think these Chinese hand bags are swell!"

"Grand. But listen, Con," said Julia, shamefacedly honest as a boy. "He's got a case on me———"

"On you?" echoed Connie. "Why, he's twenty!"

"I know it," Julia agreed.

"But, my Lord, Ju, your Mother won't stand for that!"

"Mama don't know it."

"Well, I don't think you ought to do that, Ju," Connie began gravely. But Julia, with sudden angry tears in her eyes, stopped her.

"I've *not* done anything!" she said crossly. And suddenly Connie saw the truth: that Julia, in spite of paint and powder, rings and "clubbed" hair, was only a little girl, after all, still unsexed, still young enough to resent being teased about boys.

"What's he do?" she asked presently.

"Well, he—he—I have supper with them sometimes"—Julia's words poured out eagerly—"and he'll kiss me, you know—"

"*Kiss* you! The nerve!"

"Oh, before them all, I mean—like he always has done. His mother just laughs. And then, last week, when he asked me to go to Morosco's with them, why, it was just us two—the others had gone somewhere else."

"Well, of all gall!" said Connie, absorbed.

"And I've been up there with him thousands of times," said Julia. "Maybe Hannah'd be there, or Sophy, but sometimes we'd be alone—while he was playing the piano, you know."

"Well, now you look-a-here, Julie," said Connie impressively, "you cut out that being alone business, and the kissing, too. And now how about to-night? Are you sure his whole family is going to-night?"

"Well, that's just it, I'm not," Julia confessed, flattered by Connie's interest.

"Then you don't go one step, my dear; just you fool him a bunch! You see you're like a little boy, Ju: kisses don't mean nothing to you, *yet*. But you'll get a crush some day yourself, and then you'll feel like a fool if you've got mixed up with the wrong one—see?"

"Sure," said Julia, hoarse and embarrassed. Yet she liked the sensation of being scolded by Connie, too, and tried shyly, as the conversation seemed inclined to veer toward Connie's own affairs, to bring it back to her own.

The little matter of the corsets being settled, they sauntered through the always diverting streets toward the office of Leopold Artheris, manager of the Grand Opera House, and a very good friend of both girls.

They found him idle, in a bright, untidy office, lined with the pictures of stage favourites, and with three windows open to the sun and air.

"You're placed, I think, Miss Girard?" said he, giving her a fat little puffy hand. He was a stout, short man of fifty, with a bald spot showing under a mop of graying curls, and a bushy moustache also streaked with gray.

"If you call it placed," said Connie, grinning. "We open Monday in Sacramento."

"Aha! But why Sacramento?"

"Oh, we've got to open somewhere, I suppose! Try it out on the dog, you know!" Connie said, with a sort of bored airiness.

"And you, my dear?" said Artheris, turning toward Julia.

"She's come to see you about that amachure job," said Connie, reaching over to grab a theatrical magazine from the desk, and running her eye carelessly over its pages. Artheris's blandly smiling face underwent an instant change. He elevated his eyebrows, pursed his lips, and nodded with sudden interest.

"Oh—to be sure—to be sure! The performance of 'The Amazons' for the Hospital—yes, well! And what do you think of it, Miss Page?" he said.

Julia stretched out her little feet before her, shrugged, and brought an indifferent eye to bear upon the manager.

"What's there in it?" she asked.

"Well, now, *that* you'd have to settle with them," smiled Mr. Artheris.

"Oh, rot!" said Connie cheerfully. "*You* manage that for her; what does *she* know? Go on!"

"But, my dear young lady, *I* have nothing to do with it!" the man protested. "They come to me and wish to hire my theatre, lights, ushers, orchestra, and so, and they ask me if I know of a young actress who will take a part—to give them all confidence, you see"—he made encouraging gestures with his fat little hands—"to—to carry the performance, as it were!"

"What part?" asked Connie shrewdly.

"The part of—of—a splendid part, that of the Sergeant," said Artheris cheerfully.

"Yes, I know that part," Connie said grimly.

"The idea is to have Miss Julie here understudy all the parts," said the manager quickly. "These amateurs are very apt to disappoint, do you see? They feel that there would be a sense of security in having a professional right there to fill in a gap."

"Why, that would mean she'd have to learn practically the whole play," said Connie. "They ought to be willing to pay a good price for that. Of course Miss Page is only seventeen," she continued, a calculating eye on Julia, whose appearance did not belie the statement.

"No objection at all—they are all very young! Come now, what do you say, Miss Page?"

"Oh, I don't know," said Julia discontentedly. "I'm not so crazy about acting," she went on childishly. "I'm not so sure I want all these swells to stand around and impose on me—" She hesitated, uncertain and vague. "And I don't believe Mama'd be so anxious," she submitted lamely.

Just then the door of Mr. Artheris's office was opened, and a man put in his head. He was a young man, tall, thin, faultlessly dressed, and possessed of an infectious smile.

"Excuse me, Mr. Artheris," beamed the intruder, "but could I have a look at the stage? Far be it from me to interrupt or any little thing like that," he continued easily, "but my Mother'd have me dragged out and shot if I came home without seeing it!"

"Come in, come in, Mr. Hazzard," said Artheris cordially; "you're just the man we want to see! Miss Girard—Miss Page—Mr. Hazzard. Mr. Hazzard is managing this very affair—manager, isn't that it?"

"God knows what I am!" said Carter Hazzard, mopping his forehead, and appreciative of Miss Page's beauty and the maturer charms of Miss Girard. "I'm bell-hop for the whole crowd. My sister plays Thomasine, her steady is Tweenwayes, and my Mother's a director in the hospital. Fix it up to suit yourselves; you'll see that I'm every one's goat."

Both the girls laughed, and Artheris said:

"I am glad you came in, for Miss Page is the young lady of whom I spoke to you. Unfortunately, it seems that she has just promised to sign a contract with the Alcazar people."

"Oh, shucks! Can't you put it off until after the fifteenth?" asked Mr. Hazzard in alarm.

"Too much money in it," Connie said, shaking her head.

"Well—well, we expected to—to pay, of course," Carter said, embarrassed at this crudeness. And Julia, blushing furiously, muttered, "Oh—it wasn't the *pay*!"

"In a word, Miss Page's price is twenty-five dollars a night," said Artheris. "Could your people pay it?"

"Why—why, I suppose we could," Hazzard said uncomfortably. "It's—it's for a charity, you know," he ended weakly.

"Well, Miss Page's usual price is fifty; she's already reduced it half!" Connie said briskly.

Julia was now bitterly ashamed of her manager and her friend; her face was burning.

"I'll do it, of course," she promised. "And we'll arrange the terms afterward!"

"Good work!" said Hazzard gayly. In a few moments, when they all went out to look at the stage, he dropped behind the others and began to walk beside her.

"You're sure you're old enough to be on the stage, Miss Page; no Gerry Society scandal at the last minute?" he asked banteringly. "You look about twelve!"

Julia flashed him an oblique look.

"The idea! I'm nearly seventeen!" she said, with an uncertain little laugh. His ardent eyes embarrassed her.

"Honest?" said Carter Hazzard, in a low, caressing tone. He laid his fingers on her arm. "What's your hurry?" he asked.

"We ought to keep with the others," Julia stammered, scarlet cheeked but half laughing. At the same instant his inclination to cut across her path brought her to a full stop. She backed against a heavily tasselled and upholstered old armchair that chanced to be standing in the wings, and sitting down on one of its high arms, looked straight up into his eyes. The others had gone on; they were alone in the draughty wings.

"Why ought we?" said Hazzard, still in a low voice full of significance, his eyes on her shoulder, where he straightened a ruffle that was caught under a chain of beads. "If you like me and I like you, why shouldn't we have a little talk?"

However young she might appear, the inanities of a flirtation were a familiar field to Julia. She gave him a demure and unsmiling glance from between curled lashes, and said:

"What would you like to talk about?"

By this time their faces were close together; a sort of heady lightness in the atmosphere set them both to laughing foolishly; their voices trembled on uncertain notes. An exhilarating sense of her own sex and charm thrilled Julia; she knew that he found her sweet and young and wonderful.

"I'd like to talk about *you*!" said Carter Hazzard. Julia found his audacity delightful; she began to feel that she could not keep up with the dazzling rush of his repartee. "You know, the minute I saw you—" he added.

"Now, *don't* tell me I'm pretty!" Julia begged, with another flashing look.

"No—no!" the man exclaimed, discarding mere beauty with violence. "Pretty! Lord! what does prettiness matter? Of course you're pretty, but do you know what I said to myself the minute I saw you? I said, 'I'll bet that little girl has *brains*!' You smile," said Mr. Hazzard, with passionate earnestness, "but I'll swear to God I did!"

"Oh, you just want me to believe that!" scoffed Julia, dimpling.

What they said, however, mattered as little as what might be said by the two occupants of a boat that was drifting swiftly toward rapids.

"Why do you think an unkind thing like that?" Carter asked reproachfully.

"Was that unkind?" Julia countered innocently. At which Mr. Hazzard observed irrelevantly, in a low voice:

"Do you know you're absolutely fascinating? Do you? You're just the kind of little girl I want to know—to be friends with—to have for a pal!"

Julia was quite wise enough to know that whatever qualifications she possessed for this pleasing position could hardly have made themselves evident to Mr. Hazzard during their very brief acquaintance, and she was not a shade more sincere than he as she answered coquettishly:

"Yes, that's what they all say! And then they—" She stopped.

"And then they—what?" breathed Carter, playing with the loose ribbons of her feather boa.

"Then they fall in love with me!" pouted the girl, raising round eyes.

Carter was intoxicated at this confession, and laughed out loud.

"But you're too young to play at falling in love!" he warned her. "How old are you—seventeen? And you haven't told me your name yet?"

"You know my name is Miss Page," smiled Julia.

"And do you think I'm going to call you that?" Carter reproached her.

"It might be Jane," she suggested.

"Yes, but it isn't, you little devil!" Suddenly the man caught both her wrists, and Julia got on her feet, and instinctively flung back her head. "You're going to kiss me for that!" he said, half laughing, half vexed.

"Oh, no, I'm not!" A sudden twist of her body failed to free her, and the plume on her hat brushed his cheek.

"Oh, yes, you are!" He caught both wrists in one of his strong hands, and put his arm about her shoulders like a vise, turning her face toward him at the same time. Julia, furious with the nervous fear that this scuffling would be overheard, and that Carter would make her ridiculous, glared at him, and they remained staring fixedly at each other for a few moments.

"You *dare*!" she whispered then, held so tightly that Carter could hear her heart beat, "and I'll scream loud enough to bring every one in the place!"

"All right—you little cat!" he laughed, freeing her suddenly. Julia tossed her head and walked off without speaking, but presently an oblique swift glance at him showed his expression to be all penitent and beseeching; their eyes met, and they both laughed. Still laughing, they came upon Artheris and Connie, and all walked out together on the deserted stage.

The great empty arch was but dimly lighted, draughty, odorous, and gloomy. Beyond the extinguished footlights they could see the curved enormous cavern of the house, row upon row of empty seats. In the orchestra box two or three men, one in his coat sleeves, were disputing over an opera score. High up in the topmost gallery some one was experimenting with the calcium machine; a fan of light occasionally swept the house, or a man's profile was silhouetted against a sputter of blue flame.

Artheris and young Hazzard paced the stage, consulted, and disagreed. Connie practised a fancy step in a wide circle, her skirt caught up, her face quite free of self-consciousness. Julia sat on a box, soberly looking from face to face.

Something had happened to her, she did not yet know what. She was frightened, yet strangely bold; she experienced delicious chills, yet her cheeks were on fire. Love of life flooded her whole being in waves; she was wrapped, lulled, saturated, in a new and dreamy peace.

Julia felt a sudden warm rush of affection for Connie—dear old Con—the best friend a girl ever had! She looked about the theatre; how she loved the old "Grand!" Above all possible conditions in life it was wonderful to be Julia Page, sitting here, the very hub of the world, a being to love and be loved.

There, at that hour, she came to that second birth all women know; she was born into that world of drifting sweet odours, blending and iridescent colours, evasive and enchanting sounds, that is the kingdom of the heart. Julia did not know why, from this hour on, she was no longer a little girl, she was no longer dumb and blind and unseeing. But a new and delightful consciousness woke within her, a new sense of her own importance, her own charm.

When she and Connie strolled out again, it was, for Julia at least, into a changed world. The immortal hour of romance touched even sordid Mission Street with gold. Julia walked demurely, but conscious of every admiring glance she won from the passers-by, conscious of a score of swallows taking flight from a curb, conscious of the pathetic beauty of the little draggled mother wheeling home her sleepy baby, the setting sunlight glittering in the eyes of both.

"He's nothing but a big spoiled kid, if you want to know what I think," said Connie, ending a long dissertation to which Julia had only half listened.

"He—who?" asked Julia, suddenly recalled from dreams, and feeling her heart turn liquid within her. A weakness seized her knees, a delicious chill ran up her spine.

"Hazzard—the smarty!" Connie elucidated carelessly.

"Oh, sure!" Julia said heavily. She made no further comment.

She and Connie wandered in and out of a few shops, asking prices, and fingering laces and collars. They went into the dim, echoing old library on Post Street, to powder their noses at the mirror downstairs; they went into the music store at Sutter and Kearney, and listened for a few moments to a phonograph concert; they bought violets—ten cents for a great bunch—at the curb market about Lotta's fountain.

The sweetness of the dying spring day flooded the city, and its very essence pierced Julia's heart with a vague pain that was a pleasure, too. Presently she and Connie walked to California Street, and climbed a steep block or two to the Maison Montiverte.

Julia and her mother, and a large proportion of their acquaintances, dined chez Montiverte perhaps a hundred times a year. There was a regular twenty-five-cent dinner that was extremely good, there was a fifty-cent dinner fit for a king, and there were specialties de la maison, as, for example, a combination salad at twenty cents that was a meal in itself. Irrespective of the other order, the guest of the Maison Montiverte was regaled with boiled shrimps or crabs' legs while he waited for his dinner, was eagerly served with all the delicious French bread and butter that he could eat, and had a little cup of superb black coffee without charge to finish his meal. Brilliant piano music swept the rooms whenever any guest cared to send the waiter with a five-cent piece to the old mechanical piano, and sprightly conversation, carried on from table to table, gave the place that tone that Monsieur Montiverte considered to be its most valuable asset. Monsieur himself was a dried-up little rat of a man, grizzled, and as brown as a walnut. Madame was large and superb and young, smooth faced, brown haired, regal in manner. It was said that Madame had had a predecessor, a lady now living in France, whose claim upon Jules Montiverte was still valid. However that might be, it did not seem to worry Jules, nor his calm and lovely companion, nor their two daughters, black-eyed baby girls, whose heavy straight hair was crimped at the ends into bands of brownish-black fuzz, and who wore white stockings and tasselled boots, and flounced, elaborately embroidered white dresses on Sundays. Whatever their bar sinister, the Montivertes flourished and grew rich, and a suspicion of something irregular, some high-handed disposition of the benefit of clergy, helped rather than hurt their business.

Julia and Connie were early to-night, and took their regular places at a long table that was as yet surrounded only by empty chairs. Madame, who was feeding bread and milk to a black-eyed three-year-old at a little table in a corner, nodded a welcome, and a young Frenchwoman, putting her head in through a swinging door at the back, nodded, too, and said, showing a double row of white teeth:

"Wait—een?"

"Yes, we'll wait for the others!" Connie called back. She and Julia nibbled French bread, and played with their knives and forks while they waited.

The dining-room had that aspect of having been made for domestic and adapted to general use that is so typically un-American, yet so dear to the American heart. An American manager would have torn down partitions, papered in brown cartridge, curtained in pongee, and laid a hardwood floor. Monsieur Montiverte left the two drawing-rooms as they were: a shabby red carpet was under foot, stiff Nottingham curtains filtered the bright sunlight, and an old-fashioned paper in dull arabesques of green and brown and gold made a background for framed dark engravings, "Franklin at the Court of France," and "The Stag at Bay," and other pictures of their type. The tablecloths were coarse, the china and glass heavy, and the menus were written in blue indelible pencil, in a curly French hand. From the windows at the back one could look out upon an iron-railed balcony, a garden beyond, and the old, brick, balconied houses of the Chinese quarter. At the left the California Street cable car climbed the hill, and the bell tower of old St. Mary's rose sombre and dignified against the soft sunset sky. At the right were the Park, with a home-going tide pouring through it at this hour, and Kearney Street with its jangling car bells, and below, the square roofs of the warehouse district, and the spire of the ferry building, and the bay framed in its rim of hills. Montiverte owned the house in which he conducted his business; it was one of the oldest in the city, built by the French pioneers who were the first to erect permanent homes in the new land. This had been the fashionable part of town in 1860, but its stately old homes were put to strange uses in these days. Boarding-houses of the lowest class, shops, laundries, saloons, and such restaurants as Jules Montiverte's overran the district; the Chinese quarter pressed hard upon one side, and what was always called the "bad" part of town upon the other. Yet only two blocks away, straight up the hill, were some of San Francisco's most beautiful homes, the brownstone mansion, then the only one in California, that some homesick Easterner built at fabulous cost, the great house that had been recently given for an institute of art, and the homes of two or three of the railroad kings.

Patrons of Montiverte began to saunter in by twos and threes. Some of these the girls knew, and saluted familiarly; others were strangers, and ignored, and made to feel as uncomfortable as possible. Julia's beauty was always the object of notice, and she loved to appear entirely unconscious of it, to sparkle and chatter as if no eyes were upon her. Emeline came in, with one or two older women, and Julia looked up from a great bowl of soup to nod to her.

"Sign up?" asked Emeline languidly. And two or three strangers, obviously impressed by the term, waited for the answer.

"Oh, I guess I'll do it to please Artheris!" Julia said. The girl was fairly aglow to-night, palpitating and thrilling with youth and the joy of life. Everything distracted her—everything amused her—yet now and then she found a quiet moment in which to take out her little memories of the afternoon, and to review them with a curiously palpitating heart.

"If you like me and I like you ... I want to talk about you ... do you know you're absolutely fascinating? ... you're going to kiss me for that! ..." She could still hear his voice, feel his arm about her.

Somebody producing free seats for the Alcazar Theatre, Julia allowed herself to drift along with the crowd. They were late for the performance, but nobody cared; they had all seen it before, and after commenting on it in a way that somewhat annoyed their neighbours, straggled out, in the beginning of the last act, giggling and chewing gum. Julia, raising bewildered, sweet, childish eyes to the stars above noisy O'Farrell Street, was brought suddenly to earth by a touch on her arm.

It was a dark, tall young man who stepped out of a shadowy doorway to address her, a man of twenty, perhaps, with all the ripe and sensuous beauty of the young Jew. His skin was a clear olive, his magnificent black eyes were set off with evenly curling lashes, and his firm mouth, under its faint moustache, made a touch of scarlet colour among the rich brunette tones. He was dressed with a scrupulous niceness, and carried a long light overcoat on his arm.

"Julia!" he said sombrely, coming forward, his eyes only for her.

"Why, hello, Mark!" Julia answered. And with a little concern creeping into her manner she went on, "Why, what is it?"

Young Rosenthal glanced at her friends, and, formally offering her his arm, said seriously: "You will walk with me?"

"We were going down to Haas's for ice-cream sodas," Julia submitted hesitatingly.

"Well, I will take you there," Mark said. And as the others, nodding good-naturedly at this, drifted on ahead, Julia found herself walking down O'Farrell Street on the arm of a tall and handsome man.

It was the first time that she had done just this thing—or if not the first time, it had never seemed to have any particular significance before. Now, however, Julia felt in her heart a little flutter of satisfaction. Somehow Mark did not seem just a commonplace member of the "Rosenthal gang" tonight, nor did she seem "the Page kid." Mark was a man, and—thrilling thought!—was angry at Julia, and Julia, hanging on his arm, with a hundred street lights flashing on her little powdered nose and saucy hat, was at last a "young lady!"

"What's the matter, Mark?" she asked, by way of opening the conversation.

"Oh, nothing whatever!" Mark answered, in a rich, full voice, and with elaborate irony. "You promised to go to the Orpheum with me, and I waited—and I waited—and you did not come. But that is nothing, of course!"

Julia's anger smote her dumb for a moment. Then she jerked her arm from his, and burst out:

"I'll *tell* you why I didn't meet you to-night, Mark Rosenthal, and if you don't like it, you know what you can do! Last week you asked me would I go to Morosco's with you, and I said yes, and then when it came right down to it—your mother wasn't going, and Sophy and Hannah weren't going, and Otto wasn't going—and I tell you right now that Mama don't like me to go to the theatre—"

"Well, well, well!" Mark interrupted soothingly, half laughing, half aghast at this burst of rebuke from the usually gentle Julia. "Don't be so cross about it! So—" He put her arm in his again. "I like to have you to myself, Julia," he said, his boyish, handsome face suddenly flushing, his voice very low. "Do you know why?"

"No," said Julia after a pause, the word strangling her.

"You don't, eh?" Mark said, with a smiling side glance.

"Nope," said Julia, dimpling as she returned the look, and shutting her pretty lips firmly over the little word.

"Do you know you are ador-r-rable?" Mark said, in a sort of eager rush. "Will you go to Maskey's with me, instead of joining the others at Haas's?" he asked, more quietly.

"Well," Julia said. She was her own mistress. Her mother had gone home during the play with Mrs. Toomey, who complained of a headache. So, grinning like conspirators, they stayed on the south side of the street until it joined Market, and then went by the fountain and the big newspaper buildings, and slipped into the confectioner's. Julia sent an approving side glance at herself in the mirror, as she drew a satisfied breath of the essence-laden air. She loved lights, perfumes, voices—and all were here.

An indifferent young woman wiped their table with a damp rag, as she took their order, both, with the daring of their years, deciding upon the murderous combination of banana ice-cream and soda with chopped nuts and fruit. Julia had no sooner settled back contentedly to wait for it, than her eye encountered the beaming faces of her late companions, who, finding Haas's crowded, had naturally drifted on to Maskey's.

Much giggling and blushing and teasing ensued. Julia was radiant as a rose; every time she caught sight of her own pretty reflection in the surrounding mirrors, a fresh thrill of self-confidence warmed her. She and Mark followed the banana confection with a dish apiece of raspberry ice-cream, and afterward walked home—it was not far—to the house in which they both lived.

"And so we don't quarrel any more?" Mark asked, in the dim hallway outside her door.

"Not if you won't play mean tricks on me!" Julia pouted, raising her face so that the dim light of the gas jet that burned year in and year out, in the blistered red-glass shade, fell upon the soft curves of her face.

It was a deliberate piece of coquetry, and Julia, although neither he nor any other man had ever done it before, was not at all surprised to have Mark suddenly close his strong arms about her, and kiss her, with a sort of repressed violence, on the mouth. She struggled from his hold, as a matter of course, laughed a little laugh of triumph and excitement, and shut herself into her own door.

Emeline was lying in bed, looking over some fashion and theatrical magazines. Upon her daughter's entrance she gave a comfortable yawn.

"Did Mark find you, Julie? He was sitting on the stairs when I got home, mad because you didn't go out with them."

"Yep, he found me!" Julia answered, still panting.

"It strikes me he's a little mushy on you, Julie," Emeline said, lazily, turning a page. "And if you were a little older, or he had more of a job, I'd give him a piece of my mind. You ain't going to marry *his* sort, I should hope. But, Lord, you're both only kids!"

"I guess I can mind my own business, Mama," Julia said.

"Well, I guess you can," Emeline conceded amiably. "Look, Ju, at the size of these sleeves—ain't that something fierce? Get the light out as soon as you can, lovey," she added, flinging away her magazine, and rolling herself tight in the covers, with bright eyes fixed on the girl.

Ten minutes later Emeline was asleep. But Julia lay long awake, springtime in her blood, her eyes smiling mysteriously into the dark.

CHAPTER III

By just what mental processes Emeline Page had come to feel herself a dignified martyr in a world full of oppressed women, it would be difficult to say: Emeline herself would have been the last person from whom a reasonable explanation might have been expected. But it was a fact that she never missed an opportunity to belittle the male sex; she had never had much charm for men, she had none now, and consequently she associated chiefly with women: with widows and grass widows of her own type, and with the young actresses and would-be actresses of the curious social level upon which she lived. Emeline's lack of charm was the most valuable moral asset she had. Had she attracted men she would not long have remained virtuous, for she was violently opposed to any restriction upon her own desires, no matter how well established a restriction or how generally accepted it might be. For a little while after George's going, Emeline had indeed frequently used the term "if I marry again," but of late years she had rather softened to his memory, and enjoyed abusing other men while she revelled in a fond recollection of George's goodness.

"God knows I was only a foolish girl," Emeline would say, resting cold wet feet against the open oven door while Julia pressed a frill. "But your papa never was anything but a perfect ge'man, never! I'll never forget one night when he took me to Grant's Cafe for dinner! I was all dressed up to kill, and George looked elegant—"

A long reminiscence followed.

"I hope to God you get as good a man as your papa," said Emeline more than once, romantically.

Julia, thumping an iron, would answer with cool common sense:

"Well, if I do, I want to tell you right now, Mama, I'll treat him a good deal better than you did!"

"Oh, you'll be a wonder," Emeline would concede good-naturedly.

At very long intervals Emeline dressed herself and her daughter as elaborately as possible, and went out into the Mission to see her parents. With the singular readiness to change the known discomfort for the unknown, characteristic of their class, the various young members of the family had all gone away now, and lonely old Mrs. Cox, a shrivelled little shell of a woman at sixty-five, always had a warm welcome for her oldest daughter and her beautiful grandchild. She would limp about her bare, uninviting little rooms, complaining of her husband's increasing meanness and of her own physical ills, while with gnarled, twisted old hands she filled a "Rebecca" teapot of cheap brown glaze, or cut into a fresh loaf of "milk bread."

"D'ye see George at all now, Emeline?"

"Not to speak to, Mom. But"—and Emeline would lay down the little mirror in which she was studying her face—"but the Rosenthal children say that there's a man who's *always* hanging about the lower doorway, and that once he gave Hannah———"

And so on and on. Mrs. Cox was readily convinced that George, repentant, was unable to keep away from the neighbourhood of his one and only love. Julia, dreaming over her thick cup of strong tea, granted only a polite, faintly weary smile to her mother's romances. She knew how glad Emeline would be to really believe even one tenth of these flattering suspicions.

A few weeks after Julia's long day of events with Artheris, with Carter Hazzard, and young Rosenthal, she chanced to awaken one Saturday morning to a pleasant, undefined sensation that life was sweet. She thought of Mr. Hazzard, whom she had seen twice since their first meeting, but not alone again. And she reflected with satisfaction that she knew her part of "The Amazons" perfectly, and so was ready for the first rehearsal to-day. This led to a little dream of the leading lady failing to appear on the great night, and of Julia herself in Lady Noel's part; of Julia subsequently adored and envied by the entire cast; of Carter Hazzard———

Julia had made an engagement with Mark for to-day, but the rehearsal plan must interfere. She wondered how she could send him word, and finally decided to see him herself for a moment early in the afternoon. Mark, originally employed as office boy, pure and simple, had now made himself a general handy man, reference and filing clerk, in the big piano house of Pomeroy and Parke. He had all the good traits of his race, and some of the traits that, without being wholly admirable, help a man toward success. No slur at himself or his religion was keen enough to pierce Mark's smiling armour of philosophy, no hours were too hard for him, no work too menial for him to do cheerfully, nor too important for him to undertake confidently. A wisdom far older than his years was his. Poverty had been his teacher, exile and deprivation. When other children were in school, repeating mechanically that many a little made a mickle, that genius was an infinite capacity for taking pains, and that a man has no handicaps but those of his own making, Mark *knew* these things, he knew that the great forces of life were no stronger than his own two hands, and that any work of any sort must bring him to his goal—the goal of wealth and power and position.

He knew that his father was not so clever as he was, and why. He saw that his mother was worn out with housework and child-bearing. He did not idealize their home, where father, mother, and seven children were crowded into four rooms, and where of an evening the smell of cabbage soup and herrings, of soap-suds and hot irons on woollen, of inky school books and perspiring humanity, mingled with the hot, oily breath of the lamp.

Yet Mark saw beyond this, too. The food was good, if coarse, the bills were paid, the bank account grew. Some day the girls would be married, the boys in good positions; some day the mother should have a little country house and a garden, and the father come home early to smoke his pipe and prune his rose bushes. Not a very brilliant future—no. But how brilliant to them, who could remember Russia!

As for him, Mark, there was no limit to his personal dream at all. Some day, while yet as young as Mr. Parke, he would be as rich as Mr. Pomeroy, he would have five splendid children, like the Pomeroy children, he would have a wife as beautiful as young Mrs. Parke. To his beautiful Jackson Street palace the city's best people should come, and sometimes—for a favoured few—he would play his rippling etudes and nocturnes, his mazurkas and polonaises.

Julia Page, an unnoticed little neighbour for many years, had, just at present, somewhat ruffled the surface of his dream. Julia was not the ideal wife of his mind or heart; nor was she apt to grow to fill that ideal. Mrs. Mark Rosenthal must be a Jewess, a wise, ripened, poised, and low-voiced woman, a lover of music, babies, gardens, cooking, and managing.

Yet there had been a certain evening, not long before that spring evening upon which Julia's own awakening came, when Mark had been astonished to find a sudden charm in the little girl. She was only a little girl, of course, he said to himself later; just a kid, but she was a mighty cunning kid!

Julia often had dinner with the Rosenthals; she loved every separate member of the family and she knew they all loved her. She used to run upstairs and pop her pretty head into the Rosenthal kitchen perhaps twice a week, sure of a welcome and a good meal. On the occasion so significant to Mark she had been there when he got in from work, helping his sisters Sophy and Hannah with that careless disposition of iron knives, great china sugar bowl, oddly assorted plates, and thick cups that was known as "setting the table."

Mark had noticed then that Julia's figure was getting very pretty, and he watched her coming and going with a real pleasure. She sat next him at table, and, conscious as he was of her nearness and of himself, he found her unconsciousness very charming. Julia had burned her arm serving the fried hominy, and she held it up for Mark to see, the bare, sweet young arm close to his face.

And since then, poor Mark seemed to be bewitched. He could not think of anything but Julia. It made him angry and self-contemptuous, but he was no better off for that. He did not want to fall in love with Julia Page; he would not admit that what he felt for Julia was love; he raged with disappointment at the mere thought of bondage so soon, and especially this bondage. But the sweetness of her stole upon his senses nevertheless, tangling about him like a drifting bit of vaporous mist; he had no sooner detached one section of it than another blew across his eyes, set pulses to beating in his temples, and shook his whole body with a delicious weakness.

And then came the night when she had not kept her appointment, and he had followed her to the Alcazar Theatre, and later kissed her in the dark hallway. Then Mark knew. From the instant her fresh lips touched his, and he felt the soft yielding as he drew her to him, Mark knew that he was of the world's lovers. He wanted her with all the deep passion of first love—first love in an ardent and romantic and forceful nature. His dreams did not change; Julia changed to fit them. She was everything for which he had ever longed, she was perfection absolute. She became his music, his business, his life. Every little girl, every old woman that he passed in the street, made him think of Julia, and when he passed a young man and woman full of concern for, and of shy pride in, their lumpy baby in its embroidered coat, a wave of divine envy swept Mark from head to foot.

To-day he whistled over his work, thinking of Julia. They were to meet at three o'clock, "just to bum," as the girl said, laughing. Mark thought that, as the season was well forward, they might take a car to the park or the beach, but the plan had been left indefinite.

He ate his lunch, of butterless bread and sausage, and an entire five-cent pie, in a piano wareroom, taking great bites, with dreamy studying of the walls and long delays between. Then he wandered down through the empty offices—it was Saturday afternoon and Pomeroy and Parke closed promptly at twelve—had a brief chat with the Japanese janitor, and washed his hands and combed his hair very conscientiously in the president's own lavatory.

At half-past one he went into one of the glass showrooms, a prettily furnished apartment whose most notable article of furniture was a grand piano in exquisitely matched Circassian walnut. Absorbed and radiant, Mark put back the cover, twirled the stool, and carefully opened a green book marked "Chopin." Then he sat down, and, with the sigh of a happy child falling upon a feast, he struck an opening chord.

The big flexible fingers still needed training, but they showed the result of hours and hours of patient practice, too. Through his seven years in the music house, Mark had been faithful to his gift. He made no secret of it, his associates knew that he came back after dinner to the very rooms that they themselves left so eagerly at the end of the day. Mark had indeed once asked old Mr. Pomeroy to hear him play, an occasion to which the boy still looked back with hot shame. For when his obliging old employer had settled himself to listen after hours on an appointed afternoon, and Mark had opened the piano, the performer suddenly found his spine icy, his hands wet and clumsy. He felt as if he had never touched a piano before; the attempt was a failure from the first note, as Mark well knew. When he had finished he whisked open another book.

"That was rotten," he stammered. "I thought I could do it—I can't. But just let me play you this—"

But the great man was in a hurry, it appeared.

"No—no, my boy, not to-day—some other time! Perhaps a little bit too ambitious a choice, eh? We must all be ambitious, but we must know our limitations, too. Some other time!"

Then Mr. Pomeroy was gone and Mark left to bitterest reflection.

But he recovered very sensibly from his boyish chagrin, and very sensibly went at his practicing again. On this particular Saturday afternoon he attacked a certain phrase in the bass, and for almost an hour the big fingers of his left hand rippled over it steadily. Mark, twisted about halfway on the bench, watched the performance steadily, his right hand hanging loose.

"Damn!" he said presently, with a weary sigh, as a sharp and familiar little pain sprang into his left wrist.

"Mark!" breathed a reproachful voice behind him. He whirled about, to see Julia Page.

She had come noiselessly in at the glass doorway behind him, and was standing there, laughing, a picture of fresh and demure beauty, despite the varied colours in hat and waist and gown and gloves.

"I had to see you!" said Julia, in a rush. "And nobody answered your telephone—there's a rehearsal of that play at the theatre to-day, so I can't meet you—and the janitor let me in———"

Mark found her incoherence delicious; her being here, in his own familiar stamping-ground, one of the thrilling and exciting episodes of his life. He could have shouted—have danced for pure joy as he jumped up to welcome her. Julia declared that she had to "fly," but Mark insisted—and she found his insistence curiously pleasant—upon showing her about, leading her from office to office, beaming at her whenever their eyes met. And he *must* play her the little Schumann, he said, but no—for that Julia positively would *not* wait; she jerked him by one hand toward the door. Mark had his second kiss before they emerged laughing and radiant into the gaiety of Kearney Street on a Saturday afternoon.

And Julia was not late for her rehearsal, or, if late, she was at least earlier by a full quarter hour than the rest of the caste. She took an orchestra seat in the empty auditorium at the doorkeeper's suggestion, and yawned, and stared at the coatless back of a man who was tuning the orchestra piano.

Presently two distinguished looking girls, beautifully dressed, came in, and sat down near her in a rather uncertain way, and began to laugh and talk in low tones. Neither cast a glance at Julia, who promptly decided that they were hateful snobs, and began to regard them with burning resentment. They had been there only a few moments when two young men sauntered down the aisle, unmistakably gentlemen, and genuine enough to express their enjoyment of this glimpse of a theatre between performances. Two of them carried little paper copies of "The Amazons," so Julia knew them for fellow-performers.

Then a third young woman came in and walked down the aisle as the others had done. This was an extremely pretty girl of perhaps eighteen, with dark hair and dark bright eyes, and a very fresh bright colour. Her gown was plain but beautifully fitting, and her wide hat was crowned with a single long ostrich plume. She peered at the young men.

"Hello, Bobby—hello, Gray!" she said gayly, and then, catching sight of the two other girls across the aisle, she added: "Oh, hello, Helen—how do you do, Miss Carson? Come over here and meet Mr. Sumner and Mr. Babcock!"

Babel ensued. Three or four waiting young people said, "Oh, Barbara!" in tones of great delight, and the fourth no less eagerly substituted, "Oh, Miss Toland!"

"How long have you poor, long-suffering catfish been waiting here?" demanded Miss Barbara Toland, with a sort of easy sweetness that Julia found instantly enviable. "Why, we're all out in the foyer—Mother's here, chaperoning away like mad, and nearly all the others! And"—she whisked a little gold watch into sight—"my dears, it's twenty minutes to four!"

Every one exclaimed, as they rushed out. Julia, unaccountably nervous, wished she were well out of this affair, and wondered what she ought to do.

Presently some twenty-five or thirty well-dressed folk came streaming back down the main aisle in a wild confusion of laughter and talk. Somehow the principals were filtered out of this crowd, and somehow they got on the stage, and got a few lights turned on, and assembled for the advice of an agitated manager. Dowagers and sympathetic friends settled in orchestra seats to watch; the rehearsal began.

Julia had strolled up to the stage after the others; now she sat on a shabby wooden chair that had lost its back, leaned her back against a piece of scenery, and surveyed the scene with as haughty and indifferent an air as she could assume.

"And the Sergeant—who takes that?" demanded the manager, a young fellow of their own class, familiarly addressed as "Matty."

The caste, which had been churning senselessly about him, chorussed an explanation.

"A professional takes that, Mat, don't you remember?"

"Well, where is she?" Matty asked irritably.

Julia here sauntered superbly forward, serenely conscious of youth, beauty, and charm. Every one stared frankly at her, as she said languidly:

"Perhaps it's I you're looking for? Mr. Artheris—"

"Yes, that's right!" said Matty, relieved. He wiped his forehead. "Miss—Page, isn't it?" He paused, a little at a loss, eying the other ladies of the caste dubiously. The girl called Barbara Toland now came forward with her ready graciousness, and the two girls looked fairly into each other's eyes.

"Miss Page," said Barbara, and then impatiently to the manager, "Do go ahead and get started, Matty; we've got to get home some time to-night!"

Julia's introduction was thus waived, and business began at once. The wavering voices of the principals drifted uncertainly into the theatre. "Louder!" said the chaperons and friends. The men were facetious, interpolating their lines with jokes, good-humoured under criticism; the girls fluttered nervously over cues, could not repeat the simplest line without a half-giggling "Let's see—yes, I come in here," and were only fairly started before they must interrupt themselves with an earnest, "Mat, am I standing still when I say that, or do I walk toward her?"

Julia was the exception. She had been instructed a fortnight before that she must know her lines and business to-day, and she did know them. Almost scornfully she took her cues and walked through her part. "Matty" clapped his hands and overpraised her, and Julia felt with a great rush of triumph that she had "shown those girls!" She had an exhilarating afternoon, for the men buzzed about her on every possible occasion, and she knew that the other girls, for all their lofty indifference, were keenly conscious of it.

She went out through the theatre with the others, at an early six. The young people straggled along the aisle in great confusion, laughing and chattering. Mrs. Toland, a plump, merry, handsomely dressed woman, was anxious to carry off her tall daughter in time for some early boat.

"*Do* hurry, Barbara! Sally and Ted may be on that five-fifty, and if Dad went home earlier they'll have to make the trip alone!"

At the doorway they found that the street was almost dark, and foggy. Much discussion of cars and carriages marked the breaking-up. Enid Hazzard, a rather noisy girl, who played Noel Belturbet, elected to go home with the Babcocks. This freed from all responsibility her brother Carter, who had suddenly appeared to act as escort. Julia, slipping up the darkening street, after a few moments spent in watching this crowd of curious young people, found him at her side.

"No coat, Miss Page?" said the easy tones.

"I didn't know it would be so foggy!" said Julia, her heart beginning to thump.

"And where are you going?"

"Home to get a coat."

"I see. Where is it? I'll take you."

"Oh, it's just a few blocks," Julia said. She knew nothing of the reputation of San Francisco's neighbourhoods, but Carter gave her a surprised look. When Julia, quite unembarrassed, stopped at the door beside the saloon, he was the more confused of the two, although the accident of seeing him again had set the blood to racing in Julia's veins and made speech difficult. She had been longing for just this; she was trembling with eagerness and nervousness.

"Father and Mother live here?" asked Carter.

"Just Mama—she rents rooms."

"Oh, I see!" He had stepped into the deep doorway, and catching her by the shoulders he said now, inconsequently: "Do you know you're the prettiest girl that ever *was*?"

"Am I?" said Julia, in a whisper.

"You know you are—you—you little flirt!" Hazzard said, his eyes three inches from hers. For a tense second neither stirred, then the man straightened up suddenly: "Well!" he said loudly. "That'll be about all of *that*. Good-night, my dear!"

He turned abruptly away, and Julia, smiling her little inscrutable smile, went slowly upstairs. The bedroom was dark, unaired, and in disorder. Julia looked about it dreamily, picked her library book from the floor and read a few pages of "Aunt Johnnie," sitting meanwhile on the edge of the unmade bed, and chewing a piece of gum that had been pressed, a neat bead, upon the back of a chair. After a while she got up, powdered her nose, and rubbed her finger-nails with a buffer—a buffer lifeless and hard, and deeply stained with dirt and red grease. Emeline had left a note, "Gone up to Min's—come up there for supper," but Julia felt that there was no hurry; meals at Mrs. Tarbury's were usually late.

During the ensuing fortnight there were two or three more rehearsals of "The Amazons" at the Grand Opera House, which only confirmed Julia's first impression of her fellow-players. The men she liked, and flirted with; for the girls she had a supreme contempt. She found herself younger, prettier, and a better actress than the youngest, prettiest, and cleverest among them. While these pampered daughters of wealth went awkwardly through their parts, and chatted in subdued tones among themselves, Julia rattled her speeches off easily, laughed and talked with all the young men in turn, posed and pirouetted as one born to the footlights. If Julia fancied that any girl was betraying a preference for any particular man, against that man she directed the full battery of her charms. Carter Hazzard came to every rehearsal, and was quite openly her slave. He did not offer to walk home with her again, but Julia knew that he was conscious of her presence whenever she was near him, and spun a mad little dream about a future in which she queened it over all these girls as his wife.

It was all delightful and exciting. Life had never been dark to Julia; now she found the days all too short for her various occupations and pleasures. Mark was assuming more and more the attitude of a lover, and Julia was too much of a coquette to discourage him utterly. She really liked him, and loved the stolen hours in Pomeroy and Parke's big piano house, when Mark, flinging his hair out of his eyes, played like an angel, and Julia nibbled caramels and sat curled up on the davenport, watching him. And through the casual attentions of other men, the occasional flattering half-hours with Carter Hazzard, the evenings of gossip at Mrs. Tarbury's, and round the long table at Montiverte's, Julia liked to sometimes think of Mark; his admiration was a little warm, reassuring background for all the other thoughts of the day.

At the end of the fourth or fifth rehearsal Julia noticed that pretty Barbara Toland was trying to manage a moment's speech with her alone. She amused herself with an attempt to avoid Miss Toland just from pure mischief, but eventually the two came face to face, in a garishly lighted bit of passage, Barbara, for all her advantage in years and in position, seeming the younger of the two.

"Oh, Miss Page," said Barbara nervously, "I wanted to—but were you going somewhere?"

"Don't matter if I was!" said Julia, airily gracious, but watching shrewdly.

"Well, I—I hope you won't think this is funny, but, well, I'll tell you," stammered Barbara, very red. "I know you don't know us all very well, you know—it's different with us—we've all been brought up together—but I didn't know whether you knew—perhaps you did—that Carter Hazzard is married?"

Julia felt stunned, and a little sick. She got only the meaning of the words, their value would come later. But with a desperate effort she pulled herself together, and smiled with dry lips.

"Yes, I knew that," she said, pleasantly, not meeting Barbara's eye.

"Oh, well, then it's all *right*," Barbara said hastily, relieved. "But he—he has a teasing sort of way, you know. His wife is in San Diego now, with her own people."

"Yes, he told me that," Julia said, only longing to escape before a maddening impulse to cry overpowered her. Barbara saw the truth, and laid a friendly hand on Julia's arm.

"I just wanted you to know," she said in her kindliest tone.

Suddenly Julia burst out crying, childishly blubbering with her wrists in her eyes. Barbara, very much distressed, shielded her as well as she could from the eyes of possible passers-by, and patted her shoulder with a gloved hand.

"I don't know why—perfectly *crazy*—" gulped Julia, desperately fighting the sobs that shook her. "And I've had a dreadful headache all day," she broke out, pitifully, beginning to mop her eyes with a folded handkerchief, her face still turned away from Barbara.

"Oh, poor thing!" said Barbara. "And the rehearsal must have made it worse!"

"It's splitting," Julia said sombrely. She gave Barbara one grave, almost resentful, look, straightened her hat and fluffed up her hair, and went away.

Barbara looked after her, and thought that Carter was a beast, and that there was something very pitiful about common little ignorant Miss Page, and that she wouldn't tell the girls about this, and give them one more cause to laugh at the little actress. For Barbara Toland was a conscientious girl, and very seriously impressed with the gravity of her own responsibility toward other people.

Meanwhile Julia walked toward the Mechanics' Library in a very fury of rage and resentment. She hated the entire caste of "The Amazons," and she hated Barbara Toland and Carter Hazzard more than the rest! He could play with her and flirt with her and deceive her, and while she, Julia, fancied herself envied and admired of the other girls, this delicately perfumed and exquisitely superior Barbara could be deciding in all sisterly kindness that she must inform Miss Page of her admirer's real position. Angry tears came to Julia's eyes, but she went into the Mechanics' Library and washed the evidences of them away, and made herself nice to meet Mark.

But a subtle change in the girl dated from that day; casual and foolish as the affair with Carter had been, it left its scar. Julia's heart winced away from the thought of him as she herself might have shrunk from fire. She never forgave him.

It was good to find Mark still enslaved, everything soothing and reassuring. When Julia left him, at her own door at six o'clock, she was her radiant, confident self again, and they kissed each other at parting like true lovers. To his eager demand for a promise Julia still returned a staid, "Mama'd be crazy, Mark. I ain't sixteen yet!" but on this enchanted afternoon she had consented to linger, on Kearney Street, before the trays of rings in jewellers' windows, and it was in the wildest spirits that Mark bounded on upstairs to his own apartment.

Julia had expected to find her mother at home. Instead the room was empty, but the gas was flaring high, and all about was more than the customary disorder; there were evidences that Emeline had left home in something of a hurry. The girl searched until she found the explanatory note, and read it with knitted brow.

"I'm going to Santa Rosa on important business, deary," Emeline had scribbled, "and you'd better go to Min's for a few days. I'll write and leave you know if there is anything in it, otherwise there's no use getting Min and the girls started talking. There's ten dollars in the hairpin box. With love, Mama."

"Well, I'd give a good deal to know what struck Em," said Mrs. Tarbury, for the hundredth time. It was late in the evening of the same day, and the lady and Julia were in the room shared by Miss Connie Girard and Miss

Rose Ransome. Both the young actresses had previously appeared in a skit at a local vaudeville house, but had come home to prepare for a supper to be given by friends in their own profession, after the theatres had closed. Each girl had a bureau of her own, hopelessly cluttered and crowded, and over each bureau an unshielded gas jet flared.

"Well, I'm *going* to know!" Julia added, in a heavy, significant tone. She had come to feel herself very much abused by her mother's treatment, and was inclined to entertain ugly suspicions.

"Oh, come now!" Rose Ransome said, scowling at herself in a hand mirror as she carefully rouged her lips. "Don't you get any silly notions in your head!"

"No," Mrs. Tarbury added heavily, as she rocked comfortably to and fro, "no, that ain't Em. Em is a cut-up, all right, and she's a great one for a josh with the boys, but she's as straight as a string! You'll find that she's got some good reason for this!"

"Well, she'd better have!" Julia said sulkily. "I'm going out to see my grandmother to-morrow and see if she knows anything!"

But she really gave less thought to her mother than to the stinging memory of Barbara Toland's generosity and Carter Hazzard's deception. She settled down contentedly enough, sharing the room with Connie and Rose, and sharing their secrets, and her visit to old Mrs. Cox was indefinitely postponed. The girls drifted about together, in and out of theatres, in and out of restaurants and hotels, reading cheap theatrical magazines, talking of nothing but their profession. The days were long and dull, the evenings feverish; Julia liked it all. She had no very high ideal of home life; she did not mind the disorder of their room, the jumbled bureau drawers, the chairs and tables strewn with garments, the fly-specked photographs nailed against the walls. It was a comfortable, irresponsible, diverting existence, at its worst.

Emeline did not write her daughter for nearly two weeks, but Julia was not left in doubt of her mother's moral and physical safety for that time. Only two or three days after Emeline's disappearance Julia was called upon by a flashily dressed, coarse-featured man of perhaps forty who introduced himself—in a hoarse voice heavy with liquor—as Dick Palmer.

"I used to know your Pop when you's only a kid," said the caller, "and I know where your Mamma is now—she's gone down to Santa Rosa, see?"

"What'd she go there for?" Julia demanded clearly.

Mr. Palmer cast an agitated glance about Mrs. Tarbury's dreadful drawing-room, and lowered his voice confidentially:

"Well, d'ye see—here's how it is! Your Papa's down there in Santa Rosa. I run acrost him in a boarding-house a few days ago, and d'ye see—he's sick. That's right," added the speaker heavily, "he's sick."

"Dying?" said Julia dramatically.

"No, he ain't dying. It's like this," pursued the narrator, still with his air of secrecy, "there's a party there that runs the boarding-house—her name's Lottie Clute, she's had it for years, and she's got on to the fact that George is insured for nine thousand dollars, d'ye see? Well, she's got him to promise to make the policy over to her."

"Ha!" said Julia, interested at last.

"Well, d'ye see?" said Mr. Palmer triumphantly. "So I come up to town last week, and I thought I'd drop in on your Mamma! No good letting this other little lady have it *all* her own way, you know!"

"That's right, too, she's no more than a thief!" Julia commented simply. "I don't know what Mama can do, but I guess you can leave it to Mama!"

Mr. Palmer, agreeing eagerly to this, took his leave, after paying a hoarse tribute to the beauty of his old friend's daughter, and Julia dismissed the matter from her mind.

She told Connie that she meant, as soon as this amateur affair was over, to try the stage in real earnest, and Connie, whose own last venture had ended somewhat flatly, was nevertheless very sanguine about Julia's success. She took Julia to see various managers, who were invariably interested and urbane, and Julia, deciding bitterly that she would have no more to do with her fellow-performers in the caste of "The Amazon," had Connie accompany her to rehearsals, and went through her part with a sort of sullen hauteur.

She and Connie were down in the dressing-rooms one day after a rehearsal chatting with the woman star of a travelling stock company, who chanced to be there, when Barbara Toland suddenly came in upon them.

"Oh, Miss Page," said Barbara in relief, "I *am* so glad to find you! I don't know whether you heard Mr. Pope announce that we're to have our dress rehearsal on Saturday, at the yacht club in Sausalito? There is quite a large stage."

Julia shook her head.

"I don't know that I can come Saturday," she objected, only anxious to be disobliging.

"Oh, you *must*," said Barbara brightly. "*Do* try! You take the one-forty-five from the Sausalito ferry, and somebody'll meet you! And if we should be kept later than we expect, somebody'll bring you home!"

"I have a friend who would come for me," said Julia stiffly, thinking of Mark.

For just a second mirth threatened Barbara's dignity, but she said staidly:

"That's fine! And remember, we *depend* on you!"

CHAPTER IV

The family of Dr. Robert Toland, discovered at breakfast in the Tolands' big house in Sausalito on an exquisite May morning, presented to the casual onlooker as charming a picture of home life as might be found in the length and breadth of California. The sunny dining-room, with its windows wide open to sunshine and fresh sea air, the snowy curtains blowing softly to and fro, the wide sideboard where the children's outgrown mugs stood in a battered and glittering row, the one or two stiff, flat, old oil portraits that looked down from the walls, the jars of yellow acacia bloom, and bowls of mingled wild flowers; these made a setting wonderfully well suited to the long table and the happy family about it.

There were seven children, five girls and two boys; there was the gracious, genial mother at the head and the wiry, gray-haired and gray-bearded surgeon at the foot; there was, as usual, Jim Studdiford, and to-day, besides, there was Aunt Sanna, an unmarried younger sister of the doctor, and a little black-eyed, delicate ten-year-old guest of the eleven-year-old Janie, Keith Borroughs, who was sitting near to Janie, and evidently adoring that spirited chatterbox. And there was Addie, a cheerful black-clad person in a crackling white apron, coming and going with muffins and bacon, and Toy, who was a young cousin of Hee, the cook, and who padded softly in Addie's wake, making himself generally useful.

Barbara, very pretty, very casual as to what she ate, sat next to her father; she was the oldest of the seven Tolands, and slipping very reluctantly out of her eighteenth year. Ned, a big, handsome fellow of sixteen, came next in point of age, and then a tall, lanky, awkward blond boy, Richie, with a plain thin face and the sweetest smile of them all. Richie never moved without the aid of a crutch, and perhaps never would. After Richie, and nearing fourteen, was a sweet, fat, giggling lump of a girl called Sally, with a beautiful skin and beautiful untidy hair, and a petticoat always dragging, a collar buttoned awry, and a belt that never by any chance united her pretty shirt waist to her crisp linen skirt. Only a year younger than Sally was Theodora, whose staid, precocious beauty Barbara already found disquieting—"Ted" was already giving signs of rivalling her oldest sister—then came Jane, bold, handsome, boyish at eleven, and lastly eight-year-old Constance, a delicate, pretty, tearful little girl who was spoiled by every member of the family.

The children's mother was a plump, handsome little woman with bright, flashing eyes, dimples, and lovely little hands covered with rings. There was no gray in her prettily puffed hair, and, if she was stouter than any of her daughters, none could show a more trimly controlled figure. Mrs. Toland had been impressed in the days of her happy girlhood with the romantic philosophies of the seventies. To her, as an impulsive young woman brimful of the zest of living, all babies had been "just too dear and sweet," all marriages were "simply *lovely*" regardless of circumstances, and all men were "just the dearest great big manly fellows that ever *were!*" As Miss Sally Ford, Mrs. Toland had flashed about on many visits to her girl friends admiring, exclaiming, rejoicing in their joys, and now, as a mother of growing girls and boys, there still hung between her and real life the curtain of her unquenchable optimism. She loved babies, and they had come very fast, and been cared for by splendid maids, and displayed in effective juxtaposition to their gay little mother for the benefit of admiring friends, when opportunity offered. And if, in the early days of her married life, there had ever been troublous waters to cross, Sally Toland had breasted them gallantly, her fixed, confident smile never wavering.

At first Doctor Toland had felt something vaguely amiss in this persistent attitude of radiant and romantic surety. "Are you sure the boy understands?" "D'ye think Bab isn't old enough to know that you're just making that up?" he would ask uneasily, when a question of disciplining Ned or consoling Barbara arose. But Mrs. Toland always was sure of her course, and would dimple at him warningly: "Of course it's all right, Daddykins, and we're all going to be happy, and not even think of our naughty old troubles any more!"

So the doctor gave her her way, and settled back to enjoy his children and his wife, his yacht and his roses; growing richer and more famous, more genial and perhaps a little more mildly cynical as time went on. And the children grew up, their mother, never dreaming that Barbara at eighteen was more than the sweet, light-hearted, manageable child she had been at ten; that Ned was beginning to taste of a life of whose existence she was only vaguely aware; that Sally was plotting an escape to the ranks of trained nurses; that Ted needed a firm hand and close watching if she were not to break all their hearts. No, to Mrs. Toland they were still her "rosebud garden," "just the merriest, romping crowd of youngsters that ever a little scrap of a woman had to keep in order!"

"Now, you're going to wipe that horrid frown off your forehead, Daddy," she would say blithely, if Doctor Toland confessed to a misgiving in the contemplation of any one of his seven, "and stop worrying about Richie! His bad old hip is going to get well, and he'll be walking just like any one else in no time!" And in the same tone she said to Barbara: "I know my darling girl is going to that luncheon, and going to forget that her hat isn't quite the thing for the occasion," and said to little Constance, "We're going to forget that it's raining, and not think about dismal things any more!" No account of flood or fire or outrage was great enough to win from her more than a rueful smile, a sigh, and a brisk: "Well, I suppose such things *must* be, or they wouldn't be permitted. Don't let's think about it!"

Women who knew Mrs. Toland spoke of her as "wonderful." And indeed she was wonderful in many ways, a splendid manager, a delightful hostess, and essentially motherly and domestic in type. She was always happy and always busy, gathering violets, chaperoning Sally or Barbara at the dentist's, selecting plaids for the "girlies'" winter suits. Her married life—all her life, in fact—had been singularly free from clouds, and she expected the future to be even brighter, when "splendid, honourable men" should claim her girls, one by one, and all the remembered romance of her youth begin again. That the men would be forthcoming she did not doubt; had not Fate already delivered Jim Studdiford into her hands for Barbara?

James Studdiford, who had just now finished his course at medical college, was affectionately known to the young Tolands as "Jim," and stood to them in a relationship peculiarly pleasing to Mrs. Toland. He was like a brother, and yet, actually, he bore not the faintest real kinship to—well, to Barbara, for instance. Years before, twenty years before, to be exact, Doctor Toland, then unmarried, and unacquainted, as it happened, with the lovely Miss Sally Ford, had been engaged to a beautiful young widow, a Mrs. Studdiford, who had been left with a large fortune and a tiny boy some two years before. This was in Honolulu, where people did a great deal of riding in those days, and it presently befell that the doctor, two weeks before the day that had been set for the wedding, found himself kneeling beside his lovely fiancee on a rocky headland, as she lay broken and gasping where her horse had flung her, and straining to catch the last few agonized words she would ever say:

"You'll—keep Jim—with you, Robert?"

How Doctor Toland brought the small boy to San Francisco, how he met the dashing and indifferent Sally, and how she came at last to console him for his loss, was another story, one that Mrs. Toland never tired of telling. Little Jim had his place in their hearts from their wedding day. Barbara was eleven years old when, with passionate grief, she learned that he was not her half brother, and many casual friends did not know it to this day. Jim, to the doctor's delight, chose to follow the profession of his foster father, and had stumbled, with not too much application, through medical college. Now he was to go to New York for hospital work, and then to Berlin for a year's real grind, and until the Eastern hospital should open classes, was back in his old enormous third-floor bedroom upstairs, enjoying a brief season of idleness and petting, the handsome, unaffected, sunshiny big brother of Mrs. Toland's fondest dreams.

"And he can hardly keep his eyes off Babbie," the mother confided to her sister-in-law.

Miss Toland gave her a shrewd glance.

"For heaven's sake don't get that notion in your head, Sally! Babbie may be ready to make a little fool of herself, but if ever I saw a man who *isn't* in love, it's Jim!" said Miss Toland, who was a thin, gray-haired, well-dressed woman of forty, with a curious magnetism quite her own. Miss Toland had lived in France for the ten years before thirty, and had a Frenchwoman's reposeful yet alert manner, and a Frenchwoman's art in dressing. After many idle years, she had suddenly become deeply interested in settlement work, had built a little settlement house, "The Alexander Toland Neighbourhood House," in one of the factory districts south of San Francisco, and was in a continual state of agitation and upset because worthy settlement workers were at that time almost an unknown quantity in California. Just at present she was availing herself of her brother's hospitality because she had no assistant at all at the "Alexander," and was afraid to stay in its very unsavoury environment alone. She loved Barbara dearly, but she was usually perverse with her sister-in-law.

"You may say what you like about notions in my head," Mrs. Toland answered with a wise little nod. "But the dear girl is *radiant* every time she looks at him, and both Dad and I think we notice a new *protective* quality in Jim—"

"Did Robert say so?" Miss Toland asked dryly. To this Mrs. Toland answered with a merry laugh and a little squeeze of her sister-in-law's arm.

"Oh, you old Sanna!" she chided. "You won't believe that there's a blessed time when Nature just takes the young things by the hand and pushes them right into happiness, whether or no!"

This little talk had taken place just before breakfast, and now Mrs. Toland was reassuring herself of her own position with many a glance at Barbara and at Jim. Barbara seemed serious almost to ungraciousness—that might be a sign. Jim was teasing Sally, who laughed deeply and richly, like a child, and spilled her orange juice on her fresh gown. Perhaps he was trying to pique Barbara by assuming an indifferent manner—that might be it——

"Jim!" It was Barbara speaking. Jim did not hear. "Jim," said Barbara again, patient and cold.

"I beg your pardon!" Jim said with swift contrition. His glance flashed to Barbara for a second, flashed back to Sally. "Now, you throw that—you throw that," said he to the latter young woman, in reference to a glass of water with which she was carelessly toying, "and you'll be sorrier than you ever were in your life!"

"Sally, what are you thinking of!" her mother said.

"Look out—look out!" Sally said, swinging the glass up and down. Suddenly she set it back on the table firmly. "You deserve that straight in your face, Jim, but Mother'd be mad!"

"Well, I should think Mother would!" Mrs. Toland said, in smiling reproof. "But we interrupted Bab, I think. Bab had something dreadfully important to say," she added playfully, "to judge from that great big frown!"

"It wasn't dreadfully important at all," Barbara said, in cold annoyance.

"Oh, wasn't it? And what was it, dear?"

"It was simply—it was nothing at all," Barbara protested, reddening. "I was just thinking that we have to have that rehearsal at the clubhouse this afternoon, and I was wondering if Jim would walk down there with me now, and see about getting the room ready——"

"Dad's got an eleven-o'clock operation, and I'm going to assist," said Jim.

"Did you forget that, dear?" Mrs. Toland asked.

"It's of no consequence," said Barbara, her voice suddenly thick with tears. Her hand trembled as she reached for a muffin.

"Keith, do you want to go down with us to the rehearsal this afternoon?" said Sally amiably to the little guest.

"Oh, I don't think the whole pack of us ought to go!" Ted protested in alarm. "You aren't going to let Janey and Con go, are you, Mother?"

"Oh, why not?" Mrs. Toland asked soothingly. Barbara here returned to the discussion with a tragic: "Mother, they *can't*! It would look perfectly awful!"

"Well, you don't own the yacht club, you know, Babbie," Ted supplied sweetly.

"Well," said Barbara, rising, and speaking quickly in a low voice, "of course the whole family, including Addie and Hcc, can troop down there if they want to, but I think it's too bad that I can't do a thing in this family without being tagged by a bunch of *kids*!"

The door closed behind her; they could hear her running upstairs.

- 65 -

"Now she'll cry; she's getting to be an awful cry baby," said Janey, wide eyed, pleasurably excited.

"Doesn't seem very well, does she, Mummie? Not a bit like herself," said the head of the house, raising mild eyebrows.

"Now, never mind; she's just a little bit tired and excited over this 'Amazon' thing," Mrs. Toland assured him cheerfully, "and she'll have a little talk with Mother by and by, and be her sweet self again by lunch time!"

The little episode was promptly blotted out by the rising tide of laughter and conversation that was usual at breakfast. Miss Toland presently drifted into the study for some letter writing. Jim took a deep porch rocker, and carried off the morning papers. Richie, sitting at his father's left, squared about for one of the eager rambling talks of which he and his father never tired. The doctor's blue eyes twinkled over his theories of religion, science, history, poetry, and philosophy. Richie's lean, colourless face was bright with interest. Ted volunteered, as she often volunteered of late, to go for the mail, and sauntered off under a red parasol, and Mrs. Toland slipped from the table just in time to waylay her oldest son in the hall.

"Not going to catch the 9:40, Ned?" she asked.

"Sure pop I am!" He was sorry to be caught, and she saw it under his bluff, pleasant manner.

"You couldn't take the 10:20 with Dad and Jim?"

"I've got to meet Reynolds at half-past ten, Mother," the boy said patiently.

"Reynolds!" she frowned. "Don't like my fine big boy to have friends like that—" His eyes warned her. "Friends that aren't as fine and dear and good as he is!" she finished, her hands on his shoulders.

"Reynolds is all right," said Ned, bored, and looking coldly beyond her.

"And you'll be home for dinner, Ned?"

"Sure! Unless the Orpheum should be awfully long. In that case we may get a bite somewhere."

"Try to be home for dinner," persisted the mother. And, as if to warrant the claim on his consideration, she added: "I paid the Cutter bill myself, dear, and Dad will pay Jordan next month. I didn't say anything about Cutter, but he begged me to make you *feel* how wrong it is to let these things run. You have a splendid allowance, Ned," she was almost apologetic, "and there's no necessity of running over it, dear!"

"Sure. I'm not going to do that again," Ned said gruffly, uncomfortably.

"That's right, dear! And you will—you'll try to be home for dinner?"

"Sure I'll try!" and Ned was gone, down through the roses and through the green gate.

Mrs. Toland watched him out of sight. Then she trotted off to Hee's domain. Sally straggled out into the garden, with Janey and Constance and the small boy following after. There was great distress because the little girls were all for tennis, and Keith Borroughs frankly admitted that he hated tennis.

The Tolands' rambling mansion was built upon so sharp a hill that the garden beds were bulkheaded like terraces, and the paths were steep. Roses—delicious great white roses and the apricot-coloured San Rafael rose—climbed everywhere, and hung in fragrant festoons from the low, scrub-oak trees that were scattered through the garden. Every vista ended with the blue bay, and the green gate at the garden's foot opened directly upon a roadway that hung like a shelf above the water.

Sally and the children gathered nasturtiums and cornflowers and ferns for the house. The place had been woodland only a few years ago, the earth was rich with rotting leaves, and all sorts of lovely forest growths fringed the paths. Groups of young oaks and an occasional bay or madrone tree broke up any suggestion of formal arrangement, and there were still wild columbine and mission bells in the shady places.

Presently, to the immense satisfaction of her little sisters, Sally dismissed them for tennis, and carried the music-mad small boy off to the old nursery, where he could bang away at an old piano to his heart's content, while she pasted pictures in her camera book, in a sunny window. Now and then she cast a look full of motherly indulgence at the little figure at the piano: the pale, earnest little face; the tumbled black hair, the bony, big, unchildlike hands.

The morning slipped by, and afternoon came, to find Barbara welcoming the arriving players at the yacht club, and looking her very prettiest in a gown of striped scarlet and white, and a white hat. Hello, Matty—Hello, Enid—Hello, Bobby—and did any one see Miss Page? Ah, how do you do, Miss Page, awfully good of you to make it.

The girls dressed in a square room upstairs, lined with hooks and mirrors. Julia was not self-conscious, because, while different from the crisp snowy whiteness of the other girls' linen, it did not occur to her that her well-worn pink silk underwear, her ornate corset cover, and her shabby ruffled green silk skirt were anything but adequate.

Carter Hazzard was not in evidence to-day, to Julia's relief. The rehearsal dragged on and on, everybody thrown out because Miss Dorothy Chase, the girl who was to play Wilhelmina, failed to appear. Julia took the part, when it was finally decided to go on without Dorothy, but by that time it was late, and the weary manager assured them that there must be another rehearsal that evening. Hilariously the young people accepted this decree, and Julia was carried home with the Tolands to dinner.

Good-hearted Mrs. Toland could be nothing less than kind to any young girl, and Julia's place at table was next to the kindly old doctor, who only saw an extremely pretty girl, and joked with her, and looked out for her comfort in true fatherly fashion. Julia carried herself with great dignity, said very little, being in truth quite overawed and nervously anxious not to betray herself, and after the first frightened half-hour she enjoyed the adventure thoroughly.

The evening rehearsal went much better, a final rehearsal was set for Sunday, and Julia was driven to the ten o'clock boat in the station omnibus, which smelled of leather and wet straw. She sat yawning in the empty ferry building, smiling over her recollection of dinner at the Tolands': the laughter, the quarrels, the joyous confusion of voices.

Suddenly struck by the deserted silence of the waiting-room, Julia jumped up and went to the ticket office.

"Isn't there a train at 10:03?"

The station agent yawned, eyed her with pleasant indifference.

"No train now until 12:20, lady," said he.

For a moment Julia was staggered. Then she thought of the telephone.

A few minutes later she climbed out of the station omnibus again, this time to be warmly welcomed into the Tolands' lamp-lighted drawing-room. Barbara and her mother were still at the yacht club, but the old doctor himself was eagerly apologetic. Doctor Studdiford, Ned, and Richie added their cheerful questions and regrets to the hospitable hubbub, and Sally, who had been at the piano, singing Scotch ballads to her father, took possession of Julia with heartening and obvious pleasure.

Sally took her upstairs, lighted a small but exquisitely appointed guest room, found a stiffly embroidered nightgown, a wrapper of dark-blue Japanese crepe, and a pair of straw slippers. Julia, inwardly trembling with excitement, was outwardly calm as she got ready for bed; she hung her clothes in a closet delightfully redolent of pine, and brushed and braided her splendid hair. Sally whisked about on various errands, and presently Mrs. Toland bustled in, brimful of horrified apologies and regrets, and

Barbara dawdled after, rolling her belt and starched stock, generally unhooking and unbuttoning.

Perhaps the haughty Barbara found the round-eyed, golden-haired girl in a blue wrapper a little more companionable than the dreadful Miss Page, or perhaps she was a little too lonely to-night to be fastidious in her choice of a confidante. At all events, she elected to wander in and out of Julia's room while she undressed, and presently sat on Julia's bed, and braided her dark hair. And if the whole adventure had excited Julia, she was doubly excited now, frantic to win Barbara's friendship, nervously afraid to try.

"You're an actress, Miss Page?" asked Barbara, scowling at her hairbrush.

"Will be, I guess! I've had dozens of chances to sign up already, but Mama don't want me to be in any rush."

The other girl eyed her almost enviously.

"I wish I could do something—sometimes," she sighed. And she added, giving Julia a shamefaced grin, "I've got the blues to-night."

It was from this second that Julia dated her love for Barbara Toland. A delicious sensation enveloped her—to be in Barbara's confidence—to know that she was sometimes unhappy, too; to be lying in this fragrant, snowy bed, in this enchanting room—

"Well," said Barbara presently, jumping up, "you'll want *some* sleep. If you hear us rushing about, at the screech of dawn to-morrow, it's because some of us may go out with Dad in the Crow, if there's a breeze. Do you like yachting? Would you care to go?"

"I've never been," said Julia.

"Oh, well, then, you ought to!" Barbara said with round eyes. "I'll tell you—I'll peep in here to-morrow, and if you're awake I'll give you a call!" she arranged, after a minute's frowning thought.

"I sleep awfully sound!" smiled Julia.

But she was awake when Barbara, true to her plan, peeped in at five o'clock the next morning, and presently, in a bluejacket's blouse and brief blue skirt, with a white canvas hat on her head, and a boy's old gray jersey buttoned loosely about her, followed muffled shapes through the cold house and into the wet, chilly garden. Richie was going, Sally had the gallant but shivering Jane and the dark-eyed Keith by the hand, and Barbara hung on her father's arm.

The waters of the bay were gray and cold; a sharp breeze swept their steely surfaces into fans of ruffled water. The little Crow rocked at her anchor, her ropes and brasswork beaded with dew. Julia, sitting in desperate terror upon a slanting upholstered ledge, felt her teeth chatter, and wondered why she had come.

Barbara, Sally, Richie, and their father all fell to work, and presently, a miracle to Julia, the little boat was running toward Richardson's Bay under a good breeze. Presently glorious sunlight enveloped them, flashed from a thousand windows on San Francisco hills, and struck to dazzling whiteness the breasts of the gulls that circled Sausalito's piers. Everything sparkled and shone: the running blue water that slapped the Crow's side, the roofs of houses on the hillside, the green trees that nearly concealed them.

Growing every instant warmer and more content, Julia sat back and let her whole body and soul soak in the comfort and beauty of the hour. Her eyes roved sea and sky and encircling hills; she saw the last wisp of mist rise and vanish from the stern silhouette of Tamalpais, and saw an early ferryboat cut a wake of exquisite spreading lacework across the bay. And whenever her glance crossed Sally's, or the doctor's, or Richie's glance, she smiled like a happy child, and the Tolands smiled back.

They all rushed into the house, ravenous and happy, for a nine o'clock breakfast, Julia so lovely, in her borrowed clothing and with her bright, loosened hair, that the young men of the family began, without exception, to "show off" for her benefit, as Theodora scornfully expressed it. And there was bacon and rolls and jam for every one, blue bowls of cereal, glass pitchers of yellow cream, smoking hot coffee always ready to run in an amber stream from the spout of the big silver urn.

"And you must eat at least four waffles," said Ned, "or my father will never let you come again! He has to drum up trade, you know—"

It was all delightful, not the less so because it was all tinged, for Julia, with a little current of something exquisitely painful; not envy, not regret, not resentment, a little of all three. This happy, care-free, sun-flooded life was not for her, how far, far, far from her, indeed! She was here only by accident, tolerated gayly for hospitality's sake, her coming and going only an insignificant episode in their lives. Wistfully she watched Mrs. Toland tying little Constance's sash and straightening her flower-crowned hat for church; wistfully eyed the cheerful, white-clad Chinese cook, grinning as he went to gather lettuces; wistfully she stared across the brilliant garden from her deep porch chair. Barbara, in conference with a capped and aproned maid at the end of a sunny corridor, Sally chatting with Richie, as she straightened the scattered books on the library table, Ted dashing off a popular waltz with her head turned carelessly aside to watch the attentive Keith; all these to Julia were glimpses of a life so free, so full, so invigorating as to fill her with hopeless longing and admiration.

All her affectation and arrogance dropped from her before their simple, joyous naturalness. Julia had no feeling of wishing to impress them, to assert her own equality. Instead she genuinely wanted them to like her; she carried herself like the little girl she looked in her sailor blouse, like the little girl she was.

At twelve o'clock a final rehearsal of "The Amazons" was held at the yacht club, and to-day Julia entered into her part with zest, her enthusiasm really carrying the performance, as the appreciative "Matty" assured her. She had the misfortune to step on a ruffle of her borrowed white petticoat, at the very close of the last act, and slipped into the dressing-room to pin it up as soon as the curtain descended.

The dressing-room was deserted. Julia found a paper of pins, and, putting her foot up on a chair, began to repair the damage as well as she could. The day was warm, and only wooden shutters screened the big window that gave on one of the club's wide porches. Julia, humming contentedly to herself, presently became aware that there were chairs just outside the window, and girls in the chairs—Barbara Toland and Ted, and Miss Grinell and Miss Hazzard, and one or two Julia did not know.

"Yes, Mother's a darling," Barbara was saying. "You know she didn't get this up, Margaret; she had *nothing* to do with it, and yet she's practically carrying the whole responsibility now! She'll be as nervous as we are to-morrow night!"

Julia pinned on serenely. It was in no code of hers to move out of hearing.

"The only thing she really bucked at was when she found Miss Page at our house last night," Ted said. "Mother's no snob—but I wish you could have seen her face!"

"Was she perfectly awful, Ted?" somebody asked.

"Who, Miss Page? No-o, she wasn't perfectly awful—yes, she was pretty bad," Theodora admitted. "Wasn't she, Babbie?"

"Oh, well"—Barbara hesitated—"she's—of course she's terribly common. Just the second-rate actress type, don't you know?"

"Did she call your Mother 'ma'am'?" giggled Enid Hazzard. "Do you remember when she said 'Yes, ma'am?' And did she say 'eyether,' and 'between you and I' again?" Something was added to this, but Julia did not catch it. The girls laughed again.

"Listen," said Ted, "this is the richest yet! Last night Sally said to her, 'Breakfast's at nine, Miss Page; how do you like your bath?' and she looked at Sally sort of surprised and said, '*I* don't want a bath!'"

"Oh, I don't think that's fair, Teddy," Barbara protested; "she's never had any advantages; it's a class difference, that's all. She's simply not a lady; she never will be. You'd be the same in her place."

"Oh, I would not! I wouldn't mark my eyebrows and I wouldn't wear such dirty clothes, and I wouldn't try to look twenty-five—" Ted began.

Again there was a quick commentary that Julia missed, and another laugh. Then Barbara said:

"Poor kid! And she looked so sweet in some of Sally's things."

Julia, still bent over her ruffle, did not move a muscle from the instant she first heard her name until now, when the girls dismissed the subject with a laugh. She felt as if the house were falling about her, as if every word were a smashing blow at her very soul. She felt sick and dizzy, cold and suddenly weak.

She walked across the room to the door, and stood there with her hand on the knob, and said in a whisper: "Now, what shall I do? What shall I do?"

At first she thought she would hide, then that she would run away. Then she knew what she must do: she opened the dressing-room door, and walked unchallenged through the big auditorium. Groups of chattering people were scattered about it; somebody was banging the piano; nobody paid the least attention to Julia as she went down the stairs, and started to walk to the Toland house.

She was not thinking now. She only wanted to get away.

Nobody stopped her. The house was deserted. A maid put her head in Julia's door, and finding Julia dressing immediately apologized.

"I beg your pardon, Miss Page! I thought—"

"That's all right," said Julia quietly. She was very pale. "Will you tell Mrs. Toland that I had to take the two o'clock boat?"

"Yes'm. You won't be here for dinner?"

"No," said Julia, straining to make a belt meet.

"Could I bring you a cup of tea or a sandwich?"

"Oh, no, thank you!"

The maid was gone. Julia went down through the house quietly, a few moments later. Her breath came quick and short until she was fairly on the boat, with Sausalito slipping farther and farther into the background. Even then her mind was awhirl, and fatigue and perhaps hunger, too, made it impossible to think seriously. Far easier to lean back lazily in the sun, and watch the water slip by, and make no attempt to control the confused, chaotic thoughts that wheeled dreamily through her brain. Now and then memory brought her to a sudden upright position, brought the hot colour to her face.

"I don't care!" Julia would say then, half aloud. "They're nothing to me and I'm nothing to them; and good riddance!"

May—but it was like a midsummer afternoon in San Francisco. A hot wind blew across the ferry place; papers and chaff swept before it. Julia's skirt was whisked about her knees, her hat was twisted viciously about on her head. She caught a reflection of herself in a car window, dishevelled, her hat at an ugly angle, her nose reddened by the wind.

Mrs. Tarbury's house, when she got to it, presented its usual Sunday afternoon appearance. The window curtains were up at all angles in the dining-room, hot sunshine streamed through the fly-specked panes, the draught from the open door drove a wild whirl of newspapers over the room. Cigarette smoke hung heavy upon the air.

Julia peeped into the dark kitchen; the midday meal was over, and a Japanese boy was hopelessly and patiently attacking scattered heaps of dishes and glassware. The girl was hungry, but the cooling wreck of a leg of mutton and the cold vegetables swimming in water did not appeal to her, and she went slowly upstairs, helping herself in passing to no more substantial luncheon than two soda crackers and a large green pickle.

Mrs. Tarbury, dressed in a loose kimono, with her bare feet thrust into well-worn Juliet slippers, was lying across her bed, in the pleasant leisure of Sunday afternoon, a Dramatic Supplement held in one fat ringed hand, her head supported by her pillows in soiled muslin cases, and several satin and velvet cushions from a couch. In the room also were Connie Girard and Rose Ransome, who had a bowl of soapsuds and several scissors and orange-wood sticks on the table between them, and were manicuring each other very fastidiously. A third actress, a young Englishwoman with a worn, hard face, rouged cheeks, and glittering eyes, was calling, with her little son, upon Mrs. Tarbury.

"Hello, darling!" said the lady of the house herself, as Julia came in. The girls gave her an affectionate welcome, and Julia was introduced to the stranger.

"Mrs. Cloke is my real name," said the Englishwoman briskly. "But you'd know me better as Alice Le Grange, I daresay. You'll have heard of my little sketches—the Mirror gave Mr. Cloke and I a whole page when first we came to this country, and we had elegant bookings—elegant. I'd my little flat in New York all furnished, and," she said to Mrs. Tarbury, "I was used to *everything*—the managers at home all knew me, and all, you know—" She laughed with some bitterness. "It does seem funny to be out here doing this," she added. "But there was the kiddy to consider—and, as I told you, there was trouble!"

"Parties who used their influence to get 'em out!" said Miss Girard darkly, in explanation, with a glance at Julia. "Favouritism—"

"And jealousy," added Alice Le Grange.

Julia was sympathetic, but not deeply impressed. She had heard this story in many forms before. She attracted the attention of little Eric Cloke, and showed him the pictures of the Katzenjammer Kids and Foxy Grandpa in the newspaper. Later she accompanied Rose and Connie to their room, put on loose clothing, and lay on her bed watching them dress.

The girls were to dine together, with two admirers, and urged Julia to ask a third man, and come, too. Julia refused steadily; she was very quiet and the others thought her tired.

She lay on her side, one hand falling idle over the edge of the bed, her serious, magnificent eyes moving idly from Connie's face to Rose's, and roving over the room. Hot sunlight poured through the dirty windows and the torn curtains of Nottingham lace, and flamed on the ugly wallpaper and the flawed mirrors. A thousand useless knickknacks made the room hideous; every possible surface was strewn with garments large and small, each bureau was a confusion of pins and brushes, paste and powder boxes, silk stockings and dirty white gloves, cologne bottles and powdered circles of discoloured chamois, hair kids and curls of false hair, handkerchiefs and hat pins, cheap imitations of jewellery, cheap bits of lace, sidecombs, veils and belts and collars, and a hundred other things, all wound up in an indistinguishable mass. From these somewhat sodden heaps Connie and Rose cheerfully selected what they needed, leaning over constantly to inspect their faces closely in the mirrors.

Julia watched them with a sudden, new, and almost terrifying distaste growing in her heart. How dirty and shiftless and common—yes, common—these girls were! Julia felt sick with the force of the revelation. She saw Connie lace her shabby pink-brocade corset together with a black shoestring; she saw Rose close with white thread a great hole in the heel of a black silk stocking. Their crimped hair nauseated her, their rouge and powder and cologne. She could hardly listen in patience to their careless and sometimes coarse chatter.

And when they were gone she still lay there, thinking—thinking—thinking! The sunlight crept lower and lower over the room's disorder; its last bright triangle was gone, twilight came, and the soft early darkness.

Mrs. Tarbury presently called Julia, in mellifluous accents, and the girl pulled herself stiffly from the bed, and went blinking down to an improvised supper. They two were alone in the big house, and fell into intimate conversation over their sardines and coffee and jam, discussing the characters of every person in the house with much attention to trivial detail. At nine o'clock some friends came in to see Mrs. Tarbury, and Julia went upstairs again.

She lighted the bedroom, and began idly to fold and straighten the clothes that were strewn about everywhere. But she very speedily gave up the task: there were no closets to hang things in, and many things were too torn or dirty to be hung up, anyway! Julia went down one flight of stairs to the nearest bathroom, in search of hot water, but both faucets ran cold, and she went upstairs again. She hunted through Connie's bureau and Rose's for a fresh nightgown, but not finding one, had to put on the limp and torn garment one of the girls had loaned her a week or two before.

Now she sat down on the edge of her bed, vaguely discouraged. Tears came to her eyes, she did not quite know why. She opened a novel, and composed herself to read, but could not become interested, and finally pushed up the window the two inches that the girls approved, turned out the lights, and jumped into bed. She would want her beauty sleep for "The Amazons" to-morrow night. Julia had been fully determined, when she got home, to abandon the amateur company, to fail them at the very hour of their performance, but a casual word from Connie had caused her to change her mind.

"Don't you be a fool and get in Dutch with Artheris!" Connie had said, and upon sober reflection Julia had found the advice good.

But she got no beauty sleep that night. She lay hour after hour wakeful and wretched, the jumbled memories of the last twenty-four hours slipping through her mind in ceaseless review: the green, swift-rushing water, with gulls flying over it; the coffee pot reflecting a dozen joyous young faces; the garden bright with roses—

And then, with sickening regularity, the clubhouse and the girls' voices—

How she hated them all, Julia said to herself, raising herself on one elbow to punch her sodden pillow, and sending a hot, restless glance toward the streak of bright light that forced its way in from a street lamp. How selfish, how smug, how arrogant they were, with their daily baths, and their chests full of fresh linen, and their assured speech! What had Sally and Theodora Toland ever done to warrant their insufferable conceit? Why should they have lovely parents and an ideal home, frocks and maids and delightful meals, while she, Julia, was born to the dirt and sordidness of O'Farrell Street?

Barbara—but no, she couldn't hate Barbara! The memory of that moment of confidence last night still thrilled Julia to her heart's core. Barbara had been kind to her in the matter of Carter Hazzard, had defended her to-day, in her careless, indifferent fashion. Julia's heart ached with fierce envy of Barbara, ached with fierce longing and admiration. She tortured herself with a picture of the charm of Barbara's life: her waking in the sunshine, her breakfast eaten between the old doctor and the young, her hours at her pretty writing-desk, on the porch, at the piano. Always dignified, always sweet and dainty, always adored.

Well, she, Julia, should be an actress, a great actress. But even as she flung herself on her back and stared sternly up at the ceiling, resolving it, her heart failed her. It was a long road. Julia was fifteen; she must count upon ten or fifteen years at least of slavery in stock companies, of weeks spent in rushing from one cheap hotel to another, of associating with just such women as Connie and Rose. No one that she knew, in the profession, had bureaus full of ruffled fresh linen, had a sunshiny breakfast table with flowers on it—

Julia twisted about on her arm and began to cry. She cried for a long time.

True, she could marry Mark, and Mark would be rich some day. But would Barbara Toland Studdiford—for Julia had married them as a matter of course—ever stoop to notice Julia Rosenthal? No, she wouldn't marry Mark.

Then there was her mother's home, over the saloon. Julia finally went to sleep planning, in cold-blooded childish fashion, that if her father died, and left her mother a really substantial sum of money, she would persuade Emeline to take a clean, bright little flat somewhere, and leave this neighbourhood forever.

"And we could keep a few boarders," thought Julia drowsily, "and I will learn to cook, and have nice little ginghams, like Janey's—"

The amateur performance of "The Amazons" duly took place on the following night, with a large and fashionable audience packing the old Grand Opera House, and society reporters flitting from box to box between the acts. Julia found the experience curiously flat. She had no opportunity to deliver to Barbara a withering little speech she had prepared, and received no attention from any one. The performers were excited and nervous, each frankly bent upon scoring a personal and exclusive success, and immediately after the last act they swarmed out to greet friends in the house, and Babel ensued.

Walking soberly home with Mark at half-past eleven, with her cheque in her purse, Julia decided bitterly that she washed her hands of them all; she was done with San Francisco's smart set, she would never give another thought to a single one of them.

CHAPTER V

Days of very serious thinking followed this experience. The face of the world was changed. Much that had been unnoticed, or taken for granted, became insufferable to Julia now. She winced at Connie's stories, she looked with a coldly critical eye at Mrs. Tarbury's gray hair showing through a yellow "front"; the sights and sounds of the boarding-house sickened her. She was accustomed to helping Mrs. Tarbury with the housework, not in any sense as payment for her board—for never was hospitality more generously extended—but merely because she was there, and idle, and energetic; but she found this a real hardship now. The hot, close bedrooms, odorous of perfume and cigarette smoke, the grayish sheets and thin blankets were odious to her; she longed to set fire to the whole, and start afresh, with clean new furnishings.

Presently Connie asked her if she would care to talk to a manager about going on an "eleven weeks' circuit," as assistant to a sleight-of-hand performer.

"Twenty a week," said Connie, "and a whole week in Sacramento and another in Los Angeles. All you have to do is wear a little suit like a page, and hand him things. Rose says he looks like an old devil—I haven't seen him, but you can sit on him easy enough. And the Nevilles are making the same trip, and she's a real nice woman. Not much, Ju, but it's a start, and I think we could land it for you."

"Yes, I know," Julia said vaguely.

"Well, wake up!" said Connie briskly. "Do you want it?"

"I'd rather wait until Mama gets here," the younger girl decided uncomfortably. And that afternoon, in vague hope of news of her mother, she took a Mission Street car and went out to call on her grandmother.

As usual, old Mrs. Cox's cheap little house reeked of soapsuds and carbolic acid. Julia, admitted after she had twisted the little gong set in the panels of the street door, kissed her grandmother in a stifling dark hall. Mrs. Cox was glad of company, she limped ahead into her little kitchen, chattering eagerly of her rheumatism and of family matters. She told Julia that May's children, Evelyn and Marguerite, were with her, Marguerite holding a position as dipper in a nearby candy factory, and Evelyn checking in an immense steam laundry.

"How many children *has* Aunt May now?" Julia asked, sighing.

"She's got too many!" Mrs. Cox said sharply. "A feller like Ed, who never keeps a position two weeks running, has got no business to raise such a family! For a while May had two of the boys in a home—"

"Oh, really!" said Julia, distressed.

"Lloyd and Elmer—yes, but they're home again now," the old woman pursued. "May felt dreadful when they went, but I guess she wasn't so awfully glad to get them back. Boys make a lot of work."

"Elmer and Lloyd, and then there was Muriel, and another baby?" Julia asked.

"Muriel and Geraldine, and then the baby, Regina."

"Has Aunt May seven children?" Julia asked, awed.

Mrs. Cox delayed the brewing of a pot of tea while she counted them with a bony knotted hand. Then she nodded. Julia digested the fact in frowning silence.

"Grandma," said she presently, "did you ever have enough money?"

Mrs. Cox, now drinking her tea from a saucer, smiled toothlessly.

"Oh, sure," said she, with a cackle of laughter, "Why, there's nobody knows it, but I'm rich!" But immediately the sorry joke lost flavour. The old woman sighed, and into her wrinkled face and filmed eyes there came her usual look of patient and unintelligent endurance. "I've never yet had a dollar that didn't have to do two dollars' work," said she, suddenly, in a mighty voice, staring across the kitchen, and lifting one hand as if she were taking an oath. "I've never laid down at night when I wasn't so tired my back was splitting. I've never had no thanks and no ease—the sixty years of my life! There's some people meant to be rich, Julia, and some that'll be poor the longest day of their lives, and that's all there is to it!"

"I know—but it don't seem fair," Julia mused. She presently went on an errand for her grandmother, and came back with sausages and fresh pulpy bread and large spongy crullers from the grocery. By this time the windy summer twilight was closing in, and the homegoing labourers and factory hands were filing home through the dirty streets. Julia found her two cousins in the lamp-lighted kitchen, Evelyn rather heavy and coarse looking, Marguerite reedy and thin, both wearing an unwholesome pallor. They made a little event of her coming, and the three girls chatted gayly enough throughout the meal, which was eaten at the kitchen table and washed down with strong tea.

Julia's grandfather, a gnarled old man in a labourer's rough clothes, who reeked of whiskey, mumbled his meal in silence, and afterward went into the room known as the parlour, snarling as he went that some one must come in and light his lamp. Julia went in with Evelyn to the rather pitiful room: a red rug was on the floor, and there were two chairs and a cheap little table, besides the big chair in which the old man settled himself.

"Ain't he going out, Grandma?" said Evelyn, returning to the kitchen, and exchanging a rueful look with Marguerite.

"Well, I thought he was!" Mrs. Cox made a pilgrimage to the parlour door, and returned confident. "He'll go out!" she said reassuringly.

"Comp'ny coming?" Julia asked smilingly. The other girls giggled and looked at each other.

"Well, why couldn't Grandpa sit in the kitchen?" the girl asked. "There's a better light out here!"

"Catch him doing anything decent," Evelyn said, and Marguerite added: "And, Ju, he'll sit there sometimes just to be mean, and he'll take his shoes off, and put his socks up——"

"And nights he knows we want the parlour he'll stay in on purpose," Evelyn supplemented eagerly.

"I wouldn't *stand* for it," Julia asserted.

"Pa's awfully cranky," Mrs. Cox said resignedly. "He's always been that way! You cook him corn beef—that's the night he wanted pork chops; sometimes he'll snap your head off if you speak, and others he'll ask you why you sit around like a mute and don't talk. Sometimes, if you ask him for money, he'll put his hand in his pocket real willing, and other times for weeks he won't give you a cent!"

"I wouldn't put up with it," said Julia again. "What does he *do* with his money?"

"Oh, he treats the boys, and sometimes, when he's drunk, they'll borrow it off him," said his wife. "Pa's always open-handed with the boys!"

Evelyn, who had washed her coarse, handsome face at the kitchen sink, began now to arrange her hair with a small comb that had been wedged into the sinkboard. Marguerite, having completed similar operations, offered to walk with Julia to the Mission Street car.

"The worst of Grandpa is this," said Marguerite, on the way, and Julia glancing sideways under a street lamp surprised an earnest and most winning expression on her cousin's plain, pale face, "he don't give Grandma any money, d'you see?—and that means that Ev and I have to give her pretty much what we get, and so we can't help Mamma, and that makes me awfully blue."

"But—but Uncle Ed's working, Rita?"

"Pop works when he can, Ju. Work isn't ever very steady in his line, you know. But he don't drink any more, Mamma says, only—there's five children younger'n we are, you know—"

"Sure," said Julia, heavy oppressed. But Marguerite was cheered at this point by encountering two pimply and embarrassed youths, and Julia, climbing a moment later into a Mission Street car, looked back to see her cousin walking off between the two masculine forms, and heard their loud laughter ring upon the night.

About ten days later, unannounced, Emeline came home, and with her came a stout, red-faced, grayhaired man, in whom Julia was aghast to find her father. They reached Mrs. Tarbury's at about four o'clock in the afternoon, and Julia, coming in from a call on a theatrical manager, found them in the dining-room. George had been very ill, and moved ponderously and slowly. He looked far older than Julia's memory of him. There were sagging red pockets under his eyes, and his heavy jowls were darkened with a day's growth of gray stubble. He and Emeline had had a complete reconciliation, and entertained Mrs. Tarbury with the history of their remarriage and an outline of their plans.

George took a heavy, sportive interest in his pretty girl, but Julia could not realize their relationship sufficiently to permit of any liberties. She smiled an uneasy, perfunctory smile when George kissed her, and moved away from the arm he would have kept about her.

"Don't liked to be kissed?" asked George.

"Oh, I don't mind," said Julia, in a lifeless voice, and with averted eyes. "Did you go to the flat, Mama?" she asked, clearing her throat.

"I did," Emeline answered, biting a loose thread from a finger of her dirty white gloves. "I got Toomey's rent, and told them that we might want the room on the first."

"Going to give up the flat?" Julia asked, in surprise.

"Well"—Emeline glanced at her husband—"it's this way, Ju," said she: "Papa can't stand the city, sick as he is now—"

George coughed loosely in confirmation of this, and shook his head.

"And Papa's got a half interest in a little fruit ranch down in Santa Clara Valley," Emeline pursued. "So I'm going to take him down there for a little while, and nurse him back to real good health."

"My God, Em, you'll die!" Mrs. Tarbury said frankly. "Why'n't you go somewhere where there's something doing?"

"My sporting days are over, Min," George said with mournful satisfaction. "No more midnight suppers in mine!"

"Nor mine, either. I guess I'm old enough to settle down," Emeline added cheerfully. She and Mrs. Tarbury exchanged a look, and Julia knew exactly what concessions her mother had made before the reconciliation; knew just how sincere this unworldly wifely devotion was.

"Doc says I am to have fresh air, and light, nourishing foods, and quiet nights," George explained, gravely important.

"And what about Julie?" asked Mrs. Tarbury.

"Well, we thought we'd leave Julie here, Min," Emeline began comfortably, "until we see if it works. Then in, say, a month—"

"Mama, you can't!" Julia interrupted, cheeks hot with shame. "Aunt Min's got to rent that room—"

"You see how it is, Em," the lady of the house explained regretfully: "Connie's gone off on the road now, and Rose Ransome's gone to Virginia City, and there's a party and wife that'll give me twenty a month for the room. And as it happens I'm full up now, Em—"

"Well, of course we'll pay—" George was beginning, somewhat haughtily, but Emeline, who had grown rather red, interrupted:

"It don't make the slightest difference," she said, with spirit. "I guess I'm the last woman in the world to want my child to stay where she isn't welcome!"

"It ain't that at all, Em," Mrs. Tarbury threw in pacifically, but Emeline was well launched now.

"If it hadn't been that George was all but passing away with kidney trouble," Emeline said, her voice rising, "I never would of let such an arrangement go on for five minutes! But there was days when we never knew from hour to hour that George wasn't dying, and what with having him moved and that woman holding up his clothes, and telling the doctor lies about me, I guess I had troubles enough without worrying about Julie. But I want to tell you right now, Min," said Emeline, with kindly superiority, "that this isn't the kind of a house I'm crazy about having my daughter in, anyway. It ain't you, so much—"

"Ha! that's good!" Mrs. Tarbury interpolated, with a sardonic laugh.

"But you know very well that such girls as Rosie and Con—" Emeline rushed on.

"Oh, my God, Em!" Mrs. Tarbury began in a low voice rich with feeling, but Julia took a hand.

"Don't be such a fool, Aunt Min!" she said, going over to sit on an arm of Mrs. Tarbury's chair, and putting a caressing arm about her shoulders. "And cut it out, Mama! Aunt Min's been kinder to me than any one else, and you know it—and I've felt pretty darn mean living here day after day! And now I say if Aunt Min has a chance to rent her room—"

"God knows you're welcome to that room as long as you'll stay, Julie," Mrs. Tarbury said tremulously; "it's only—"

"If every one was as good to me as you are, Aunt Min!" Julia said, beginning to cry. Mrs. Tarbury burst into sobs, and they clung together.

"I never meant that you wasn't awfully good to her, Min," Emeline said stiffly. Then her eyes watered, and she, too, began to cry, and groped for her handkerchief. "I'm just worn out with worrying and taking care of George, I guess," sobbed Emeline, laying her head on the arm she flung across a nearby table.

"Don't cry, Mama!" Julia gulped, leaving Mrs. Tarbury's lap to come and pat her mother's shoulder. Emeline convulsively seized her, and their wet cheeks touched.

"If any one ever says that I don't appreciate what you've done for me and mine," choked Emeline, "it's a lie!"

"Well, it didn't *sound* like you, Em," Mrs. Tarbury said, drying eyes between sniffs.

Emeline immediately went over and kissed her, and all three laughed shakily over a complete reconciliation, which was pleasingly interrupted by George's gallant offer to take the whole crowd to dinner, if they didn't mind his eating only tea and toast.

Still, it was decided that Julia should not stay at Mrs. Tarbury's, but should spend the next week or two with her grandmother in the Mission. Julia's quiet acceptance of this arrangement was both unexpected and pleasing to her parents.

But as a matter of fact the girl was rather dazed, at this time, too deeply sunk in a miserable contemplation of her own affairs to be conscious of the immediate discomfort of the moment. She had dreamed many a happy dream, as the years went by, of her father: had thought he would claim her some day, be proud of her. She had fancied a little home circle of which she would be the centre and star, spoiled alike by father and mother. Dearer than any dream of a lover had been to Julia this hope for days to come, when she should be a successful young actress, with an adoring Daddy to be proud of her. Now the dream was clouded; her father was an old man, self-absorbed; her mother—but Julia had always known her mother to be both selfish and mercenary. More than this, her little visit in Sausalito had altered her whole viewpoint. Ignorant of life as she was, and bewildered by the revelations of that visit, she was still intelligent enough to feel an acute discontent with her old world, an agonizing longing for that better and cleaner and higher existence. How to grasp at anything different from life as it was lived in her mother's home—in her grandmother's, in Mrs. Tarbury's—Julia had not the most remote idea. Until a few months ago she had not known that she wanted anything different.

She brooded over the problem night and day; sometimes her hours of gloomy introspection were interrupted by bursts of rebellious fury. She would *not* bear it, she would *not* be despised and obscure and ignorant, when, so close to her, there were girls of her own age to whom Fate had been utterly kind; it was not her fault, and it was not *right*—it was not right to despise her for what she could not help! But usually her attitude was of passive if confused endurance.

Julia pored over the society columns of the Sunday papers, in these days, and when she came across the name of Barbara Toland or Enid Hazzard, it was as if a blow had been struck at her heart. Barbara's face, smiling out at her from a copy of the News Letter, made Julia wretched for a whole day, and the mere sight of the magazine that contained it was obnoxious to her for days to come. Walking with Mark, she saw in some Kearney Street window an enlarged photograph of a little yacht cutting against a stiff breeze, and felt a rush of unwelcome memories suddenly assail her.

Mark was very much the devoted lover just now, but the contemplation of marriage with Mark never for a moment entered Julia's head. She had really liked him much better when he was only Hannah's big brother, who ignored all small girls in kindly, big-boy fashion. His adoring devotion embarrassed her, and his demand for a definite answer to his suggestion of marriage worried and perhaps a little frightened her.

One summer Sunday Mark asked her to go to the Park with him, and the two made the trip on a Geary Street dummy front, and wandered through wide, sunny stretches of lawn and white roadway to the amphitheatre, where several thousand persons of all ages and conditions were already listening to the band. Benches were set in rows under a grove of young maple and locust trees, and Julia and Mark, sauntering well up to the front, found seats, and settled themselves to listen.

Julia, enjoying the sunshine and the good hour, looked lazily at the curiously variegated types about them: young men who lay almost horizontally in their seats, their eyes shut, newspapers blowing about their feet; toddling babies in Sunday white; young fathers and mothers with tiny coats laid across their laps; groups of middle-aged Teutons critically alert, and, everywhere, lovers and lovers and lovers. Mark was pleasantly aware that his companion's beauty made her conspicuous, even though Julia was plainly, almost soberly, dressed to-day, and showed none of her usual sparkle and flash. She wore a trim little gown of blue serge, with a tiny white ruffle about its high collar for its only relief, her gloves were black, her small hat black, and she wore no rings, no chains, and no bangles, a startling innovation for Julia. The change in her appearance, and some more subtle change in face and voice and manner, affected Mark like a strong wine.

"Do you know you're different from what you uster be, Julie?" he said, laying his arm about her shoulders, on the back of the bench, and squaring about so that his handsome black eyes could devour her.

"Getting older, maybe," Julia smiled indifferently. "I'll be sixteen in no time, now!"

"My mother was only fifteen when she was married," Mark said, in a deep and shaken voice, yet with pride and laughter in his eyes. Julia flushed and looked at the toe of her shoe.

"Well, what about it—eh?" Mark pursued in an eager undertone. Julia was silent. "What about it?" he said again.

"Why—why, I don't know," Julia stammered, uncomfortably, with a nervous and furtive glance about her; anywhere but at his face.

"Suppose I *do* know?" he urged, tightening a little the arm that layabout her. "Suppose I know for us both?"

Julia straightened herself suddenly, evading the encircling arm.

"Don't, Mark!" she pleaded, giving him a glimpse of wet blue eyes.

"I'm not teasing you, darling," he said tenderly. "I'm not going to tease you! But you do love me, Julia?"

A silence, but she tightened the hold of the little glove that rested on his free hand.

"Don't you, Julie?" he begged.

"Why—you know I do, Mark!" the girl said, and both began to laugh.

"But then what's the matter?" Mark asked, serious again.

"Well—" Julia looked all about her, and finally brought her troubled eyes to rest on his.

"Well, what, you darling?"

"Well, it's just this, Mark. I don't know whether I can get it over to you." The girl interrupted herself for a little puzzled laugh. "I don't know that I can get it over to myself," she said. "But it's this: I feel as if I didn't know *myself* yet, d'ye see? I don't know what I want, myself, and of course I don't know what I want my husband to be like—d'ye see, Mark? I—I feel as if I didn't know *anything*—I don't know what's good and what's just common. I haven't read books, I haven't had any one to tell me things, and show me things!" She turned to him eyes that he was amazed to see were brimming again. "My mother never told me about things," she burst out incoherently, "about how to talk, and taking baths—and not using cologne!"

Mark could not quite follow this argument, but he was quick with soothing generalities.

"Aw, pshaw, Julie, as if you aren't about as good as they make 'em, just as you are! Why, I'm crazy about you—I'm crazy about the way you look and about the way you act; you're good enough for *me*! Julie," his voice sank again, "Julie, won't you let me pick out a little flat somewheres? Pomeroy said I could have any one of the old squares for nothing; we could get some rugs and chairs from the People's Easy Payment Company. Just you and me, Julie; what do you think?"

"I-I'd like to have a cute little house," said Julia, with a shaky smile.

"Sure you would! And a garden—"

"Oh, I'd love a little garden!" The girl smiled again.

"Well, then, why not, Julia?"

She looked at him obliquely.

"Suppose I stopped loving you, Mark?"

Mark gave a great laugh.

"Once I have you, Ju, I'll risk it!"

Child that she was, a glimpse of that complete possession stained her cheeks crimson.

"I have to go down to Mama in Santa Clara next week," she submitted awkwardly.

"Well, go down. But—how about New Year's, Julie? Will you marry me then?"

Julia got up, and they walked away across the soft green of the grass.

"I don't honestly know what I want to do, Mark," she said a little drearily. "I'm not crazy to go to Santa Clara, and yet it's something awful—living at my grandmother's house! I'd like to kill my grandfather, I know that. He's the meanest old man I ever saw. I suppose I could keep at Artheris for an engagement—he's awfully decent—but now that Rose and Connie have gone, I have to go round alone, and—it isn't that I'm afraid of anything, but I simply don't seem to care any more! I don't believe I want to be an actress. Artheris offered me small parts with the Sacramento Star Stock, playing fourteen weeks and twenty plays, this winter, but I thought of getting up there, and having to hunt up a boarding-house—" Her voice sank indifferently. "I don't believe I'd take anything less than ingenue," she added presently. "Florence Pitt played ingenue in stock when she was only fifteen!"

"You could work up, Ju," Mark suggested, honestly anxious to console.

"Yes, the way Connie and Rose have!" the girl answered dryly. "Con's been in the business six years and Rose nine!" Her eyes travelled the blue spaces of the summer sky. "I wish I could go to New York," she said vaguely.

"They say New York is jam-packed with girls hanging round theatrical agencies," Mark submitted, to which Julia answered with a dispirited, "I know!"

George had promised to send five dollars each week to old Mrs. Cox for Julia's board, so that her stay in the Mission Street house was agreeable for more than one reason, and her cousins understood perfectly that Julia was to remain idle while they continued to be self-supporting. They had no room in their crowded lives for envy of the prettier and more fortunate Julia, but Julia vaguely envied them, seeing them start off for work every morning, and joined by other girls and young men as they reached the corner. Evelyn and Marguerite had each an admirer, and between the romance of their evenings and the thousand little episodes of the factory day, they seemed to find life cheerful enough.

Julia tried, early in her stay, to make the room she shared with her cousins, and her grandmother's kitchen, a little more attractive. But the material to her hand was not very easily improved. In the bare bedroom there was an iron bed, large enough to be fairly comfortable for three tenants, two chairs, a washstand, and a chest of drawers that would not stand straight. The paper was light, and streaked with dirt and mould, and the bare wooden floor was strewn with paper candy bags and crumpled programs from cheap theatres. There were no curtains at the two windows, and the blue-green roller shades were faded by the sun. Not a promising field for a reformer whose ideal was formed on a memory of the Tolands' guest room!

The kitchen was quite as bad; worse in the sense that while Julia might do as she pleased in the bedroom, her grandmother resented any interference in what old Mrs. Cox regarded as her own domain. The old woman found nothing amiss in the dirty newspapers that covered the table, the tin of melting grease on the stove, the odds and ends of rags and rope and clothespins and stockings that littered the chairs and floor, the flies that walked on the ceiling and buzzed over the sugar bowl. Julia quite enraged her on that morning that she essayed to clean a certain wide shelf that, crowded to its last inch, hung over the sink.

"Do you need this, Grandma—can I throw this away?" the girl said over and over, displaying a nearly empty box of blacking, a moist bag tightly rolled over perhaps a pound of sugar, a broken egg beater, a stopped alarm clock, a bottle of toothache drops, a dog's old collar, a cracked saucer with a cake of brown soap tightly adhering to it, a few dried onions, a broken comb, the two halves of a broken vase, and a score of similarly assorted small articles.

"Jest don't meddle with 'em, Julia," Mrs. Cox said over and over again uneasily. "I'm going to give all that a thorough cleaning when I get around to it!"

She was obviously relieved when Julia gave the whole thing up as a bad job, and went back to her aimless wandering about the house. Mrs. Cox never went out except to church, but now and then Julia went down to Mrs. Tarbury's and vaguely discussed the advisability of taking a theatrical engagement, exactly as if several very definite offers were under consideration.

Just at this time Julia's youngest uncle, Chester Cox, wrote his mother from the big prison at San Quentin that he was coming home. The letter, pencilled on two sheets of lined, grayish paper, caused a good deal of discussion between Mrs. Cox, her husband, and her granddaughters. Chester, now about thirty years old, had been pardoned because of late evidence in his favour, when a five-year term for burglary was but one quarter served, but in his old father's eyes a jailbird was a jailbird, and Chester was still in some mysterious way to blame. Mrs. Cox was only concerned because the boy was ill and out of a job and apt to prove a burden, but the three girls, frankly curious about him, nevertheless reserved judgment. He had always been an idler, he had always been a weakling, but if he really were accused falsely, they could champion him still.

The day he had set for his return was a Sunday, but he arrived unexpectedly on the Saturday afternoon, to find great trouble in the Mission Street house. Evelyn and Marguerite were free for the afternoon, and were in the kitchen with Julia and their grandmother. It had lately come to Evelyn's ears that her grandfather had been borrowing money on the little property, and old Mrs. Cox was beside herself with anger and fear. The house was her one hope against a destitute old age. She fairly writhed at the contemplation of her husband's treachery in undermining that one stay. While she was slaving and struggling, he had airily disposed of three hundred dollars. She was stifled by the thought.

"He'd ought to be sent to jail for it!" the old woman said bitterly.

"You can't do it," Evelyn, the bearer of the badnews, assured her impatiently.

"Well, he'll see what I can do, when he gets home!" Mrs. Cox muttered. Julia, distressed by the scene, laid her hand over her grandmother's old knotted one, as she sat beside her at the table, but could find no words with which to comfort her. Her soul was sick with this fresh sordid revelation; she felt as if she must scream in another minute of existence in this dreary, dirty house, with the glaring sunshine streaming in the kitchen window and a high summer wind howling outside.

The talk was ended by a ring at the door, and Julia went through the dark, stifling passage to admit a lean, pale young man, with a rough growth of light hair on his sunken cheeks, and a curious look of not belonging to his clothes.

"It's Uncle Chess, Grandma," said she, leading the way back to the kitchen. Mrs. Cox gave her youngest child a kiss, assuring him that she never would have known him, he looked like a ghost, she said, and Chester sat down and talked a little awkwardly to his mother and nieces. His voice was husky, full of apologetic cadences; he explained painstakingly the chance that had brought him home twenty-four hours early, as if it were the most important thing in the world. Julia, helping her grandmother with preparations for dinner, did not know why she found Chester's presence unendurably trying; she did not know that it was pity that wrung her heart; she only wished he were not there.

An hour's talk cheered the newcomer amazingly, as perhaps did also the dinner odours of frying potatoes and bacon. He was venturing upon a history of his wrongs when a damper fell upon the little company with the arrival of the man of the house. Her husband's return brought back in a flood to old Mrs. Cox's heart the memory of his outrageous negotiations regarding the house; the three girls all cordially detested the old man and were silent and ungracious in his presence, and Chester flushed deeply as his father came in, and became dumb.

Old Cox made no immediate acknowledgement of the newcomer's arrival, but grunted as he jerked a chair to the table, indicating his readiness for dinner, and dinner was served with all speed. It was only when he had drunk off half a cup of scalding strong tea that the man of the house turned to his last born and said:

"So, you're out again?"

"I should never have been in!" Chester said, eagerly and huskily.

"Yes, I've heard lots of that kind of talk," the old man assured him. "'Cording to what you hear there's a good many up there that never done nothing at all!"

Julia saw the son shrink, and a look of infinite wistfulness for a moment darkened his eyes. He was a stupid-looking, gentle-faced fellow, pitiable as a sick child.

"Perhaps you'll read these, Pa," he said, fumbling in his pockets for a moment before producing two or three short newspaper clippings from an inner coat pocket. "There—there's the truth of it; it's all there," he said eagerly. "'Cox will immediately be given his freedom—after sixteen months as an innocent victim of the law'—that's what it says!"

"I'll read nothin'," the old man said, sweeping back the slips with a scornful hand, his small, deep-set eyes blinking at his son like a monkey's.

"Well, all right, all right," Chester answered, his thin face burning again, his voice hoarsely belligerent.

"That's the jestice you'll get from your father!" the old woman said, with a cackle. Julia gathered up the newspaper clippings.

"Aren't you mean, Grandpa!" she said, indignantly, beginning to read.

"Maybe I am, maybe I am," he retorted fiercely. "But you'll find there's no smoke without some fire, my fine lady, and when a boy that's always been a lazy, idle shame to his father and mother gets a taste of blame, you can depend that no newspaper is going to make a saint of him!"

"Grandma, don't let him talk that way!" Julia protested, her breast rising and falling. Chester turned to his father.

"Maybe if you'd a-give me a better chance," he said sullenly, "maybe if us boys hadn't been kicked around so much, shoved into the first job that came handy, seeing Ma and the girls afraid to breathe while you was in the house—"

Both men were now standing, their faces close together.

"Well, you ain't going to have another chance here!" the old man shouted. "I'll have no jailbirds settin' around here to be petted and babied! Get that into your head! Don't you let me come into the house and find you here again——"

"Pa!" protested Mrs. Cox, fired by the eyes of her granddaughters. "Yes—an' 'Pa'!" he snarled, pulling on his old hat, and opening the kitchen door. "But it'll be Pa on the wrong side of your face if you make any mistake about it! Jailbird!" he muttered to himself, with a final slam at the door. The others looked at each other.

"That's a sweet welcome home," said Chester, with a bitter laugh. He was standing, his head lowered; there was bewilderment as well as anger in his look.

"Pa's got to be a terrible crank," said Mrs. Cox, returning to her teapot, after a glance through the window at her retiring lord. "He carries on something terrible sometimes."

"Well, he won't carry on any longer as far as I am concerned!" Chester said, a little vaguely.

"I don't know what's got into Pa!" his wife complained.

"Don't you care, Uncle Chess," Marguerite submitted with timid sympathy.

"Oh, no, sure I don't care," the man said with a short laugh. "Of course it's nothing to me! A man comes home to his own folks, he's had a tough time—" His voice sank huskily. The sleeves of his coat were too short for him, and Julia noticed how thin his wrists were, as he gathered up his newspaper clippings and restored them to his inside pocket. The women watched him in silence. Presently he stooped down and kissed his mother's forehead, at the edge of her untidy, grizzled hair.

"Good-bye, Ma!" he said. "Good-bye, girls!"

"It'll be a judgment on your father," Mrs. Cox protested. "I don't know what's gotten into him!"

But she made no further objection; she did not get up from her place at table when Chester crossed the kitchen, opened the street door, and went out.

"Grandpa's a prince, all right!" said Marguerite then, and Evelyn added, "Wouldn't it give you a pain?"

"But I notice that none of us did anything about it!" Julia said bitterly.

"If your grandpa found Chess here when he got home to-night, there'd be a reckoning!" the old woman asserted dully.

"And what is Uncle Chess supposed to do?" Julia demanded.

"I betcher he kills himself," Evelyn submitted.

"I betcher he does," her sister agreed.

"Well, it'll be on your grandfather's head!" the old woman said. She began to cry, still drinking her tea.

"I wonder if he has any money?" speculated Julia.

"Where'd he get money?" Evelyn said. Julia, following an uncomfortable impulse, went to the window in the close little parlour and looked out into the street. It was about six o'clock, and still broad day. The wind had died down, but the street was dirty, and the glaring light of the sinking sun fell full on the faces of the home-going stream of men and women. Julia's quick eye found Chester instantly. He had loitered no farther than the corner, a hundred feet away, and was standing there, irresolute, stooped, still wearing his look of vague bewilderment.

The girl ran upstairs, and snatched her hat and a light coat. Two minutes later she was downstairs again, the chatelaine bag in which all girls carried their money in those days jumping at her belt.

But in those two minutes Chester had disappeared. Julia felt sick with disappointment as she reached the corner only to find him gone. She stood looking quickly about her: up the street, down the street; he was gone. It seemed to the girl that she could not go back to her grandmother's house again; a disgust for everything and everybody in it shook her from head to foot. She was sorry for them, her grandmother, her cousins, but the simple fact remained that they could bear this sort of existence and she could not; it was stifling her; it was killing her.

"If they minded things as I do they would change them, somehow!" said Julia to herself, walking on blindly. "My grandmother should never have let things get to such a pass—I can't bear it! The smells and the fights—"

She stopped a car, one of the cable cars that ran out into the factory district. Julia had no idea where she was going, nor did she care. She got on because one of the small forward outside seats was empty, and she could sit there comfortably. The car went on and on, through a less and less populated district, but Julia, buried in unhappy thought, paid no attention to route or neighbourhood.

"All off!" shouted the conductor presently. Julia had meant to keep her seat for the return trip, but the man's glance at her young beauty annoyed her, and she got off the car.

She walked aimlessly along a battered cement sidewalk, between irregularly placed and shabby little houses. These were of too familiar a type to interest Julia, but she presently came to a full stop before a wide, one-story brick building, with a struggling garden separating it from the street, and straggling window boxes at every one of the wide windows. A flight of steps led up from the garden to the pretty white front door, and a neat brass plate, screwed to the cement at the turn of the steps, bore the words: "Alexander Toland Neighbourhood House."

It would have been a pretty house anywhere, with its crisp dotted muslin curtains, its trim colonial walls, but in this particular neighbourhood it had an added charm of contrast, and Julia stood before it literally spellbound by admiration, and smitten, too, with that strange sick fascination to which the mere name of Toland subjected her.

And while she stood there, Miss Anna Toland came to the door and stood looking down at the street. Julia's heart began to beat very fast, and the blood rushed to her face. She bowed, and Miss Toland bowed.

"Oh, Miss Page!" said Miss Toland then, crisply ready with the name and the request. "This is very fortunate! I wonder if you won't come in and help me a moment? I've been trying for one hour to make the hall key work."

Julia said nothing. She mounted the steps and followed Miss Toland into the hall.

CHAPTER VI

The Alexander Toland Neighbourhood House, familiarly known by all who had anything to do with it as The Alexander, was small, as neighbourhood houses go, but exceptionally pretty and complete, and financially so well backed by a certain group of San Francisco's society women as to be entirely free from the common trouble of its kind. Miss Toland had built it, and had made it her personal business to interest some of her friends in its success, but she now found herself confronted by an unexpected problem: it seemed impossible to get an experienced woman as resident worker with whom Miss Toland could live in peace. The few women who had been qualified to try the position had all swiftly, quietly, and firmly resigned, with that pained reticence that marks the trained worker. Miss Toland told her committees, with good-humoured tolerance, that Miss Smith or Mrs. Brown had been a splendid person, perfectly splendid, but unable to understand the peculiar conditions that made social work in San Francisco utterly—and totally—different from social work elsewhere. Meanwhile, she did the best she could with volunteer workers, daily bewailing the fact that, without the trained worker, her girls' clubs and classes, her boys' and mothers' clubs, had been difficult to start, and maintained but a languishing existence. She was a sanguine woman, and filled with confidence in the eventual success of The Alexander, and with energy to push it toward a completely fruitful existence, but she herself was inexperienced, and Julia had chanced upon her in a thoroughly discouraged mood.

Julia's first aid—in climbing through a transom and opening a stubborn door—being entirely successful, Miss Toland kept her to show her the little establishment, and was secretly soothed and pleased by the girl's delight.

The front door opened into a wide square hall, furnished with neat Mission chairs and tables, and with a large brown rug. There were two doors on each side, and a large double door at the back. One door on the right led to a model kitchen, floored in bright blue-and-white linoleum, and with a shining stove, a shining dresser full of blue-and-white china, a tiled sink, a table, and two chairs. The other right-hand door opened into a little committee room, where there were wall closets full of ginghams and boxes of buttons and braid, and more Mission furniture. On the left each door opened into a bedroom, one occupied by Miss Toland and littered by her possessions, one empty and immaculate. The two were joined by a shining little bath. Julia looked at the white bed in the unoccupied room, the white bureau, the white chairs, the white dotted curtains at the windows, the dark-blue rugs on a painted floor, and a gasp of honest admiration broke from her. Miss Toland gave her a quick approving glance, but said nothing.

Through the big double door they stepped straight on the stage that filled one end of the tiny auditorium, Miss Toland touching an electric button that flooded the room with light, for Julia's benefit. There were wide windows, curtained in crisp dotted white, all about the hall, and a door at the far end that gave, as Julia afterward learned, on a side street. An upright piano was on the stage, and at one side a flight of three or four steps led down to the hall. The main floor was broken by tables and benches, a hundred sewing bags of blue linen hung on numbered hooks on the wall, and at the far end there were two deep closets for kindergarten materials and sewing supplies.

The tour of inspection was ended in the kitchen, where Miss Toland put several paper bags on the table, dropped into a chair, and asked Julia also to be seated.

"Well, what do you think of it?" she said, reaching behind her to get a knife from a drawer. With the knife she cut a spongy crust from a loaf of bread, without fairly withdrawing it from the bag, and subtracting a thin pink slice of ham from some oiled paper in another bag, she folded it into the crust and began to eat it. "I picnic here—when I come," said Miss Toland, unembarrassed. "You've had your dinner?"

"Oh, yes," said Julia, "but do let me—" And without further words she took two plates from the dresser, served the ham neatly, cut a slice or two of bread, and removed the bags.

"Ah, yes, that's *much* better!" Miss Toland said. "There's tea there. I suppose you couldn't manage a cup?"

A deep and peculiar pleasure began to thrill through Julia. She stepped to the entrance hall, laid aside her hat and jacket, and returned to set about tea-making with deftness and quickness. She found a wilted slice of butter in a safe, and set out cups and sugar beside it. Miss Toland stopped eating, and watched these preparations with great satisfaction. Presently she stood up to pin her handsome silk-lined skirt about her hips, and pushed her face veil neatly above the brim of her hat. The water in the white enamelled kettle boiled, and Julia made tea in a blue Japanese pot.

"This is *much* better!" said Miss Toland again. "I get to be a perfect barbarian—eating alone!" She rummaged in a closet. "Here's some jam Sally sent," said she, producing it. "They are always sending me pies and fresh eggs and jelly; they are always afraid of my starving to death."

They began the meal again, and this time Julia joined her hostess, and really enjoyed her tea and bread and jam. It was dark now, and they drew the shades at the two street windows and turned on the electric light. Julia knew by some instinct that she need not be afraid of the gray-haired, eccentric, kindly woman opposite; in that very hour she assumed a maternal attitude that was to be the key to her relationship with Miss Toland for many years. The two, neither realizing it, instantly liked each other. Never in her rather reserved little life had Julia shown her heart as she showed it in this hour over the teacups.

"So you like it?" said Miss Toland. "It's small, but it's the most complete thing of the kind in the State. I've been scrambling along here as best I might for three months, but as soon as I get a resident head worker, we'll get everything straightened out." She gave her nose a sudden rub with her hand, frowned in a worried fashion.

"Girls—regularly appointed girls ought to take care of all this!" she went on, indicating the kitchen with a wave of her hand. "But no! You can't get them to systematize! Now I tell you," she added sternly, "I am going to lay down the law in this house! They do it in other settlement houses, and it shall be done here! Every yard of gingham, every thimble and spool of thread, is going to be *accounted* for! Do you suppose that at the Telegraph Hill House they allow the children to run about grabbing here and grabbing there—poh! They'd laugh at you!"

"Of course," said Julia vaguely.

"Classes of the smaller girls should keep this kitchen and bathroom like a *pin*," said Miss Toland sharply. "And, as soon as we get a regular manager in here—Now that's what I tell my sister Sally, that is Mrs. Toland," she broke off to say. "Here's Barbara, home from a finishing school and six months abroad. Why couldn't she step in here? But no! Barbara'll come in now and then if it's a special occasion—"

"But she has such wonderful good times at home; she has everything in the world now," Julia said wistfully. Miss Toland gave her a shrewd glance; it was as if she saw Julia for the first time.

"Barbara?" Barbara's aunt poured herself another cup of tea, and fell into thought for a few moments. Then she set down her cup, straightened herself suddenly, and burst forth: "Barbara! That's one of the most absurd things in the world, you know—the supposition that a girl like Barbara is perfectly happy! Perfectly wretched and discontented, if you ask me!"

"Oh, no!" Julia protested.

"Oh, yes! Barbara's idle, she's useless, she doesn't know what to do with herself. No girl of her age does. I know, for my mother brought me up in the same way. She got a lot of half-baked notions in school; she had a year of college in which to get a lot more; she came home afraid to go back to college for fear of missing something at home, afraid of staying home for fear of missing something at college; compromised on six months in Europe. Now, here she is, the finished product. We've been spending twelve years getting Barbara ready for something, and, as a result, she's ready for nothing! What does she know of the world? Absolutely nothing! She's never for one instant come in contact with anything real—she can't. She's been so educated that she wouldn't know anything real if she saw it! Mind you," said Miss Toland, fixing the somewhat bewildered Julia with a stern eye, "mind you, I admit it's hard for people of income to bring a girl up sensibly. 'But,' I've said to my sister-in-law, 'hand me over one of the younger girls—I'll promise you that she'll grow up something more than a poor little fashionably dressed doll, looking sidewise out of her eyes at every man she meets, to see whether he'll marry her or not!' Of course there's only one answer to that. I've never married, and I don't know anything about it!"

"Miss Toland will marry," Julia submitted.

"Perhaps she will," her aunt said. "Perhaps, again, she won't. But at all events, it's a rather flat business, all this rushing about to dinners and dances; it'll last a few years perhaps—then what? I tell you what, my dear, there's only one good thing in this world, and that's *work*—self-expression. It hurts my pride every time I see a nice girl growing older year after year, idle, expensive, waiting for some man to miraculously happen along and take her out of it. I tell you the interesting lives are those of people who've had to work up from the bottom. A working girl may have her troubles, but they're *real*. Why, let's suppose that Barbara marries, that she marries the man her mother has picked out, for example, still she doesn't get away from the tiring, the sickening conventions that all her set has laid down for her! I wish I had my own girlhood to live over—I know that!" finished the older woman, with a gloomy nod.

"Miss Toland seems to me to have everything in the world," Julia said, in childish protest. "She's—she's beautiful, and every one loves her. She's always been rich enough to do what she pleased, and go places, and wear what she liked! And—and"—Julia's eyes watered suddenly—"and she's a lady," she added unsteadily. "She's always been told how to do things, she's—she's different from—from girls who have had no chances, who—"

Her voice thickened, speech became too difficult, and she stopped, looking down at her teacup through a blur of tears. Miss Toland watched her for a silent moment or two; despite all her oddities, no woman who ever lived had a kinder heart or a keener insight than Anna Toland. It was in a very winning tone that she presently said:

"Tell me a little something about yourself, Miss Page!"

"Oh, there's nothing interesting about *me*!" Julia said, ashamed of showing emotion. She jumped up, and began to put the kitchen in order. But the recital came, nevertheless, beginning with Chester, and ending with Julia's earliest memories of the O'Farrell Street house. The girl tumbled it out regardless of sequence, and revealing far more than she knew. Julia told of the episode of Carter Hazzard; she repeated the conversation she had overheard at the club.

Miss Toland did not once interrupt her; she listened in an appreciative silence. They washed and put away the dishes, straightened the kitchen, and finally found themselves standing in the reception room, Julia still talking.

".... so you see why it sounds so funny to me, your talking about your niece," Julia said. "Because she—she seems to me such *miles* ahead—she seems to have everything I would like to have!" She paused, and then said awkwardly: "I'll never be a lady, I know that. I—I wish I had a chance to be!"

And she sat down at the little Mission table, and flung her arms out before her, her face tired and wretched, her blue eyes dark with pain. Miss Toland's face, from showing mere indulgent interest, took on a sharper look. She was a quick-witted woman, and this chanced to touch her in a sensitive spot.

"As for a lady, ladies are made and not born," she said decidedly. "Don't ever let them fool you. Barbara may run around until she's tired talking about belonging to the Daughters of Southern Officers; she can stick a sampler up here, and lend a Copley portrait to a loan exhibition now and then; but you mark my words, Barbara had to learn things like any other girl. One sensible mother in this world is worth sixteen distinguished great-grandmothers!"

Julia said nothing; she began to think it was time for her to go. But Miss Toland was well launched in a favourite argument.

"Why, look here," said the older woman, who was enjoying herself, "you're young, you're pretty, you're naturally inclined to choose what is nice, what is refined. You say you're not a lady—how do you know? You may take my word for it—Julia, your name is?—Julia, then, that if you make up your mind to be one, nothing can stop you. Now I've been thinking while we talked. Why couldn't you come here and try this sort of thing? You could keep things running smoothly here; you could work into the girls' clubs, perhaps; no harm to try, anyway. Do you sing?"

Julia had to clear her throat before she could say huskily:

"I can play the piano a little."

"You see—you play. Well, what do you think of it, then?"

"Live here?" stammered Julia.

"Certainly, live right here. I want some one right *here* with me. You can arrange your own work, you can read all the books you want, you'll come in contact with nice people. I'm afraid to be here alone at night very much, and I've come to the conclusion that we'll never accomplish anything until I can stay, day out and in. Why don't you try it, anyway? Telephone your grandmother—sleep right here to-night!"

Julia struggled for absolute control of her facial muscles.

"Here?" she asked, a little thickly.

"Right in here—you can but try it!" Miss Toland urged, throwing open the door of the immaculate, unused bedroom. Julia looked again at the fresh white bed, the rug, the bureau. Her own—her own domain! Just what entering it meant to her she never tried to say, but the moment was a memorable one in her life. She presently found herself telephoning a message to the drug store that was nearest her grandmother's home. She selected a flannelette nightgown from a deep drawer marked: "Nightgowns and petticoats—Women's." She assured Miss Toland that she could buy a toothbrush the next day, and when the older woman asked her how she liked her bath in the morning, Julia said very staidly: "Warm, thank you."

"Warm? Well, so do I," said Miss Toland's approving voice from the next room. "This business of ice-cold baths! Fad. There's a gas heater in the kitchen."

Julia, laying her underwear neatly over a chair, was struck by the enormity of the task she had undertaken. A great blight of utter discouragement swept over her—she never could do it! Her mother—all her kin—seemed to take shadowy shape to menace this little haven she had found. Chester—suppose he should find her! Suppose Mark should! Sooner or later some one must discover where she was.

And clothes! These clothes would not do! She had no money; she must borrow. And how was she to help in sewing classes and cooking classes, knowing only what she knew?

".... said to her as nicely as I could, but firmly," Miss Toland was saying, above the rasp of a running faucet in the bathroom, "'Well, my dear Miss Hewitt, you may be a trained worker and I'm not, but you can't expect your theories to work under conditions—'"

"What a bluffer I am," thought Julia, getting into bed. She snapped her light off, but Miss Toland turned it on again when she came to the door to look at Julia with great satisfaction.

"Comfortable, my dear?"

"Oh, yes, thank you."

"Have you forgotten to open your window?"

Julia raised herself on an elbow.

"Well, I believe I have," said she.

Miss Toland flung it up.

"We're as safe as a church here," she said, after a moment's study of the street. "Sometimes the Italians opposite get noisy, but they're harmless. Well, I'm going to read—you'll see my light. Sleep tight!"

"Thank you," said Julia.

Miss Toland went back to her room, and Julia, wide awake, lay staring at her own room's pure bare walls, the triangle of light that fell in the little passageway from Miss Toland's reading lamp, and the lights in the street outside. Now and then a passing car sent lights wheeling across her ceiling like the flanges of a fan; now and then a couple of men passing just under her window roused her with their deep voices, or a tired child's voice rose up above the patter of footsteps like a bird's pipe in the night. Cats squalled and snarled, and fled up the street; a soprano voice floated out on the night air:

"But the waves still are singing to the shore As they sang in the happy days of yore—"

To these and a thousand less sharply defined noises, to the constant, steady flicking of stiff pages in Miss Toland's room, Julia fell asleep.

Miss Toland told her family of the arrangement some three months later. She met her sister-in-law and oldest niece downtown for luncheon one day in November, and when the ladies had ordered their luncheon and piled superfluous wraps and parcels upon a fourth chair, Barbara, staring about the Palm Room, and resting her chin on one slender wrist, asked indifferently:

"And how's The Alexander, Aunt Sanna?"

"Why don't you come and see?" asked her aunt briskly. "You've all deserted me, and I don't know whether I'm on speaking terms with you or not! We're getting on splendidly. Nineteen girls in our Tuesday evening club; mothers' meetings a great success. I've captured a rare little personality in Julia."

She enlarged upon the theme: Julia's industry, her simplicity, her natural sympathy with and comprehension of the class from which the frequenters of The Alexander were drawn. Mrs. Toland listened smilingly, her bright eyes roving the room constantly. Barbara did not listen at all; she studied the scene about her sombrely, with heavy-lidded eyes.

Barbara was at an age when exactly those things that a certain small group of her contemporaries did, said, and thought, made all her world. She wished to be with these young people all the time; she wished for nothing else, to-day she was heartsick because there was to be a weekend house party to which she was not invited. A personal summons from the greatest queen of Europe would have meant nothing to Barbara to-day, except for its effect upon the little circle she desired so eagerly to impress. Parents, sisters, and brothers, nature, science, and art, were but pale shapes about her. The burning fact was that Elinor Sparrow had asked the others down for tennis Saturday and to stay overnight, and had asked her, Barbara, to join them on Sunday for luncheon—

"Tell Aunt Sanna about the wedding, dear!" commanded Mrs. Toland suddenly. Barbara smiled with mechanical brightness.

"Oh, it was lovely! Every one was there. Georgie looked stunning—ever so much prettier than Hazel!" she said, rather lifelessly.

"Tell Aunt Sanna who got the bride's bouquet!"

"Oh," Barbara again assumed an expression of animation. "Oh, I did."

"Jim go?"

"Oh, yes, he went with the Russells. That's getting to be quite a case, you know," Barbara said airily.

"I *thought* that was Elinor Sparrow and her mother," Mrs. Toland said, bowing to two ladies who were now at some distance, and were leaving the room. "They were at that table, but I couldn't be sure who they were until they got up."

"Was Elinor right there?" Barbara asked quickly.

"Why, yes; but as I say—"

Barbara pushed back her broiled bird with a gesture of utter exasperation.

"I think you might have *said* something about it, Mother," she said, angry and disappointed.

"Why, my darling," Mrs. Toland began, fluttered, "how could I dream—besides, as I say, I couldn't see—"

"You knew how I felt about Saturday," Barbara said bitterly, "and you let them sit there an hour! I could have turned around—I could have—"

"Listen to Mother, dear. You—"

"And I can't understand why you wouldn't naturally mention it," Barbara interrupted, in a high, critical voice. Tears trembled into her eyes. "I would have given a great deal to have seen Elinor to-day," she said stiffly.

Mrs. Toland, smitten dumb with penitence, could only eye her with sympathy and distress.

"Listen, dear," she suggested eagerly, after a moment. "Suppose you run out and see Elinor in the cloakroom? Mother's so sorry she—"

"No, I couldn't do that," Barbara answered moodily. "It would have been all right to have it just seem to happen—No, it doesn't make any difference, Mother. Please—*please*—don't bother about it."

"I'm sure Elinor didn't see you," Mrs. Toland continued. Barbara, throwing her a glance of utter weariness, begged politely:

"*Please* don't bother about it, Mother. *Please.* I'd rather not."

"Well," Mrs. Toland conceded, with dissatisfaction. An uncomfortable silence reigned, until Miss Toland began suddenly to talk of Julia.

"She's a very unusual girl," said she. "She's *utterly* and *entirely* satisfactory to me."

"I think you're very fortunate, Sanna," Mrs. Toland commented absently. She speculated a little as to Julia; there really must be something unusual about the girl; Sanna was notoriously difficult to live with.

"She's not stiff—she's amenable to reason," Miss Toland said, smiling vaguely. "We—we have really good times together."

"I hope she's improved in appearance," Mrs. Toland remarked severely. "You remember how dreadfully she looked, Barbara?"

Barbara smiled, half lifted dubious brows, and shrugged slightly.

"She's *enormously* improved," Miss Toland said sharply. "She wears an extremely becoming uniform now."

"She's evidently got *your* number, Auntie," Barbara said, watching three young men who were entering the room. "She evidently knows that you're nutty about appearances!"

"I am not nutty about appearances at all," her aunt responded, as she attacked an elaborate ice. "I like things done decently, and I like to see Julia in her nice, trim dresses. That Eastern woman I tried, Miss Knox, wouldn't hear of wearing a uniform—not she! Julia has more sense."

"I expect that Julia hasn't an idea in her head that you haven't put there," Barbara said dryly.

"Don't you believe it!" her aunt said with fire. She seemed ready for further speech, but interrupted herself, and was contented with a mere repetition of her first words, "Don't you *believe* it."

"Your geese are all swans, Sanna," Mrs. Toland said, with a tolerant smile.

"Very likely," Miss Toland said briefly, drinking off her black coffee at a draught. "Now," she went on briskly, "where are you good people going? Julia's to meet me here in the Turkish Room at two; we have to pick out a hundred books, to start our library."

"It's after that now," Barbara said. "She's probably waiting. Let's go out that way, Mother, and walk over to Sutter?"

They sauntered along the wide passage to the Turkish Room, and just before they reached it a young woman came toward them, a slender, erect person, under whose neatly buttoned long coat showed the crisp hem of a blue linen dress. Julia bowed briefly to the mother and daughter, but her eyes were only for Miss Toland. She was nervous and constrained; bright colour had come into her cheeks; she could not speak. But Barbara merely thought that the cheap little common actress had miraculously improved in appearance and manner, and noted the blue, blue eyes, and the glittering sweep of hair under Julia's neat hat, and Miss Toland felt herself curiously touched by the appealing look that Julia gave her.

"Now for the books, Julia," said she, beaming approval. The two went off together, chattering like friends and equals.

"What does Aunt Sanna *see* in her?" marvelled Barbara, watching.

"Your aunt is peculiar," Mrs. Toland said, with vague disapproval, compressing her lips.

"Well, the way she runs The Alexander is curious, to say the least," Barbara commented vigorously. "I couldn't stay out there one *week*, myself, and have Aunt Sanna carrying on the way she does, planning a thing, and forgetting it in two seconds, and yelling at the children one day, and treating them to ice-cream the next! Why, the last time I went out there Aunt Sanna was in bed, at eleven o'clock, because she felt like reading, and she'd called off the housekeeping class for no reason at all except that she didn't feel like it!"

"Yes, I know, I know," Mrs. Toland said, picking her way daintily across Market Street. "But she has her own money, and I suppose she'll go her own gait!" But she looked a little uneasy, and was silent for some moments, busy with her own thoughts.

Long before this Julia's whereabouts had been discovered by her own family, and by at least one of her friends, Mark Rosenthal. Mark walked in upon her one Sunday afternoon, when she had been about a month at The Alexander. Miss Toland had gone for a few hours to Sausalito, and Julia was alone, and had some leisure. She put on her hat, and she and Mark walked through the noisy Sunday streets; everybody was out in the sunshine, and saloons everywhere were doing a steady business.

"Evelyn told me where you were," Mark explained. Julia made a little grimace of disapproval, and the man, watching her, winced.

"Are you so sorry to have me know?" he asked, a sword in his heart.

"Oh, it's not that, Mark! But"—Julia stammered—"but I only went home to see grandma Thursday, and it struck me that Evelyn hadn't lost much time!"

"Wouldn't you ever have written me?" Mark asked, his dark eyes caressing her.

"Oh, of course I would. Only I wanted to get a start first. Why do you laugh?" Julia broke off to ask offendedly.

"Just because I love you so, darling. Just because I've been hungry for you all these weeks—and it's just ecstasy to be here!" Mark's eyes were moist now, though he was still smiling. "You don't know it, but I just *live* to see you, Julie. I can't think of anything else. This—this new job isn't going to make any difference about our marrying, is it, darling?"

Julia surveyed a stretch of dirty street lined with dirty yet somewhat pretentious houses. Women sat on drifts of newspapers on the steps, white-stockinged children quarrelled in the hot, dingy dooryards.

"I wish you didn't care that way, Mark," she said, uncomfortably.

"Why, dearest?" he said eagerly. "Because I care more for you than you do for me? I know that, Julie." He watched the cool little cheek nearest him. "But wait until we're married, Julie, you'll love me then; I'll *make* you!"

But all his young fire could not touch her. He could only win an occasional troubled glance.

"I want to stay here a long, long time, you know, Mark—if I can. I want to read things and study things. I want to be let alone. It'll be *years* before I want to marry!" Julia raised her anxious, harassed eyes to his. "I don't really think of men or of marriage at all," said she.

"Well, that's all right, darling," Mark said, smiling down at her, a little touched. "I'm going to be sent up to Sacramento for a while; I'll not worry you. But see here, if I go back to the house with you again, do I get a kiss?"

Julia gave him a grave smile, and let him follow her into the settlement house. But Mark did not get his kiss, for Miss Toland was there, and a group of eager club girls who had something to arrange for a meeting the following night. Mark left the lady of his delight staidly discussing the relative merits of lemonade and gingersnaps and two pounds of "broken mixed" candy, as evening refreshments, and carried away a troubled heart. He wrote Julia, at least twice a week, shyly affectionate and honestly egotistical letters, but it was some months before he saw her again.

Julia's visit to her grandparents, through which Mark had been able to trace her, had taken place some days before, on a certain Wednesday afternoon. Suddenly, after the daily three o'clock sewing class had had its meeting in the big hall, the thought had come to her that she must see her own people. It was a still autumn afternoon, a little chilly, and Julia, setting forth, felt small relish for her errand.

Her grandmother's house presented a dingy, discouraging front. Julia twisted the familiar old bell, and got the familiar old odours of carbolic acid and boiling onions, superimposed upon a basis of thick, heavy, stale air. But the hour she spent in the dirty kitchen was nevertheless not an unpleasant one. Her grandmother was all alone, and was too used to similar vagaries on the part of all her family to resent Julia's disappearance and long silence.

"We had your postal," she admitted, in answer to her granddaughter's embarrassed query. "You look thin, me dear; you've not got your old bold, stylish look about you."

And she wrinkled her old face and studied Julia with blinking eyes. "The girls was glad enough to use your dresses. Marguerite looked real nice in the one she took. Your Mama wrote in to know what kind of a job you had— Sit down, Julia," she said as she poked about the stove with a lid lifter.

Julia, who had drawn a long breath to recount her experiences, suddenly expelled it. It occurred to her, with a great relief, that her grandmother was not interested in details. Her hard life had left her no curiosity; she was only mildly satisfied at finding her granddaughter apparently prosperous and well; Mrs. Cox was never driven to the necessity of borrowing trouble.

Julia learned that her own father and mother were in Los Angeles, where George was looking for employment. Evelyn had developed a sudden ambition to be a dressmaker, Marguerite had a new admirer. Pa, Mrs. Cox said, was awful cross and cranky. Julia, with a premonition of trouble, asked for Chester.

"He's fine; he's the only one Pa'll speak to," her grandmother said, unexpectedly.

"Oh," said Julia eagerly, "he's here?"

"Sure, he come back," Mrs. Cox assured her indifferently. "He's got good work."

Walking home in the early darkness, Julia could have danced for very lightness of heart. She had dreaded the call, dreaded their jealousy of her new chance, dreaded the possibility of their wishing to share the joys of The Alexander with her. She found them entirely uninterested in her problems, and entirely absorbed in themselves. Marguerite remarked that she did not see why Julia "let them make" her wear the plain linen uniform of which Julia was secretly so proud. Evelyn was fretting because dressmakers' apprentices could depend upon such very poor pay, and vouchsafed Julia a moment's attention only when Julia observed that the Tolands patronized a very fashionable dressmaker, and might say a good word to her for Evelyn. This excited Evelyn very much, and she suggested that perhaps she herself had better see Miss Toland.

"No—no! I'll do it," Julia said hastily.

Mrs. Cox, upon her departure, extended her granddaughter a warm invitation.

"If they don't treat you good, dearie, you come right back here and Grandma'll take good care of you," said she, and Evelyn and Marguerite, eying Julia over their cups of tea, nodded half pityingly. They thought it a very poor job that did not permit one to come home to this kitchen at night, even less desirable than their own despised employments. Julia's being kept at night only added one more item to the long total that made the helplessness of the poor. It was as if Julia, dancing back to The Alexander in the early darkness, hugged to her heart the assurance that these kinswomen were as contentedly independent of her as she of them.

These experiences belonged to early days at The Alexander. There were other experiences, hours of cold discouragement and doubt, hours of bitter self-distrust. Julia trembled over mistakes, and made a hundred mistakes of which she never knew. But by some miracle, she never chanced to offend her erratic superior. To Miss Toland there was small significance in the fact of an ill-cut pattern or a lost key. At the mothers' meetings, when Julia was dismally smitten with a sense of her own uselessness, Miss Toland thought her shy little attempts at friendliness very charming, and when she casually corrected the faults of Julia's speech, she gave no further thought to the matter, although Julia turned hot and cold at the recollection for many a day to come.

Julia never made any objection, never hinted by so much as a reproachful eyelid, that Miss Toland's way of doing things was not that usually adopted. Julia would show her delight when a shopping tour and a lunch downtown were substituted for a sewing lesson; she docilely pushed back her boiling potatoes and beef stew when Miss Toland was for delaying supper while they went out to buy a waffle iron, and made some experiments with batter. On three or four mornings each week there were no classes, and on these mornings the two loitered along over their coffee and toast, Miss Toland talking, Julia a passionately interested listener. Perhaps the older woman would read some passage from Meredith or de Balzac, after which Julia dipped into Meredith for herself, but found him slow, and plunged back into Dickens and Thackeray. It amused Miss Toland to watch her read, to have Julia burst out, with flaming cheeks:

"Oh, I *hope* Charles Darney won't be such a fool as to go to Paris *now*—oh, *does* he?" or:

"You wouldn't catch *me* marrying George Osborne—a spoiled, selfish pig, that's what *he* is!"

So the months went by, and the day came when Julia, standing shyly beside Miss Toland, said smilingly:

"Do you know what day *this* is, Miss Toland?"

"To-day?" Miss Toland said briskly. "No, I don't. Why?"

"I've been here a year to-day," Julia said, dimpling.

"You *have*?" Miss Toland, handling bolts of pink-and-white gingham at a long table, straightened up to survey her demure little assistant. "Well, now I'll tell you what we'll do to celebrate," she said, after a thoughtful interval. "I understand that the Sisters over on Lake Merritt have a very *remarkable* sewing school. Now, we ought to see that, Julia, don't you think so?"

"We might get some ideas," Julia agreed.

"Precisely. So you put the card—'No Classes Today'—on the door, and we'll go. And put your milk bottle out, because we may be late. I hate to do it, but I really think we should know what they're doing over there."

"I do, too," Julia said. This form preceded most of their excursions. A few moments later they were out in the open air, with the long sunny day before them.

The months sped on their way again, and Julia had been in the settlement two years—three years. She was eighteen, and the world did not stand still. She was nineteen—twenty. She changed by slow degrees from the frightened little rabbit that had fled to Miss Toland for refuge to an observant, dignified young woman who was quietly sure of herself and her work. The rumpled ashen glory that had been her hair was transformed into the soft thick braids that now marked Miss Page's head apart from those of the other girls of her day. The round arms were guiltless of bracelets; Julia wore her severe blue uniform, untouched by any ornament; her stockings and shoes were as plain as money could buy.

Her beauty, somewhat in eclipse for a time, presently shone out again. But there were few to see it. Miss Watts, the simple, sweet, middle-aged teacher of the kindergarten, admired it wistfully, and Miss Toland watched it with secret pride. But the society girls and young matrons who flitted in once or twice a week to teach their classes never saw it at all, or, seeing it, merely told each other that little Miss Page would be awfully pretty in decent things, and the women and girls and children who formed the classes at The Alexander never saw her at all. The women were too much absorbed in their own affairs, children are proverbially blind to beauty, and the girls who came to the monthly dances, the evening sewing classes and reading clubs, thought their sober little guardian rather plain, as indeed she was, when judged by their standard of dress, their ruffled lace collars and high-heeled shoes, their curls and combs and coloured glass jewellery.

Julia's amazing detachment from the ordinary ideals of girlhood was an unending surprise to Miss Toland.

"She has simply and quietly set that astonishing little mind of hers upon making herself a lady," Miss Toland said now and then to her sister-in-law. Mrs. Toland would answer with only an abstracted smile. If she had any convictions at all in her genial view of life, she certainly believed a lady to be a thing born, not made. But she was not concerned about Julia; she hardly realized the girl's existence.

Miss Toland, however, was keenly concerned about Julia. Julia had come to be the absorbing interest of her life. It was quite natural that Julia should love her, yet to the older woman it always seemed a miracle, tremulously dear. That any one so young, so lovely, so ardent as Julia should depend so utterly upon her was to Anna Toland an unceasing delight. Julia had been bewildered and heartsick when she turned to The Alexander, but she had never in her life known such an aching loneliness as had been Miss Toland's fate for many years. To such a nature the solitary years in Paris, the solitary return to California, the tentative and unencouraged approaches to her nieces, all made a dark memory. Rich as she was, independent and popular as she was, Miss Toland's life had brought her nothing so sweet as this young thing, to teach, to dominate, to correct, and to watch and delight in, too. As Julia's grammar and manner and appearance rapidly improved, Miss Toland began to exploit her, in a quiet way, and quietly gloried in the girl's almost stern dignity. When the members of the board of directors were buzzing about, Julia, with her neatly written report, was a little study in alert and silent efficiency.

"She's a cute little thing," said Mrs. von Hoffmann, president of The Alexander Toland Neighbourhood House, after one of these meetings of the board, "but she never has much to say."

"No, she's a very silent girl," Miss Toland agreed, with that little warmth at her heart the thought of Julia always brought.

"You imported her, Sanna?"

"Oh, no. She's a Californian."

"Really? And what do we pay her?"

"Forty."

"Forty? And didn't we pay that awful last creature sixty-five?"

"Seventy-five—yes." Miss Toland smiled wisely. "But she had been specially trained, Tillie."

"Oh, specially trained!" Mrs. von Hoffmann, flinging a mass of rich sables about her throat, began to work on the fingers of her white gloves. "This girl's worth two of her," she asserted, "with her nice little silent ways and her little uniform!"

"I'll see that she's treated fairly," Miss Toland promised.

"Well, do! Don't lose her, whatever you do! I suppose she has beaus?"

"Not Julia! She's entirely above the other sex. No; there's a young Jew in Sacramento who writes her now and then, but that's a mere boy-and-girl memory."

"Well, let's hope it remains one!" And the great lady, sailing out to her waiting coupe, stopped on the outer steps to speak to Miss Page, who was tying up some rain-beaten chrysanthemums in the little front garden.

"How crushed they are! Do you like flowers, Miss Page?"

"Oh, yes," smiled Julia, looking like a flower herself in the clear twilight.

"You must come and see Mr. von Hoffmann's orchids some day," Mrs. von Hoffmann volunteered. Julia smiled again, but did not speak. The older woman glanced up and down the desolate street, and shuddered. "Dreadful neighbourhood!" she said with a rueful smile and a shake of the head, and climbing into her carriage, she was gone. Julia looked about her, but found the neighbourhood only interesting and friendly, as usual, and so returned to her flowers.

When her chrysanthemums were trim and secure once more, perhaps—if this were one of the club evenings—she put on her long coat, and the hat with the velvet rose, and went upon a little shopping expedition, a brown twine bag dangling from one of her ungloved arms. The bakery was always bright and odorous, and at this hour filled with customers. The perspiring Swedish proprietress and a blond-haired daughter or two would be handling the warm loaves, the flat, floury pies, and the brown cookies as fast as hands could move; the cash register behind the counter rang and rang, the air was hot, the windows obscured with steam. Men were among the customers, but the Weber girls had no time to flirt now. They rustled the thin large sheets of paper, snapped the flimsy pink string, lifted a designated pie out of the window, or weighed pound cake with serious swiftness.

From the bakery Julia crossed an indeterminate street upon which shabby scattered houses backed or faced with utter disregard of harmony, and entered a dark and disorderly grocery, which smelled of beer and brooms and soap and stale cakes. Tired women, wrapped in shawls, their money held tight in bony, bare hands, sat about on cracker boxes and cheese crates, awaiting their turn to be served. A lamp, with a reflector, gave the only light. The two clerks, red-faced young men in their shirt sleeves, leaned on the dark counter as they took orders, listening with impatient good nature to whispered appeals for more credit, grinding coffee in an immense wheel, and thumping each loaf of bread as they brought it up from under the counter.

Julia, out in the street again and enjoying, as she always did enjoy, the sense of being a busy householder, facing the tide of home-goers, would perhaps have an errand in the damp depth of the big milk depot, would get chops or sausages at some small shop, or stop a fruit cart, driving by in the dimness, for apples or oranges.

Then home to the brightly lighted little kitchen, the tireless little gas stove. Julia, cheerfully attempting to do ten things at once, would look up to see Miss Toland, comfortably wrappered and corsetless, in the doorway.

"Don't forget your window shades, Julie."

"I know, but I wanted to get this oven started—if these sweets are to bake."

"Give me something to do!" And the older woman, seated, was pleased to cut bread and fill salt shakers at the request of her busy assistant. "To-night's the older girls, is it?" she would yawn. "Is Miss Pierce coming? Good! Well, tell me if you need me, and I'll dress and come out."

"Oh, we're not doing much to-night," Julia invariably assured her. Miss Toland never questioned the verdict that freed her for an evening of restful reading. Julia it was who lighted the hall and opened the street door, and welcomed the arriving club girls. Sometimes these young women brought their sewing—invariably fancywork. Sometimes there was a concert to rehearse, or they danced with each other, or stood singing about Julia at the piano while she banged away at the crude accompaniments of songs. Miss Pierce or Miss Watts, older women, usually came in for a little while to see what was going on, but again it was Julia alone who must bid the girls good-night and lock and darken the hall.

Once a month there was a dance for the older girls, to which their "friends," a word which meant to each girl her foremost male admirer, were asked, and at which cake and ice-cream were served. Julia always wore her uniform to these dances, but she also danced, when asked, and never attempted to deny that she enjoyed herself. But that there was an immense gulf already widening between her and these other girls, one of whom she might have been, she soon began to perceive. They were noisy, ignorant, coarse young creatures, like children unable to see beyond the pleasure or the discomfort of the day, unable to help themselves out of the sordid rut in which they had been born. Julia watched them soberly, silently, as the years went by. One by one they told her of their wedding plans, and introduced the boyish, ill-shaven, grinning lads who were to be husbands and fathers soon. One by one Julia watched the pitifully gay little weddings, in rooms poisonous with foul air and crowded with noisy kinspeople. One by one she welcomed old members of the Girls' Club as new members of the Mothers' Club. The young mother's figure would be curiously shapeless now, her girlish beauty swept away as by a sponge, her nervous pride in the beribboned baby weakened by her own physical weakness and clouded by the fear that already a second child's claim was disputing that of the first. And already her young voice would borrow some of the hopeless whining tones of the older women's.

Julia was really happiest in her relationship with the children. She frequently peeped into the kindergarten during the morning, and had her dearly loved favourites among the tiny girls and boys, and she could never be absent from the sewing class every afternoon when some forty small girls scattered themselves about the assembly hall, and chattered and sang as they worked. Volunteers from among the city's best families were usually on hand to inspect the actual sewing—vague, daintily dressed girls who alternately spoiled and neglected their classes, who came late and left early—but Julia kept order, supplied materials, recited the closing prayer, and played the marches by which the children marched out at five o'clock. Now and then she incited some small girl to sing or recite for the others, and two or three times a year the sewing classes gave an evening entertainment—extraordinary affairs at the memory of which Julia and Miss Toland used to laugh for weeks. To drill the little, indifferent, stupid youngsters in songs and dances, to spangle fifty costumes of paper cambric and tissue, to shout emphatic directions about the excited murmurings of the churning performers, to chalk marks on the stage, and mark piano scores, were all duties that fell to the two resident workers. Julia sacrificed her immaculate bedroom for a green room, the perspiration would stream from her face as she whipped off one dirty little frock after another, fastened the fairy regalia over unspeakable undergarments, and loosened sticky braids of black or yellow hair into something approaching a fairylike fluffiness. One second to straighten her own tumbled hair at a mirror, another to warn her carefully ranged performers in the passage, and Julia was off to light the hall and open the street door to the clamorous audience. Opening the performance with a crash of chords from the piano, fifteen minutes later, she would turn her face to the stage, that the singers might see her lips framing the words they were so apt to forget, and manage to keep a watchful eye upon the noisy group of boys that filled the back benches and the gaslights that might catch a fairy's spear or a witch's wand.

"Well, we've had some *awful* performances in the place, but really I think to-night's was *about* the worst!" Miss Toland might remark, when the last dirty little garment had been claimed by its owner, and the last fairy had reluctantly gone away.

"Well, the mothers and fathers thought it was fine," Julia would submit, with a weary grin.

"When that awful Cunningham child, with her awful, flat, slapping feet, began to dance the Highland Fling, I truly thought I would strangle, trying not to laugh!" Miss Toland, gazing absently over her book, would add reflectively.

"And the Queen of the Elves in those *dirty* pink stockings! And poor Hazel, bursting into tears as usual!" Julia, collapsed in a chair, dishevelled and rosy, would give a long sigh of relaxation and relief.

"But we don't do the slightest good this way," Miss Toland sometimes said with asperity. "We merely amuse them; it goes no further. Now, next time, we will make it an absolute condition that every child has a bath before coming, and wears clean clothes!"

"But we made that a condition this time, and it didn't do any good."

"Very well. Next time"—flushed at the merest hint of opposition, Miss Toland would speak with annoyance—"next time every child who hasn't had a bath will go straight into that tub, I don't care if the performance doesn't begin until midnight!"

"Well," Julia would concede tolerantly. She very speedily learned not to dispute these vigorous resolutions. Miss Toland always forgot them before morning; she would not have considered them seriously in any case.

"We are the laughing-stock of the city," she would frequently say with bitterness, upon being informed that more thimbles were needed, or that the girls hated to sew on the ugly gray ginghams. But sometimes Julia found her giving out candy and five-cent pieces, without regard for the girls' merits and achievements, for the mere pleasure of hearing their thanks.

Or sometimes, when for any reason the attendance upon the sewing classes was poor, Miss Toland bought herself a new blank book, dated it fiercely, and proceeded to ransack the neighbourhood for children in a house-to-house canvass. Julia and she would take a car into Mission Street, eat their dinner at the Colonial dining-room, where all sorts of wholesome dairy dishes were consumed by hungry hundreds every night, and where a white-clad man turned batter cakes in the window.

"They do that everywhere in New York," said Miss Toland, thereby thrilling Julia. "What, d'you like New York?" asked the older woman.

"I've never seen it!" Julia breathed.

"Well, some day we'll go on—study methods there. Spring's the time," said Miss Toland, raising gold-rimmed eyeglasses to study the grimy and spotted menu. "Spring afternoons on the Avenue, or driving in the Park—it's quite wonderful! I see they have chicken pie specially starred, thirty-five cents; shall we try that?"

After the meal the canvassing began, Miss Toland doing all the talking, while Julia stared about the small, stuffy interiors, and smiled at the babies and old women. Miss Toland jotted down in her book all the details she gathered in each house, and only stopped in her quest when the hour and the darkened houses reminded her that the evening was flying.

This might keep up every free evening for two weeks; it would end as suddenly as it began, and Miss Toland enter upon a lazy and luxurious phase. She would spend whole mornings and even afternoons in bed, reading and dozing, and fresh from a hot bath at four o'clock, would summon her assistant and make a suggestion or two.

"Julia, suppose we go down to the Palace for tea?"

Julia, standing gravely in the doorway, considered.

"The girls won't be gone for another hour, Miss Toland!"

"The—Oh, the girls, to be sure. Of course. Who else is there, Julia?"

"Miss Parker and Miss Chetwynde. And Mrs. Forbes Foster was here for a little while."

Miss Toland, drawing on silk stockings, would make a grimace.

"What did you tell them?"

"Sick headache."

"Oh, yes, quite right! Well, get through out there, and we'll go somewhere."

The assistant, about to depart, would hesitate:

"I have nothing to wear but my tailor-made and a white waist, Miss Toland."

"And quite good enough! No one will notice us."

Perhaps truly no one noticed the eagerly talking, middle-aged woman and her pretty and serious little companion, as they sat in a quiet corner of the big grill-room, eating their dinner, but Julia noticed everything, and even while she answered Miss Toland politely, her eyes were moving constantly to and fro. She watched the cellarer, in his leather apron, the well-dressed, chattering men and women who came and went; she drank in the warm, perfumed air as if it were the elixir of life. The music enchanted her, the big room with its lofty ceiling, its clustered lights and flowers, swam in a glorious blur before her.

Miss Toland would bow now and then, and tell Julia about the people to whom she bowed. Once they saw Doctor Studdiford laughing and talking at a distant table with a group of young men, and once it was Barbara, lovely in a blue evening gown, who came across the room to speak to her aunt.

"And hello, Julia!" said Barbara pleasantly, on this occasion, resting her armful of blue brocade and eiderdown upon a chair back. "It's awfully nice to see you two enjoying yourselves!"

"What are you doing, dear?" her aunt asked.

"Mrs. Maitland's party—and we're going to the Orpheum. I don't care much for vaudeville, though" And idly eying Julia, she added, "Do you, Julia?"

Julia's heart leaped, her mouth felt dry.

"I like plays," she stammered, trying to smile, and clearing her throat.

"Well, so do I." Barbara shrugged, gathered up her coat again, and drifted away. Julia heard nothing else that night but the kindly, insolent little voice that seemed to make a friend and equal of her, and when she was alone in bed in the dark, she went over and over the little scene again, and thrilled again at Barbara's graciousness.

Perhaps six times a year Miss Toland went to Sausalito for a few days, and then, during her first year as a settlement worker, Julia went to her grandmother's house. Evelyn was now working with Ryan, the Tolands' fashionable dressmaker, and doing extremely well. Marguerite was engaged to be married, and as foolishly happy as if her eyes had been fixed upon ideal unions since the days of her childhood. Nobody paid very much attention to Julia except Marguerite's promised husband, who disgusted her by hoarsely assuring her that she was a little peach, and attempting to kiss her. There were several letters from her mother, from which Julia learned that her father was well again, but that he had left her mother, who had entered, with a friend, upon the boarding-house business in Los Angeles. She wrote her mother an affectionate letter, and, after a few months, stopped going to her grandmother's house.

Miss Pierce, a delicate, refined, unmarried woman, was a daily teacher in the kindergarten, and grew very fond of the grave, demure, silent Miss Page. Julia felt enormously flattered when Miss Pierce suggested that she come home with her during one of Miss Toland's brief absences, and as merry, impulsive, affectionate little Miss Scott followed suit, she usually had the choice of two pleasant places in which to spend her holidays.

Miss Pierce lived with her old mother in a handsome upper flat on Broadway. Julia liked the quiet, dignified neighbourhood, and thought Mrs. Pierce a lovely old lady. She chattered with Adachi, the Japanese boy, tried the piano, whistled at the canary, and sat watching Mrs. Pierce's game of patience with the absorption of a rosy-cheeked, wide-eyed child. Miss Pierce, glancing up now and then from her needlework, thought it very nice to see pretty Miss Page there and Mamma so well amused, and wished that she had more inducements to offer her young guest. But Julia found the atmosphere, the quiet voices and quiet laughter, inducement enough, and quite touched Mrs. Pierce with her gratitude.

The first visit to Miss Scott's house, however, was a revelation, and the memory of it stood out in such bold colours as made the decorous pleasures of the visit to Miss Pierce turn pale. Julia was rushed into the centre of a group of eager, noisy, clever young people, six brothers and sisters who had been motherless from babyhood, and were in mourning now for their father. The Scotts were bold and outspoken in their grief as in everything else; they showed Julia their father's picture before she had been ten minutes in the house, and Kennedy—Julia's "Miss Scott" of The Alexander—flung open the big desk so violently as to bring two vases and a calendar to the floor, and read Julia various notes and letters that had been sent them at the time of their father's death, until tears stood in more than one pair of lovely black eyes. Dinner was somehow cooked in a Babel of voices, served in a rush, and afterward their chatter rose above the hissing of dishwater and the clash of hot plates. Julia laughed herself tired at the nonsense, the mad plans, and untrammelled dreams. Kennedy was to be a writer, 'Lizbeth the president of a girls' college, little Mary wanted to live in "Venith." The boys were all to be rich; Peter, the oldest, drew his brothers into a long, serious discussion as to the exact proportions of the ideal private car.

"We'll have the finish mahogany, d'ye see?" said Peter, "and the walls and curtains of dark green velvet."

"Dark green velvet!" Kennedy said, from the couch where she was sitting, busy with a torn sleeve lining. "Oh, horrors! Why not red velvet and gold braid!"

"Well, what would *you* have?" Peter asked belligerently.

"Oh, grayish blue velvet," 'Lizbeth suggested rapturously.

"Very pale, you know, and silvery curtains," Kennedy agreed, "and one gorgeous bluish-grayish-pinkish rug, like the two-thousand-dollar one at the White House!"

"Well," Peter said, satisfied. "And what colour upholstery?"

"Dark blue might be beautiful," Julia submitted timidly.

"Dark blue—you're on, Miss Page!"

"Or a sort of blue brocade," 'Lizabeth said dreamily.

"And I'll tell you what we'll name the cars," George, the second brother, suddenly contributed; "you know they've got to be named, Pete. We'll call the dining-car, 'Dinah,' and the sleeper, 'Bertha'; do you see?"

The others shouted approval, Peter adding with a grin, a moment later:

"And we might call the observation car 'Luke'!"

"Oh, *Peter!*" Kennedy expostulated, laughing. She presently interrupted the completing details of the private train by general suggestions of bed. The four girls went upstairs together.

"Oh, Mary, you've fixed everything, you little angel, you!" said Kennedy, seeing that hats and wraps had been put away, and a couch made up in a large shabby bedroom. 'Lizabeth, professing that she loved a couch, settled herself upon it with great satisfaction, Julia had a single bed, and Kennedy and the little Mary shared a somewhat larger one.

Julia watched the sisters with deep admiration; they were all tired, she knew, yet vigorous ablutions went on in the cold little bathroom, and clothes were brushed and made ready for to-morrow's need. Their joyous talk was pitifully practical, Mary raising the dread topic of new shoes for Stephen, the youngest, and Kennedy somewhat ruefully conceding that the shoes must be had, even at the cost of the needed gallon of olive oil.

"No salads for a month, and they're so cheap!" she mourned. "And that young terror seems to me to need shoes every week! Don't ever have sons, Miss Page, they're a heart scald wid the bould ways av thim! Stephen had nine pairs of shoes in eight months—that's true, isn't it, 'Lizabeth? For we were keeping accounts then—while Dad's will was in probate, we had to."

"A good thing to have a will to fall back on," said Julia.

"Even if we only inherited one hundred and sixteen dollars apiece," 'Lizabeth added.

"Dad had had losses—it wasn't any one's fault—everything went to smash," Kennedy supplemented instantly. "And of course when we found that Steve had been braking his coaster with his feet, that helped. But me—I'm going to have only girls—five darling little gray-eyed girls with brown hair!"

"I'd like a boy to start off with," 'Lizabeth said. "He could take his sisters to parties—"

"Yes, but they never do; they take other girls to parties!" the fifteen-year-old Mary said suddenly, and the older girls laughed together at her sapience.

"Peter has a girl," Kennedy said. "But naturally he won't desert the bunch. Next year, when some bills we simply couldn't help—"

"Doctor and nurse when George and Mary had typhoid," 'Lizabeth explained.

"—are paid off," Kennedy continued. "Then, if he still likes her, he might. But he never stays in love very long," she ended hopefully.

The four girls talked late into the night, and after a picnic the next day, a Sunday, Julia felt as if she loved them all, and she and Kennedy began shyly to call each other by their given names. Peter and George did not go on the picnic, having plans of their own for the day, but the others spent a dreamy day on Baker's Beach, and the two older boys, joining the group at dinner, ended the holiday happily. Julia carried away definite impressions to be brooded over in her quiet times. The Scotts were "ladies," of course. Somehow, although they were very poor, they all worked very hard, and all dressed very shabbily, they were "ladies," and knew only nice people. The sisters were really stronger and braver than the brothers, and loved their brothers more than they were loved. Julia wondered why. Also she came a little reluctantly to the conclusion, as girls at twenty, whether they be Julias or Barbaras, usually do, that if there were a great many nice young men in the world, there were a great many marriageable girls, too. No girl could expect a very wide choice of adorers, there were too many other girls. And affairs of the heart, and offers of marriage, occurred much more often in books than in life.

Two or three times a week Miss Toland liked to rise early and go to the beautiful eight o'clock mass at St. Anne's, the big institution for unfortunate girls that was not far from The Alexander Toland Neighbourhood House. There was no church in the immediate vicinity, and in asking for permission to come to the convent chapel, Miss Toland had felt herself doing no extraordinary thing, had felt almost within her rights.

But the good nuns in charge of St. Anne's had whetted her appetite for the experience by interposing unexpected objections. Their charges, they explained, about two hundred in number, were very impressionable, very easily excited. A stranger in the chapel meant a sensation. Of course, the lay workers of the institution and the old people from the Home across the way sometimes came in, but they were so soberly dressed. Perhaps if Miss Toland and Miss Page would dress in dark things, and assure Good Mother that they would not speak to the girls—

"Oh, certainly!" Miss Toland had agreed eagerly. Julia, awed by the airy, sombre interior of the great building, the closed doors, the far-away echoes of footsteps and subdued voices, was a little pale.

"And this is your little assistant?" said Good Mother, suddenly, turning a smile of angelic brightness upon Julia. "Well, come to mass by all means, both of you. And pray for our poor children, dear child; we are always in need of prayers."

"You must have extraordinary experiences here," Miss Toland said.

"And extraordinary compensations," said the nun. "Of course, some of our poor children are very wild—at first. We do what we can. I had a little pet of mine here until yesterday, Alice, ten years old; she is—"

"*Ten*!" ejaculated Miss Toland.

"Oh, yes, my dear! And younger; she was but eight when she came. What I was going to say was that her mother took her away yesterday, and Sister Philip Neri was amused to see how sad I was to have her go. She reminded me that when Alice first came here she had bitten my hand to the bone, so that I could not use it for three weeks. Ah, well!" And Good Mother gave the sweet toneless laugh of the religious. "That is not the worst of it—a clean bite on the hand!"

Miss Toland bought an alarm clock on the way home, and she and Julia went to early mass on the very next morning. Julia found this first experience an ordeal; she and Miss Toland were in a side pew before the big gong struck, and Julia did not raise her eyes from her book as the girls filed in. The steady rustle of frocks and shuffle of feet made her feel cold and sick.

A day or two later she could watch them, although never without profound emotion. Two hundred girls, ranging in years from ten to twenty, with roughly clipped hair, and the hideous gray-green checked aprons of the institution. Two hundred faces, sullen or vacuous, pretty, silly faces, hard faces, faces tragically hopeless and pale. These young things were offenders against the law, shut away here behind iron bars for the good of the commonwealth. Julia, whose life had made her wise beyond her years, watched them and pondered. Here was an almost babyish face; what did that innocent-looking twelve-year-old think of life, now that she had thrown her own away? Here was a sickly looking girl a few years older, coughing incessantly and ashen cheeked; why had some woman borne her in deathly anguish, loved her and watched her through the years that least need loving and watching? This thing that they had all done—this treasure they had all thrown away—what did they think about it?

She would come out very soberly into the convent garden, and walk home, through the delicious airs of a spring morning, without speaking, perhaps to break out, over her belated coffee:

"Oh, I think it's horrible—their being shut up there, the poor little things!"

"They have sensible work, plenty to eat, and they're safe," Miss Toland might answer severely. "And that's a great deal more than they deserve!"

"Nobody worried about them until it was too late," Julia suggested once, in great distress. "Lots of them never would have done anything wrong if they'd had work and food *then*!"

"Well, the nuns are very kind to them," Miss Toland answered comfortably; and Julia knew this was true, as far as possible.

One morning, when Julia slipped into her place in St. Anne's, she saw, two feet away from her, on an undraped trestle, a narrow coffin, and in the coffin the rigid form of a girl who had been prayed for a few mornings earlier as very ill. There was not a flower on the still, flat young breast, and no kindly artifice beautified the stern face or the bare, raw little hands that protruded from the blue-green gingham sleeves. The ruined little tenement that had served some man's pleasure and been flung aside lay there as little beholden to the world in death as it had been in life. And as if the usual silence of the chapel would be too hard to bear, the living girls chanted to-day the "Dies Irae" and the "Libera me."

When winter came, the little trestle was often in requisition, for the inmates of St. Anne's were ill-fitted to cope with any sickness. Once it was a nun, in her black robes, who lay there, her magnificent still face wearing its usual deep, wise smile, her tired hands locked about her crucifix. For her there were flowers, masses of flowers, and more than one black-robed priest, and a special choir, and Julia knew that the other nuns envied that one of their number who had gone on to other work in other fields.

She grew grave, who was always grave, thinking of these things, and talked them over with Kennedy Scott. Kennedy was deeply, even passionately, concerned for a while, and she and Julia decided to establish a home some day for girls who were still to be saved.

Time went very swiftly now: years were not as long as they used to be, one birthday was in sight of another. Sometimes Julia was astonished and a little saddened, as is the way of youth, at the realization of the flying months. She was busy, contented, beloved; she was accomplishing her ambition—but at what a cost of years! The great moment might come now at any time—Prince Charming might be on his way to her now, but meantime she must work and eat and sleep—and the birthdays came apace. Sometimes she grew very restless; this was not life! But a visit to her grandmother's house usually sent her back to The Alexander with fresh courage. No possible alternative offered itself anywhere.

Just at first she had hoped for inspiring frequent glimpses of her adored Tolands, but these were very few. Sometimes Barbara or the younger girls would come to Easter or Christmas entertainments at the settlement, but Julia, always especially busy on these occasions, saw no more than Barbara's pretty, bored face, framed in furs, across a room full of people, or returned a dignified good-bye to Sally's hasty, "Mother and the others have gone on, Miss Page; they asked me to say good-bye!" But then there was the prospect of a day with Kennedy Scott, to console her, or perhaps the reflection that little Mr. Craig, who came out on Tuesday evenings to the meetings of the Boys' Club, was in love with her. She did not wish to marry Mr. Craig, still it was nice of him to admire her; it was nice to have a new hat; it was pleasant to visit the San Jose convent, with Miss Toland, and be petted by the nuns. So Julia cheated herself, as youth forever cheats itself, with the lesser joys.

She went home for three or four days at the time of her father's death, and afterward deliberately decided not to accompany her mother on a trip south. Emeline had nine thousand dollars of life insurance, and thought of buying a half interest in a boarding-house in Los Angeles.

"All the theatrical trade goes there," said Emeline, "and you could get a berth as easy as not!"

"Yes, I know," Julia said, gently, concealing an inward shudder. She went quietly back to The Alexander, when the funeral was over, to her mother's disgust. Emeline did not go south, but lingered on at home, drinking tea and gossiping with her mother, quarrelling with her old father, and gradually eating into her bank account. She called upon her daughter, to Julia's secret embarrassment, though the girl introduced this overdressed, sallow, hard-eyed mother with what dignity she could muster to Miss Pierce, Miss Scott, and Miss Toland. Emeline laughed and talked with an air of ease, was forced into silence when Julia said the closing prayer, and burst out laughing at its close.

"That does sound so funny, dolling! But I mustn't laugh," said Emeline. "I'm sure you do wonders for these girls, and they need it," she added graciously to Miss Toland. She followed Julia into the little kitchen.

"Don't she help you cook?" she asked in a low tone, indicating Miss Toland with a jerk of her much-puffed head.

"Sometimes she does," Julia answered, annoyed.

"H'm!" Emeline said. And she asked curiously a moment later, "Why you do it is what gets me! Here's Marguerite going to get married, and Ev has an elegant job, and I want you to go south with me; you'd have a *grand* time!"

She stopped on a complaining note, her eyes honestly puzzled. Julia closed the oven door upon some potatoes, and stood up.

"I'm perfectly satisfied, Mama," said she briefly. "I'm doing what I want to do."

"Lord!" Emeline ejaculated, discontentedly, vaguely baffled by the girl's definiteness and dignity. She left soon after, Julia dutifully walking with her to her car. Miss Toland said nothing of the visitor when Julia came back, but she knew the girl was troubled, and lay awake a long time herself that night, conscious that Julia, in the next room, was restless and wakeful.

Besides a certain troubled consciousness of her failure to please her own people, Julia had in these years a more definite source of worry. Mark Rosenthal was still her patient adorer, and if, like Julia, he allowed the flying months to steal a march upon him, and drifted along in the comfortable conviction that "a little while" would bring a change in Julia's feeling, still he was none the less a watchful and ardent lover, with whom she sometimes found it very difficult to deal.

Mark, always tall, was broad as well now, an imposing big fellow, prosperous, shrewd, and self-confident. He had handsome dark eyes, and showed white teeth when he laughed; he dressed well, but not conspicuously; his shoes might be well worn, but they were always bright; and if his suit were shabby, still he was never without gloves. He liked to talk business; he had long ago given up his music and devoted himself with marvellous success to his work. He was no longer with the piano house, but had an excellent position as adjuster of damages, out of court, for one of the street railway companies. The history of his various promotions and his favour with his employers was absorbing to him; but the time came, when Julia was about twenty-two, when his determination to win her became a serious menace to her peace.

His manner, which had once been boyish and uncertain, was in these days good-humouredly proprietary. He laughed at little Julia's earnest explanations, and would answer her most eager appeal only with a lover's fond comment upon her eyes.

"Yes, darling, I wasn't listening—forgive me!" he said one day, when, with a spark of real anger, Julia had begged him to make his calls at the settlement house a little less frequent and less conspicuous. "What was it?" And with twinkling eyes he caught up the hand that lay near him on the table and kissed it.

"I want you not to do that, Mark," said Julia gravely, moving a little farther away, "and please don't call me darling!"

"All right, darling!" smiled Mark.

"I'm not joking," Julia said resentfully, two red spots in her cheeks.

Mark moved to lay his hand over hers penitently, and said, in the low, gentle voice Julia dreaded:

"Do you know what's the matter with you, Julie? I'll tell you. You love me and you won't admit it. Girls never will. But that's what makes you so unhappy—you won't let yourself go. Ah, Julia! be fair to yourself, darling! Tell me that you care for me. I've waited seven years for you, dear—"

"Oh, you have not!" Julia said impatiently.

"I'd like to know why I haven't!" Mark said challengingly. "Ah, but you know I have, darling. And I want my wife." It was a Saturday afternoon, and Miss Toland was dozing in her own room. Julia and Mark were alone in the deserted assembly hall. Suddenly he slipped on his knees beside her, and locked one arm about her waist. "You will, won't you, Julia?" he stammered.

Julia, scarlet cheeked, tried to rise, and held him off with her hands.

"Oh, please, *please*," she begged. "I can't, Mark. You are awfully good to me—I'm not worth it, and all that—but I *can't*. I—it's not my fault I don't want to, is it? It would be wrong to do it, feeling this way—"

She was on her feet now, and Mark stood up, too. Both were breathing hard; they looked at each other through a widening silence. Flies buzzed against the closed windows, a gust of summer wind swept along the street outside. Suddenly Mark caught Julia fiercely in his arms, and felt her heart beating madly against him, and forcing up her chin with a gentle big hand, kissed her again and again upon her unresponsive lips.

"There!" he said, freeing her, a laugh of triumph in his voice. "Now you belong to me! That's the kind of a man that's in love with you, my girl, and don't you think for one instant that you can play fast and loose with him!"

Julia sat still for a long time after the street door banged, staring straight ahead of her. She was going for this week-end to the little house the Scotts had been loaned in Belvedere for the season, and she dressed and packed her suitcase very soberly. Miss Toland went with her to the ferry, both glad to get the fresh breath of the water, and Julia had a riotous dinner with the Scotts, and a wonderful evening drifting about in their punt between the stars in the low summer sky and the stars in the bay. When they were in their porch beds she told Kennedy all about Mark, and Kennedy commented that he certainly was a gratifyingly ardent admirer.

"Ardent? I should think so!" sighed Julia, and went to sleep, not ill-pleased with her role of the inaccessible lady. But the fact that Mark's persistence could not be discouraged fretted her a good deal. He rarely gave her a chance for a definite snub; if she was ungracious, his humble patience waited tirelessly upon her mood; and if she smiled, he showed such wistful delight that even Julia's cool little heart was stirred. That he never stirred her in any deeper way, that his kisses did not warm her, was not a serious trouble to Mark. She would be all the sweeter to win; he would wake her in his arms to the knowledge that she loved him! And Julia won, as his little wife, would be dearer even than the demure and inaccessible Julia of to-day. Mark fed his hungry heart on love tales; many a man had won a harder fight than his; these cold, shy girls made the best wives in the world!

Julia began seriously to consider the marriage. She visioned a safe and pleasant life, if no very thrilling one. Mark was handsome, devoted, he was making money, he would be faithful to his wife and adore his children. Julia would have no social position, of course. She sighed. She would be a comfortable little complacent wife among a thousand others. She would have her silk gowns, her cut glass; she could afford an outing at Pacific Grove with the children; some day she and Mark would go to New York—

No, not she and Mark! She couldn't; she didn't love him enough to sit opposite him all the mornings of her life, to sell her glowing dreams for him! She had come so far from the days that united her childhood with all the Rosenthals—she had not seen Mrs. Tarbury, nor Rose, nor Connie for years. She was climbing, climbing, away from all those old associations. And she could climb faster alone!

CHAPTER VII

One warm morning in August, when Miss Toland was stretched out on the reception-room couch, and Julia, who had washed her hair, was shaking it, a flying, fluffy mop, over the sill of the bathroom window, a sudden hubbub broke out in the kindergarten. Miss Toland flung down her book and Julia gathered her loose wrapper about her, and both ran to the door of the assembly hall. The children, crying and frightened, were gathered in a group, and in the centre of it Julia, from the elevation of the stage, could see Miss Pierce half-kneeling and leaning over as if she tried to raise something from the floor. While they watched she arose, holding the limp body of a five-year-old child in her arms.

"What is it—what is it?" screamed Miss Toland, but as every one else was screaming and crying, and Julia's automatic, "Is she dead?" was answered over and over again only by Miss Pierce's breathless, "No—no—no—I don't think so!" it was some time before any clear idea of the tragedy could be had. The small girl was carried in to Julia's bed, where she lay half-conscious, moaning; great bubbles of blood formed from an ugly skin wound in her lip, and her little frock was stained with blood. As an attempt to remove her clothes only roused her to piercing screams, Julia and Miss Pierce gave up the attempt, and fell to bathing the child's forehead, which, with the baby curls pushed away from it, gave a ghastly look to the little face.

"Well, you've killed her, Miss Pierce!" said Miss Toland, beside herself with nervousness. "That's a dying child, if I ever saw one. That ruins *this* Settlement House! That ends it! Poor little thing!"

"I was at the board," said Miss Pierce, white-lipped, and in a low tone.

"I don't care where you were," said Miss Toland. "There, there, darling! I pay you to watch these children! It's a fine thing if a child is going to be killed right here in the house! Where was Miss Watts?" she broke off to ask.

"Miss Watts is at home, sick," Miss Pierce said eagerly. "And I was at the board, when some of those bigger boys set a bench up on top of another bench. I heard the noise and turned around; this child—poor little Maude Daley, it is—was standing right there, and got the full weight of both benches as they fell."

"This boy is back," said Julia, coming from the front door, "and he says that Doctor White is out and Doctor McGuire is out, too!"

"Great heavens!" Miss Toland began despairingly. "No doctor! of course, eleven o'clock they're all out on morning rounds! And the child's mother, where is she? Am I the only person here who can do something except sit around and say 'I'm sorry, I'm sorry!'"

"She has no mother, and her grandmother's out," Julia said soothingly. "Miss Toland, if I telephone do you think I can catch Doctor Studdiford at the City and County?"

"A two hours' trip from Sausalito!" Miss Toland said scornfully. "You must be crazy, that's all! No! Go into Mission Street—"

"I don't mean in Sausalito," Julia said firmly; "he's at the City and County on Wednesday mornings, you know. I could get him there."

Miss Toland stared at her unblinkingly for a second.

"Yes, do that!" she said then. "Yes, that's a good idea!" And as Julia ran to the telephone she called after her, "Yes, that's a very good idea!"

Julia's heart thumped as she called the big institution, thumped when after a long wait a crisp voice, out of utter silence, said:

"Yes? This is Doctor Studdiford!"

She explained as concisely as she could, feeling that he listened attentively.

"Keep the child flat, no pillow," he said, as Julia concluded. "Tell my aunt I'll be there in fifteen minutes."

Julia, thrilled by she knew not what, knotted her flying hair loosely on her neck and buttoned on a fresh uniform. Ten minutes later she admitted Doctor Studdiford to the sickroom.

He had laid aside his hat and washed his hands. Now he sat down by the bed and smiled at the dazed, moaning little Maude. Julia felt something expand in her heart as she watched him, his intense, intelligent face, his singularly winning smile, the loose lock of dark hair on his forehead.

"Now, then, Maude," said he, his clever, supple fingers on her wrist, "where does it hurt?"

Maude whimpered something made unintelligible by the fast-stiffening cut in her lip.

"Her back's broken, Jim, no doubt about it," said Miss Toland grimly.

"I think her side hurts," Miss Pierce submitted eagerly.

"Well, we'll see—we'll see!" Doctor Studdiford said soothingly. "Now, if you'll help me, Miss Page, we'll get off these clothes—ah!" For an anguished moan from the sufferer coincided with his discovery that the little left arm hung limp. Julia loosened the sleeve as the surgeon's scissors clipped it away, and she held the child while the arm was set and bandaged. Miss Pierce was faint, and Miss Toland admitted freely that she hated to see a child suffer, and went away. "Only a clean dislocation, Aunt Sanna!" said Jim, cheerfully, when he came out of the sickroom. "She'll have to lie still for a while, but that's all. The cut on her mouth doesn't amount to anything. She's all right, now—Miss Page is telling her stories. She ought to have a glass of milk, or soup, or something; then she'll go to sleep. I'll be in to-morrow. By the way, you have a little treasure there in Miss Page!"

"Julia? Glad you have the sense to see it, Jim!"

"She—is—a—peach!" the doctor mused, packing his very smart little instrument case. "Who is she?"

"A little girl I found. Yes, she's a nice child, Julia. She's been here six years now."

"Six years! Great Scott! How old is she?"

"Twenty-two—twenty-three—something like that."

"It doesn't sound much of a life for a young girl, Aunt Sanna. Imagine the Barbary-flower!" Doctor Studdiford shook his thermometer, looked at it, and screwed it into its case.

"How *is* Barbara?" Miss Toland asked dryly.

"Fine! Mother came to me with a long tale, the other day, about her being run down, or blue, or something, but I don't see it. She has a dandy time."

"Why doesn't she marry? Barbara must be twenty-six," her aunt said, with directness.

"Oh, I don't know; why don't all the girls? The fellows they run with are an awfully bum lot," Jim said contentedly. "Look at me! Why don't I?" he added, laughing.

"Well, why don't you?"

"I'm waiting to settle the others off, I guess. Besides, you know, I've been working like the devil! Sally's been worrying Mother with her affairs lately," said Jim.

"*Sally*—and who?"

"Keith Borroughs!" Jim announced, grinning.

"Keith Borroughs? Why, he's ten years younger!"

"He's about three years younger, and he's an awful fool," said Jim, "but he's very much in love with Sally, and she certainly seems to like it!"

"I think that's disgusting!" said Miss Toland. "Has he a *job*?"

"Job? He's a genius, my dear aunt. His father pays for his music lessons, and his mother gives him an allowance. He's a pianist."

"H'm!" commented the lady briefly.

"Ned has definitely announced his intention of marrying his Goldfield girl," pursued Jim.

"Yes, I knew that. Kill your mother!"

"It'll just about kill her. And the latest is Ted—falling in love with Bob Carleton!"

"Carleton! Not the lumber man? But he's fifty!"

"He's forty-five, forty-seven perhaps."

"But he's married, Jim!"

"Divorced, Aunt Sanna."

"Oh, Jim, that's awful!" said his aunt, horrified.

"Well, it may come to nothing. Ted's only twenty—I hope devoutly it will. There—that's all the news!" Jim jumped up from his chair, and gave his aunt a kiss. "Why don't you come over and get it for yourself, now and then! I don't know how much there is in any of this stuff, because I use my rooms at the club a good deal, but it's all in the wind. That little Julia Page is a peach, isn't she?"

"You said that once," Miss Toland said dispassionately. Jim grinned, unabashed. He had been in love with one girl or another since his fourteenth year, and liked nothing so much as having his affairs of the heart discussed.

"Well, it's true, and I'll say it again for luck!" said he. "Who is she? I suppose Pius Aloysius Maloney, or some good soul who comes to teach the kids boxing, has got it all framed up with her?"

"I don't know any Mr. Maloney," Miss Toland answered imperturbably. "Mr. Craig is director of the Boys' Club, and I know he admires her, and she has another admirer, too, who comes here now and then. But how likely she is to marry I really can't say! She's an extremely ambitious girl, and she has determined to raise herself."

"Raise herself!" Jim said, with a casual laugh. "I don't suppose she started much lower than other people?"

"Oh, I imagine she did. Her father was a—I don't know—a sort of drummer, I guess, but her mother is an awful person, and her grandfather was a day labourer!"

"Ha!" Jim said, discomfited. "Well, see you tomorrow!" he added, departing. He walked briskly to the corner of the street, and experienced a thump at the heart when a casual backward glance discovered Julia, in a most fetching hat, coming out of the settlement house with a market basket on her arm. She did not see him, and Jim decided not to see her. Of course she *was* a little peach, but that labourer grandfather was too much.

That same evening Julia used the accident to little Maude as an excuse to break a half engagement with Mark. He was to be given only a few moments' chat before the Girls' Club met for a rehearsal, but he showed such bitter disappointment at losing it that Julia, half against her will, promised to spend at least part of her Sunday afternoon with him.

This was on Wednesday, and on Thursday and Saturday Doctor Studdiford came to see his little patient, and both times saw Julia, too. He asked Julia what books she liked, and, surprised that she knew nothing of Browning, he sent her a great volume of his poetry, a leather-bound exquisite edition that Jim had taken some trouble to find. With the book came a box of violets, and Julia, opening the package, suddenly remembered that he was a rich man, and stood, flushed and palpitating to a thousand emotions, looking down at the damp, fragrant flowers.

She wore a few violets at the breast of her sober little gown when she met Mark on Sunday for the promised walk. Julia had been most reluctant to go, but Maude had been moved to her own home, and the child's father was sitting with her, so that Julia had no excuse to visit her.

"I want to show you something—something you'll like!" said Mark eagerly. "We take the Sixteenth Street car and transfer down Sacramento."

Julia accepted his guidance good-naturedly, and they crossed the city, which lay in a clear wash of the warm September sunlight. Mark led Julia finally to the ornate door of a new apartment house in Sacramento Street.

"What is it, Mark?" the girl asked, as they went in. "Some one we know live here?"

"You wait!" Mark said mysteriously. He went to a desk in the handsome entrance hall, and talked for a few moments to a clerk who sat there. Then a quiet-looking, middle-aged woman came out, and Mark and Julia went upstairs with her, in a little elevator.

The woman turned a key in a door, and led them into a charmingly bright front apartment of four good-sized rooms and a shining bathroom. There was a bedroom with curly-maple furniture, a dining-room with a hanging lamp of art glass on a brass chain, and Mission oak table and chairs, a kitchen delightfully convenient and completely equipped, and a little drawing-room, with a gas log, a bookshelf, a good rug, a little desk, and some rocking chairs and small tables. The sun shone in through fresh net curtains, and the high windows commanded a bright view of city roofs and a glimpse of the bay.

Julia began to feel nervous and uncomfortable. She did not understand at all what Mark meant by this, but it was impossible to doubt, from his beaming face, that some plan involving her was afoot. He couldn't have furnished this apartment in the hope—?

"Whose place *is* this, Mark?" she asked, trying to laugh naturally.

"Do you like it?" Mark countered, his eyes dancing.

"Like it? It's simply sweet, of course! But whose is it?"

"Well, now listen," Mark explained. "It's Joe Kirk's furniture; he's just been married, you know. He and his wife had just got back from their honeymoon when Joe got an offer of a fine job in New York. He asked me to see if I couldn't find a tenant for this—two years' lease to run—just as it stands; no raise in rent. And the rent's fifty-five?" he called to the woman in the next room.

"Fifty, Mr. Rosenthal," she answered impassively.

"Fifty!" Mark exulted. "Think of getting all this for fifty! Ah, Julia"—he came close to her as she stood staring down from the window, and lowered his voice—"will you, darling? Will you? You like it, don't you? Will you marry me, dearest, and make a little home here with me?" "Oh, Mark!" Julia stammered, a nervous smile twitching her lips.

"Well, why won't you, Ju? Do you doubt that I love you? Answer me that!"

"Why, no—no, I don't, of course." Julia moved a little away.

"Don't go over there; she'll hear us! And you love me, don't you, Ju?"

"But not that way I don't, Mark," Julia said childishly.

"Oh, 'not that way'—that's all rubbish—that's the way girls talk; that's just an expression they have! Listen! Do you doubt that I'll always, *always* love you?"

"Oh, no, Mark, of course not!" Julia admitted. "But I don't want to marry any one—"

"Well, what do you want? Haven't I loved you since you were a little girl?"

"Yes, I know—of course you have! Only"—Julia gave him a desperate smile—"only I can't discuss such things here," she pleaded, "with that woman so near!"

"You're right!" Mark said, with military promptness, and as one who loves to receive his lady's orders. "We'll go out. Only—I wanted you to see it!"

And as they went out he must stop to show her the admirably deep drawers of the little sideboard and the ingenious arrangement by which the gas was electrically lighted.

They thanked the woman, and began the long ride back to the settlement house, for Julia never left Miss Toland long alone. In the Sacramento Street car they both had to stand, but Mark found seats without difficulty on the dummy of the Fillmore Street car, and laying his arm along the back of Julia's seat, swung about so that his face was very close to hers. A world of wistful tenderness filled his voice as he said again:

"Well, darling, what do you think of it?"

Poor Mark! Perhaps if he had asked her only a week earlier, his lady might have given him a kinder answer. But Julia was walking in a golden dream to-day, a dream peopled only by herself and one other, and she hardly noticed his emotion. She fixed her blue eyes vaguely on the black eyes so near, and smiled a little.

"Oh, answer me, Julia!" Mark said impatiently. And a second later he asked alertly: "Where'd you get the violets?"

"Oh—somebody," Julia temporized. Pink flooded her cheeks.

"Who?" said Mark, very calm.

"Oh, Mark, what a tone! Nobody you know!" Julia laughed.

"Is he in love with you?" Mark asked fiercely.

"Oh, don't be so silly! No, of course he's not."

"Tell me who he is!" Mark commanded grimly.

"Now, look here, Mark," Julia said sternly, "you stop that nonsense, or you can get straight off this car, and I'll go home alone! And don't you sulk, either, for it's too ridiculous, and I won't have it!"

Mark succumbed instantly.

"It's because I love you so," he said humbly. There was a little silence, then Julia, watching the Sunday streets, said suddenly:

"Look, Mark, look at the *size* of that hat!"

Mark, disdaining to turn his eyes for the fraction of a moment from her face, said reproachfully:

"Are you going to answer me, Julia?"

"How do you mean?" Julia said nervously.

"You know what I mean," Mark answered, with an impatient nod.

"No, I don't," Julia said, with a little laugh.

"Now, you look-a-here, Julia—you look-a-here," Mark began, almost angrily. "I am going to ask you to marry me! You've fooled about it, and you've laughed about it, and I've got a right to *know*! I think about it all the time; I lie awake at night and think about it. I"—his voice softened suddenly—"I love you awfully, Julia," he said. And then, with a sort of concentrated passion that rather frightened the girl, he added, "So I'm going to ask you once more. I want you to answer me, d'ye see?"

The car sped on, clanged across Market Street, turned into the Mission. Julia had grown a little pale. She gave Mark a fleeting glance, looked away, and finally brought her eyes back to him again.

"I wish you wouldn't take things so *seriously*, Mark," she began uneasily. "You're always forcing me to say things—and I don't want to—I don't want to get married *at all*—"

"Nonsense!" said Mark harshly.

"It's not nonsense!" Julia protested, glad to feel her anger rising. Mark saw her heightened colour, and misread it.

"Yes," he said sneeringly. "That's all very well, but I'll bet you'd feel pretty badly if I never came near you again—if I let the whole thing drop!"

"Oh, Mark," said Julia fervently, "if you only *would*—I don't mean that!" she interrupted herself, compunction seizing her at the look of mortal hurt on his face. "But I mean—if you only didn't love me! You see, I'm perfectly happy, Mark, I've got what I want. And if Miss Toland takes me abroad with her next year, why, it'll mean more to me than *any* marriage could, don't you see that? You know what my childhood was, Mark; my mother didn't love my father—" And as a sudden memory of the old life rose to confront her, Julia's tone became firm; she felt a certain sureness. "Married people ought to love each other, Mark," she said positively. "I *know* that. And I won't—I *never* will marry a man I don't love. If everything goes wrong, after that, you have only yourself to blame. And so many times it goes wrong, Mark! I should be unhappy, I should keep wondering if I wouldn't be happier going my own way—wondering if I wouldn't have—have gotten farther—do you understand me?"

This was a long speech for Julia, and during it Mark had twisted about, and pulled his hat over his face. Now, in a voice curiously dead and hard, he asked briefly:

"Gotten farther—*where?*"

"I don't know," said Julia candidly. "But the more I read, and the more I think, the more it seems to me that anyone can be anything in this world; there's some queer rule that makes you rise if you want to rise, if only you don't compromise! The reason so many people *don't* ultimately get what they want is because they stop trying for it, and take something else!"

"And marriage with me would be a compromise, is that it?" Mark muttered sullenly.

"It would be for me," Julia answered serenely. "Because staying where I am keeps me nearer what I want."

"Money, huh?" asked Mark.

"Oh, money, *no*! Books and talk—things. And—and if I loved you, Mark, then don't you see it *would* be the right thing to marry you?" she added brightly. "But now, it would only be because it was easier, or because I was tired of The Alexander, do you see?"

"I suppose so," Mark answered drearily.

A long silence ensued. In silence they got off the car, and walked through the cheerless twilight of the dirty streets, and they were almost in sight of the settlement house before Mark burst out, a little huskily:

"Then there's no chance for me at all, Julie?"

"Oh, Mark, I feel rotten about it!" said Julia frankly, her eyes full of pity and regret, and yet a curious relief evident in her voice. "I *am* so sorry! I've just been thinking of girls who like this sort of thing—I don't see how they *can*! I *am* so sorry! But you won't mind very long, Mark; you won't always care; you'll—why, there's Doctor Studdiford's automobile!"

For they were in sight of The Alexander now, and could see the electric runabout at the door. Motor cars were still new to San Francisco and to the world, and a crowd of curious children surrounded the machine.

"What's he there for?" Mark asked gruffly.

Julia explained: the accident—the emergency call.

"Well, but the kid is not there now, you say?"

"Yes, I know. But he didn't know that. I suppose he's calling on his aunt."

To this Mark made no immediate answer. Presently he said:

"City and County! I'll bet the city pays for his automobile!"

"Oh, no!" Julia protested. "He's a rich man in his own right, Mark."

They were at the house now, and went up the steps together. Doctor Studdiford was in the little reception hall with Miss Toland. He looked very handsome, very cheerful, as he came forward with his fine eyes on Julia. And Julia stood looking up at him with an expression Mark never had won from her, her serious, beautiful little face flooded with light, her round eyes soft and luminous. A woman at last, she seemed as she stood there, a grave and wise and beautiful woman, ripe for her share of loving and living, ready to find her mate.

"You got the book?" Jim said, with a little laugh. He laughed because his heart was shaking curiously, and because the sudden sight of Julia disconcerted him so that he hardly knew what he said.

Julia did not answer; she only touched the wilting and fragrant violets on her breast with her free hand. Jim still held one hand.

"You—you'll like Browning," added Jim. And inconsequentially he added, "I was thinking of our little talk yesterday—all night."

"So was I," Julia breathed. They turned suddenly and self-consciously to Miss Toland and Mark. Julia introduced the men; her breath was coming unevenly and her colour was exquisite; she talked nervously, and did not meet Mark's eye. Mark was offered a lift in Doctor Studdiford's motor car, and declined it. The doctor seemed to be in no hurry to go; wandered into her room to advise his aunt upon the placing of a telephone extension. Julia and Mark loitered about the assembly hall for a few empty moments, and then Mark said he must go, and Julia, absently consenting, went with him toward the stage door.

"And he's rich, is he?" said Mark.

Julia came out of a brief dream.

"He's very rich—yes!" she smiled.

She mounted to the stage as she spoke, and Mark held out his hand and turned about as if to say goodbye. The next instant Julia felt as if the dull twilight room had turned to brass and was falling with a wild clamour; she felt as if her heart were being dragged bodily to her lips, and she heard her own wild scream.

Silence fell, and Mark was still staring at her, still smiling. But now he toppled slowly toward her and stumbled, and as his body, with a hideous, slithering sound, slipped down to the floor, his arm fell lax, and the still smoking revolver slid to Julia's very feet.

"*Stop*, Julia—what is it?—what is it?" Miss Toland was crying. She locked her arms tight about the girl, and drew her back into the reception hall. Julia was silent, suddenly realizing that she had been screaming. She moved her tongue over her dry lips, and struggled to explain.

"Now we understand perfectly!" Doctor Studdiford said soothingly. "He shot himself, poor fellow. I'm going to take care of him, do you see? Just keep *still*, Aunt Sanna, or we'll have a crowd here. Aunt Sanna, do you want this to get into the papers?" For Miss Toland's surmises were delivered at a sort of shriek.

"Oo—oo—oo!" shuddered Julia, fearful eyes on the assembly room door. "He was—we were just talking—"

"Is he dead, Jim?" asked Miss Toland fearfully.

"I think so. I'm going to call the hospital for an ambulance, anyway." Doctor Studdiford was all brisk authority.

"But what ever possessed him?" shrilled Miss Toland again. "Of all *things*!"

"Had you quarrelled?" asked Jim, keen eyes on Julia as he rattled the telephone hook.

"No," Julia said shortly, like a child who holds something back. Then her face wrinkled, and she began to cry. "He wanted to marry me," she said piteously. "He wanted me to promise! But he always has asked me—ever since I was fifteen years old, and I always said no!"

"Well, now," Jim said soothingly. "Don't cry. You couldn't help it. Do you know why he carried a revolver?"

"He has to carry it, his business isn't a very safe one," Julia said shakily. "He's shown it to me once or twice!" Her voice dropped on a trembling note, and her eyes were wild with fright.

"Now, Aunt Sanna," said Jim quietly, after telephoning, "I think that you and Miss Page ought to get out of here. You'll have a raft of reporters and busybodies here to-morrow. It's a ghastly thing, of course, and the quieter we keep it the better for every one. I'll manage my end of it. I'll have as conservative an account as I can in the papers—simply that he was despondent over a love affair and, in a fit of temporary aberration—and so on. Could you close this place up for a week?"

"Certainly!" said Miss Toland, with Spartan promptness, beginning to enjoy the desperate demand of the hour.

"And could you take that poor child somewhere, out of the public eye?"

"I will indeed, Jim!"

"Well, that's the best way to do. You're a trump, Aunt Sanna! I will say that Miss Page is naturally prostrated, and gone away to friends."

"Jim, has that poor boy a chance?"

"A chance? No. No; he died instantly. It was straight through the brain. Yes, terrible—naturally. Now, will you take what you need—" "Instantly!" said Miss Toland, with a shudder. "Oh, Jim, I'm so glad you're a doctor," she added weakly, clutching his arm, "and so cold blooded and reliable!"

"I'm glad I was here," Jim answered simply. "Hello, look at poor little Miss Page! She's fainted!"

CHAPTER VIII

It was Christmas time before Julia saw Doctor Studdiford again, and then it was but for a few minutes. Christmas Eve was wet and blowy out of doors, but the assembly hall of The Alexander looked warm and bright; there were painfully made garlands of green looped about the windows, bells of red paper hung from all the chandeliers, and on the stage an enormous Christmas tree glittered with colour and light. Six hundred people were crowded into the room, more than half of them children. Babies twisted and climbed on the laps of their radiant mothers, small girls and boys everywhere were restless with excitement and anticipation. Miss Toland only appeared at intervals, spending most of the afternoon with a few chosen guests in the reception hall, but Julia was everywhere at once. She wore a plain white linen gown, with a bit of holly in her hair and on her breast, and whether she was marshalling small girls into groups, stopping to admire a new baby, meeting the confectioner's men and their immense freezers at the draughty side door, talking shyly with the directors in Miss Toland's room, or consoling some weeping infant in the hall, she was followed by admiring eyes.

At three o'clock the general restlessness visibly increased, and the air in the hall, between steaming wet garments and perspiring humanity, became almost insufferable. Julia experimentally opened a door and let in a wet blast of air, but this was too drastic, and her eyes were brought back from a wistful study of the high windows by a voice that said:

"Merry Christmas! Give me a stick, and I'll do it for you!"

The girl found her hand in Doctor Studdiford's, and their eyes met.

"I didn't know you were here!" said Julia, in swift memory of their last meeting.

"Just come." He looked at her, all kindliness. "How goes it?"

"Finely," Julia answered. When he had opened a window, he followed her across the room. "I may stay near you, mayn't I?"

"I am just going to begin," Julia said, taking her place at the piano, and facing the room across the top of it. Her small person seemed suddenly fired with authority. She struck a full chord. "Children!" she said. "*Children*! Who is talking? Some one is still talking! Keep still, everybody, please! Keep still, every one.

"Now we are going to sing the 'Adeste'—four verses. And then we'll give out the presents. Listen, every one! We are going to sing the 'Adeste,' and then give out the presents. The presents, of course, go only to our own girls and boys, do you understand that? Listen, children, please!

"But we have a box of candy for every child here, whether that child comes to any of the classes or not! So don't go home without your candy. And don't come up for your present until you hear your name called, do you understand that? If I see any child coming up before Miss Pierce calls her name, I'll send her right back to her seat! Now, the 'Adeste,' please!"

Jim had listened in intense amusement. How positive she was and how authoritative! Her straight little back, her severe braids, her stern blue eyes roving the hall as she touched the familiar chords, were all so different from the vague young women who were Barbara's friends. She played a few wandering chords after the distribution of gifts began, watching the children file up the aisle, and listening, with only an occasional lifting of her blue eyes to his face, to Doctor Studdiford's smiling comments. Her heart was beating high under a flood of unsensed joy, she did not know why— but she was happy beyond all words.

"I'm afraid I'll have to go help Miss Pierce and Miss Furey, Doctor," she said presently, standing up. "Our Miss Scott, who got married two years ago, used to be a perfect wonder at times like this! Here, little girl, little girl! You don't come to the classes, do you? No? Well, then, go back to your seat and wait—you see!" She turned despairingly to Jim. "You see, they're simply making a *mess* of it!"

"I have to go, anyway," said Jim.

"Oh?" Julia turned surprised eyes toward him, and said the one thing she meant to avoid. "But Mrs. Toland and Miss Barbara are coming," she submitted.

"And what of it?" Jim said meaningly. It was his turn to say the awkward thing. "How are the nerves these days?" he asked quickly.

Colour flooded Julia's face.

"Much better, thank you! I gave the tonic up weeks ago. It was just nerves," explained Julia, "a sort of breakdown after we came back from Cloverdale! And I'm so much obliged to you!" she ended shyly.

"Oh, not at all, not at all!" Jim protested gruffly. An unmanageable silence hung between them for a few seconds; then Julia, with a murmured excuse, went to the extrication of Miss Pierce, now hopelessly involved in a surge of swarming children, and Jim went on his way. He carried with him a warm memory of the erect young figure in white, and the thick twisted braid, set against a background of Christmas green. For Julia the rest of the afternoon was enchanted; an enchantment subtly flavoured with the odour of evergreen, and pierced by rapturous voices, and by the glowing colours of the Christmas tree, and the slapping rain at the window.

She and Miss Toland sat down, exhausted and well satisfied, at seven o'clock, to a scrappy little supper in the littered dining-room: one director had left chocolates, another violets; a child's soiled hair ribbon, still tied, lay on the floor; the chairs were pushed about at all angles.

"Give me some more coffee, dear, and open that box of candy," said Miss Toland luxuriously. "We'll sleep late, and go to high mass at the Cathedral. Alice always has room in her pew. And then we might go over to Sausalito and say 'Merry Christmas.' They'll all be scattered; Jim tells me he and my brother have an operation at twelve, poor wretches! And I suppose Barbara and little Sally will be off somewhere. Sally always tries to keep them together for Christmas Eve, but in my opinion they're all bored by this tree and stocking business. But of course Ned and his extraordinary wife will be all over the place!"

"I've not been in Sausalito, except once, for eight years," Julia said reflectively.

"I know you've not. Well, we'll go to-morrow." Miss Toland reached for a cigarette; yawned as she lighted it. But Julia's heart began to beat fast in nervous anticipation.

Mrs. Toland received them very graciously the next day, and Julia was at once made to feel at home in the pretty house, which was littered charmingly to-day with all sorts of Christmas gifts, and bright with open fires. Barbara was there, and the crippled Richie, but Sally had gone to a Christmas concert with her devoted little squire, Keith Borroughs, and Mrs. Toland presently took Miss Sanna aside for a long, distressed confidence. Theodora, it seemed, had had a stormy argument with her father on the subject of her admirer, Robert Carleton, some days before, and yesterday had left, in defiance of all authority, to meet him for a walk, and lunch with him. She and her father had not spoken to each other since, and Ted was keeping her room. Julia met Ned's wife, a pretentious, complacent little gabbling village belle, and was dragged about by the younger sisters to look at everybody's presents.

"Must be a long time since we saw you here, Miss Page?" said the old doctor, smiling at her over his glasses, as he carved at luncheon.

"I was here two years ago, one afternoon," Julia smiled. "But I think I haven't seen *you* since 'The Amazons'—eight years ago!"

"Eight years!" Barbara said, struck. "Mother, do you realize that it is eight years since I was in that play with the Hazzards and Gray Babcock and the Grinells? Isn't that *awful*?" She fell into sombre thought.

Julia went through the day in a sort of deep study. This was the enchanted castle that had stood to her for so long as the unattainable height of dreams; these were the envied inhabitants of that castle. Everything was the same, except herself, yet how incredibly the change in her affected everything about her! She was at home here now, could answer the table pleasantries with her ready, grave smile, could feel that her interest in Constance and Jane was a pleasure to them, or could pick a book from the drawing-room table with the confidence that what she said of it would not be ridiculous. She could even feel herself happier than Barbara, who listened so closely to what Julia said of the settlement house, and sighed as she listened.

After luncheon Richie took her driving over cold country roads, behind a big-boned gray mare, and adored her, though she never dreamed it, because she neither offered to take the reins nor asked him at intervals if his back was tired. He was finishing work at the school of medicine now, and although he could never hope to be in regular practice, his thin, bony face was very bright as he outlined his plans. Julia listened to him sympathetically, and said good-bye to him at the boat with a sense of genuine liking on both sides. Miss Toland was waiting for her on the upper deck, her long nose nipped and red in the cold air.

"Well, he saw that you didn't miss it, after all!" said she, with a welcoming light for Julia in her sharp eyes, though she did not smile. "Sit down! I've been hearing nice things about you, my dear! I said to Sally, 'So there *is* something in old maids' children, eh?'" Miss Toland chuckled; she was well pleased with her protegee. Julia settled herself comfortably beside her. She liked to watch the running gray water, and to feel the cold December wind in her face. The thought of Mark was always with her, poor Mark! so much more in her heart dead than living! But to-day his memory seemed only a part of the tender past; it was toward the future that her heart turned; she felt young and strong and full of hope.

In the new year Jim began to come pretty regularly to the settlement house. Sometimes he stayed but for two minutes, never for more than ten, and usually, even if Julia was out, he left some little gift for her, a book or a magazine, flower seeds, or violets, or a box of candy. She would glance up from the soiled and rumpled sewing of some small girl to find Jim smiling at her from the stage door, or come back from her little shopping round and have a moment's chat with him on the steps. She grew more and more silent, more and more self-contained, but her beauty deepened daily, and her eyes shone like blue stars.

"God, I will not believe it—I *cannot* believe it!" said Julia, on her knees, at night, her hands pressed tight against her eyes. "But I think he is beginning to love me!" And she walked in a strange dazzle of happiness, rejoicing in every sunny morning that, with its warmth and blueness and distant soft whistles from the bay, seemed to promise the spring, and rejoicing no less when rain beat against the windows of The Alexander, and the children rushed in upon her at three o'clock with raindrops in their hair and on their glowing cheeks. The convent garden, in the February mornings, the assembly room, with late uncertain sunlight checking its floor in the long afternoons, the Colonial restaurant filled with lights and the odours of food at night, all these familiar things seemed strangely new and thrilling, and the arrival of the postman was, twice a day, a heart-shaking event.

In April Doctor Toland went on a fortnight's trip to Mexico, and took his third daughter with him, in the undisguised hope of winning some small share of her confidence, and convincing her of his own disinterested affection. Two days later Barbara telephoned her aunt the harrowing news of Sally's elopement with Keith Borroughs, and Miss Toland went at once to Sausalito, taking Julia along.

They found the big house full of excitement. Richie was with his mother, who had retired to her room and was tearful and hysterical; Ned and his wife had gone back after Christmas to the country town, where he held a small position under his father-in-law; and Jim was doing both his own work and that of his foster father for the time being, and could not be found by telephone; so Julia was received by Barbara and the two younger girls, who were not inclined to make light of the event.

"Four years younger than Sally!" said Constance, not for the first time.

"It's not *that*," Barbara contributed disgustedly. "But he's only nineteen—not of age, even! And he hasn't one single penny! Why, Mrs. Carter was thinking of sending him abroad for two years' work with his music. I *see* her doing it now! Little sloppy-haired, conceited idiot, that's what *he* is!"

"And Richie says he'll have to have his mother's consent before he can marry her," said Jane with a virtuous air.

"It's too disgusting!" Barbara added, giving Jane a sharp glance. "And you oughtn't talk that way, Jane; it doesn't sound very well in a girl your age to talk about any one's having to marry any one!"

"I know this," said Constance gloomily. "It's going to give this family a horrible black eye. A fine chance we'll have to marry, we younger ones, with Sally disgracing every one this way!" Constance was the handsomest of all the Tolands, and felt keenly the disadvantages of being the youngest of four unmarried sisters.

"Don't worry about your marriage until it comes along, Con," said Barbara wearily.

"I'll bet I marry before you do!" said Constance, without venom.

"I long ago made up my mind never to marry at all," Barbara said, with a bored air. Julia chuckled.

"It is so funny to hear you go at each other," she explained. "It sounds so cross—and it really isn't at all! Don't worry, Miss Toland," she added soothingly, "Miss Sally wouldn't marry him if she didn't love him—"

"Oh, she loves him fast enough!" Barbara admitted, consoled.

"And if people love each other, it's all right," Julia went on. Barbara sighed.

"Oh, I hope it is, Julia!" said she, as conscious of the little familiarity for all her abstracted air as Julia was, and suspecting that it thrilled Julia, as indeed it did.

"And it's all the result of idleness, that's what it is, and that's what I've been telling your mother," said Miss Toland, coming in. "You've all got nothing to do except sit about and think how bored you are!"

"Oh, Auntie, aren't you low?" Barbara said tranquilly, going to take an arm of her chair. "All sorts of people elope—there's nothing so disgraceful in *that*."

"It's disgraceful considering what a father you've got, and what a mother!" Miss Toland said vexatiously. "And Ted worrying your father to death about that scamp, too! I declare it's too much!"

"He's a pretty rich scamp, and a pretty attractive scamp," Barbara said in defence of Theodora's choice. "He's not like that *kid* of a Keith!"

Julia heard the garden gate slam, and a quick, springing step on the porch before the others did, but it was Jane who said, "Here's Jim!" and Barbara who went to let him in.

"Oh, Jimmy, have you heard of Sally?" she faltered, and as they came in from the hall Julia's quick eye saw that she was half clinging to his shoulder, sister fashion, and that his arm was half about her.

"Hello, every one!" said his big, reassuring voice. "How's Mother? Hello, Aunt Sanna—and Miss Page, too! Well, this is fun, isn't it? Yes, Miss Babbie, I've heard of Sally, Sally Borroughs, as she is now—"

"What! Married?" said every one at once, and Mrs. Toland, making an impressive entrance with Richie, sank into a deep chair and echoed: "Married?"

"Married, Mother dear," said Jim. "They found me in Dad's office at five o'clock; Keith's father, a fierce sort of man, was with them, and was for calling the whole thing off. Sally was crying, poor girl, and Keith miserable—"

"Oh, poor old Sally!" said Barbara's tender voice.

"You should have brought her straight home to me!" Mrs. Toland added severely.

"Well, so I thought at first. But they had their license, which would be in the morning papers anyway, and Sally had done the fool thing of mailing letters to two girl friends when she left here this morning—"

"She left me a mere scribble, pinned to her pin-cushion," said her mother, magnificently. "Just as any common actress—"

"Oh, Mother! it wasn't pinned to her cushion at all!" Barbara protested. "She had no pincushion, she has a pin tray."

"I hardly see how it matters, Babbie; it was on her bureau, anyway! Just like a servant girl!" Mrs. Toland persisted.

"Well, anyway, it seemed best to push it right through," said Jim, "especially as they persisted that they would do it again or die—or rather, Sally did!"

"Oh, Jim, *don't!*" wailed Sally's mother. "Poor, deluded child!"

"I don't mean that Keith wasn't fiery enough," Jim hastened to say. "He's a decent enough little fellow, and he's madly in love. So we all went up to the French church, and Father Marchand married them—"

"A child of mine!" said Mrs. Toland, stricken.

"Keith's father and I witnessed," pursued Jim, "and we both kissed the bride—"

"Sally! And she was such a dear sweet baby!" whispered Mrs. Toland, big tears beginning to run down her cheeks.

"Ah, Mother!" Constance said soothingly, at her mother's knees.

"Sally's of age, of course," Jim argued soothingly, "and one couldn't bring her home like a child. The thing would have gotten out, and she'd have been a marked girl for life! There's really no *reason* why they shouldn't marry, and the boy—Keith, that is, put her into a carriage quite charmingly, and they drove off. They'll go no farther than Tamalpais or the Hotel Rafael, probably, for Keith has to be back at work on Monday, and I made him promise to bring Sally here on Sunday night."

"And what will they live on?" Mrs. Toland asked stonily.

"That isn't worrying them. Sally has—what? From those bonds of her grandfather's?"

"Three hundred a year," Mrs. Toland said discouragingly.

"And Keith gets fifty-five a month. That's eighty—h'm!" pursued Jim.

"Well, some of us simply will have to help them," suggested Mrs. Toland, with a swift, innocent glance at Miss Sanna.

"His father will have to help," Miss Toland countered firmly.

They presently adjourned to the dining-room, all still talking—even Julia—of Sally. Sally would have to take the Barnes cottage, at fifteen dollars a month, and do her own cooking, and her own sewing—

"They can dine here on Sundays," said Sally's mother, sniffing and wiping her eyes.

"And wouldn't it be awful if they had a baby!" Jane flung out casually.

Every one felt the indelicacy of this, except Julia, who relieved all Jane's hearers by saying warmly:

"Oh, don't say awful! Why, you'd all go wild over a dear little baby!"

Doctor Studdiford gave her a curious look at this, and though Julia did not see it, Barbara did. After dinner the doctor and Barbara played whist with the older ladies, and Julia sat looking over their shoulders for a few minutes, and then went upstairs with Constance and Jane for a long, delightful gossip. The girls must show her various pictures of Keith and Sally, books full of kodak prints, and everywhere Julia saw Jim, too: Jim from the days of little boyhood on to to-day, Jim as camp cook, Jim as tennis champion, Jim riding, yachting, fishing; a younger Jim, in the East at college, a small, stocky, unrecognizable Jim, in short trousers and straw hat. And everywhere, with him, Barbara.

"That's when they gave a play—I was only five," Constance said. "See, this is Jim as Jack Horner, and Babbie as Mother Goose. And look! here's Jim on a pony—that's at his grandfather's place in Honolulu, He stayed there a month every year, when he was a little boy, and Mother and Barbara visited there once. Here we all are, swimming, at Tahoe. And here's Bab in the dress she wore at her coming-out tea—isn't it dear? And look! here she is in an old dress of Jim's mother, and see the old pearls; aren't they lovely? Jim gave them to her when she was twenty."

"Jim was crazy about her then," said Jane.

"*I* don't think he was," Constance said perversely.

"Oh, Con, you know he was!" Jane protested. "He *was*, too," she added, to Julia.

"*I* don't think he was," persisted Constance lightly.

Barbara came in a second later, and again the talk went back to Sally.

"Mother and Aunt Sanna said good-night," reported Barbara, "and Aunt Sanna said to leave the door between your rooms open, and—oh, yes, Doctor Studdiford has been teasing Aunt Sanna to stay for a few days, Miss Page; he says you look as pale as a little ghost!"

"I liked so much to have you call me Julia," was Julia's extremely tactful answer to this. Barbara, perhaps glad to find her message so casually dismissed, smiled her prettiest.

"Julia—then!" and Barbara sat down on a bed, and began to roll up her belt. "Aunt Sanna says she gives Sally and Keith about three months—" she began.

Two days later, on Sunday, the bride and groom came home. Sally, who looked particularly well and was quite unashamed, rushed into her mother's arms, and laughed and cried like a creature possessed. She kissed all her sisters, and if there was a note of disapproval in her welcome, she did not get it. Richie having charitably carried off the somewhat sullen young husband, the bride was presently free to open her heart to the women of the house.

"It's all so different when you're married, isn't it, Mother?" bubbled Sally. "Going into hotels and everything—you don't care who looks at you, you know you've a perfect right to go anywhere with your husband! Now, that look that Keith just gave me, as he went off with Richie—*blazing*! Well, it would just have amused me when we were engaged, but now I know that he's simply wretched with jealousy, and I'll have to pet him a little and quiet him down! He is a perfect child about money; he *will* spend too much on everything, and if we go abroad I'll simply have to—"

"Go abroad?" every one echoed.

"Oh, I think we must, for Keith's music," Sally said gravely. "He can't settle down here, you know. He's got to live abroad, and he's got to have lessons—expensive lessons. Office work makes him too nervous, anyway."

"Well, my dear, I hope you have money enough to carry out these pleasing plans," said Miss Toland dryly.

"Well, we have my twenty-five a month," Sally said capably, "and Keith's father *ought* to give him another twenty-five, because the expense of having Keith live at home will be gone, and"—Sally fixed a hopeful eye on her mother—"and I should think Dad would give me at least that, Mother," said she. "I must cost him much more than that!"

"Oh, I—don't—know!" said Mrs. Toland guardedly, taken unawares, and slowly shaking her head.

"Then I thought," pursued the practical Sally, "that if you would give me half the clothes of a regular trousseau, and if Dad would give us our travelling expenses to Berlin for a wedding present—why, there you are!"

"But you two couldn't live on seventy-five dollars a month, Sally!"

"Oh, Mother, Jeannette said you could get a lovely room for two—in a pension—for a dollar a day! And that leaves forty for lessons, two a week, and five dollars over!"

"For laundry and carfare and doctor's bills," said Miss Toland unsympathetically.

"Well!" Sally flared, resentful colour in her cheeks.

"And Dad will never consent to anything so *outrageously* unfair as living on thirty-five and spending forty for lessons!" said Barbara.

Poor little Sally looked somewhat crushed.

"For heaven's sake don't let Keith hear you say that, Babbie!" she said nervously. "It makes him frantic to suggest that you can get decent lessons in harmony for nothing! I don't know what you know about it, anyway. I'll fix it with Dad!"

"If Dad allows Sally so much, he ought to do the same for the rest of us," Constance suggested. Julia, foreseeing a scene, slipped out of the room.

In the hallway she encountered Doctor Studdiford, who was just downstairs after a late sleep. Jim had the satisfied air of a man who has had a long rest, a shave and a bath, and a satisfactory breakfast.

"Family conference?" he said, nodding toward the sitting-room door.

"Sally and Keith are here," Julia announced.

"Oh, are they? Well, I ought to go in. But I also ought to walk up to the Ridge, and see that poor fellow who ran a shaft into his leg." Jim hesitated. "I suppose you wouldn't like to go with me?" he asked, with his sudden smile. Julia's heart jumped; her eyes answered him. "Well, wrap up snug," said Jim, "for there's the very deuce of a wind!"

So Julia tied herself into the most demure of hats, and buttoned her long coat about her, and Jim shook himself into his heaviest overcoat, and pulled an old cap down over his eyes. They let themselves out at a side door, and a gust of wet wind howled down upon them, and shook a shower from the madly rippling ivy leaves. The sky was high and pale, and crossed by hurrying and scattered clouds; a clean, roaring gale tore over the hills, and ruffled the rain pools in the road, and bowed the trees like whips. The bay was iron colour; choppy waves chased each other against the piers. Now and then a pale flicker of sunlight brightened the whole scene with blues and greens and shadows spectacularly clear; then the clouds met again, and the wind sang like a snapped wire.

Julia and the doctor climbed the long flights of stairs that cut straight up through the scattered homes on the hill. These earthen steps were still running with the late rain, and moss lay on them like a green film. Julia breathed hard, a veil of blown hair crossed her bright eyes, her stinging cheeks glowed.

"I love this kind of a day!" she shouted. Jim's gloved hand helped her to cross a wide pool, and his handsome eyes were full of all delight as he shouted back.

Presently, when they were in a more quiet bit of road, he told her of some of his early boyish walks. "Listen, Julia!" he said, catching her arm. "D'you hear them? It's the peepers! We used to call them that, little frogs, you know—sure sign of the spring!"

And as the wind lulled Julia heard the brave little voices of a hundred tiny croakers in some wet bit of meadow. "We'll have buttercups next week!" said Jim.

He told her something of the sick man to whom they were going, and spoke of other cases, of his work and his hopes.

"Poor Kearney!" said Jim, "his oldest kid was sick, then his wife had a new baby, and now this! You'll like the baby—he's a nice little kid. I took him in my arms last time I was here, and I wish you could have seen the little lip curl up, but he wouldn't cry! A kid two months old can be awfully cunning!" He looked a little ashamed of this sentiment, but Julia thought she had never seen anything so bright and simple and lovable as the smile with which he asked her sympathy.

She was presently mothering the baby, in the Kearneys' little hot living-room, while Doctor Studdiford caused the patient in the room beyond to shout with pain. The howling wind had a sinister sound, heard up here within walls, and Julia was glad to be out in it, and going down the hills again.

"Well, how do you like sick calls?" asked Jim.

"I was glad not to have to see him," Julia confessed. "But it is a darling baby, and such a nice little wife! She has a sister who comes up every afternoon, so she can get some sleep, poor thing. His mother is going to pay their rent until he gets well, and he gets two dollars a week from his union. But she said that if you hadn't—"

"Well, you know now, for such a quiet little mouse of a girl, Julia, you are a pretty good confidence woman!"

"And the baby's to be named for you!" Julia ended triumphantly.

"Lord, they needn't have done that!" said the doctor, with his confused, boyish flush. "Look, Julia, how the tide has carried that ferryboat out of her course!"

Julia's heart flew with the winds; she felt as if she had never known such an hour of ecstasy before. They had crossed the upper road, and were halfway down the last flight of steps, when Jim suddenly caught her hand, and turned her about to face him. Dripping trees shut in this particular landing, and they were alone under the wind-swept sky. Jim put his arms about her, and Julia raised her face, with all a child's serene docility, for his kiss.

"*Do* you love me, Julie?" said Jim urgently, then. "Do you love me, little girl? Because I love you *so* much!"

Not the words he had so carefully chosen to say, but he said them a score of times. If Julia answered, it was only with a confused murmur, but she clung to him, and her luminous eyes never moved from his own.

"Oh, my God, I love you so!" Jim said, finally releasing her, only to catch her in his arms again. "Won't you say it once, Julia, just to let me hear you?"

"But I did say it," Julia said, dimpling and rosy.

"Oh, but darling, you don't know how *hungry* I am to hear you!"

"How—how could I help it?" Julia stammered; and now the blue eyes she raised were misty with tears.

Jim found this satisfactory, intoxicatingly so. They went a few steps farther and sat on a bit of dry bulk-heading, and began to discuss the miracle. About them the winds of spring shouted their eternal promise, and in their hearts the promise that is as new and as old as spring came to dazzling flower.

"My clever, sweet, little dignified girl!" said Jim. "Julia, do you know that you are the most fascinating woman in the world? I never saw any one like you!"

"I—Oh, Jim!" was all that Julia said, but her dimples and the nearness of the blue eyes helped the stammered words.

"Among all the chattering, vapid girls I know," pursued Jim, "you stand utterly alone, you with your ambitions, and your *wiseness*! By George! when I think what you have made of yourself, I could get down and worship you. I feel like a big spoiled kid beside you! I've always had all the money I could spend, and you, you game little thing, you've grubbed and worked and made things do!"

"I never had any ambition as high as marrying *you*," Julia said, with the mysterious little smile that at once baffled and enchanted him. "When I think of it, it makes me feel giddy, like a person walking in a valley who found himself set down on top of a mountain! I never thought of marriage at all!"

"But you are going to marry me, sweet, aren't you?" Jim asked anxiously. "And you *are* happy, dear? For I feel as if I would die of joy and pride!"

"Oh, I'm happy!" Julia said, and instantly her lip quivered, and her eyes brimmed with tears. She jumped to her feet, and caught him by the hand. "Come on!" she said. "We *mustn't* be so long!"

"But darling," said Jim, infinitely tender, "why the tears?"

For answer she caught his coat in her shabbily gloved little hands.

"Because I love you so, Jim," she faltered, trying to smile. "You don't know how much!" Her voice had dropped to a whisper, and for a moment her eyes looked far beyond him, down into the valley, and at the iron-cold bay with its racing whitecaps. Then she took his hand, and they began to descend the steps.

"I may tell my mother, Julie?" Jim asked joyously. "And Aunt Sanna? And do you know that Julia is one of my favourite names—"

"No, I want you not to tell any one," Julia decided quickly. "You must promise me that. Nobody." Something in her tone surprised, a little chilled, him.

"Julie—but why?"

"Well, because we want to be *sure*—"

"Oh, sure! Why, but, dearest, *aren't* you—"

"No, but wait a moment," Julia interrupted, and Jim, turning toward her, saw a real trouble reflected in her face. "I want you to meet my mother, and my own people," she said, scarlet cheeked. Jim's grave, comprehensive look met hers.

"And I want to, dear," he said. And then, as her face did not brighten: "Why, my dearest, you aren't going to worry because your people aren't in the Social Register, and don't go to the Brownings'? I know all sorts of people, Ju—Kearney, up there, is a good friend of mine! And I know from Aunt Sanna that you're a long way ahead of your own people."

"I don't know whether it's 'ahead' or not," said Julia, with a worried laugh. "I suppose only God knows the real value of finger bowls and toothbrushes and silk stockings! I *suppose* it's 'ahead'!"

She opened the Tolands' side gate as she spoke, and they went into the bare garden.

"Well—but *don't* go in," pleaded Jim, "there'll be a mob about us in no time, and I've never had you to myself before! When may I come see your people?"

"Will you write?" Julia asked at the side door.

"Oh, but darling, when we've just begun to talk!" fretted Jim. "Would you dare to kiss me right here—no one could possibly see us!"

"I would *not*!" And Julia flashed him one laughing look as she opened the door. A moment later he heard her running up the stairway.

Julia found Miss Toland upstairs, hastily packing. "Well, runaway!" said the older lady. And then, in explanation, "I think we'd best go, Julia, for my brother and Teddy have just got home, and there'll have to be a great family council to-night."

"Would you stay if I went?" Julia asked, coming close to her.

"No, you muggins! I'd pack you off in a moment if that was what I meant! No, I'm glad enough to get out of it!" Miss Toland stood up. "What's Jim Studdiford been saying to you to give you cheeks like that?" she asked.

"I don't know," Julia whispered, with a tremulous laugh. And for the first time she went into Miss Toland's open arms, and hid her face, and for the first time they kissed each other.

"Anything settled?" the older woman presently asked in great satisfaction.

"Not—quite!" Julia said.

"Not quite! Well, that's right; there's no need of hurry. Oh, law me! I've seen this coming," Miss Toland assured her; "he all but told me himself a week ago! Well, well, well! And it only goes to show, Julia," she added, shaking a skirt before she rolled it into a ball and laid it in her suitcase, "that if you give a girl an occupation, she's better off, she's more useful, and it doesn't keep her fate from finding her out! You laugh, because you've heard me say this before, but it's true!"

Julia had laughed indeed; her heart was singing. She would have laughed at anything to-day.

Four days later, at four o'clock in the afternoon, Doctor Studdiford called at The Alexander, and Miss Page joined him, in street attire, at once. They walked away to the car together, in a street suddenly flooded with golden sunshine.

"Did you tell your mother I was coming, dear?"

"Oh, Jim, of course! I never would dare take them unawares!"

"And did you tell her that you were going to be my adored and beautiful little wife in a few months?"

"In a few months—hear the man! In a few years! No, but I gave them to understand that you were my 'friend.' I didn't mention that you are a multi-millionaire and a genius on leg bones—"

"Julia, my poor girl, if you think you are marrying a multi-millionaire, disabuse your mind, dear child! Aren't women mercenary, though! Here I thought I—No, but seriously, darling, why shouldn't your mother have the satisfaction of knowing that your future is pretty safe?"

"Well, that's hard to say, Jim. But I think you will like her better if she takes it for granted that you are just—well, say just the sort of doctor we might have called in to the settlement house, establishing a practice, but quite able to marry. I feel," said Julia, finding her words with a little difficulty, "that my mother might hurt my feelings—by doubting my motives, otherwise—and if she hurt my feelings she would anger you, wouldn't she?"

"She certainly would!" Jim smiled, but the look he gave his plucky little companion was far removed from mirth.

"And I do dread this call," Julia said nervously. "I came down here yesterday, just to say we were coming, and it all struck me as being— However, there's the house, and you'll soon see for yourself!"

The house itself was something of a shock to Jim, but if Julia guessed it, he gave her no evidence of his feeling, and was presently taken into the stifling parlour, and introduced to Julia's mother, a little gray now, but hard lipped and bright eyed as ever, and to Mrs. Cox, who had been widowed for some years, and was a genial, toothless, talkative old woman, much increased in her own esteem and her children's as the actual owner of the old house.

"Mother, we want some air in here!" Julia said, going to a window.

"Julia's a great girl for fresh air," said Emeline. "Sit down, Doctor, and don't mind Ma!" Mrs. Cox, perhaps slightly self-conscious, was wandering about the room picking threads from the carpet, straightening the pictures on the walls, and dubiously poking a small stopped clock on the mantel.

"How's your arm to-day?" Julia asked, stopping behind her mother's chair, and laying two firm young hands on her shoulders.

"What do you think of a girl that runs off and doesn't see her mother for weeks at a time, Doctor?" Mrs. Page demanded a little tartly. "Her papa and I was devoted to her, too! But I suppose if she marries, she'll be too grand for us altogether!"

"Now, Mother!" said Julia pleadingly, half vexed, half indulgent.

"I had an elegant little place myself when I was first married," Mrs. Page continued, in a sort of discontented sing-song. "Julia must have told you about her papa—"

Julia's serious eyes flashed a look to Jim, and he saw something almost like humour in their blue deeps.

"That's a crayon enlargement of my youngest son," the old woman was presently saying, "Chess. A better boy never lived, but he got in with bad companions and they got him in jail. Yes, indeed they did! On'y the governor let him out again—"

The call was not long. Doctor Studdiford shook hands with both the ladies, in departing, and Julia kissed her mother and grandmother dutifully. The two walked almost in silence to the car.

"Downtown?" asked Julia, in surprise.

"Downtown, for tea," Jim said. And when they were comfortably established in a secluded corner of the Golden Pheasant, he expelled a long breath from his lungs, and sent Julia his sunniest smile as he said:

"Well, you're a wonder!"

"I?" Julia touched her heart with her fingers, and raised her eyebrows.

"Oh, yes, you are!" Jim repeated. "You're a little wonder! To make yourself so sweet and fine and dear, it shows that you're one of the big people of the world, Julie! Some one of the writers, Emerson I guess it was, says that when you find a young person who is willing to accept the wisdom of older people, and abide by it, why, you may watch that young person for great things. And you see, I propose to!"

Julia had no answering smile ready. Instead her face was very grave as she said musingly:

"I hardly know why I wanted you to meet my mother and grandmother, Jim. I don't know quite what I expected when you *did* meet them, but—but you mustn't make light of the fact that they *are* different from your people, and different from me, too. For three or four days and nights now I've been thinking about—us. I've been wondering whether this engagement would be a—a happy thing for you, Jim. I've wondered—"

"But, sweetheart!" he interrupted eagerly, "I love you! You're the only woman I ever wanted to marry! I love you just because you *are* different, you are so much wiser and deeper and truer than any other girl I ever knew, and if your people and your life have made you that, why I love them, too! And you do love me, Julie?"

Julia raised heavy eyes, and he could see that tears were pressing close behind them. She did not speak, but her look suddenly enveloped him like a cloud. Jim felt a sudden prick of tears behind his own eyes.

"Sweetness," he said gravely, "I know you love me! And Julia, my whole soul is simply on fire for you. Don't—*don't* let any mere trifle come between us now. Let me tell my mother and father to-morrow!"

A clear light was shining in Julia's eyes. Now, as she automatically arranged the tea things before her, and poured him his first cup of tea, she said:

"Jim, I told you that I haven't thought much about marriage for myself. I suppose it's funny that I shouldn't, for they say most girls do! But perhaps it was because the biographies and histories I began to read when I came to the settlement house were all about men: how Lincoln rose, how Napoleon rose, how this rich man sold newspapers when he was a little boy, and that other one spent his first money in taking his mother out of the poorhouse. And of course marriage doesn't enter so much into the lives of men. It came to me years ago that what wise men are trying to din into young people everywhere is just this: that if you make yourself ready for anything, that thing will come to you. Just do your end, and somewhere out in the queer, big, incomprehensible machinery of the world your place will mysteriously begin to get ready for you—Am I talking sense, Jim?"

"Absolutely. Go on!" said Jim.

"Well, and so I thought that if I took years and years I might—well, you won't see why, but I wanted to be a lady!" confessed Julia, her lips smiling, but with serious eyes. "And, Jim, everything comes so much more easily than one thinks. Your aunt knew I wasn't, but I happened to be what she needed, and I kept quiet, and listened and learned!"

"And suppose you *hadn't* happened upon the settlement house?" asked Jim, his ardent eyes never moving from her face.

"Why, I would have done it somehow, some other way. I meant to take a position in some family, and perhaps be a trained nurse when I was older, or study to be a librarian and take the City Hall examinations, or work up to a post-office position! I had lots of plans, only of course I was only a selfish little girl then, and I thought I would disappear, and never let my own people hear from me again!"

"But you softened on that point, eh?" asked Jim.

"Oh, right away!" Julia's wonderful eyes shone upon him with something unearthly in their light. "Because God decides to whom we shall belong, Jim," said she, with childish faith, "and to start wrong with my own people would mean that I was all wrong, everywhere. But my highest ambition then was to grow, as the years went on, to be useful to nice people, and to be liked by them. I never dreamed every one would be so friendly! And when Miss Pierce and Miss Scott have asked me to their homes, and when Mrs. Forbes took me to Santa Cruz, and Mrs. Chetwynde asked me to dine with them, well, I can't tell you what it meant!"

"It meant that you are as good—and better, in every way—than all the rest of them put together!" said the prejudiced Jim.

"Oh, Jim!" Julia looked at him over her teacup, a breach of manners which Jim thought very charming. "No," she said, presently, pursuing her own thoughts, "but I never thought of marriage! And now you come along, Jim, so—so good to me, so infinitely dear, and I can't—I can't help caring—" And suddenly her lip trembled, and tears filled her eyes. She looked down at her teacup, and stirred it blindly.

"You angel!" Jim said.

"Don't—make—me—cry—!" Julia begged thickly. A second later she looked up and laughed through tears. "And I feel like a person who has been skipped over four or five grades at school; I don't know whether I *can* be a rich man's wife!" she said whimsically. "I know I can go on as I am, reading and thinking, and listening to other people, and keeping quiet when I have nothing to say, but—but when I think of being Mrs. James Studdiford—"

"Oh, I love to hear you say it!" Jim leaned across the table, and put one warm big hand over hers. "My darling little wife!"

The word dyed Julia's cheeks crimson, and for the long hour that they lingered over their tea she seemed to Jim more charming than he had ever found her before. Her gravity, with its deep hint of suppressed mirth, and her mirth that was always so delicate and demure, so shot with sudden pathos and seriousness, were equally exquisite; and her beauty won all eyes, from the old waiter who hovered over their happiness, to the little baby in the street car who would sit in Julia's lap and nowhere else. Jim presently left Julia to her Girls' Club, consoling himself with the thought that on the following night they were to make their first trip to the theatre together.

But when, at half-past seven the next evening, Jim presented himself at the settlement house, he found Julia alone, and obviously not dressed for the theatre. She admitted him with a kiss that to his lover's enthusiasm was strangely cool, and drew him into the reception hall.

"Your aunt had to go out with Miss Parker," said Julia. "But she'll positively be here a little after eight."

"My darling, I didn't come to see Aunt Sanna!" Jim caught her to him. "But, sweetheart," he said, "how hot your face is, and your poor little hands are icy! Aren't you well?"

"No, I don't believe I'm very well!" Julia admitted restlessly, lighting the shaded lamp on the centre table, and snapping off the side lights that so mercilessly revealed her pale face and burning eyes.

"Not well enough for the theatre? Well, but darling, I don't care one snap for the theatre," Jim assured her eagerly. "Only I hate to see you so nervous and tired. Has it been a hard day? Aunt Sanna—?"

"No, your aunt's an angel to me—no, it's been an easy day," Julia said, dropping into a chair, and pushing her hair back from her face with a feverish gesture. A second later she sprang up and disappeared into the assembly hall. "I thought I mightn't have locked the door," she said, returning.

"Why, sweetheart," Jim said, in great distress, "what is it? You're not one bit like yourself!"

"No, I know I'm not," Julia said wildly. She sat down again. "I've been thinking and thinking all day, until I feel as if I must go *crazy*!" she said with a desperate gesture. "And it's come to this, Jim—Don't think I'm excited—I mean it. I—we can't be married, Jim. That's all. Don't—don't look so amazed. People break engagements all the time, don't they? And we aren't really engaged, Jim; nobody knows it. And—and so it's *all* right!"

Anything less right than Julia's ashen face and blazing eyes, and the touch of her cold wet little hands, Jim thought he had never seen. He stepped into the bathroom, and ran his eye along the trim row of labelled bottles on the shelf.

"Here, drink this, dear," he said, coming back to her with something clear and pungent in a glass. "Now, come here," and half lifting the little figure in his arms he put her on the couch, and tucked a plaid warmly about her. "Don't forget that your husband is also a doctor," said Jim, sitting down so that he could see her face, and hold one hand in both of his. "You're all worn out and excited, and no wonder! You see, most girls take out their excess emotion on their families, but my little old girl is too much alone!"

Julia's eyes were fixed on him as if she were powerless to draw them away. It was sweet—it was poignantly sweet—to be cared for by him, to feel that Jim's warm heart and keen mind were at her service, that the swift smile was for her, the ardour in his eyes was all her own. For perhaps half an hour she rested, almost without speaking, and Jim talked to her with studied lightness and carelessness. Then suddenly she sat up, and put her hands to her loosened hair.

"I must look wild, Jim!"

"You look like a ravishing little gipsy! But I wish you had more colour, mouse!"

"Am I pale?" Julia asked, with a little nervous laugh. Jim dropped on one knee beside her, and studied her with anxious eyes, and she pushed the hair off his forehead, and rested her cheek against it with a long sigh as if she were very tired.

"What is it, dear?" asked Jim, with infinite solicitude.

"Well!" Julia put the faintest shadow of a kiss on his forehead, then got abruptly to her feet and crossed the room, as if she found his nearness suddenly insufferable. "I can't break my engagement to you this way, Jim," said she. "For even if I told you a thousand times that I had stopped loving you"—a spasm of pain crossed her face, she shut her hands tightly together over her heart—"even then you would know that I love you with my whole soul," she said in a whisper with shut eyes. "But you see," and Julia turned a pitiful smile upon him, "you see there's something you don't understand, Jim! You say I have climbed up alone, from being a tough little would-be actress, who lived over a saloon in O'Farrell Street, to this! You say—and your aunt says—that I am wise, wise to see what is worth having, and to work for it! But has it never occurred to *one* of you—" Julia's voice, which had been rising steadily, sank to a cold, low tone. "No," she said, as if to herself, sitting down at the table, and resting her arms upon it. "No, it has never occurred to one of them to ask *why* I am different—to ask just what made me so! Life boils itself down to this, doesn't it?" she went on, staring drearily at the shadowy corner of the room beyond her. "That women have something to sell, or give away, and the question is just how much each one can get for it! That's what makes the most insignificant married woman feel superior to the happiest and richest old maid. She says to herself, 'I've made my market. Somebody chose me!' That's what motherhood and homemaking rest on: the whole world is just one great big question of sex, spinning away in space! And even after a woman is married, she still plays with sex; she likes to feel that men admire her, doesn't she? At dinners there must be a man for every woman; at dances no two girls must dance together! And here, the minute a new girl comes to join my clubs, I try to read her face. Is she pure, or has she already thrown away—"

"Julia, *dear*!" said Jim, amazed and troubled, but she silenced him with a quick gesture. Her cheeks were burning now, and her words came fast.

"Those poor little girls at St. Anne's," she said feverishly, "they've thrown their lives away because this thing that is in the air all about them came too close. They were too young legally to be trusted as Nature has trusted them for years! They heard people talk of it, and laugh about it—it didn't *seem* very dangerous—"

"Julia!" Jim said again, pleadingly.

"Just one moment, Jim, and I'll be done! When they had learned their lesson, when they had found out what sorrow it brought, when they knew that there was only loss and shame in it for them—then it was too late! Then men, and women, too, expected them to go on giving; there was nothing else to do. Oh," said Julia, in a heartbreaking voice, bringing her locked hands down upon the table as if she were in physical agony, "if the law would only take a hand before and not afterward! Or if, when they are sick to death of men, they could believe that time would wash it all away; that there was clean, good work for them somewhere in the world!"

"My darling, why distress yourself about what can't possibly concern you?" Jim said. Julia stared at him thoughtfully for a few silent seconds.

"It *does* concern me. That's how I bought my wisdom," she said quietly then, with no emotion deeper than a mild regret visible in her face. Voice and manner were swept bare of passion; she seemed infinitely fatigued. "That's why I can't marry you, Jim."

"What do you mean?" Jim said easily, uncomprehendingly, the indulgent smile hardly stricken from his lips.

Julia's eyes met his squarely across the lamplight.

"That," she said simply.

There was a silence, and no change of expression on either face. Then Jim stood up.

"I don't believe it!" he said, with a short laugh.

"It's true," said Julia. "I was not fifteen. How long ago it was! Nobody has ever known—you need not have known. But I am glad I told you. I have been thinking of nothing else but telling you for two days and two nights. And sometimes I would say to myself that what that old little ignorant Julia did would not concern you—"

Jim made an inarticulate sound, from where he sat with his elbows on his knees, with his face dropped in his hands.

"But I see it does concern you!" Julia said, quickly, with great simplicity. "I—luckily I decided to tell you this morning," she said, "for I am absolutely exhausted now. It was a terrible thing to keep thinking about, and I could not have fought it out any longer! There were extenuating circumstances, I suppose. I was a spoiled little empty-headed girl; the girls all about me were reckless in everyway; I did not know the boundary-line, or dream that it mattered very much, so long as no one knew! My mother had been unhappy in my childhood, and used to talk a good deal about the disappointment of marriage. Perhaps I don't make myself clear?"

"*You*! Julia!" Jim whispered, his hands still over his face.

"Yes, I know," Julia said drearily. "I don't seem like that sort of a girl, I know."

Then there was a long silence.

"You—poor—little—kid!" Jim said, after a while, getting up and beginning to walk the floor. "Oh, my God! My God! Poor little kid!"

"I suppose there are psychological moments when one wakes up to things," Julia went on, in a tone curiously impersonal. "I was in some theatricals with your sister, years ago. Every one snubbed me, and no wonder! There was a man named Carter Hazzard—and I suddenly seemed to wake up at about that time—"

"Carter Hazzard!" The horror in Jim's voice rang through the room. Julia frowned.

"I only saw him two or three times," she said. "No. But he flirted with me, and flattered me, and then Barbara told me he was married, and then I found out that they all thought I was vulgar and common—and so I was. And I suppose I wanted to be loved and made much of, and he—this man—was good to me!"

"Not you—of all women!" Jim said dully, as if to himself.

"I know how you feel," Julia said without emotion, "because of course I feel that way, too—now! And I never loved him, never even thought I did! It was only a little while—two weeks or three, I guess—before I told him I couldn't ever love him. I said I thought I might, but it was like—like realizing that I had been throwing away gold pieces for dimes. Do you know what I mean? And the most awful disgust came over me, Jim—a sort of disappointment, that this talked-of and anticipated thing was no more than that! And then I came here, and I knew that keeping still about it was my only chance, and oh, how sick I was, soul and body, for a fresh start! And then your aunt talked to me, and said what a pity it is that young girls think of nothing but love and lovers, and so throw away their best years, and I thought that I was done with love; no more curiosity—no more thrill—and that I would do something with my life after all!"

Her voice dropped, and again there was silence in the room. Jim continued to pace the floor.

"Why, there's never been a morning at St. Anne's that I haven't looked at those girls," Julia presently resumed, "and said to myself that I might have been there, with my head shaved and a green check dress on! Lots of them must be better than I!"

"Don't!" Jim said sharply, and there was a silence until Julia said wonderingly:

"Isn't it funny that all last night, and the night before, I thought I was going to *die*, telling you this—and now it just doesn't seem to matter at all?"

"That's why you've never married?" Jim said, clearing his throat.

"I've never wanted to until now," Julia said. "And I—I am so changed now that somehow I would never think of that—that bad old time, in connection with marriage! It was as if that part of my life was sealed beyond opening again—

"And then you came. I only wanted no one to guess that I cared at first. And then, when I saw that you were beginning to care, too, oh, my God! I thought my heart would burst!"

And with sudden terrible passion in her voice, she got up in her turn and began to pace the room. Jim, who had flung himself into a chair opposite hers, rested his elbows on the table, and his face in his hands.

"But I feel this about your caring for me, Jim," Julia said. "In a strange, mysterious way I feel that giving you up—giving you up, my best and dearest, is purification! When—when this is over, I shall have paid! It may be"—tears flooded her eyes, and she came back to her chair and laid her head on her arm—"it may be that I can't bear it, and that I will die!" sobbed Julia. "But I shall always be glad that I told you this to-night!" There was a long silence, and then again Jim came to kneel beside her, and put one arm about her.

"My own little girl!" said he. At his voice Julia raised her head, and put her arms about his neck like a weary child, and rested her wet face against his own.

"My own brave girl!" Jim said. "I know what courage it took to have you tell me this! It will never be known to any one else, sweetheart, and we will bury it in our hearts forever. Kiss me, dearest, and promise me that my little wife will stop crying!"

For a moment it was as if she tried to push him away.

"Jim," she whispered, tears running down her face, "have you thought—are you *sure*?"

"Quite sure, sweetheart," he said soothingly and tenderly. "Why, Julie, wouldn't you forgive me anything I might have done when I was only an ignorant little boy?"

Julia tightened her arms about him, and sobbed desperately for a long while. Then her breathing quieted, and she let Jim dry her eyes with his own handkerchief, and listened, with an occasional long sigh, to his eager, confident plans. They were still talking quietly when the street door was flung open and Miss Toland came in, on a rush of fresh air.

"Rain!" said Miss Toland. "Terrible night! Not an umbrella in the Parker house until Clem came home—it's quarter to ten!"

"Congratulate us, Aunt Sanna," said Jim, rising to his feet with his arm still about Julia. "Julia has promised to marry me!"

End of Part One

PART TWO

CHAPTER I

Yet Dr. James Studdiford, walking down to his club, an hour later, with the memory of his aunt's joyous congratulations ringing in his ears, and of Julia's last warm little kiss upon his cheek, was perhaps more miserable than he had been before in the course of his life. Julia was his girl—his own girl—and the thrill of her submission, the enchanting realization that she loved him, rose over and over again in his heart, like the rising of deep waters—only to wash against the firm barrier of that hideous Fact.

Jim could do nothing with the Fact. It did not seem to belong to him, or to Julia, to their love and future together, or to her gallant, all-enduring past. Julia was Julia—that was the only significant thing, the sweetest, purest, cleverest woman he knew. And she loved him! A rush of ecstasy flooded his whole being; how sweet she was when he made her say she loved him—when she surrendered her hands, when she raised her gravely smiling blue eyes! What a little wife she would be, what a gay little comrade, and some day, perhaps, what a mother!

Again the Fact. After such a little interval of radiant peace it seemed to descend upon him with an ugly violence. It was true; nothing that they could do now would alter it. And, of course, the thing was serious. If anything in life was serious, this was. It was frightful—it seemed sacrilegious to connect such things for an instant with Julia. Dear little Julia, with her crisp little uniforms, her authority in the classroom, her charming deference to Aunt Sanna! And she loved him——

"Damn it, the thing either counts or it doesn't count!" Jim muttered, striding down Market Street, past darkened shops and corners where lights showed behind the swinging doors of saloons. Either it was all important or it was not important at all. With most women, all important, of course. With Julia—Jim let his mind play for a few minutes with the thought of renunciation. There would be no trouble with Julia, and Aunt Sanna could easily be silenced.

He shook the mere vision from him with an angry shake of the head. She belonged to him now, his little steadfast, serious girl. And she had deceived them all these years! Not that he could blame her for it! Naturally, Aunt Sanna would never have overlooked that, and presumably no other woman would have engaged her, knowing it, even to wash dishes and sweep steps.

"Lord, what a world for women!" thought Jim, in simple wonder. Hunted down mercilessly, pushed at the first sign of weakening, they know not where, and then lost! Hundreds of thousands of them forever outcast, to pay through all the years that are left to them for that hour of yielding! Hundreds of thousands of them, and his Julia only different because she had made herself so—

It seemed to Jim, in his club now, and sunk in a deep chair before the wood fire in the quiet library, that he could never marry her. It must simply be his sorrow to have loved Julia—God, how he did love her!

But, through all their years together, there must not be that shadow upon their happiness; it was too hideous to be endured. "It must be endured," mused Jim wretchedly. "It is true!

"Anyway," he went on presently, rousing himself, "the thing is no more important than I choose to make it. Ordinarily, yes. But in this case the thing to be considered is its effect on Julia's character, and if ever any soul was pure, hers is!

"And if we marry, we must simply make up our minds that the past is dead!" And suddenly Jim's heart grew lighter, and the black mood of the past hour seemed to drop. He stretched himself luxuriously and folded his arms. "If Julia isn't a hundred per cent, sweeter and better and finer than these friends of Babbie's, who go chasing about to bad plays and read all the rottenest books that are printed," he said, "then there's no such thing as a good woman! My little girl—I'm not half worthy of *her*, that's the truth!"

"Hello, Jim!" said Gray Babcock, coming in from the theatre, and stretching his long cold hands over the dying fire. "We thought you might come in to-night. Hazzard and Tom Parley had a little party for Miss Manning, of the 'Dainty Duchess' Company, you know—awfully pretty girl, straight, too, they say. There were a couple of other girls, and Roy Grinell—things were just about starting up when I came away!"

Jim rose, and kicked the scattered ends of a log toward the flame.

"I've not got much use for Hazzard," he observed, frowning.

Babcock gave a surprised and vacant laugh.

"Gosh! I thought all you people were good friends!"

"Hazzard's an ass," observed Jim irritably. "There are some things that aren't any too becoming to college kids—however, you can forgive them! But when it comes to an ass like Hazzard chasing to every beauty show, and taking good little girls to supper—"

"Alice don't care a whoop what he does," Babcock remarked hastily.

"Yes, so of course that makes everything all right," Jim said ironically. But Mr. Babcock was in no mood to be critical of tones.

"Sure it does!" he agreed contentedly. And when Jim had disgustedly departed, he remained still staring into the fire, a pleased smile upon his face.

Julia spent the next day in bed fighting a threatened nervous breakdown, and Jim came to see her at two o'clock, and they had a long and memorable talk, with Jim's chair drawn close to the couch, and the girl's lax hand in his own. She had not slept all night, she told him, and he suspected that she had spent much of the long vigil in tears. Tears came again as she begged a hundred times to set him free, but he quieted her at last, and the old tragedy that had risen to haunt them was laid. And if Julia felt a rush of blind gratitude and hope when they sealed their new compact with a kiss, Jim was no less happy—everything had come out wonderfully, and he loved Julia not less, but more than he had ever loved her. The facts of her life, whatever they had been, had made her what she was; now let them all be forgotten.

"Still, you are not sorry I told you, Jim?" Julia asked.

"No, oh, no, dearest! If only because you would have been sure to want to do it sooner or later—it would have worried you. But now I do know, Julie, you little Spartan! And this ends it. We'll never speak of it again, and we'll never think of it again. You and I are the only two who know—And we love each other. When all's said and done, it's I that am not good enough for you, darling, not worthy to tie your little shoe laces!"

"Oh, *you*!" Julia said, in great content.

The rest followed, as Julia herself said, like "a house-maid's dream." Jim went home to tell his own people that night, and the very next morning Julia, surprised and smiling, took in at the door a trim little package that proved to be a blue-and-white Copenhagen teacup, with a card that bore only the words "Miss Barbara Lowe Toland." Julia twisted it in her fingers with a curious little thrill at the heart. The "nicest" people sent cups to engaged girls, the "nicest" people sent their cards innocent of scribbled messages. She, Julia Page, was one of the "nicest" people now, and these were the first tentacles of her new estate reaching out to meet her.

Notes and flowers from the Tolands and the warm-hearted Tolands

themselves followed thick and fast, and in a day or two notes and cups—cups—cups—were coming from other people as well. The Misses Saunders, the Harvey Brocks, the George Chickerings, Mr. Peter Coleman, Mr. Jerome Phillips, Mrs. Arnold Keith, and Miss Mary Peacock—all had found time to go into Nathan Dohrmann's, or Gump's, or the White House, and pick out a beautiful cup to send Miss Julia Page.

Six weeks—five weeks—three weeks to the wedding, sang Julia's heart; the time ran away. She had dreaded having to meet Jim's friends, and had dreaded some possible embarrassment from an unexpected move on the part of her own family, but the days fled by, and the miracle of their happiness only expanded and grew sweeter, like a great opening rose. Their hours together, with so much to tell each other and so much to discuss, no matter how short the parting had been, were hours of exquisite delight. And as Julia's beauty and charm were praised on all sides, Jim beamed like a proud boy. As for Julia, every day brought to her notice something new to admire in this wonderful lover of hers: his scowl as he fixed his engine, the smile that always met hers, the instant soberness and attention with which he answered any question as to his work from the older doctor—all this was delightful to her. And when he took her to luncheon, his careless big fingers on the ready gold pieces and his easy nod to the waiter were not lost upon Julia. She had loved him for himself, but it was additionally endearing to learn that other people loved him, too, to be stopped by elderly women who smiled and praised him, to have young people affectionately interested in his plans.

"You know you are nothing but a small boy, Jim," Julia said one day, "just a sweet, happy kid! You were a spoiled and pitied little boy, with your big eyes and your velvet suits and your patent leathers; you loved every one—every one loved you; you had your allowance, you were born to be a surgeon, and chance made your guardian a doctor—"

"I fell down on my exams," Jim submitted meekly. "And there was a fellow at college who said I bored him!"

"Oh, dearest," Julia said, beginning to laugh at his rueful face, "and are those the worst things that ever happened to you?"

"About," said Jim, enjoying the consolatory little kiss she gave him.

"And your youngness baffles me," pursued Julia thoughtfully. "You're ten years older than I am, you've been able to do a thousand things I never did, you're a rising young surgeon, and yet—and yet sometimes there's a sort of level—level isn't the word!—a sort of *positive* youth about you that makes me feel eighty! It's just as if you had been born everything you are, ready made! When you have to straighten a child's hip, you push your hair back like a nice little kid, and say to yourself, 'Sure—I can do that!' You seem as pleased and surprised as any one else when everything comes out right!"

"Well, gosh! I never can put on any lugs!" said James, rumpling his hair in penitential enjoyment.

"I have to learn things so *hard*," Julia mused, "they dig down right into the very soul of me—"

"You're implying that I'm shallow," said the doctor sternly. "You think I'm a pampered child of luxury, but I'm not! I just think I'm a pretty ordinary fellow who came in for an extraordinary line of luck. I would have made a pretty good bluff at supporting myself in any sort of life; as it was, when I was a youngster, growing up, I used to say to myself, 'You think you're going to be rich, but half the poor men in the world are born rich, anything may happen!' However, I enjoyed things just the same, and I went to medical college just because Dad said every man ought to be able to support himself. Then I got interested in the thing, and old Fox was a king to me, and told me I ought to go in for surgery. My own father was a surgeon, you know. Some hands are just naturally better for it than others, and his were, and mine are. And at twenty-five I came of age, and found that my money was pretty safely fixed, and that Dad was kind of counting on my going in with him. So there you are! Things just come my way; as I say, I'd have been satisfied with less, but I've got in the habit of taking my luck for granted."

"And some people, like—well, like my grandmother, for instance, just get in the habit of bad luck," Julia said, with a sigh. "And some, like myself," she added, brightening, "are born in the bad belt, and push into the good! And we're the really lucky ones! I shall never put on a fresh frock, or go downtown with you to the theatre, without a special separate joy!"

Jim said, "You angel!" and as she jumped up—they had been sitting side by side in the hall at The Alexander—he caught her around the waist, and Julia set a little kiss on the top of his hair.

"But you do love me, Ju?" Jim asked.

"But I do indeed!" she answered. "Why do you always ask me in that argumentative sort of way? But me no buts!"

"Ah, well, it's because I'm always afraid you'll stop!" Jim pleaded. "And I do so want you to begin to love me as much as I do you!"

"You must have had thousands of girls!" Julia remarked, idly rumpling his hair.

"I never was engaged before!" he assured her promptly. "Except to that Delaware girl, as I told you, and after five years she threw me over for a boy named Gregory Biddle, with several millions, but no chin, Julia, and had the gall to ask me to the wedding!"

"Jim, and you went?"

"Sure I went!" Jim declared.

"Oh, Jim!" and Julia gave him another kiss, through a gale of laughter, and ran off to change her gown and put on her hat.

It was a Saturday afternoon, and they were going to Sausalito. But first they went downtown in the lazy soft spring afternoon, to buy gloves for Julia and a scarf pin for Richie, who was to be Jim's best man, and to go into the big railroad office to get tickets for the use of Dr. and Mrs. James Studdiford three days later.

"Where are we going?" Julia asked idly, her eyes moving about the bright pigeonholed office, and to the window, and the street beyond. Jim for answer put his thumb upon the magic word that stared up at her from the long ticket.

"New York!" she whispered; her radiant look flashed suddenly to him. "Oh, Jim!" And as they went out he heard a little sigh of utter content beside him. "It's too much!" said Julia. "To go to New York—with you!"

"Wherever you go, you go with me," he reminded her, with a glance that brought the swift colour to her face.

Then they went down to the boat. It was the first hot afternoon of the season; there was a general carrying of coats, and people were using the deck seats; there was even some grumbling at the heat. But Sausalito was at its loveliest, and Julia felt almost oppressed by the exquisite promise of summer that came with the sudden sound of laughter and voices in lanes that had long been silent, and with the odour of dying grass and drooping buttercups beside the road. The Toland garden was full of roses, bright in level sunshine, windows and doors were all wide open, and the odours from bowls of flowers drifted about the house. Barbara, lovely in white, came to meet them.

"Come in, you poor things, you must be roasted! Jim, you're as red as a beet; go take a bath!" said Barbara. "And Julia, Aunt Sanna is here, and she says that you're to lie down for not less than an hour. And there are some packages for you, so come up and lie down on my bed, and we'll open them!"

"Barbara, I am so happy I think my heart will burst!" said Julia, ten minutes later, from Barbara's pillows.

"Well, you ought to be, my good woman! Jim Studdiford—when he's sober—is as good a husband as you're likely to get!" said Barbara, laughing. "Now, look, Julia, here's a jam pot from the Fowlers—Frederic Fowlers—I call that decent of them! Janey, come in here and put this jam pot down on Julia's list! And this heavy thing from the Penroses. I hope to goodness it isn't more carvers!"

It was Barbara who said later to Julia, in a confidential undertone:

"You know you've got to write personal notes for every bit of this stuff, Julia, right away? Lots of girls do it on their honeymoons."

"Well, I wanted to ask you, Barbara: how do I sign myself to these people I've never seen: 'Yours truly'?"

"Oh, heavens, no! 'Sincerely yours' or 'Yours cordially' and make 'em short. The shorter they are the smarter they are, remember that."

"And if I sign J. P. Studdiford, or Julia P. Studdiford—then oughtn't 'Mrs. J. N.' go in one corner?"

"Oh, *no*, you poor webfoot! No. Just write a good splashy 'Julia Page Studdiford' all over the page; they'll know who you are fast enough!"

"Thanks," said Julia shyly.

"You're welcome," Barbara said, smiling. "Are you ready to go down?"

After dinner the young Tolands, augmented by several young men, and by Julia and the doctor, all wandered out into the thick darkness, rejoicing in the return of summer. Sausalito's lanes were sweet with roses, lights shone out across the deep fresh green of gardens, and lights moved on the gently moving waters of the bay. A ferryboat, a mass of checkered brightness, plowed its way from Alcatraz—far off the city lay like a many-stranded chain of glittering gems upon the water. Julia and Doctor Studdiford let the others go on without them, and sat together in the dim curve of the O'Connell seat, and the heartbreaking beauty of the night wrapped them both in a happiness so deep as to touch the borderland of pain.

"Was there ever such a night?" said little Julia. "Shall we ever be so happy again?"

Jim could not see her clearly, but he saw her bright, soft eyes in the gloom, the shimmer of her loosened hair, the little white-clad figure in the seat's wide curve, and the crossed slim ankles. He put his arm about her, and she rested her head on his shoulder.

"Don't say that, darling!" said Jim. "This is great, of course. But it's nothing to all the happy months and years that we'll belong to each other. Nothing but death will ever come between you and me, Julie!"

"And I shouldn't be afraid of death," murmured Julia, staring up at the stars. "Strange—strange—strange that we all must go that way some day!" she mused.

"Well, please God, we'll do some living first," Jim said, with healthy anticipation. "We'll go to New York, and gad about, and go to Washington and Boston, and pick up things here and there for the house, do you see? Then we'll come back here and go to a hotel, and find a house and fix it up!"

"That'll be fun," said Julia.

"You bet your life it'll be fun! And then, my dear, we'll give some corking dinners, and my beautiful wife will wear blue velvet, or white lace, or peachy silk—"

"Or all three together," the prospective wife suggested, "with the flags of all nations in my hair!"

"Then next year we'll visit old Gilchrist, at Monterey, and go up to Tahoe," continued Jim, unruffled. "Or we could take some place in Ross—"

"And then I will give a small and select party for one guest," said Julia whimsically, "and board him, free, for fifteen or twenty years—"

"Julia, you little *duck*!" Jim bent his head over her in the starlight, and felt her soft hair brush his face, and caught the glint of her laughing eyes close to his own, and the vague delicious little perfume of youth and beauty and radiant health that hung about her. "Do you know that you are as cunning as a sassy kid?" he demanded. "Now, kiss me once and for all, and no nonsense about it, for I can hear the others coming back!"

Two days later they were married, very quietly, in the little Church of Saint Charles Borromeo, where Julia's father and mother had been married a quarter of a century ago. They had "taken advantage," as Julia said, of her old grandfather's death, and announced that because the bride's family was in mourning the ceremony would be a very quiet one. Even the press was not notified; the Tolands filled two pews, and two more were filled by

Julia's mother, her grandmother, and cousins. Kennedy Scott Marbury and her husband were there, and sturdy two-year-old Scott Marbury, who was much interested in this extraordinary edifice and impressive proceeding, but there were no other witnesses. Julia wore a dark-blue gown, and a wide black hat whose lacy brim cast a most becoming shadow over her lovely, serious face. She and Miss Toland drove from the settlement house, and stopped to pick up Mrs. Page, who was awed by Julia's dignity, and a little resentful of the way in which others had usurped her place with her daughter. However, Emeline had very wisely decided to make the best of the situation, and treated Miss Toland with stiff politeness. Julia was in a smiling dream, out of which she roused herself, at intervals, for only a gentle, absent-minded "Yes" or "No."

"I tried to persuade her to be married at the Cathedral, by His Grace," said Miss Toland to Mrs. Page. "But she wanted it this way!"

"Well, I'm sure she feels you've done too much for her as it is," Emeline said mincingly. "Now she must turn around and return some of it!"

To this Miss Toland made no answer except an outraged snort, and a closer pressure of her fine, bony hand upon Julia's warm little fingers. They presently reached the church, and Julia was in Barbara's hands.

"You look lovely, darling, and your hat is a dream!" said Barbara, who looked very handsome herself, in her brown suit and flower-trimmed hat. "We go upstairs, I think. Jim's here, nervous as a *fish*. You're wonderful—as calm! I'd simply be in spasms. Ted was awful; you'd think she had been married every day, but Robert—his collar was *wilted*!"

They had reached the upper church now, and Miss Toland and Mrs. Page followed the girls down the long aisle to the altar. Julia saw her little old grandmother, in an outrageous flowered bonnet, and Evelyn who was a most successful modiste now, and Marguerite, looking flushed and excited, with her fat, apple-faced young husband, and three lumpy little children. Also her Aunt May was there, and some young people: Muriel, who was what Evelyn had been at fifteen, and a toothless nine-year-old Regina, in pink, and some boys. On the other side were the elegant Tolands, the dear old doctor in an aisle seat, with his hands, holding his eye-glasses and his handkerchief, fallen on either knee; Ted lovely in blue, Constance and Jane with Ned and Mrs. Ned, frankly staring.

As Julia came down the aisle, with a sudden nervous jump of her heart, she saw Jim and Richie, who was limping badly, but without his crutch, come toward her. The old priest came down the altar steps at the same time. She and Jim listened respectfully to a short address without hearing a word of it, and found themselves saying the familiar words without in the least sensing them. Julia battled through the prayer with a vague idea that she was losing a valuable opportunity to invoke the blessing of God, but unable to think of anything but the fact that the bride usually walked out of church on the groom's arm, and that St. Charles's aisle was long and rather dismal in the waning afternoon light.

"Here, darling, in the vestry!" Jim was whispering, smiling his dear, easy, reassuring smile as he guided her to the nearby door. And in a second they were all about her, her first kiss on the wet cheek of Aunt Sanna, the second to her mother—"Evelyn, you were a darling to come way across the city, and Marguerite, you were a darling to bring those precious angels"— and then the old doctor's kiss, and Richie's kiss, and a pressure from his big bony fingers. Julia half knelt to embrace little Scott Marbury. "He's beautiful, Kennedy; no wonder you're proud!" And she tore her beautiful bunch of roses apart, that each girl might have a few.

"I've got to get her to the train!" Jim protested presently, trying patiently to disengage his wife's hands, eyes, and attention. "Julia! Julia Studdiford!"

"Yes, I know!" Julia laughed, and was snatched away, half laughing and half in tears, and hurried down to the side street, where a carriage was waiting. And here there was one more delay: Chester Cox, a thin shambling figure, came forward from a shadowy doorway, and rather timidly held out his hand.

"I couldn't get away until jest now," said Chester. "But of course I wish you luck, Julia!"

"Why, it's my uncle!" Julia said, cordially clasping his hand. "Mr. Cox— Doctor Studdiford. I'm so glad you came, Chess!"

"Glad to know you, Mr. Cox," Jim said heartily.

"And I brought you a little present; it ain't much, but maybe you can use it!" mumbled Chester, terribly embarrassed, and with a nervous laugh handing Julia a rather large package somewhat flimsily wrapped and tied.

"Oh, thank you!" Julia said gratefully. And before she got in the carriage she put her hand on Chester's arm, and raised her fresh, exquisite little face for a kiss.

"Now, about this—" Doctor Studdiford began delicately, glancing at Chester's gift, which Julia had given him to hold. "I wonder if it wouldn't be wise to ask your uncle to send this to my mother's until we get back, Ju. You see, dear—"

"Oh, no-no!" Julia said eagerly, leaning out of the carriage, and taking the package again. She sent Chester a last bright smile, as Jim jumped in and slammed the door, but it was an April face that she turned a second later to her husband.

"They're all so good to me, and it just breaks my heart!" she said.

"At last—it's all over—and you belong to me!" exulted Jim. "I have been longing and *longing* for this, just to be alone with you, and have you to myself. Are you tired, sweetheart?"

"No-o. Just a little—perhaps."

"But you do love me?"

"Oh, Jim—you idiot!" Julia slipped her hand into his, as he put one arm about her, and rested against his shoulder. "When I think that I will often ride in carriages," she mused, half smiling, "and that, besides being my Jim, you are a rich man, it makes me feel as if I were Cinderella!"

"You shall have your own carriage if you want it, Pussy!" he smiled.

"Oh, don't—don't give me anything more," begged Julia, "or a clock somewhere will strike twelve, and I'll wake up in The Alexander, with the Girls' Club rehearsing a play!"

When she had examined every inch of her Pullman drawing-room, and commented upon one hundred of its surprising conveniences, and when her smart little travelling case, the groom's gift, had been partly unpacked, and when her blue eyes had refreshed themselves with a long look at the rolling miles of lovely San Mateo hills, then young Mrs. Studdiford looked at her Uncle Chester's wedding gift. She found a brush and comb and mirror in pink celluloid, with roses painted on them, locked with little brass hasps into a case lined with yellow silk.

"Look, Jim!" said Julia pitifully, not knowing whether to laugh or to cry.

"Gosh!" said the doctor thoughtfully, looking over the coat he was neatly arranging on a hanger. "I've often wondered who buys those things!"

"I'll give it to the porter," Julia decided. "He may like it. Dear old Chess!" And Jim grinned indulgently a few minutes later at the picture of his beautiful little wife enslaving the old coloured porter, and gravely discussing with him the advantages and disadvantages of his work.

"You know, we could have our meals in here, Ju," Jim suggested. "Claude here"—all porters were "Claude" to Jim—"would take care of us, wouldn't you, Claude?"

"Dat I would!" said Claude with husky fervour. But Julia's face fell.

"Oh, Jim! But it would be such fun to go out to the dining-car!" she pleaded.

Jim shouted. "All right, you baby!" he said. "You see, my wife's only a little girl," he explained. "She's—are you eight or nine, Julia?"

"She sho' don't look more'n dat," Claude gallantly assured them, as he departed.

"I'll be twenty-four on my next birthday," Julia said thoughtfully, a few moments later.

"Well, at that, you may live three or four years more!" Jim consoled her. "Do you know what time it is, Loveliness? It's twenty minutes past six. We've been married exactly two hours and twenty minutes. How do you like it?"

"I love it!" said Julia boldly. "Do I have to change my dress for dinner?"

"You do not."

"But I ought to fix my hair, it's all mashed!" Julia did wonders to it with one of the ivory-backed brushes that had come with the new travelling case, fluffing the thick braids and tucking the loose golden strands about her temples trimly into place. Then she rubbed her face with a towel, and jumped up to straighten her belt, and run an investigating finger about the embroidered "turn-down" collar that finished her blue silk blouse. Finally she handed Jim her new whisk-broom with a capable air, and presented straight little shoulders to be brushed.

Jim turned her round and round, whisking and straightening, and occasionally kissing the tip of a pink ear, or the straight white line where her hair parted.

"Here, you can't keep that up all night!" Julia suddenly protested, grabbing the brush. "I'll do you!" But Jim stopped the performance by suddenly imprisoning girl and whiskbroom in his arms.

"Do you know I think we are going to have great fun!" said he. "You're such a good little sport, Ju! No nerves and no nonsense about you! It's such fun to do things with a person who isn't eternally fussing about heat and cold, and whether she ought to wear her gloves into the dining-car, and whether any one will guess that she's just married!"

"Oh, I have my nervous moments," Julia confessed, her eyes looking honestly up into his. "It seems awfully strange and queer, rushing farther and farther away from home, alone with you!" Her voice sank a little; she put up her arms and locked them about his neck. "I have to keep reminding myself that you are just you, Jim," she said bravely, "who gave me my

Browning, and took me to tea at the Pheasant—and then it all seems right again! And then—such lots of nice people *have* got married, and gone away on honeymoons," she ended, argumentatively.

The laughter had gone from Jim's eyes; a look almost shy, almost ashamed, had taken its place. He kept her as she was for a moment, then gave her a serious kiss, and they went laughing through the rocking cars to eat their first dinner together as man and wife. And Jim watched her as she radiantly settled herself at table, and watched the frown of childish gravity with which she studied her menu, with some new and tender emotion stirring at his heart. Life had greater joys in it than he had ever dreamed, and greater potentialities for sorrow, too. What was bright in life was altogether more gloriously bright, and what was dark seemed to touch him more closely; he felt the sorrow of age in the trembling old man at the table across the aisle, the pathos of youth in the two young travelling salesmen who chattered so self-confidently over their meal.

Several weeks later young Mrs. Studdiford wrote to Barbara that New York was "a captured dream." "I seem to belong to it," wrote Julia, "and it seems to belong to me! I can't tell you how it *satisfies* me; it is good just to look down from my window at Fifth Avenue, every morning, and say to myself, 'I'm still in New York!' For the first two weeks Jim and I did everything alone, like two children: the new Hippodrome, and Coney Island, and the Liberty Statue, and the Bronx Zoo. I *never* had such a good time! We went to the theatres, and the museums, and had breakfast at the Casino, and *lived* on top of the green 'busses! But now Jim has let some of his old college friends know we are here, and we are spinning like tops. One is an artist, and has the most fascinating studio I ever saw, down on Washington Square, and another is an editor, and gave us a tea in his rooms, overlooking Stuyvesant Square, and Barbara, everybody there was a celebrity (except us) and all so sweet and friendly—it was a hot spring day, and the trees in the square were all such a fresh, bright green.

"They make a great fuss about the spring here, and you can hardly blame them. The whole city turns itself inside out; people simply stream to the parks, and the streets swarm with children. Some of the poorer women go bareheaded or with shawls, even in the cars—did you ever see a bareheaded woman in a car at home? But they are all much nearer the peasant here. And after clean San Francisco, you wouldn't believe how dirty this place is; all the smaller stores have shops in the basements, and enough dirt and old rags and wet paper lying around to send Doctor Blue into a convulsion! And they use pennies here, which seems so petty, and paper dollars instead of silver, which I hate. And you say 'L' or 'sub' for the trains, and always 'surface cars' for the regular cars—it's all so different and so interesting.

"Tell Richie Jim is going to assist the great Doctor Cassell in some demonstrations of bone transplanting, at Bellevue, next week—oh, and Barbara, did I write Aunt Sanna that we met the President! My dear, we did. We were at the theatre with the Cassells, and saw him in a box, and Doctor Cassell, the old darling, knows him, and went to the President's box to ask if we might be brought in and presented, and, my dear, he got up and came back with Doctor Cassell to our box, and was simply *sweet*, and asked me if I wasn't from the South, and I nearly said, 'Yes, south of Market Street,' but refrained in time. I had on the new apricot crepe, and a black hat, and felt very Lily-like-a-princess, as Jane says.

"But we're both getting homesick; it will seem good to see the old ferry building again—and Sausalito, and all of you."

Early in July they did start homeward, but by so circuitous a route, and with such prolonged stops at the famous hotels of Canada, that it was on a September afternoon that they found themselves taking the Toland household by storm. And Julia thought no experience in her travels so sweet as this one: to be received into the heart of the family, and to settle down to a review of the past five months. Richie was so brotherly and kind, the girls so admiring of her furs and her diamonds, so full of gay chatter, the old doctor so gallant and so affectionate! Mrs. Toland chirped and twittered like the happy mother of a cageful of canaries; and Julia, when they gathered about the fire after dinner, took a low stool next to Miss Toland's chair and rested a shoulder, little-girl fashion, against the older woman's knee.

"It was simply a tour of triumph for Ju," said Doctor Jim, packing his pipe at the fireplace, with satisfied eyes on his wife. "She has friends in the Ghetto and friends in the White House. We went down to the Duponts', on Long Island, and Dupont said she—"

"Oh, please, Jim!" Julia said seriously.

"Dupont said she was one of the most interesting women he ever talked to," Jim continued inexorably, "and John Mandrake wanted to paint her!"

"Tell me the news!" begged Julia. "How's The Alexander, Aunt Sanna—how is Miss Striker turning out?"

"She's turned out," said Miss Toland grimly, her knitting needles flashing steadily. "She came to me with her charts and rules, and oh, she couldn't lie in bed after half-past six in the morning, and she couldn't put off the sewing class, and she would like to ask me not to eat my breakfast after nine o'clock! A girl who never cared what she ate—sardines and tea!—and she wouldn't come in with me to dinner at the Colonial because she was afraid they used coal tar and formaldehyde—ha! Finally she asked me if I wouldn't please keep the expenditures of the house and my own expenditures separate, and that was the *end*!"

Jim's great laugh burst out, and Julia dimpled as she asked demurely:

"What on *earth* did you say?"

"Say? I asked her if she knew I built The Alexander, and sent her packing! And now"—Miss Toland rubbed her nose with the gesture Julia knew so well—"now Miss Pierce is temporarily in charge, but she won't stay there nights, so the clubs are given up," she observed discontentedly.

"And what's the news from Sally?" Julia pursued.

"Just the loveliest in the world," Mrs. Toland said. "Keith is working like a little Trojan; and Sally sent us a perfectly charming description of the pension, and their walks—"

"Yes, and how she couldn't go out because she hadn't shoes," Jane added, half in malice, half in fun. "*Don't* look so shocked, Mother dear, you know it's true. And the landlady cheating them out of a whole week's board—"

"Gracious me!" said Mrs. Toland, in a low undertone full of annoyance. "Did any one ever hear such nonsense! All that is past history now, Janey," she reminded her young daughter, in her usual hopeful voice. "Dad sent a cheque, like the dear, helpful daddy he is, and now everything's lovely again!"

Julia did not ask for Ted until she saw Barbara alone for a moment the next day. It was about ten o'clock on a matchless autumn morning, and Julia, stepping from her bedroom's French window to the wide sunny porch that ran the width of the house, saw Barbara some forty feet away sitting just outside her own window, with a mass of hair spread to the sun.

Julia joined her, dragged out a low, light chair from Barbara's room, and settled herself for a gossip.

"Had breakfast?" Barbara smiled. "Jim downstairs?"

"Oh, hours ago!" Julia said to the first question, and to the second, with the young wife's conscious blush, "Jim's dressing. He's the most impossible person to get started in the morning!"

Barbara did not blush but she felt a little tug at her heart.

"Come," she said, "I thought Jim had no faults?"

"Well, he hasn't," Julia laughed. And then, a little confused by her own fervent tone, she changed the subject, and asked about Ted.

"Why, Ted's happy, and rich, and simply adored by Bob Carleton," Barbara summarized briefly, in a rather dry voice, "but Mother and Dad never will get over it, and I suppose Ted herself doesn't like the idea of that other wife—she lives at The Palace, and she's got a seven-year-old girl! It's *done*, you know, Julie, and of course Ted's accepted everywhere; she'll go to the Brownings' this year, and Mrs. Morton has asked her to receive with her at some sort of dinner reception next month, you'll meet her everywhere. But I do think it's terribly hard on Mother and Dad!"

"But how *could* she, that great big black creature?"

"Oh, she loves him fast enough! It was perfectly legal, of course. I think Dad was at the wedding, and I think Richie was, but we girls never knew anything until it was all over. Mother simply announced to us one night that Ted was married, and that there was to be no open break, but that she and Dad were just about *sick*! I never saw Mother give way so! She said—and it's true—that if ever there was a mother who deserved her children's confidence, and so on! All the newspapers blazed about it—Ted's picture, Bob's picture—and, as I say, society welcomed her with open arms. They've got a gorgeous suite at the St. Francis, and Ted really looks stunning, and acts as if she'd done something very smart. Con says that when she called, it reminded her of the second act of a bad play. Ted came here with Bob, one Saturday afternoon, but Mother hasn't been near her!"

"It seems too bad," Julia said thoughtfully, "when your father and mother are always so sweet!"

"There must be some reason for it," Barbara observed, "I suppose we were all spoiled as kids, with our dancing schools and our dresses from Paris, and so now when we want things we oughtn't have, we just take 'em, from habit! I remember a governess once, a nice enough little Danish woman, but Ned and I got together and decided we wouldn't stand her, and Mother let her go. It seems funny now. Mother used to say that never in her life did she allow her children to want anything she could give them; but I'm not at all sure that's a very wise ideal!"

"Nor I," said Julia earnestly. Barbara had parted and brushed her dark hair now, and as she gathered it back, the ruthless morning sunlight showed lines on her pretty face and faint circles about her eyes.

"Because life gets in and gives you whacks," Barbara presently pursued, "you're going to want a lot of things you can't have before you get through, and it only makes it harder! Sally's paying for her jump in the dark, poor old Ned is condemned to Yolo City and Eva for the rest of his life, and somehow Ted's the saddest of all—so confident and noisy and rich, boasting about Bob's affection, buying everything she sees—and so *young*, somehow! As for me," said Barbara, "my only consolation is that nearly every family has one of me, and some have more—a nice-looking, well-liked, well-dressed young woman, who has cost her parents an enormous amount of money, to get—nowhere!"

"Why, Lady Babbie!" Julie protested. "It's not like you to talk so!"

Barbara patted the hand that had been laid upon her knee, and laughed.

"And the moral of that is, Ju," she said, "if you have children, don't spoil them! You've had horribly hard times, but they've given you some sense. As for Jim, he's an exception. It's a miracle he wasn't ruined—but he wasn't!" And she gathered up her towels and brushes to go back into her room. "But I needn't tell you that, Julie!" said she.

"Ah, well, Jim!" Julia conceded, smiling.

Jim had no faults, of course. Yet the five-months wife sighed unconsciously as she went back to her room. Jim had qualities that had now and then caused a faint little cloud to drift across Julia's life, but that sheer loyalty had kept her from defining, even in her inmost heart. Now this talk with Barbara had suddenly seemed to make them clear. Jim was—spoiled was too harsh a word. But Jim wanted his own way, in little things and big—all the time. The world just now for Jim held only Julia. What she wanted he wanted, and, at any cost, he would have. If her gown was not right for the special occasion, she should have a new gown; if the motor car was out of order, telephone for another; if the steward assured them that there was not another table in the dining-room—tip him, tip everybody, make a scene, but see that the "Reserved" card comes off somebody's table, and that the Studdifords are seated there in triumph.

At first Julia had only laughed at her lord's masterful progress. It was very funny to her to see how quickly his money and his determination won him his way. A great deal of money was wasted, of course, but then, this was their honeymoon, and some day they would settle down and spend rationally. Jim, like all rich men, had an absolute faith in the power of gold. The hall maid must come in and hook Mrs. Studdiford's gown; oh, and would she be here at, say, one o'clock, when Mrs. Studdiford came home? She went off at twelve, eh? Well, what was it worth to her to stay on to-night, until one? Good. And by the way, Mrs. Studdiford had torn a lace gown and wanted it to-morrow; could the maid mend it and press it? She didn't think so? Well, come, there must be somebody who would rush it through for Mrs. Studdiford? Ah, that was fine, thank you very much, that would do very nicely. Or perhaps it was a question of theatre tickets, and Jim would stop his taxicab on Broadway at the theatre's door. Here, boy! Boy, come here! Go up and ask him what his best for to-night are? There's a line of people waiting, eh?—well, go up and ask some fellow at the top of the line what it's worth to him to get two seats for me. Oh, fine. Much obliged to you, sir. Thank you. And here—boy!

"Do you think the entire world circles about your convenience, Jim?" Julia asked amusedly one day, after some such episode. "Sure," he answered, grinning.

"Jim, you don't think you can go through life walking over people this way?"

"Why not, my good lady?"

"Well," said Julia gravely, "some day you may find you want something you *can't* buy!"

"There ain't no such animal," Jim assured her cheerfully.

Only a trifling cloud, after all, Julia assured herself hardily. But there was a constant little sensation of uneasiness in her heart. She tried to convince herself that the sweetness of his nature had not been undermined by this ability to indulge himself however fast his fancies shifted; she reasoned that because so many good things were his, he need not necessarily hold them in light esteem. Yet the thought persisted that he knew neither his own mind nor his own heart; there had been no discipline there, no hard-won battles—there were no reserves.

"I call that simply borrowing trouble!" said Kennedy Scott Marbury healthily, one day when she and the tiny Scott were lunching with Julia at the hotel. Kennedy was close to her second confinement, and the ladies had lunched in Julia's handsome sitting-room. "Lord, Julie dear! It seems sometimes as if you have to have *something* in this world," Kennedy went on cheerfully; "either actual trouble or mental worries! Anthony and I were talking finances half last night: we decided that we can't move to a larger house, just now, and so on—and we both said *what* would it be like to be free from money worries for ten minutes—"

"But, Ken, don't you see how necessary you are to each other!" said Julia, kneeling before the chair in which her fat godson was seated, and displaying a number of gold chains and bracelets for his amusement. "You have to take a turn at everything—cooking and sewing and caring for old Sweetum here—Anthony couldn't get on without you!"

"And I suppose you think Doctor Studdiford could find twenty wives as pretty and clever and charming as you are, Ju?"

"Fifty!" Julia answered.

"Well, now, that just shows what a little idiot you are!" Mrs. Marbury scolded. "Not but what most women feel that way sooner or later," she added, less severely. "I remember that phase very well, myself! But the thing for you to do, Julie, is to remember that you're exactly the same woman he fell in love with, d'you see? Just mind your own affairs, and be happy and busy, and try not to fancy things!"

"What a sensible old thing you are, Ken!" said Julia gratefully. And as Kennedy came over to stand near her, Julia gave her a little rub with her head, like an affectionate pony. "I think it's partly this hotel that's demoralizing me," Julia went on, a little shamed. "I feel so useless—getting up, eating, dressing, idling about, and going to bed again. Jim has his work, and I'll be glad when I have mine again!"

CHAPTER II

In these days, the Studdifords were househunting in all of Jim's free hours; confining their efforts almost entirely to the city, although a trip to San Mateo or Ross Valley made a welcome change now and then. It was not until late in October that the right house was found, on Pacific Avenue, almost at the end of the cable-car line. It was a new house, large and square, built of dignified dark-red brick, and with a roomy and beautiful garden about it. There was a street entrance, barred by an iron gate elaborately grilled, and giving upon three shallow brick steps that led to the heavily carved door. On the side street was an entrance for the motor car and tradespeople, the slope of the hill giving room for a basement kitchen, with its accompanying storerooms and laundries.

Upstairs, the proportions of the rooms, and their exquisite finish, made the house prominent among the city's beautiful homes. Even Jim could find nothing to change. The splendid dark simplicity of the drawing-room was in absolute harmony with the great main hall, and in charming contrast to the cheerful library and the sun-flooded morning-room. The dining-room had its own big fireplace, with leather-cushioned ingle seats, and quaint, twinkling, bottle-paned windows above. On the next floor the four big bedrooms, with their three baths and three dressing-rooms and countless closets, were all bright and sunny, with shining cream-coloured panelling, cretonne papers in gay designs of flowers and birds, and crystal door knobs. Upstairs again were maids' rooms, storerooms lined in cedar, and more baths.

"Perfect!" said Jim radiantly, on the afternoon when, the Studdifords first inspected the house. "It's just exactly right, and I'm strong for it!" He came over to Julia, who was thoughtfully staring out of a drawing-room window. Her exquisite beauty was to-day set off by a long loose sealskin coat, for the winter was early, and a picturesque little motor bonnet, also of seal, with a velvet rose against her soft hair. "Little bit sad to-day, sweetheart?" Jim asked, kissing the tip of her ear.

"No—o. I was just thinking what a lovely, sheltered backyard!" Julia said sensibly, raising her blue eyes. But she had brightened perceptibly at his tenderness. "I love you, Jim," she said, very simply.

"And I adore you!" Jim answered, his arms about her. "I've been thinking all day how rotten that sounded this morning!" he added in a lower tone. "I'm so sorry!"

"As if it was your fault!" Julia protested generously. And a moment later she charmed him by declaring herself to be entirely satisfied with this enchanting house, and by entering vigorously upon the question of furnishings.

The little episode to which Doctor Studdiford had made a somewhat embarrassed allusion had taken place in their rooms at the hotel that morning, while they were breakfasting. Plans for a little dinner party were progressing pleasantly, over the omelette and toast, when Jim chanced to suggest that a certain Mrs. Pope be included among the guests.

"Oh, Jim—not Mrs. Jerry Pope?" Julia questioned, wide eyed.

"Yes, but she calls herself Mrs. Elsie Carroll Pope now. Why not?"

"Oh, Jim—but she's divorced!"

"Well, so are lots of other people!"

"Yes, I know. But it was such a horrid divorce, Jim!"

"Horrid how?"

"Oh, some other man, and letters in the papers, and Mr. Pope kept both the children! It was awful!"

"Oh, come, Ju—she's a nice little thing, awfully witty and clever. Why go out of your way to knock her!"

"I'm not going out of my way," Julia answered with dignity. "But she was a great friend of Mary Chetwynde, who used to teach at The Alexander, and she came out there two or three times, and she's a noisy, yelling sort of woman—and her hair is dyed—yes, it *is*, Jim!"

"Lord, you women do love to rip each other up the back!" Jim smiled lazily, as he wheeled his chair about, and lighted a cigarette.

"I'm not ripping her up the back at all," Julia protested with spirit. "But she's not a lady, and I hate the particular set she goes with—"

"Not a lady—ha!" Jim ejaculated. "She was a Cowdry."

Julia leaned back in her chair, and opened a fat letter from Sally Borroughs in Europe, that had come in her morning's mail.

"Ask her by all means to dinner," she said calmly. "Only don't expect me to admire her and approve of her, Jim, for I won't do it; I know too much about her!"

"It's just possible Mrs. Pope isn't waiting for your admiration and approval, my dear," Jim said, nettled "But I doubt, whatever she knew of you, if she would speak so unkindly about *you*!"

Julia turned as scarlet as if a whip had fallen across her face. She stared at him for a moment with fixed, horrified eyes, then crushed her letter together with a spasmodic gesture of the hands, and let it fall as she went blindly toward the bedroom door. Jim sat staring after her, puzzled at first, then with the red blood surging into his face. He dropped his cigarette and his newspaper, and for perhaps three minutes there was no sound in the apartment but the coffee bubbling in the percolator, and the occasional clank of the radiator.

Then Jim jumped up suddenly and flung open the door of the bedroom. Julia was sitting at her dressing-table, one elbow resting upon it, and her head dropped on her hand. She raised heavy eyes and looked at him.

"Don't be a fool, Ju," Jim said, solicitous and impatient. "You know I didn't mean anything by that. I wouldn't be such a cad. You know I wouldn't say a thing like that—I couldn't. Come on back and finish your coffee."

But he did not kiss her; he did not put his arm about her; and Julia felt curiously weary and cold as she came slowly back to her place. Jim immediately lighted a fresh cigarette, and began to rattle away somewhat nervously of his plans for the day. He was going over to the Oakland Hospital to look at his man with the spine—better not try to meet for lunch. But how about that Pacific Avenue house? If Julia took the motor and stopped at the agent's for the key, he would meet her there at four—how about it?

Agreed. Gosh! It was nearly ten o'clock, and Jim had to get out to the Children's Hospital before he went to Oakland. Julia had a quick kiss, and was advised to take good care of herself. Then Jim was gone, and she could fling her arm across the table and sob as if her heart would break.

Julia cried for a long time. Then she stopped resolutely, and spent a long half hour in serious thought, her fingers absently tracing the threads of the tablecloth with a fork, her thoughts flying.

Presently she roused herself, telephoned Jim's chauffeur and the agent of the Pacific Avenue house, bathed her reddened eyes, and inspected her new furs, just home from the shop. Now and then her breast rose with a long sigh, but she did not cry again.

"I'll wear my new furs," she decided soberly. "Jim loves me to look pretty. And I *must* cheer up; he hates me to be blue! Who can I lunch with, to cheer up? Aunt Sanna! I'll get a cold chicken and some cake, and go out to The Alexander!"

So the outward signs of the storm were obliterated, and no one knew of the scar that Julia carried from that day in her heart. Only a tiny, tiny scar, but enough to remind her now and then with cold terror that even into her Paradise the serpent could thrust his head, enough to prove to her bitter satisfaction that there was already something that Jim's money could not buy.

The furnishing of the Pacific Avenue house proceeded apace—it was an eminently gratifying house to furnish, and Jim and Julia almost wished their labours not so light. All rugs looked well on those beautiful floors; all pictures were at their best against the dull rich tones of the walls. Did Mrs. Studdiford like the soft blue curtains in the library, or the dull gold, or the coffee-coloured tapestry? Mrs. Studdiford, an exquisite little figure of indecision, in a great Elizabethan chair of carved black oak, didn't really know; they were all so beautiful! She wondered why the blue wouldn't be lovely in the breakfast room, if they used the gold here? Then she wouldn't use the English cretonne in the breakfast room? Oh, yes, of course, she had forgotten the English cretonne!

At last it was all done, from the two stained little Roman marble benches outside the front door, to the monogrammed sheets in the attic cedar closet. The drawing-room had its grand piano, its great mahogany davenport facing the fire, its rich dark rugs, its subdued gleam of copper and crystal, dull blue china and bright enamel. The little reception room was gay with yellow-gold silk and teakwood; Jim's library was severely handsome with its dark leather chairs and rows of dark leather bindings. A dozen guests could sit about the long oak table in the dining-room; the great sideboard with its black oak cupids and satyrs, and its enormous claw feet, struck perhaps the only pretentious note in the house. A wide-lipped bowl, in clear yellow glass, held rosy pippins or sprawling purple grapes on the table in the window, the sideboard carried old jugs and flagons in blackened silver or dull pottery.

Upstairs the sunny perfection of the bedrooms was not marred by the need of so much as a cake of violet soap. Julia revelled in details here: flowers in the bedrooms must match the hangings; there must be so many fringed towels and so many plain, in each bathroom. She amused as well as edified Jim with her sedate assurance in the matter of engaging maids; her cheeks would grow very pink when interviews were afoot, but she never lost her air of calm.

"We are as good as they are," said Julia, "but how hard it is to remember it when you are talking to them!"

Presently Foo Ting was established supreme in the kitchen, Lizzie secured as waitress, and Ellie, Lizzie's sister, engaged to do upstairs work. Chadwick, Jim's chauffeur, was accustomed occasionally to enact also the part of valet, so that it was with a real luxury of service that the young Studdifords settled down for the winter.

Julia had anticipated this settling as preceding a time of quiet, when she and Jim should loiter over their snug little dinners, should come to know the comforts of their own chairs, at each side of the library fire, and laugh and cry over some old book, or talk and dream while they stared into the coals. The months were racing about to her first wedding anniversary, yet she felt that she really knew Jim only in a certain superficial, holiday sense—she knew what cocktail he liked best, of course, and what seats in the theatre; she was quite sure of the effect of her own beauty upon him. But she longed for the real Jim, the soul that was hidden somewhere under his gay mask, under the trim, cleanshaven, smiling face. When there was less confusion, less laughing and interrupting and going about, then she would find her husband, Julia thought, and they would have long silent hours together in which to build the foundation of their life.

Her beautiful earnest face came to have a somewhat strained and wistful look, as the weeks fled past without bringing the quiet, empty time for which she longed. All about her now stretched the glittering spokes of the city's great social wheel, every mail brought her a flood of notes, every quarter hour summoned her to the telephone, every fraction of the day had its appointed pleasure. Julia must swiftly eliminate from her life much of the rich feminine tradition of housewifery; it was not for her to darn her husband's hose, to set exquisite patches in thinning table linen, to gather flowers for jars and vases. Julia never saw Jim's clothing except when he was wearing it, the table linen was Ellie's affair, and Lizzie had the entire lower floor bright and fragrant with fresh flowers before Jim and Julia came down to breakfast. Young Mrs. Studdiford found herself readily assuming the society woman's dry, brief mannerisms. Jim used to grin sometimes when he heard her at the telephone:

"Oh, that would be charming, Mrs. Babcock," Julia would say, "if you'll let me run away at three, for I must positively keep an appointment with Carroll at three, if I'm to have my gown for dear Mrs. Morton's bal masque Friday night. And if I'm just a tiny bit late you won't be cross? For we all do German at twelve now, you know, and it *will* run over the hour! Oh, you're very sweet! Oh, no, Mrs. Talcott spoke to me about it, but we can't—we're both *so* sorry, but this week seems to be just *full*—no, she said that, but I told her that next week was just as bad, so she's to let me know about the week after. Oh, I know she is. And I *did* want to give her a little tea, but there doesn't seem to be a *moment*! I think perhaps I'll ask Mrs. Castle to let us dine with her some other time, and give Betty a little dinner Monday—"

And so on and on, in the quick harassed voice of one who must meet obligations.

"You're a great social success, Ju," Jim said, smiling, one morning.

Julia made a little grimace over her letters.

"Oh, come off, now!" her husband railed good-naturedly. "You know you love it. You know you like to dress up and trot about with me and be admired!"

"I like to trot about with you," Julia conceded, sighing in spite of her smile. "But I get very tired of dinners. Some other woman gets you, and some other woman's husband gets me, and we say such *flat* things, about motor cars, or the theatre—nothing friendly or intimate or interesting!"

"Wait until you know them all better, Ju. Besides, you couldn't get intimate at a dinner, very well. Besides"—Jim defended the institutions of his class—"you didn't look very gay when young Jo Coutts seemed inclined to get very friendly at dinner the other night!"

"Jo Coutts was drunk," Julia asserted briefly. "As they very often are," she added severely. "Not raging drunk, but just silly, or sentimental and important, you know."

"I know," Jim laughed.

"And it makes me furious!" Julia said. "As for knowing them better, they aren't one bit more interesting when they're old friends. They're more familiar, I admit that, but all this cheeky yelling back and forth isn't interesting—it's just tiresome! 'I'm holding your husband's hand, Alice!' 'All right, then I'm going to kiss your husband!'" Her voice rose in mimicry. "And then Kenneth Roberts tells some little shady story, and every one screams, and every one goes on telling it over and over! Why, that little silly four-line verse Conrad Kent had last night—every one in the room had to learn it by heart and say it six hundred times before we were done with it!"

"You're a cynic, woman," Jim said, kissing his wife, who by this time had come around to his chair. "It's all too easy for you, that's the trouble! They've accepted you with open arms; you're the rage! You ought to have been kept for a while on the anxious seat, like the poor Groves, and Mrs. McCann; then you'd appreciate High Sassiety!"

"Well, I wouldn't make myself ridiculous and pathetic like the Groves, trying to burst into society, and giving people a chance to snub me!" Julia said thoughtfully. "Never mind," she added, "next month Lent begins, and then there must be some let-up!"

However, Lent had only begun when the Studdifords made a flying trip to Honolulu, where Jim had a patient. The great liner was fascinating to Julia, and, as usual, her beauty and charm, and the famous young surgeon's unostentatious bigness, made them friends on all sides, so that the life of cocktail mixing and card playing and gossip went on as merrily as it had in San Francisco. Julia could not spend the empty days staring dreamily out at the rolling green Pacific; every man on board was anxious to improve her acquaintance, from the Captain to the seventeen-year-old little English lad who was going out to his father in India, and to not one of them did it ever occur that lovely little Mrs. Studdiford might prefer to be left alone.

But the sea air shook Julia into splendid health and energy, and she was her sweetest self in Honolulu; she and Jim both seemed to recapture here some of the exquisite tenderness of their honeymoon a year ago. Neither would admit that there had been any drifting apart, they had never been less than lovers, yet now they experienced the delights of a reconciliation. Julia, in her delicate linens and thin embroidered pongees, with a filmy parasol shading her bright hair, seemed more wonderful than ever before, and lovely Hawaii was a setting for one of their happiest times together.

On the boat, coming home, however, there occurred a little incident that darkened Julia's sky for a long time to come. On the very day of starting she and Jim, with some other returning San Franciscans, were standing, a laughing group on the deck, when a dark, handsome young woman came forward from a nearby cabin doorway, and held out her hand.

"Do you remember me, Julia?" said she, smiling.

Julia, whose white frock was draped with a dozen ropes of brilliant flowers, and who looked like a little May Queen in her radiant bloom, looked at the newcomer for a few moments, and then said, with a clearing face:

"Hannah! Of course I know you. Mrs. Palmer, may I present Doctor Studdiford?"

Jim smilingly shook hands, and as the rest of the group melted away, Mrs. Palmer explained that her husband's business was in Manila, but she was bringing up her two little children to visit her parents in Oakland.

"She's extremely pretty," Jim said, when he and Julia were alone in their luxurious stateroom. "Who is she?"

"I don't know why I supposed you knew that she is one of Mark's sisters," Julia said, colouring. "I saw something of them all, after—afterward, you know."

"Oh!" Jim's face, which he chanced to be washing, also grew red; he scowled as he plunged it again into the towel. Julia proceeded with her own lunch toilet in silence, humming a little now and then, but the brightness was gone from the day for her; the swift-flying green water outside the window had turned to lead, the immaculate little apartment was bleak and bare. Jim did not speak as they went down to lunch, nor was he himself when they met again, after a game of auction, at dinner. In fact, this marked Julia's first acquaintance with a new side of his character.

For Jim's sunny nature was balanced by an occasional mood so dark as to make him a different man while it lasted. Barbara had once lightly hinted this to Julia—"Jim was glooming terribly, and did nothing but snarl"—and Miss Toland had confirmed the hint when she asked him, at Christmas dinner, when he and Julia had been eight months man and wife: "Well, Jim, never a blue devil once, eh?"

"Never a one. Aunt Sanna!" Jim had responded gayly.

"What should he have blue devils about?" Julia had demanded on this occasion, presenting herself indignantly to them, and looking in her black velvet and white lace like a round-eyed child.

She thought of that happy moment this afternoon, with a little chill at her heart. For there was no doubt that Jim had blue devils now. When she came back to her stateroom at six o'clock, he was already there, flung across the bed, his arms locked under his head, his sombre eyes on the ceiling, where green water-lights were playing.

"Jim, don't you feel well, dear?"

"Perfectly well, thank you!" Jim said coldly.

Slightly angered by his tone, Julia fell silent, busied herself with her brushes, hooked on a gown of demure cherry colour and gray, caught up a great silky scarf.

"Anything I can do for you, Jim?" she said then, politely.

"Just—*let me alone*!" Jim answered, without stirring.

Hurt to the quick, and with sudden colour in her face, Julia left the room. She held her head high, but she felt almost a little sick with the shock. Five minutes later she was the centre of a chattering group on the deck. A milky twilight held the sea, the skyline was no longer to be discerned in the opal spaces all about them, the ship moved over a vast plain of pearl-coloured smooth waters. Where staterooms were lighted, long fingers of rosy brightness fell across the deck; here and there in the shelter of a bit of wall were dark blots that were passengers, wrapped and reclining, and unrecognizable in the gloom.

Julia and a young man named Manners began to pace the deck. Mr. Manners was a poet, and absorbed in the fascinating study of his own personality, but he served Julia's need just now, and never noticed her abstraction and indifference. He described to Julia the birth of his own soul, when he was what the world considered only a clumsy, unthinking lad of seventeen, and Julia listened as a pain-racked fever patient might listen with vague distress to the noise of distant hammers.

Presently they were all at dinner; soup, but no Jim; fish, but no Jim. Here was Jim at last, pale, freshly shaven, slipping into his place with a muttered apology and averted eyes. With a sense of impending calamity upon her, Julia struggled through her dinner; after a while she found herself holding cards, under a bright light; after a while again, she reached her stateroom.

Julia turned up the light. The room was close and empty, littered with the evidences of Jim's hasty toilet. She opened a window, and the sweet salt air filtered in, infinitely soothing and refreshing. She began to go about the room, picking up Jim's clothes, and putting the place in order. Once or twice her face twitched with pain, and once she stopped and pressed Jim's coat to her heart with both hands, as if to stop a wound, but she did not cry, and presently began her usual preparations for bed in her usual careful fashion. The cherry-coloured gown had been put away, and Julia, in an embroidered white kimono almost stiff enough to stand alone, was putting her rings into their little cases when Jim came in. She looked at him over her shoulder.

"Where have you been, Jim?" she asked quietly, noticing his white face, his tumbled hair, and a certain disorder in his appearance. Jim did not answer, and after a puzzled moment Julia repeated her question.

"Up on deck," Jim said, a bitter burst of words breaking through his ugly silence. He dropped into a chair, and put his head in his hands.

Julia watched him for a few moments in silence, while she went on with her preparations. She wound her little watch and put it under her pillow; she folded the counterpanes neatly back from both beds, and got out her slippers. Then she sat down to put trees into the little satin slippers she had been wearing, and carried them to the closet.

Suddenly Jim sat up, dropped his hands, and stared at her haggardly.

"Julia," said he hoarsely, "I've been up there thinking—I'm going mad, I guess—"

He stopped, and there was silence. Julia stood still, looking at him.

"Tell me," Jim said, "was it Mark?"

The hideous suddenness of it struck Julia like a bodily blow; she stood as if she had been turned to ice. A great weight seemed to seize her limbs, a sickening vertigo attacked her. She had a suffocating sense that time was passing, that ages were going by in that bright, glaring room, with the sea air coming in a shuttered window, and the two beds, with their smooth white pillows, so neatly turned down—Still, she could not speak—not yet.

"Yes, it was Mark," she said tonelessly and gently, after a long silence. "I thought you knew."

"Oh, my God!" Jim said, choking. He flung his hands madly in the air and got on his feet. Then, as if ashamed, through all the boiling surge of his emotions, at this loss of control, he rammed his hands into the pockets of his light overcoat, and began to pace the room. "You—you—you!" he said, in a sort of wail, and in another moment, muttering some incoherency about air, he had snatched up his cap and was gone again.

Julia slowly crossed the room, and sat down on her bed. She felt as a person who had swallowed a dose of poison might feel: agonies were soon to begin that would drive the life from her body, but she could not feel them yet. Instead she felt tired, tired beyond all bearing, and the lights hurt her eyes. She slipped her kimono from her, stepped out of her slippers, and plunged the room into utter darkness. Like a tired child she crept into bed, and with a great sigh dropped her head on the pillow.

The ship plowed on, its great lights cutting a steady course over the black water, its whole bulk quivering to the heartbeat of the mighty engines; whispered good-nights and laughing good-nights were said in the narrow, hot hallways. Lights went out in cabin after cabin. The decks were dark and deserted. Below stairs the world that never slept hummed like a beehive; squads of men were washing floors, laying tables; the kitchen was as hot and busy as at midday; the engine rooms were filled with silhouetted forms briskly coming and going. Up on one of the dark decks, with the soft mist blowing in his face, Jim spent the long night, his folded arms resting on the rail, his sombre eyes following the silent rush of waters, and in her cabin Julia lay wide awake and battling with despair.

She had thought the old dim horror over and done with. Now she knew it never would be that; now she knew there was no escape. The happy little castle she had built for herself fell about her like a house of cards; she was dishonoured, she was abased, she was powerless. In telling Jim her whole history, on that terrible night at the settlement house, she had flung down her arms; there was no new extenuating fact to add to the story; it was all stale and unchangeable; it must stand before their eyes forever, a hideous fact. And it seemed to Julia, tossing restlessly in the dark, that a thousand sleeping menaces rose now to terrify her. Perhaps Hannah Palmer knew! Julia's breath stopped, her whole body shook with terror. And if Hannah, why not others? A letter of Mark's to some one—to any one— might be in existence now, waiting its hour to appear, and to disgrace her, and Jim, and all who loved them!

And was it for this, she asked herself bitterly, that she had so risen from the past, so studied and struggled and aspired? Had she been mad all these years to forget the danger in which she stood, to imagine that she had buried her tragedy too deep for discovery? Had she been mad to marry Jim, her dear, sweet, protecting old Jim, who was always so good to her?

But at the thought of him, and of her bitter need of him in this desolate hour, Julia fell to violent crying, and after her tears she drifted into a deep sleep, her lashes wet, and her breast occasionally rising with a sharp sigh as a child's might.

When she awakened, dawn was breaking, the level waste of the sea was pearl colour and rose under a slowly rising mist. Julia bathed and dressed, and went out to the deck, where, with a great plaid wrapped about her, she might watch the miracle of the birth of day. And as the warming rays of the sun enveloped her, and the newly washed decks dried under its touch, and as signs of life began to be heard all about, slamming doors and gay greetings, laughter and the crisp echoes of feet, hope and self-confidence crept again into her heart. She was young, after all, and pretty, and Jim's very agony of jealousy only proved that he loved her. She had never deceived him, he could not accuse her of one second's weakness there. He had only had a sudden, terrible revelation of the truth he had known so long; it could not affect him permanently.

"Going down?" said a voice gayly.

Julia turned to smile upon a group of cheerful acquaintances.

"Thinking about it," she smiled.

"Where's Himself?" somebody asked.

"Still asleep—the lazy bones!" Julia answered calmly. They all went downstairs together, and Julia was perhaps a little ashamed to find the odours of coffee and bacon delightful, and to enjoy her breakfast.

Afterward she went straight to her room, not at all surprised to find Jim there, flung, dressed as he was, across his bed, and breathing heavily. Julia studied him for a moment in silence. Then she set about the somewhat difficult task of rousing him, quite her capable wifely little self when there was something she could do for him.

"Jim! You'll have to get these damp things off, dear! Come, Jim, you can't sleep this way. Wake up, Jim!"

Drowsily, heavily, he consented to be partially undressed, and covered with a warm rug. Julia grew quite breathless over her exertions, tucked him in carefully.

"I'm going to tell the chambermaid not to come in until I ring, Jim. But shall I send you in a cup of coffee?"

"Ha!" Jim said, already asleep.

"Do you want some coffee, Jim?"

"No—no coffee!"

Julia tiptoed about the room a moment more, took her little sewing basket and a new magazine, and giving a departing look at her husband, found his eyes wide open and watching her. Instantly a rush of tears pressed behind her eyelids, and she felt herself grow weak and confused.

"Thank you for fixing me up so nicely, darling," Jim said meekly.

"Oh, you're welcome!" Julia answered, with a desperate effort to appear calm.

"Will you kiss me, Julie?" Jim pursued, and a second later she was on her knees beside him, their arms were locked together, and their lips met as if they had never kissed each other before.

"You little angel," Jim said, "what a beast I am! As if life hadn't been hard enough for you without my adding to it! Oh, but what a night I've had! And you'll forgive me, won't you, sweetheart, for I *love* you so?"

Julia put her face down and cried stormily, her wet face pressed against his, his arms holding her close. After a while, when the sobs lessened, they began to talk together, and then laugh together in the exquisite relief of being reconciled. Then Jim went to sleep, and Julia sat beside him, his hand in hers, her eyes idly following the play of broken bright lights that quivered on the wall.

She leaned back in her big chair, feeling weary and spent, broken, but utterly at peace. From that hour life was changed to her, and she dimly felt the change, accepted it as stoically as an Indian might the loss of a limb, and adjusted herself to all it implied. If Jim was a little less her god, he was still hers, hers in some new relationship that appealed to what was protective and maternal in her. And if the burden of her secret had grown inconceivably heavy for her to bear, she knew by some instinct that this burst of jealous frenzy had somehow lightened its weight for Jim; she, not he, would henceforth pay the price.

"And life isn't easy and gay, say what you will," thought Julia philosophically. "There is no use grumbling and groaning, and saying to yourself, 'Oh, if only it wasn't just this or that thing worrying me!' for there is always this or that. Kennedy and Bab think I am the most fortunate girl in the world, and yet, to be able to go back ten years, and live a few weeks over again, I'd give up everything I have, even Jim. Just to start *square*! Just to feel that wretched thing wasn't there like a layer of mud under everything I do, making it a farce for me to talk of uplifting girls by settlement work, as people are eternally making me talk! Or if only every one *knew* it, it would be easier, for then I would feel at least that I stood on my own feet! But now, of course, that's impossible, on Jim's account. What a horrible scandal it would be, what a horrible thing it *is*, that any girl can cloud her own life in this way!

"As for boys, I suppose mighty few of them are pure by the time they're through college, by the time they're through High School, perhaps! It's all queer, for that involves girls and women, too, thousands of them! And how absurd it would be to bring such a charge as this against a man, ten years after it happened, when he was married and a respectable citizen!

"Well, society is very queer; civilization hasn't got very far; sometimes I think virtue is a good deal of an accident, and that people take themselves pretty seriously!" And so musing, Julia dozed, and wakened, and dozed again. But in her heart had been sowed the seed that was never to be uprooted, the little seed of doubt: doubt of the social structure, doubt of its grave authorities, its awe-inspired interpreters. What were the mummers all so busy about and how little their mummery mattered! This shall be permitted, this shall not be permitted; what is in your heart and brain concerns us not at all; where your soul spends its solitudes is not our affair; so that you keep a certain surface smoothness, so that you dress and talk and spend as we bid you, you—for such time as we please—shall be one of us!

CHAPTER III

Nevertheless, the young Studdifords, upon their return to San Francisco, entered heartily upon the social joys of the hour. Barbara had been only waiting their arrival to demurely announce her engagement, and Julia's delight immediately took the form of dinners and theatre parties for the handsome Miss Toland and her fiance. A new and softened sweetness marked Barbara in these days; she was more gentle and more charming than she had ever been before. Captain Edward Francis Humphry Gunther Fox was an officer in the English army, a blond, silent man of forty, with kind eyes and a delightfully modulated voice. He had a comfortable private income, a "place" in Oxfordshire, an uncle, young and healthy to be sure, but still a lord, and an older sister who had married a lord, so that his credentials were unexceptionable, and Mrs. Toland was nearly as happy as her daughter was.

"It's curious," said Barbara to Julia, in one of their first hours alone, "but there *is* a distinction and an excitement about getting engaged, and you enjoy it just as much at thirty as at twenty—perhaps more. People—or persons, as Francis says—who have never paid me any attention before, are flocking to the front now with presents and good wishes, and some who never have seen Captain Fox congratulate me—it amounts to congratulation—as if *any* marriage were better than none!"

"Well, there is a something about marriage," Julia admitted; "you may not have any reason for feeling so, but you *do* feel superior, 'way down in your secret heart! And yet, Babbie," and a little shadow darkened her bright face, "and yet, once you *are* married, you see a sort of—well, a sort of uncompromising brightness about girlhood, too! When I go out to The Alexander now, and remember my old busy days there, and walking to chapel with Aunt Sanna, in the fresh, early mornings—I don't know—it makes me almost a little sad!"

"Don't speak of it," said Barbara. "When I think of leaving Dad, and home, and going off to England, and having to make friends of awful women with high cheek bones, and mats of crimps coming down to their eyebrows, it scares me to death!"

And both girls laughed gayly. They were having tea in Julia's drawing-room on a cold bright afternoon in May.

"I'll miss Dad most," pursued Barbara seriously. "Mother's so much with Ted now, anyway." She frowned at the fire. "Mother's curious, Ju," she added presently. "Every one says she's an ideal mother, and so on, and I suppose she is, but—"

"You're more like your father, anyway," Julia suggested in the pause.

"It's not only that," said Barbara slowly, "but Mother has never been in sympathy with any one of us! Ned deceived her, Sally deceived her, Theodora went deliberately against her advice, and broke her heart, and Con and Jane don't really respect her opinion at all! I'm the oldest, her first born—"

"And she loves you dearly," Julia said soothingly.

"Used to Ju, when I was a baby. And loves me theoretically now. But she has taken my not marrying to heart much more than the curious marriages Ned and the girls have made! Hints about old maids, and stories about her own popularity as a girl, regardless of the fact that no one wanted me—"

"Oh, Babbie!"

"Well, no one did!" Barbara laughed a little dryly. "Why, not two months ago," she went on, "that little sprig of a Paul Smith called on Con, and Mother engineered me out of the room, and said something laughingly to Richie and Ted about not wanting to stand in Con's way, 'one old maid was enough in a family!'"

"Maddening! Yes, I know," Julia said, laughing and shaking her head. "I've heard her a hundred times!"

"Of course it's all love and kisses, now," Barbara added, "and Francis is a bold, big thief, and how can she give up her dear big girl—"

"Oh, Barbara, don't be bitter!"

"Well," Barbara flung her head back as if she tossed the subject aside, "I suppose I am bitter! And why you're not, Ju, I can't understand, for you never had one tenth the chance I did!"

"No," Julia assented gravely, "I never did. If my mother had kept me with her—and she could have done it—if she hadn't left my father—he loved me so—it would all have been different. Mothers are strange, Babby, they have so much power—or seem to! It seems to me that one could do so much to straighten things out for the poor little baby brains; this is worth while, and this isn't worth while, and so on! Suppose"—Julia poured herself a fresh cup of tea, and leaned back comfortably in her chair—"suppose you had young daughters, Bab," said she, "what would you do, differently from your mother, I mean?"

"Oh, I don't know!" Barbara said, "only it seems funny that mothers can't help their daughters more. Half my life is lived now, probably, yet Mother goes right on theorizing, she—she doesn't get down to *facts*, somehow! I don't know—"

"It all comes down to this," Julia said briskly, as Barbara's voice trailed into silence, "sitting around and waiting for some one to ask her to marry him is not a sufficiently absorbing life work for the average young woman!"

"She isn't expected to do anything else," Barbara added, "except—attract. And it isn't as if she could be deciding in her own mind about it; the decision is in *his* mind: if he chooses he can ask her; if he doesn't, all right! It's a *shame*—it's a shame, I say, not to give her a more dignified existence than that!"

"Yes, but, Bab, your mother couldn't have put you into a shop to sell ribbons, or made a telephone girl of you!"

"No; my brothers didn't sell ribbons, or go on a telephone board, either. But I don't see why I shouldn't have studied medicine, like Jim and Richie, or gone into the office at the works in Yolo City, like Ned."

"Yes, but, Babby, you've no leaning toward medicine!"

"Well, then, something else, just as Jim would have done something else, in that case! Office hours and responsibility, and meeting of men in some other than a social way. You and I have somehow dragged a solution out of it, Julie: we are happy in spite of all the blundering and stumbling, but I've not got my Mother to thank for it, and neither have you!"

"No, neither have I!" Julia said, with a long sigh, and for a few moments they both watched the coals in silence. The room was quite dark now; the firelight winked like a drowsy eye; here and there the gold of a picture frame or the smooth curve of a bit of copper or brassware twinkled. The windows showed opaque squares of dull gray; elsewhere was only heavy shadow, except where Barbara's white gown made a spot of dull relief in the gloom, and Julia's slipper buckles caught the light. A great jar of lilacs, somewhere in the room, sent out a subtle and delicious scent.

"Funny world, isn't it, Julie?"

"Oh, *funny*!" Julia put out her hand, and met Barbara's, and their fingers pressed. "Nothing better in it, Barbara, than a friend like you!" she said affectionately.

"That's what I was thinking," said Barbara.

The Studdifords went to San Mateo after the wedding, and Julia, who had taken herself seriously in hand, entered upon the social life of the summer with a perfectly simulated zest. She rode and drove, played golf and tennis and polo, gossiped and spent hours at bridge, she went tirelessly from luncheon to tea, from dinner to supper party, and when Jim was detained in town, she went without him; a little piece of self-reliance that pleased him very much. If society was not extremely popular with Julia, Julia was very popular with society; her demure beauty made her conspicuous wherever she went, and in July, prominent in some theatricals at the clubhouse, she earned all honours before her.

Julia found the theatricals perilously delightful; the grease paint and the ornate costume seemed like old friends; she was intoxicated and enchanted by the applause. For several days after her most successful performance she was thoughtful: what if she had never joined the "Amazon" caste, never gone to Sausalito, followed naturally in the footsteps of Connie Girard and Rose Ransome? She might have been a great actress; she would have been a great beauty.

San Mateo, frankly, bored her, although she could not but admire the beautiful old place, the lovely homes set in enchanting old gardens, the lawns and drives stretching under an endless vista of superb oaks. There, alone with Jim, in a little cottage—ah, there would have been nothing boring about that!

But the Hardesty cottage never seemed like home to her, they had rented the big, shingled brown house for only three months, and Jim was anxious that she should not tire herself with altering the arrangement of furniture and curtains for so casual a tenancy. The Hardesty's pictures looked down from the wall, their chairs were unfriendly, their books under lock and key. Not a lamp, not a cup or saucer was familiar to Julia; she felt uncomfortable in giving dinner parties with "H" on the silver knives and forks; she never liked the look of the Hardesty linen. Life seemed unreal in the "Cottage"; she seemed to be pushed further and further away from reassuring contact with the homely realities of love and companionship; chattering people were always about her, pianoplayers were rippling out the waltz from "The Merry Widow," ice was clinking in cocktail shakers, the air was scented with cigarettes, with the powder and perfumery of women. She and Jim dined alone not oftener than once a week, and their dinner was never finished before friendly feet crisped on the gravel curve of the drive, and friendly invaders appeared to invite them to do something amusing: to play cards, to take long spins in motor cars, or to spend an idle hour or two at the club. Sometimes they were separated, and Julia would come in, chilled and tired after a long drive, to find Jim ahead of her, already sound asleep. Sometimes she left him smoking with some casual guest, and fell asleep long before the voices downstairs subsided. Even if they went upstairs together, both were tired; there was neither time nor inclination for confidences, for long and leisurely talk.

"Happy?" Jim said to his wife one day, when Julia, looking the picture of happiness, had come downstairs to join him for some expedition.

"Happy enough," Julia said, with her grave smile. She took the deep wicker chair next his, on the porch, and sat looking down the curve of the drive to the roadway beyond a screen of trees.

"Heavenly afternoon," she said. "Just what are we doing?"

"Well, as near as I got it from Greg," Jim informed her a little uncertainly, "we go first to his place, and then split up into about three cars there; Mrs. Peter and Mrs. Billings will take the eats, Peter will have a whole hamper of cocktails and things, and we go up to the ridge for a sort of English nursery tea, I think."

"Doing it all ourselves?" Julia suggested, brightening.

"Well, practically. Although Greg's cook is going ahead with a couple of maids in the Peters' car. They're going to broil trout or something; anyway, I know Greg has been having fits about seeing that enough plates go, and so on. I know Paula Billings is taking something frozen—"

"Oh, Lord, what a fuss and what a mess!" Julia said ungratefully.

"Well, you know how the Peters always do things. And then, after tea, if this glorious weather holds, we'll send the maids and the hampers home, and all go on down to Fernand's."

"Fernand's! Forty miles, Jim?"

"Oh, why not? If we're having a good time?"

"Well, I hope Peter Vane and Alan Gregory keep sober, that's all!" Julia said. "The ride will be lovely, and it's a wonderful day. But Minna Vane always bores me so!"

"Why, you little cat!" Jim laughed, catching her hand as it hung loose over the arm of her chair.

"They've no brains," complained Julia seriously; "they were born doing this sort of thing, they think they like it! Buying—buying—buying—eating—dancing—rushing—rushing—rushing! It's no life at all! I'd rather pack a heavy basket, and lug it over a hot hill, and carry water half a mile, when I picnic, instead of rolling a few miles in a motor car, and then sitting on a nice camp-chair, and having a maid to pass me salads and ices and toast and broiled trout!"

"Well, if you would, I wouldn't!" Jim said good-naturedly.

"I wasn't born to this," Julia added thoughtfully; "my life has always been full of real things; perhaps that's the trouble. I think of all the things that aren't going right in the world, and I *can't* just turn my back on them, like a child—I get thinking of poor little clerks whose wives have consumption—"

"Oh, for heaven's sake!" Jim protested frowningly, biting the end from his cigar with a clip of firm white teeth.

"It isn't as if I had never been poor," Julia pursued uncertainly. "I know that there are times when a new gown or a paid bill actually would affect a girl's whole life! I think of those poor little girls at St. Anne's—"

"I would like to suggest," Jim said incisively, "that the less you let your mind run on those little girls from St. Anne's, the better for you! If you have no consideration for my feelings in this matter, Julie, for your own I should think you would consider such topics absolutely—well, absolutely in poor taste!"

Silence. Jim puffed on his cigar. Julia sat without stirring, feeling that every drop of blood in her body had rushed to her head. The muscles of her temples and throat ached, her eyes saw only a green-and-gold dazzle, her wet little hands gripped the arms of her chair.

"It is all very well to criticise these people," pursued Jim sententiously, after a long silence, "although they have all been kindness and graciousness itself to you! They may be shallow, they may be silly; I don't hold any brief for Minna Vane and Paula Billings. But I know that Minna is on the Hospital Board, and Paula a mighty kind-hearted, good little woman, and they don't sit around pulling long faces, and wishing they were living south of Market Street!"

Julia sat perfectly still. She could not have battled with the lump in her throat if life had depended upon her speaking. She felt her chest strain with a terrible rush of sobbing, but she held herself stiffly, and only prayed that her tears might be kept back until she was alone.

"Hello! Here's Greg," Jim said cheerfully, after another silence. And here, truly, was Alan Gregory, a red-faced, smooth-shaven young man, already slightly hilarious and odorous of drink, and very gallant to beautiful Mrs. Studdiford. A great silky veil must be tied over Julia's hat; sure she was warm enough? Might be late, might get cold, you know.

"Shall I get you your white coat, dear?" Jim asked solicitously.

"Oh, no, thank you, Jim!"

Then they were off, and Julia told herself that men and their wives often quarrelled this way; it was a common enough thing to have some woman announce, with a casual laugh, that she and her husband had had a "terrible scene," and "weren't speaking." Only, with Jim it seemed so different! It seemed so direfully, so hopelessly wrong!

She felt a hypocrite when they joined the others, and when she presently found herself laughing and talking with them all, even with Jim. And through the jolly afternoon and noisy evening she found herself watching her husband, when she could do so unobserved, with gravely analytical eyes. No barbed sentence of his could long affect her, for Julia had pondered and prayed too long over this matter to find any fresh distress in a reminder of it. Her natural simple honesty very soon adjusted the outraged sensibilities. But Jim could hurt himself with his wife, and this afternoon he had done so. Unconsciously Julia said to herself, over and over, "Oh, he should not have said that! That was not kind!"

Mrs. Vane had a great favour to ask the men of the party to-night. She proffered it somewhat doubtfully, like a spoiled child who is almost sure of being denied, yet risks its little charms in one more entreaty. She and Paula, yes, and Mrs. Jerome, and little Julia—wasn't that so, Julia?—wanted to see a roadhouse. No—no—no—not the sort of place where nice women went, but a regular roadhouse—oh, please, please, please! They had their veils to tie over their faces, and they would keep very unobtrusively in the background, and there was a man apiece and two men over to protect them.

"All the girls in town are doing it!" argued Mrs. Vane, "and they say it's perfectly killing! Dancing, you know, and singing. You have to keep your veil down, of course! Betty said they'd been three times!"

"Nothing doing," Jim said good-naturedly, shaking his head.

"Oh, now, don't say that, Doctor!" Mrs. Vane commanded animatedly; "it's too *mean*! Well, if you couldn't take us to the very worst, where *could* you take us—Hunter's?"

"Hunter's!" the three men echoed, laughing and exchanging glances.

"Well, where then?" the lady pursued.

"Look here, Min," said her husband uneasily, "there's nothing to it. And you girls might get insulted and mixed into something—"

"Oh, divine!" Mrs. Billings said; "now I *will* go!"

"White's, huh, Jim?" Greg suggested tentatively.

"White's?" Jim considered it, shook his head. "Nothing doing there, anyway!" was his verdict.

"Larry's, where the pretty window boxes are," suggested Mrs. Vane, hopeful eyes upon the judges. "Come on! *Oh, come on*! You see such flossy ladies getting out of motor cars in front of Larry's!"

"There's this about Larry's," Mr. Billings contributed; "we could get one of those side places, and then, if things got too hot, just step out on to the porch, d'ye see, and get the girls away with no fuss at all."

"That's so," Jim conceded; "but I'll be darned if I know why they want to do it. However—"

"However, you're all angels!" sang Mrs. Vane, and catching Julia about the waist, she began to waltz upon the pleasant meadow grass where they had just had their high tea. "Come on, everybody! We won't be at Fernand's until nearly night, then dinner, and then Larry's!"

"Mind now," growled one of the somewhat unwilling escort, "you girls keep your veils down. Nix on the front-page story to-morrow!"

"Oh, we'll behave!" Mrs. Billings assured him. And slipping an affectionate arm about Julia's waist, as they walked to the motor cars, she murmured: "My dear, there isn't one decent woman in the place! Isn't this fun!"

Julia did not answer. She got into the car and settled herself for the run; so much of the day at least would be pleasant. It was the close of a lovely summer afternoon, the long shadows of the trees lay ahead of them on the road, the sky was palest blue and palest pink, a flock of white baby clouds lay low against the eastern horizon. The warm air bore the clean good scent of wilting grass and hot pine sap. The car rolled along smoothly, its motion stirring the still air into a breeze. Mr. Billings, sitting next to Julia, began an interested disquisition upon the difficulties of breeding genuine, bat-eared, French bulldogs. Julia scarcely heard him, but she nodded now and then, and now and then her blue eyes met his; once she gratified him with a dreamy smile. This quite satisfied Morgan Billings, to whom it never occurred that Julia's thoughts might be on the beauties of the rolling landscape, and her smile for the first star that came prickling through the soft twilight.

And after a while some aching need of her soul grew less urgent, and some of the wistfulness left her face. She forgot the ideals that had come with her into her married life, and crushed down the conviction that Jim, like all men, liked his wife to slip into the kitchen and concoct some little sweet for his supper, even with an artist like Foo Ting at his command. She realized that when she declined old Mrs. Chickering's luncheon invitation for the mere pleasure of rushing home to have lunch with Jim, her only reward might be a disapproving: "My Lord! Julia, I hope you didn't offend Mrs. Chickering! She's been so decent to us!"

It was as if Julia, offering high interest on her marriage bond, had at last learned that one tenth of what she would pay would satisfy Jim. Feeling as she did that no demonstration on his part, no inclination to monopolize her, would do more than satisfy her longing to be all in all to him, it was not an easy lesson. For a while she could not believe that he knew his own happiness in the matter, and a dispassionate onlooker might have found infinitely pathetic the experimental temerity with which she told him that this invitation had been accepted, this social obligation incurred, this empty Sunday filled to overflowing with engagements.

And now Jim approved, and Julia had to hide in the depth of her hurt soul the fact that she had never dreamed he *could* approve. However tired, he liked to come home to the necessity of immediately assuming evening dress, and going out into the night again. He and Julia held a cheerful conversation between their dressing-rooms as they dressed; later they chattered eagerly enough in the limousine, Jim enthusiastic over his wife's gown, and risking a kiss on her bare shoulder when the car turned down a dark street. Jim, across a brilliant table, in a strange house, did not seem to Julia to belong to her at all; but it was almost as if he found his wife more fascinating when the eyes of outsiders were upon her, and admired Julia in a ballroom more than he did when they had the library and the lamplight to themselves, at home.

They would come home together late and silent. Ellie would come in to help her lovely mistress out of the spangled gown, to lift the glittering band from her bright hair. And because of Ellie, and because Jim usually was dressed and gone before she was up in the morning, Julia had a room to herself now. She would have much preferred to breakfast with her lord, but Jim himself forbade it.

"No, no, no, Ju! It's not necessary, and you're much better off in bed. That's the time for you to get a little extra rest. No human being can stand the whole season without making some rest up somehow! You'll see the girls begin to drop with nervous prostration in January; Barbara used to lose twenty pounds every winter. And I won't *have* you getting pale. Just take things easy in the morning, and sleep as late as you can!"

Julia accepted the verdict mildly. With the opening of her second winter in San Francisco's most exclusive set, she had tried to analyze the whole situation, honestly putting her prejudices on one side, and attempting to get her husband's point of view. It was the harder because she had hoped to be to Jim just what Kennedy Marbury was to Anthony, united by a thousand needs, little and big, by the memory of a thousand little comedies and tragedies. Kennedy, who worried about bills and who dreaded the coming of the new baby, could stop making a pie to administer punishment and a lecture to her oldest son, stop again to answer the telephone, stop again to kiss her daughter's little bumped nose, and yet find in her tired soul and body enough love and energy to put a pastry "A. M." on the top of her pie, to amuse the head of the house when he should cut into it that night.

But this mixture of the ridiculous and the sublime was not for Julia. And just as Kennedy had adjusted herself to the life of a poor man's wife, so Julia must adjust herself to her own so different destiny.

And adjust herself she did. Nobody dreamed of the thoughts that went on behind the beautiful blue eyes, nobody found little Mrs. Studdiford anything but charming. With that steadfast, serious resolution that had marked her all her life, Julia set herself to the study of gowns, of dinners, of small talk. She kept a slim little brown Social Register on her dressing-table, and pored over it at odd moments; she listened attentively to the chatter that went on all about her. She drew infinitely less satisfaction from the physical evidences of her success—her beauty, her wealth, her handsome husband, and her popularity—than any one of the women who envied her might have done, yet she did draw some satisfaction, loved her pretty gowns, the freedom of bared white neck and shoulders, the atmosphere of perfumed drawing-rooms and glittering dinner tables. She wrote long letters to Barbara, was a devoted godmother to Theodora Carleton's tiny son, loved to have Miss Toland with her for an occasional visit, and perhaps once a month went over to Sausalito, to spoil the old doctor with her affectionate attentions, hold long conferences with their mother on the subject of the girls' love affairs, and fall into deep talks with Richie—perhaps the happiest talks in her life, for Richie, whose mind and body had undergone for long years the exquisite discipline of pain, was delightfully unexpected in his views, and his whole lean, ungainly frame vibrated with the eager joy of expressing them.

Perhaps once a month, too, Julia went to see her own mother, calls which always left her definitely depressed. Emeline was becoming more and more crippled with rheumatism, the old grandmother was now the more brisk of the two. May's two younger girls, Muriel and Geraldine, were living there now, as Marguerite and Evelyn had done; awkward, dark, heavy-faced girls who attended the High School. Julia's astonishing rise in life had necessarily affected her relatives, but much less, she realized in utter sickness of spirit, than might have been imagined. She and Jim were paying for the schooling of two of May's boys, and a substantial check, sent to her mother monthly, supposedly covered the main expenses of the entire household. Besides this, Chess was working, and paying his mother something every week for board.

It had been Julia's first confident plan to move the family from the Mission entirely. There were lovely roomy flats in the Western Addition, or there were sunny houses out toward the end of Sutter Street, where her mother and grandmother would be infinitely more comfortable and more accessible. She was stunned when her grandmother flatly refused. Even her mother's approval of the plan was singularly wavering and half hearted. Mrs. Cox argued shrilly that they were poor folks, and poor folks were better off not trapesing all over the city, and Emeline added that Ma would feel lost without her backyard and her neighbours, to say nothing of the privilege of bundling up in a flat black bonnet and brown shawl, hot weather or cold, and trotting off to St. Charles's Church at all hours of the day and night.

"I don't care, Julie," Mrs. Page made her daughter exquisitely uncomfortable by saying very formally, "but there's no girl in God's world that wouldn't think of asking her mother to stay with her for a while—till things got settled, anyway. You haven't done it!"

"Well, I'll tell you, Mama—" Julia began, but Emeline interrupted her.

"You haven't done it, Julie, and let me tell you right now, it looks queer. I'm not the one that says it; every one says it. I don't want to force myself where I'm not—"

"But, Mama *dear*, we're only at the hotel now!" Julia protested, feeling a hypocrite.

"I see," said Emeline, "and I'm not good enough, of course. I couldn't meet your friends, of course!" She laughed heartily. "That's *good*!" she said appreciatively.

Julia used to flush angrily under these withering comments, at first; later, her poor little mother's attitude filled her only with a great pity. For Emeline was suffering a great deal now, and Julia longed to be able to take her with her to the Pacific Avenue house, if only to prove that its empty splendour held no particular advantages over the life on Shotwell Street, for Emeline. She was definitely better off in her mother's warm kitchen, gossiping and idling her days away, than she would have been limping aimlessly about in Julia's house, and catching glimpses of Julia only between the many claims of the daughter's day.

More than this, Jim would not hear of such a visit; it never even came to a discussion between husband and wife; he would have been frankly as much surprised as horrified at the idea. So Julia did what was left to her, for her mother: listened patiently to long complaints, paid bills, and supplemented Jim's generous cheque with many a gold piece pressed into her mother's hand or slipped into her grandmother's dreadful old shopping-bag. She carried off her young cousins to equip them with winter suits and sensible shoes, aware all the while that their high-heeled slippers and flimsy, cheap silk dresses, the bangles that they slipped over dirty little hands, and the fancy combs they pushed into their untidy hair, were infinitely more prized by them.

The Shotwell Street house was still close and stuffy, the bedrooms as dark and horrible as Julia remembered them, and no financial aid did more than temporarily soften the family's settled opinion that poor folks were poor folks, and predestined to money trouble. Julia knew that when the clothes she bought her cousins grew dirty they would not be cleaned; she knew that her grandmother had never taken a tub bath in her life and rather scorned the takers of tub baths; she knew that such a thing as the weekly washing of clothes, the transformation of dirty linen into piles of fragrant whiteness, never took place in the Shotwell Street house. Mrs. Cox indeed liked to keep a tub full of gray suds standing in the kitchen, and occasionally souse in it one of her calico wrappers, or a shirt waist belonging to the girls. These would be dried on a rope stretched across the kitchen, and sooner or later pressed with one of the sad irons that Julia remembered as far back as she remembered anything; rough-looking old irons, one with a broken handle, all with the figure seven stamped upon them with a mould. Mrs. Cox had several ironholders drifting about the kitchen, folds of dark cloth that had been so often wet and singed that the covering had split, and the folded newspaper inside showed its burned edges, but she never could find one when she wanted it, and usually improvised a new one from a grocery bag or the folds of her apron, and so burned her veined old knotted hands.

Julia came soon to see that her actual presence did them small good, and did herself real harm, and so, somewhat thankfully, began to confine her attentions more and more to mere financial assistance. She presently arranged for the best of medical care for her mother, even for a hospital stay, but her attitude grew more and more that of the noncommittal outsider, who helps without argument and disapproves without comment. Evelyn had made a great success of her dressmaking, but such aid as she could give must be given her sister, for Marguerite's early and ill-considered marriage had come to the usual point when, with an unreliable husband, constantly arriving and badly managed babies, and bitter poverty and want, she found herself much in the position of her mother, twenty years before. May was still living in Oakland, widowed. Her two sons were at home and working, and with a small income from rented rooms as well, the three and her youngest daughter, Regina, somehow managed to maintain the dreary cottage in which most of the children were born.

"They all give me a great big pain!" Evelyn said one day frankly, when Julia was at Madame Carroll's for a fitting, and the cousins—one standing in her French hat and exquisite underlinen, and the other kneeling, her gown severely black, big scissors in hand, and a pincushion dangling at her breast—were discussing the family. "Gran'ma isn't so bad, because she's old, but Aunt Emeline and Mama have a right to get next to themselves! Mama had a fit because I wouldn't take a flat over here, and have her and Regina with me; well, I could do it perfectly well; it isn't the money!" Evelyn stood up, took seven pins separately and rapidly from her mouth, and inserted them in the flimsy lining that dangled about Julia's arm. "You want this tight, but not too tight, don't you, Julie?" said she. "That can come in a little, still. No," she resumed aggrievedly, "but I board at a nice place on Fulton street; the Lancasters, the people that keep it, are just lovely. Mrs. Lancaster is so motherly and the girls are so jolly; my wash costs me a dollar a week; I belong to the library; I've got a lovely room; I go to the theatre when I want to; I buy the clothes I like, and why should I worry? I know the way Mama keeps house, and I've had enough of it!"

"It's awfully hard," Julia mused, "Marguerite's just doing the same thing over again. It's just discouraging!"

"Well, you got out of it, and I got out of it," Evelyn said briskly, "and they call it our luck! Luck? There ain't any such thing," she went on indignantly. "I'm going to New York for Madame next year—me, to New York, if you please, and stay at a good hotel, and put more than twenty thousand dollars into materials and imported wraps and scarfs and so on—is there any luck to that? There's ten years' slavery, that's what there is! How much do you suppose you'd have married Jim Studdiford if you hadn't kept yourself a little above the crowd, and worked away at the settlement house for years and years?" she demanded. "I can put a little hook in here, Ju, where the lace comes, to keep that in place for you!" she added, more quietly.

"Well, it's true!" Julia said, sighing. She looked with real admiration at the capable, black-clad figure, the clear-skinned, black-eyed face of Madame Carroll's chief assistant. "Why don't you ever come and have lunch with me, Evelyn?" she demanded affectionately.

"Oh, Lord, dearie!" Evelyn said, in her most professional way, as she pencilled a list of young Mrs. Studdiford's proportions on a printed card, "this season Madame has our lunches, and even our dinners, sent in—simply one rush! But some time I'd love to."

"You like your work, don't you, Evelyn?" Julia said curiously.

"You go tell Madame I'm ready for Mrs. Addison," Evelyn said capably to a small black-clad girl who answered her bell, "and then carry this to Minnie and tell her it's rush—don't drop the pins out. I love my work," she added, when she and Julia were alone again; "I'm crazy about it! The girls here are awfully nice, and some of the customers treat me simply swell—most of them do. This way, Julia. Christmas time we get more presents than you could shake a stick at!" said Evelyn, opening a door. "Good afternoon, Mrs. Addison, I'm all ready for you."

"That's a good girl!" the woman who was waiting in Carroll's handsome parlour said appreciatively; she recognized Julia. "Well, how do you do, Mrs. Studdiford?" she smiled, "so sorry not to see you on Saturday, you bad little thing!"

Julia gave her excuse. "You know Evelyn here is my cousin?" she said, in her quiet but uncompromising way, as she hooked her sables together.

"About eleven times removed!" Evelyn said cheerfully. "Right in here, please, Mrs. Addison! At the same time to-morrow, Mrs. Studdiford. Thank you, good-night."

"Good-night!" Julia said, smiling. For some reason she could not fathom, Evelyn never seemed willing to claim the full relationship; always assumed it to be but a hazy and distant connection. It was as if in her success the modiste wished to recognize no element but her own worth; no wealthy or influential relative could claim to have helped *her*! Julia always left her with a certain warmth at her heart. It was good to come in contact now and then with such self-confidence, such capability, such prosperity. "I could almost envy Evelyn!" thought Julia, spinning home in the twilight.

CHAPTER IV

The Studdifords, with some four hundred other San Francisco society folk, regarded the Browning dances as quite the most important of the winter's social affairs, and Julia, who thoroughly liked the host and the brilliant assembly, really enjoyed them more than the smaller and more select affairs. The Brownings were a beloved and revered institution; very few new faces appeared there from year to year, except the very choice of the annual crop of debutantes. Little Mrs. Studdiford had made a sensation when she first came, at her handsome husband's side, a year ago, her dazzling prettiness set off by the simplest of milk-white Paris gowns, her wonderful crown of hair wound about with pearls. Now she was a real favourite, and at the January ball, in her second winter in society, a score of admirers assured her that her gown was the prettiest in the room.

"That pleases you, doesn't it, Jim?" she smiled, as he put her into a red velvet armchair, at the end of the long ballroom, and dropped into a chair beside her.

"Well, it's true," Jim assured her, "and, what's more, you're the most beautiful woman in the room, too!"

"Oh, Jeemy! What a story! But go get your dances, dear, if we're not going to stay for supper. Here's Mrs. Thayer to amuse me," said Julia, as a magnificent old woman came toward her with a smile.

"Not dancing, dear?" said the dowager, as she sank heavily into the seat Jim left. "Whyn't you dancing with the other girls? I"—she panted and fanned, idly scanning the room—"I tell Brownie I don't know how he gets the men!" she added, "lots of 'em; supper brings 'em, probably! Whyn't you dancing, dear?"

"She's implying that her ankle was sprained," Jim grinned, departing. Julia dimpled. The dowager brought an approving eye to bear upon her.

"Well—well, you don't say so? Now that's very nice indeed," she said comfortably; "well, I declare! I hadn't heard a word of it—and you're glad, of course?"

"Oh, very glad!" Julia assured her, colouring.

"That's nice, too!" Mrs. Thayer rumbled on, her eyes beginning again to rove the room. "Fuss, of course, and lots of trouble, but you forget all that! Yes, I love children myself, used to be the most devoted mother alive, puttin' 'em to bed, and all that, yes, indeed!"

"You had two?" Julia hazarded. The dowager gave her a surprised glance.

"I, me dear? I had five—Rose there, that's Mrs. St. John, and Kate, you know her? Mrs. Willis, and my boy that's in Canada now, and the boy I lost, and Lillian—Lily we called her, she was only three. Diphtheria."

"Oh!" Julia said, shocked.

"Yes, indeed, I thought it would break Colonel Thayer's heart," pursued Mrs. Thayer, fanning regally, and watching the room. "She was the first—Lily would be nearly forty now! Look, Julia, who is that with Isabel Wallace? Who? Oh, yes, Mary Chauncey. See if you can see her husband anywhere. I'd give a good deal to know if she came with him!"

"Mrs. Thayer," said Julia presently, "how long have you been coming to the Brownings?"

"I? Oh, since they were started, child. There was a little group of us that used to dance round at each other's houses, then some of the men got together and formed a little club—Brownie was one of them. The Saunders used to come. Ella was about eighteen, and Sally and Anna Toland, and the Harts, and the Kirkwoods. Who's that with young Brice, Julia, me dear? Peter Coleman, is it?"

"Talking to Mr. Carter, yes, that's Mr. Coleman. He's a beautiful dancer," said Julia.

"Peter is? Yes, well, then, why don't you—But you're not dancing, of course," Mrs. Thayer said. "There's Gordon Jones and his wife! Why Brownie ever let them in I don't—Ah, Ella, how are you, dear?"

"Fine, thank you!" said the newcomer, a magnificent woman of perhaps forty, in a very beautiful gown. "How do you do, Mrs. Studdiford?" she added cordially, as she sat down. "Dancing, surely?"

"Now she's got the best reason in the world for not dancing," said old Mrs. Thayer, with a protective motion of her fan.

"Oh—so?" Miss Saunders said, after a quick look of interrogation. "Well, that's—dutiful, isn't it?" She raised her eyebrows, made a little grimace, and laughed.

"Now, Ella, don't ye say anything wicked!" Mrs. Thayer warned her, and the fan was used to tap Miss Saunders sharply on her smooth, big arm.

"Wicked!" Miss Saunders said negligently, watching the dancers, "I think it's fine. I always said I'd have ten. Is Jim pleased?"

"He's perfectly delighted—yes," Julia assented, suddenly feeling that this careless talk, in this bright, hot room, was not fair to the little one she already loved so dearly.

"Is that Mrs. Brock or Vera?" Mrs. Thayer asked. "I declare they look alike!"

"That's Alice," Ella answered, after a glance, "don't you know that blue silk? They've got the Hazzards with them."

"Gets worse every year, absolutely," the old lady declared, "doesn't it, Ella? Emily here?"

"No, she's wretched, poor kid. But Ken's here somewhere. There are the Geralds," Miss Saunders added, leaning toward the old woman and sinking her tone to a low murmur. "Have you heard about Mason Gerald and Paula Billings—oh, *haven't* you? Not about the car breaking down—*haven't* you? Well, my *dear*—"

Julia lost the story, and sat watching the room, a vague little smile curving her lips, her blue eyes moving idly to and fro. She saw Mrs. Toland come in with her two lovely daughters. Julia had had tea with them that afternoon at the hotel, where they would spend the night. The orchestra was silent just now, and the dancers were drifting about the room, a great brilliant circle. Some of the men were clapping their hands, all of them were laughing as they bent their sleek heads toward their partners, and all the girls were laughing, too, and talking animatedly as they raised wide-open eyes. Julia admired the gowns: shining pink and cloudy pink, blue with lace and blue with spangles, white alone, and white with every colour in the world; a yellow and black gown that was indescribably dashing, and a yellow and black gown that somehow looked very flat and dowdy. She noticed the Ripley pearls on Miss Dolly Ripley's scrawny little lean neck, and that charming Isabel Wallace danced a good deal with her own handsome, shy young brothers, and seemed eager that they should enjoy what was evidently their first Browning. She studied the old faces, the hard faces, the faded faces, the painted cheeks and powdered necks; she read the tragedy behind the drooping head of some debutante, the triumph in the high laugh of another. There was poor Connie Fox, desperately eager and amiable, dancing with the youngest men and the oldest men, glittering and jolly in her dingy blue silk; and Connie's mother, who was her chaperon, a little fluttering fool of a woman, nervously eager to ingratiate, and nervously afraid to intrude her company upon these demi-gods and goddesses; and Theodora Carleton, handsome in too low cut a gown, laughing with Alan Gregory, and aware, as every one in the room was aware, that her husband's first wife was also at the dance. The room grew warm, the air heavy with delicate perfumes. Men were mopping their faces; some of the debutantes looked like wilting roses; the faces of some of the older women were shining. It was midnight, the latest comers had arrived, the floor was well filled.

"I wonder if I will be doing this twenty years from now," thought Julia. "I wonder if my daughter will come to the Brownings, then?"

"... which I call disgraceful, don't you, Mrs. Studdiford?" asked Miss Saunders suddenly.

"I beg your pardon!" Julia said, startled into attention, "I didn't hear you!"

"I know you didn't," the other said, laughing, "nevertheless, it was a low trick," she added to Mrs. Thayer, "and Leila Orvis can wait a long time before she makes the peace with *me*! Charity's all very well, but when it comes to palming off girls like that upon your friends, it's just a little too much!"

"How's it happen ye didn't ask the girl for any references, me dear?" asked Mrs. Thayer.

"Because Leila told me she knew all about her!" snapped Miss Saunders.

"What was she, a waitress?" Julia asked, amused.

"No, she was nothing!" Miss Saunders said in high scorn; "she'd had no training whatever—not that I mind *that*. She was simply supposed to help with the pantry work and make herself generally useful. Well, one day Carrie, a maid Mother's had for *years*, told Mother that something this Ada had said she fancied Ada had been in some sort of reform school—imagine! Of course poor Mother collapsed, and Emily telephoned for me—the kid always rises to an emergency, I will say that. So I rushed home, and got the whole story out of Ada in five minutes. At first she cried a good deal, and pretended it was an orphans' home; orphans' home—ha! Finally I scared her into admitting that it was a place just for girls of her sort—"

"Fancy!" said Mrs. Thayer, fanning. Julia had grown a little pale.

"What did you do, Miss Saunders?" said she.

"Do? I sent her packing, of course!" said that lady, smiling as she bowed to an acquaintance across the room. "I told her to go straight back to Mrs. Orvis, and say I sent her. However, she didn't, for I telephoned Leila at once—Lucy Bacon is trying to bow to you, Mrs. Studdiford—over there, with your husband!"

"I wonder where she did go?" pursued Julia.

"I really have no idea!" Miss Saunders said.

"You may be sure she knew just where to go, a creature like that!" old Mrs. Thayer said wisely. "How de do, Peter, Auntie here?" she called to a smiling man who went by.

"Oh, she wouldn't go utterly bad," Julia protested; "you can't tell, she may have been decent for years. It may have been years ago—"

"Still, me dear," old Mrs. Thayer said comfortably, "one doesn't like the idea—one can't overlook that, ye know."

"Of course, it's too bad," Miss Saunders added briskly, "and it's a great pity, and things ought to be different from what they are, and all *that*; but at the same time you couldn't have a girl like that in the house, now could you?"

"Oh, yes, I could!" said Julia, scarlet cheeked, "I was just thinking how glad I would be to give her a trial!"

She stopped because Jim, very handsome in evening dress and with his pretty partner beside him, had come up to them.

"Tired, dear?" Jim said, smiling approval of the little figure in white lace, and the earnest eyes under loosened bright hair.

"Just about time you came up, Jim!" Ella Saunders said cheerfully, "here's your wife championing the cause of unfortunate girls—*she* wouldn't care what they'd done, she'd take them right into her home!"

"And very sweet and nice of her," Mrs. Thayer observed, with a consolatory pat on Julia's arm, "only it isn't quite practical, me dear, is it, Jim?"

"Julia'd like to take in every cat and dog and beggar and newsboy she sees," said Jim, with his bright smile. But Julia knew he was not pleased. "Do you want to come speak to Mother and the girls, dear, before I take you home?" he added, offering his arm. Julia stood up and said her good-nights, and crossed the room, a slender and most captivating little figure, at his side. It was not until she was bundled into furs and in the motor car that she could say, with an appealing hand on his arm:

"Don't blame me, Jimmy. I didn't start that topic. Miss Saunders happened to tell of a poor girl who—"

"I don't care to discuss it," Jim said, removing her hand by the faintest gesture of withdrawing.

Julia sighed and was silent. The limousine ran smoothly past one lighted corner after another; turned into Van Ness Avenue. After a while she said, a little indignation burning through her quiet tone:

"I've said I was not responsible for the conversation, Jim. And it seems to me merely childish in you to let a casual remark affect you in this way!"

"All right, then, I'm childish!" Jim said grimly, folding his arms as he leaned back in his seat.

Julia sighed again. Presently Jim burst out:

"I'm affected by a casual remark, yes, I admit it. But my God, doesn't it mean anything to you that I have my pride, that when I think of my wife I want to feel that she is more perfect in every way—in *every* way—than all the other women in the world?" He stopped, breathing hard, and resumed, a little less violently: "All I ask is, Julia, that you let such subjects *alone*. You're not called upon to defend such girls! Surely that's not too much to ask!"

Julia did not answer; she sat silent and sick. And as Jim did not speak again, except to mutter "My God!" once or twice, they reached the house in silence, and separated with a brief "Good-night." Ellie was waiting for Julia, eager to hear what Miss Jane wore, and Miss Constance wore, and how "Miss Teddy" looked.

"I am absolutely done, Ellie," said the mistress, when the filmy lace gown was back in its box, and she was comfortably settled on her pillows, "so don't come in until I ring."

"And I hope you'll get a long sleep," Ellie said approvingly, "you've got to take care of yourself now!"

Julia's little daughter was born on a June day in the lovely Ross Valley house the Studdifords had taken for the summer.

They had moved into the house in April, because Julia's hopes made a later move unwise, and, delighted to get into the sweet green country so early in the year, and to have the best of excuses for leading the quiet life she loved, she bloomed like a rose. She was in splendid health and in continual good spirits; her exultant confidence indeed lasted until the very day of the baby's birth.

The day was late, and the pretty nurse, Miss Wheaton, had been in the house for nearly two weeks before Julia herself came to her door, in the first pearl dawning to say, still laughingly, that the hour had come. A swift, well—ordered period of excitement ensued; the maids were silent, awed, efficient; Miss Wheaton authoritative, crisp, ready with technical terms; and Jim as nervous and upset as if he were absolutely ignorant of all things physiological, utterly dependent upon the skill and knowledge of the nurse, humbly obedient to her will. The telephone rang and rang. Julia, the centre of this whole thrilling drama, wandered about in her great plum-coloured silk dressing-gown, commenting cheerfully enough upon the various rapid changes that were being made in her room. She picked up the little pink blanket that had been hung upon a white-enamelled clothes-horse, by the fire, and pressed it to her cheek. But now and then she stopped walking, and put her hand out toward the back of a chair as if she needed support, and then an expression crossed her face that made Jim's soul sicken within him: an expression of fear and wonderment and childish surprise. At nine o'clock Miss Toland came in, a little pale, but very cheerful and reassuring.

"I'm afraid—my nerve—will give out, Aunt Sanna!" Julia said, beginning her restless march again, after a hot quick kiss.

"Hear her!" said the nurse, with a laugh of bright scorn. "Don't talk any nonsense like that, Mrs. Studdiford. Why, she's the coolest of us all!"

"Oh, no—I'm not—oh, no—I'm not!" Julia moaned.

"Your doctor says you're doing splendidly, and that another two hours ought to see everything well over!" Miss Toland said, trying to keep the acute distress she felt out of her tone.

"I feel so—nauseated!" Julia complained. "So—uncertain!"

"Yes, I know," the nurse said soothingly, whisking out of the room. Miss Toland followed her into the hall.

"She's in great pain, she won't have much of this?" asked the older woman anxiously.

"She's not suffering much," the nurse said brightly, after a cautious glance at Julia's closed door. "This isn't much—yet. She's a little scared, that's all!"

Hating the nurse from the depth of her heart, Miss Toland went downstairs to see the doctor. Jim was sitting with a newspaper on the porch, trying to smoke. He jumped up nervously.

"Where's Doctor Lippincott?" demanded Miss Toland. "He ran in to San Rafael. Back directly."

"Ran in to San Rafael? And you let him! Why, I don't see how he dared, Jim!"

"Oh, I guess he knows his business, Aunt Sanna!" Jim said miserably. "Do you suppose I can go up for a while?"

"Yes, go," said Miss Toland. "I think she wants you, God bless her!"

But Julia wanted nobody and nothing. Jim's presence, his concerned voice and sympathetic eyes, only vaguely added to her distress. She was frightened now, terrified at the recurring paroxysms of pain; she recoiled from the breezy matter-of-factness of the doctor and the nurse; the elaborate preparations for the crisis offended every delicate instinct of her nature. She felt that the room was hot, and complained of the fire; but a few moments later her teeth chattered with a chill, and Miss Wheaton closed the wide windows through which a June breeze was wandering.

The day dragged on. The doctor came back, talked to Jim and Miss Toland during luncheon about mushroom-raising, went upstairs to send Miss Wheaton down to her lunch, and to watch the patient a little while for himself. Jim went up, too, but was sent down to reassure Mrs. Toland, who had arrived, and with Miss Sanna was holding a vigil in the pretty cretonne-hung drawing-room. He was crossing the hall to go upstairs again, when a sound from above held him rigid and cold. A long low moan of utter weariness and anguish drifted through the pleasant silence of the house, died away, and rose again.

Slowly the sense of tragedy deepened about them. Mrs. Toland was white; Miss Toland's face was streaked with tears. The moaning was almost incessant now, but Jim in the hall could hear the nurse murmur above it, and now and then the doctor's voice, short and sharp.

"I wonder if you could come in and give her a little chloroform, Jim?" said Doctor Lippincott, a pleasant, middle-aged man in a white linen suit and cap, appearing suddenly in the door of Julia's room. "I think we can ease her along a little now, and I need Miss Wheaton."

Jim pushed his hair back with a wet hand; cleared his throat.

"Sure. D'you want me to scrub up?" he asked huskily.

"Oh, no—no, my dear boy! Everything's going splendidly." The doctor beckoned him in, and shut the door. "Now, Mrs. Studdiford," said he, "we'll be all right here in no time!"

Julia did not answer; she did not open her eyes even when Jim took her moist hot hand in one of his, and brushed back the lovely tumbled hair from her wet forehead. She was breathing deep and violently, as if she had been running. Presently she beat upon the bed with one clenched fist, and began to toss her head from side to side. Then the stifled moan began to escape from her bitten lips again, her face worked pitifully, and she began to cry.

"Now, crowd it on, Jim!" Doctor Lippincott said, nodding toward the chloroform.

"Breathe deep, breathe it in, my darling!" Jim urged, pouring the sweet, choking stuff upon the little mask he held above the tortured face.

"You aren't—helping me—at all!" Julia muttered, in a deep hoarse voice. But her shrill thin cry sank to a moan again; she stammered incoherent words.

So struggling and sobbing, now quieter under the anaesthetic, now crying aloud, the next long hour somehow passed for the helpless, suffering little animal that was Julia. A climax came, and the kindly chloroform smothered the last terrible cry.

Julia awoke to a realization that something was snapping brightly, like wood on a fire; that the cottony fumes in her head were breaking, drifting away; that commonplace cheerful voices were saying things very near her. She seemed to have fallen from infinite space to this wretchedly uncomfortable bed and this wretchedly uncomfortable position. She wanted a pillow; her head was rocking with pain, and her forehead was sticky with moisture. Yet under and over all other sensations was the heavenly relief from the familiar agonies of the day. She felt so tired that the mere thought of beginning to rest distressed her; she would not open her eyes; her lids seemed sealed. She felt faintly worried because she could not seem to intelligently grasp the subject of Honolulu.

"Honolulu? Honolulu?" This was the doctor's pleasant drawl. "No. I haven't. Mrs. Lippincott's people live in New York, so our junketings are usually in that direction."

"Ah, well, you'd like Honolulu," Miss Wheaton's voice answered. A pause. Then she said, "I put some wood on. It's not so warm to-day as it was yesterday."

Julia strove in vain to pierce the meaning of these cryptic words. Presently the doctor said, "Perfectly normal?" more as a statement than a question, and Miss Wheaton answered in a matter-of-fact voice, "Oh, absolutely."

Julia opened her eyes, looked up into the nurse's face, and with returning consciousness came self-pity.

"I couldn't do it, Miss Wheaton," she whispered pitifully, with trembling lips.

"Hello, little girlie, you're beginning to feel better, aren't you?" Miss Wheaton said. "Here she is, Doctor, as fine as silk."

Julia's languid eyes found the doctor's kindly face.

"But the baby?" she faltered, with a rush of tears.

"The baby is a very noisy young woman," said Doctor Lippincott cheerfully. "I wrapped her in her pink thingamagig, and she's right here in Jim's room, getting her first bath from her granny."

"Really?" Julia whispered. "You wouldn't—fool me?"

"Listen to her!" Miss Wheaton said. "Now, my dear, don't you be nervous. You've got a perfectly lovely little girl, and you've come through *splendidly*, and everything's fine. If you want to go look at that baby, Doctor," she added, "ask Doctor Studdiford to send Ellie in here to me and we'll straighten this all out. Then we can let him in here to see this young lady!"

Presently Jim came in, to kneel beside Julia's bed, and gather her little limp hands to his lips, and murmur incoherent praise of his brave girl, his darling little mother, his little old sweetheart, dearer than a thousand babies. Julia heard him dreamily, raised languid eyes, and after a little while stroked his hair. She was spent, exhausted, hammered by the agony of a few short hours into this pale ghost of herself, and he was strong and well, the red blood running confident and audacious in his veins. Their spirits could not meet to-night. But she loved his praise, loved to feel his cheek wet against her hand, and she began to be glad it was all over, that peace at last had found the big pleasant room, where firelight and the last soft brightness of the June day mingled so pleasantly on rosy wall paper and rosy curtains.

"She's a little darling," said Jim. "Mother says she's the prettiest tiny baby she ever saw. Poor Aunt Sanna and Mother had a great old cry together!"

"Ah!" said Julia hungrily. For Miss Toland had come stepping carefully in, the precious pink blanket in her arms.

"I'm to bring her to say 'Good-night' to her mother!" said Miss Toland. "How are you, dear? All forgotten now?"

The pink miracle was laid beside Julia; she shifted her sore body just a trifle to make room, and spread weak fingers to raise the blanket from the baby's face. A little crumpled rose leaf of a face, a shock of soft black hair, and two tiny hands that curved warmly against Julia's investigating finger. All the rest was delicate lawn and soft wool.

The baby wrinkled her little countenance, her tiny mouth opened, and Julia heard for the first time her daughter's rasping, despairing, bitter little cry. A passion of ecstasy flooded her heart; she dropped her soft pale cheek close to the little creased one.

"Oh, my darling, my *darling*!" she breathed. "Oh, you little perfect, helpless, innocent thing! Oh, Jim, she's crying, the angel! Oh, I do thank God for her!" she ended softly.

"I thank God you're so well," said Miss Toland. "Here, you can't keep her!"

"Anna, go with Aunt Sanna," Julia said weakly.

"Anna, eh?" Miss Toland said, wrapping up the pink blanket.

"Anna Toland Studdiford," Jim answered. "Julia had that all fixed up weeks ago!"

"Well—now—you children!" Miss Toland said, looking from one to the other, with her half-vexed and half-approving laugh. "What do you want to name her that for?"

"*I* know what for," Julia smiled, as she watched the pink blanket out of sight.

A little later Mrs. Toland crept in, just for a kiss, and a whimpered, "And now you must forget all the pain, dear, and just be happy!"

Then Julia was left to her own thoughts.

She watched Miss Wheaton come and go in the soft twilight. A shaded light bloomed suddenly, where it would not distress her eyes. The curtains were drawn, and Ellie came softly in with a pitcher of hot milk on a tray. Now and then the baby's piercing little "Oo-wah-wah!" came in from the next room, and when she heard it, Julia smiled and said faintly, "The darling!"

And as a ship that has been blown seaward, to meet the gales and to be battered upon rocks, might be caught at last by friendlier tides and carried safely home, so Julia felt herself carried, a helpless little wreck, too tired to care if the waves flung her far up on shore or drew her out to their mad embraces again.

"All forgotten?" Miss Toland had asked, from her fifty years of ignorance, and "Now you must forget all the pain," Mrs. Toland had said, with her motherly smile.

Queer, drifting thoughts came and went in her active brain during these quiet days of convalescence. She thought of girls she had known at The Alexander, girls who had cried, and who had been blamed and ostracised, girls who had gone to the City and County Hospital for their bitter hour, and had afterward put the babies in the Asylum! Julia's thoughts went by the baby in the next room, and at the picture of that tender helplessness, wronged and abandoned, her heart seemed to close like a closing hand.

Anna Toland Studdiford would never be abandoned, no fear of that. Never was baby more closely surrounded with love and the means of protection. But the other babies, just as dear to other women, what of them? What of mother hearts that must go through life knowing that there are little cries they will never hear, tears they may never dry, tired little bodies that will never know the restfulness of gentle arms? The terrible sum of unnecessary human suffering rose up like a black cloud all about her; she seemed to see long hospital wards, with silent forms filling them day and night, night and day, the long years through; she had glimpses of the crowded homes of the poor, the sick and helpless mothers, the crying babies. She suddenly knew sickness and helplessness to be two of the greatest factors in human life.

"What if Heaven is only this earth, clean and right at last," mused Julia, "and Hell only the realization of what we might have done, and didn't do—for each other!" And to Jim she said, smiling, "This experience has not only given me a baby, and given me my own motherhood, but it seems to have given me all the mothers and the babies in the world as well! I wish you were a baby doctor, Jim—the preservation of babies is the most important thing in the world!"

Slowly the kindly tides brought her back to life, and against her own belief that it would ever be so, she found herself walking again, essaying the stairs, taking her place at the table. Miss Wheaton went away, the capable Caroline took her place, and Julia was well.

Caroline was a silent, nice-looking, efficient woman of forty. She knew everything there was to know about babies, and had more than one book to consult when she forgot anything. She had been married, and had two handsome sturdy little girls of her own, so that little Anna's rashes and colics, her crying days and the days in which she seemed to Julia alarmingly good, presented no problems to Caroline. There was nothing Julia could tell her about sterilizing, or talcum powder, or keeping light out of the baby's eyes, or turning her over in her crib from time to time so that she shouldn't develop one-sidedly.

More than this, Anna was a good baby; she seemed to have something of her mother's silent sweetness. She ran through her limited repertory of eating, sleeping, bathing, and blinking at her friends with absolute regularity.

"I'd just like you to leave the door open so that if she *should* cry at night—" Julia said.

"But she never *does* cry at night!" Caroline smiled.

Julia persisted for some time that she wanted to bathe the baby every day, but before Anna was two months old she had to give up the idea. It became too difficult to do what nobody in the house wanted her to do, and what Caroline was only too anxious to perform in her stead. Jim liked to loiter over his breakfast, and showed a certain impatience when Julia became restive.

"What is it, dear? What's Lizzie say? Caroline wants you?"

"It's just that—it's ten o'clock, Jim, and Caroline sent down to know if I am going to give Anna her bath this morning!"

"Oh, bath—nothing! Let Caroline wait—what's the rush?"

"It's only that baby gets so cross, Jim!" Julia would plead.

"Well, let her. You know you mustn't spoil her, Julie. If there's one thing that's awful it's a house run by a spoiled kid! Do let's have our breakfast in peace!"

Julia might here gracefully concede the point, and send a message to Caroline to go on without her. Or she might make the message a promise to perform the disputed duty herself, "in just a few minutes."

She would run into the nursery breathlessly, and take the baby in her arms. Everything would be in readiness, the water twinkling in the little bathtub, soap and powder, fresh little clothes, and woolly bath apron all in order.

"But *hush*, Sweetest! How cross she is this morning, Caroline!"

"Yes, Mrs. Studdiford. You see she ought to be having her bottle now, it's nearly eleven! Dear little thing, she was *so* good and patient."

"Well, darling, Mudder'll be as quick as she can," Julia might console the baby, and under Caroline's cool eye, and with Anna screaming until she was scarlet from her little black crown to the soles of her feet, the bath would somehow proceed. Ellie might put her head in the door.

"Well—oh, the poor baby, were they 'busing Ellie's baby?" she would croon, coming in. "Don't you care, because Ellie's going to beat 'em all with sticks!"

Caroline anticipated Julia's every need on these occasions: the little heap of discarded apparel was whisked away, band and powder were promptly presented, the bath vanished, the clothes-rack with its tiny hangers was gone, and Julia had a moment in which to hug the weary, sleepy, hungry, fragrant little lump of girlhood in her arms.

"Bottle ready, Caroline?"

"Yes, Mrs. Studdiford. She goes out on the porch now, for her nap. Come to Caroline, darling, and get something goody-good."

And so Julia had no choice but to go, wandering a little disconsolately to her own room, and wishing the baby took her nap at another hour and could be played with now.

Presently outside interests began to claim her again, dressmakers and manicures, shopping and the essential letter writing filled the mornings, luncheons kept her late into the afternoons, there were calls and card playing and teas. Julia would have only a few minutes in the nursery before it was time to dress for dinner; sometimes Jim came in to feast his eyes on the beautiful, serene little Anna, in her beautiful mother's arms; more often he was late, and Julia, trailing her evening gown behind her, would fly for studs, and pull the boot-trees from Jim's shining pumps.

In September they went to Burlingame for the polo tournament, and here, on an unseasonably hot day, Jim had an ugly little touch of the sun, and for two or three days was very ill. They were terrible days to Julia. Richie came to her at once, and they took possession of the house of a friend, where Jim had chanced to be carried, and sent to San Rafael for Julia's servants; but two splendid nurses kept her out of the sickroom, and the baby was in San Rafael, so that Julia wandered about utterly at a loss to occupy heart or hands.

On the third day the fever dropped, and Julia crept in to laugh and cry over her big boy. Jim got well very quickly, and just a week from the day of the accident he and Julia went home to the enchanting Anna, and began to plan for a speedy removal to the Pacific Avenue house, so that the little episode was apparently quite forgotten by the time they were back in the city and the season opened.

But looking back, months later, Julia knew that she could date a definite change in their lives from that time. Whether his slight sunstroke had really given Jim's mind a little twist, or whether the shock left him unable to throw off oppressing thoughts with his old buoyancy, his wife did not know. But she knew that a certain sullen, unresponsive mood possessed him. He brooded, he looked upon her with a heavy eye, he sighed deeply when she drew his attention to the lovely little Anna.

Julia knew by this time that marriage was not all happiness, all irresponsible joy. She had often wondered why the women she knew did not settle themselves seriously to a study of its phases, when the cloudless days inevitably gave place to something incomprehensible and disturbing. Even lovers like Kennedy and her husband had their times of being wholly out of sympathy with each other, she knew, and she and Jim were not angels; they must only try to be patient and forbearing until the dark hour went by.

With a sense of unbearable weight at her heart she resigned herself to the hard task of endurance. Sometimes with a bitter rush would come the memory of how they had loved each other, and then Julia surrendered herself to long paroxysms of tears; it was so hard, so bewildering, to have Jim cold and quiet, to live in this painful alternation of hope and fear. But she never let Jim see her tears, and told herself bravely that life held some secret agony for every one, and that she must bear her share of the world's burden. How had it all come about, she wondered. Her thoughts went back to the honeymoon, and she had an aching memory of Central Park in its fresh green, of Jim laughing at her when she tried to be very matronly, in her kimono, over their breakfast tray. Oh, the exquisite happy days, the cloudless, wonderful time!

She left the thought of it for the winter that followed. That had been happy, too. Not like the New York months, not without its grave misgivings, not without its hours of bitter pain, yet happy on the whole. Then Honolulu, all so bright a memory until that hour on the ship—that first horrible premonition of so much misery that was to follow. The San Mateo summer had somehow widened the wordless, mysterious gap between them, and the winter! Julia shuddered as she thought of the winter. Where was her soul while her body danced and dressed and dined and slept through those hot hours? Where was any one's soul in that desperate whirl of amusement?

But she had found her soul again, on the June day of Anna's coming. And with Anna had come to her what new hopes and fears, what new potentialities and new sensibilities! She had always been silent, reserved, stoical by nature, accepting what life brought her uncomprehendingly, only instinctively and steadily fighting toward that ideal that had so long ago inspired her girlhood. Now she was awake, quivering with exquisite emotions, trembling with eagerness to adjust her life, and taste its full delicious savour. Now she wanted to laugh and to talk, to sit singing to her baby in the firelight, to run to meet her husband and fling herself into his arms for pure joy in life, and joy that she was beautiful and young and mother of the dearest baby in the world, and wife of the wisest and best of men. The past was blotted out for Julia now; her place in society was undisputed, not only as the wife of the rich young consulting surgeon, but for herself as well, and she could make as little or as much as she pleased of society's claim. From her sickness she felt as if she had learned that there is suffering and sorrow enough in the world without the need of deliberately sustaining the old and long-atoned wrongs. More than that, she had come to regard her own fine sense of right as a safer guide than any other, and by this she was absolved of the shadowy sin of her girlhood: the years, the hours she had prayed, the long interval, absolved her. Julia felt as if she had been born again.

In this mood Jim did not join her. As the weeks went by his aspect grew darker and more dark, and life in the Pacific Avenue house became a thing of long silences and rare and stilted phrases, and for the brief time daily that they were alone together, husband and wife were wretchedly unhappy, Jim watching his wife gloomily, Julia feeling that his look could chill her happiest mood. She had sometimes suspected that this state of affairs existed between other husbands and wives, and marvelled that life went smoothly on; there were dinners and dances, there were laughter and light speech. Jim might merely answer her half-timid, half-confident "Good-morning" with only a jerk of his head; he might eat his breakfast in silence, and accord to Julia's brief outline of dinner or evening engagements only a scowling monosyllable. Yet the day proceeded, there was the baby to visit, a dressmaker's appointment to keep, luncheon and the afternoon's plans to be gotten through, and then there was the evening again, and Jim and herself dressing in adjoining rooms in utter silence, silently descending to welcome their guests, or silently whirling off in the limousine.

Sometimes she fancied that when she resolutely assumed a cheerful tone, and determined to fight this unwholesome atmosphere with honest bravery, she merely succeeded in making Jim's mood uglier than ever. Often she tried a shy tenderness, but with no success.

One day when Miss Toland was lunching with her Julia made some allusion to the subject, in answer to the older woman's comment that she did not look very well.

"I'm *not* very well, Aunt Sanna," said Julia, pushing her plate away, and resting both slim elbows on the table. "I'm worried."

"Not about Anna?" Miss Toland asked quickly.

"No-o! Anna, God bless her, is simply six-months-old perfection!" Julia said, with a brief smile. "No—about myself and Jim."

Miss Toland gave her a shrewd glance.

"Quarrelled, eh?" she said simply.

"Oh, no!" Julia felt her eyes watering. "No. I almost wish we had. Because then I could go to him, and say 'I'm sorry!'" she stammered.

"Sorry for what?" demanded Miss Toland.

"For whatever I'd done!" elucidated Julia, with her April smile.

"Yes, but suppose he'd done it, what then?" Miss Toland asked.

"Ah, well," Julia hesitated. "Jim doesn't do things!" she said vaguely.

"Jim's in one of his awful moods, I suppose?" his adopted aunt asked, after a pause.

"Oh, in a dreadful one!" Julia confessed.

"How long—days?"

"Weeks, Aunt Sanna!"

"Weeks? For the Lord's sake, that's awful!" Miss Toland frowned and rubbed the bridge of her nose. "What gets into the boy?" she said impatiently. "You don't know what it's about, I suppose?"

Julia hesitated. "I think it's that he gets to thinking of my old life, when I was a little nobody, south of Market Street," she hazarded with as much truth as she could.

"Oh, *really*!" Miss Toland said, in a tone of cold satire. But her look fell with infinite tenderness and pity upon the drooping little figure opposite. "Yet there's nothing of the snob about Jim," she mused unhappily.

"Oh, *no*!" Julia breathed earnestly.

"There isn't, eh?" Miss Toland said. "I'm not so sure. I'm not at all sure. He isn't working too hard, is he?"

"He isn't working hard at all," Julia said. "Jim doesn't have a case, to worry over, twice a year. You see it's either City and County cases, that he just goes ahead and *does*, or else it's rich, rich people who have one of the older doctors, and just call Jim in to assist or consult. He was a little nervous over a demonstration before the students the other day, but at the very last second," Julia's quick smile flitted over her face, "at the very last second the assisting nurse dropped the cold bone—as they call it—that Jim was going to transplant. Doctor Chapman told him he'd bet Jim bribed the girl to do it!"

"H'm!" Miss Toland said absently. "But his father was just another such moody fellow, queer as Dick's hatband!" she added, suddenly, after a pause.

"Jim's father? I didn't know you knew him!"

"Knew him? Indeed I did! We all lived in Honolulu in those days. Charming, charming fellow, George Studdiford, but queer. He was very musical, you know; he'd look daggers at you if you happened to sneeze in the middle of one of his Beethoven sonatas. Tim's mother was very sweet, beautiful, too, but spoiled, Julia, spoiled!"

"Too much money!" Julia said, shaking her head.

"Exactly—there you have it!" Miss Toland assented triumphantly. "I've seen too much of it not to know it. There's a sort of dry rot about it; even a fine fellow like Jim can't escape. But, my dear"—her tone became reassuring—"don't let it worry you. He'll get over it. Just bide your time!"

"Well, that's just what I *am* doing," Julia said, with a rueful laugh. "But it's like being in a bad dream. There is sorrow that you have to bear, don't you know, Aunt Sanna, like crippled children, or somebody's death, or being poor; and then there are these other unnatural trials, that you just *rebel* against! I say to myself that I'll just be patient and sweet, and go on filling my time with Anna and calls and dinner parties, until Jim comes to his senses and tells me what an angel I am, but it's awfully hard to do it! Sometimes the house seems like a vault to me, in the mornings, even the sunshine"—Julia's eyes watered, but she went steadily on—"even the sunshine doesn't seem right, and I feel as if I were eating ashes and cotton! I go about looking at other houses, and thinking, 'I wonder what men and women are being wretchedly unhappy behind *your* plate-glass windows!' I watch other men and their wives together," pursued Julia, smiling through tears, "and when women say those casual things they are always saying, about not loving your husband after the first few months, and being disillusioned, and meaning less and less to each other, I feel as if it would break my heart!"

"Well," Miss Toland said, somewhat distressed, "of course, I'd rather walk into a bull fight than advise—"

"I know you would," Julia hastened to assure her. "That's why I've been talking," she added, "and it's been a real relief! Don't think I'm complaining, Aunt Sanna—"

"No, my dear," Miss Toland said. "I'll never think anything that isn't good of you, Julie," she went on. "If Jim Studdiford is so selfish as to—to make his wife unhappy for those very facts that made him first love her and choose her, well, I think the less of Jim, that's all! Now give me a kiss, and we'll go and pick out something for Barbara's boy!"

"Well, it may be a pretty safe general rule not to discuss your husband with your women friends," Julia said gayly. "But I feel as if this talk had taken a load off my heart! In books, of course," she went on, "the little governess can marry the young earl, and step right into noble, not to say royal, circles, with perfect calm. But in real life, she has an occasional misgiving. I never can quite forget that Jim was a ten-year-old princeling, with a pony and a tutor and little velvet suits, and brushes with his little initials on them, when I was born in an O'Farrell Street flat!"

"Well, if you remember it," said Miss Toland, in affectionate disapproval, "you're the only person who does!"

Either the confidential chat with Miss Toland had favourably affected Julia's point of view, or the state of affairs between Jim and herself actually brightened from that day. Julia noticed in his manner that night a certain awkward hint of reconciliation, and with it a flood of tenderness and generosity rose in her own heart, and she knew that, deeply as he had hurt her, she was ready to forgive him and to be friends again.

So a not unhappy week passed, and Julia, with more zest than she had shown in some months, began to plan a real family reunion for Thanksgiving, now only some ten days off. She wrote to the Doctor and Mrs. Toland, to the Carletons and Aunt Sanna, and to Richie, who had established himself in a little cottage on Mount Tamalpais, and who was somewhat philanthropically practising his profession there. She very carefully ordered special favours for the occasion, and selected two eligible and homeless young men from her list of acquaintances to fill out the table and to amuse Constance and Jane. Jim had to go to Sacramento on the Saturday before Thanksgiving for an important operation, but would be home again on Tuesday or Wednesday to take the head of his own table on the holiday.

Julia offered, when the Friday night before his departure came, to help him with packing. They had dined very quietly with friends that night, and found themselves at home again not very long after ten o'clock. But Jim, sinking into a chair beside the library fire, with an assortment of new magazines at his elbow, politely declined.

"Oh, no, thank you! Plenty of time for that in the morning. I don't go until nine."

"Let Chadwick do it, anyway, Jim. Shall I tell Ellie to send him up at eight?"

"If you will. Thank you! Good-night!"

"Good-night!" And Julia trailed her satins and laces slowly upstairs, unfastening her jewels as she went. A little sense of discouragement was fighting for possession; she fought it consciously as she had fought such waves of despondency a hundred times before. She propped herself comfortably in pillows, turned on a light, and began to read.

Ellie fussed about the room for a few minutes, and then was gone. The big house was very still. Eleven o'clock struck from the little mahogany clock on her mantel, midnight struck, and still Jim's footstep did not come up the stairs, and there was no welcome sound of occupancy in the room adjoining her own.

Suddenly terror smote Julia; she flung her book aside and sat up erect in bed. Her heart was thundering with fear; the silence of the house was like that that follows an explosion.

For a few dreadful seconds she sat motionless; then she thrust her bare feet in the slippers of warm white fox that Ellie had put out, and caught up a Japanese robe of black crepe, in which her figure was quite lost. Fastening the wide obi with trembling fingers, she slipped out into the hall, dimly lighted and very still. Then she ran quickly downstairs.

What sight of horror she expected to find in the library she did not know, but the shock of revulsion, when the opened door showed her nothing more terrible than Jim, musing in the firelight, was almost as bad as a fright could have been.

"Oh, Jim!" she panted, coming in, one hand pressed against her heart, "I thought something—I got frightened!"

Jim looked up with his old, tender, whimsical smile, the smile for which she had hungered so long, and held out a reassuring hand.

"Why, no, you poor kid!" he said. "I've been sitting right here!"

"I thought—and it was so still—and you didn't come up!" Julia said, beginning to sob. And in a moment she was in his arms, clinging to him in an ecstasy of love and relief. For a long blissful time they remained so, the soft curve of Julia's cheek against Jim's face, her heart beating quick above his own, her warm little figure, in its loose, soft robe, gathered closely to him.

"Feeling better now, old lady?"

"Oh, fine!" But Julia's face quivered with tears again at the tone.

"Well, then, what's this for?" He showed her a drop on the back of his hand.

"Be—because I love you so, Jim!"

"Well, you needn't cry over it!" said Jim gently. "I'm the one that ought to do the crying, Judy," he added, with a significant glance at her lovely flushed face and tear-bright blue eyes.

Julia leaned against him with a long, happy sigh.

"Oh, I'm so glad I came down!" she breathed contentedly.

"'Glad!'" Jim echoed soberly. "God! You don't know what it meant to me to look up and see my little Geisha coming in. I was going crazy, I think!"

"Ah, Jimmy, why do you?" she coaxed, one slender arm about his neck.

"I don't know," he said thoughtfully. "Made that way, I guess!"

For a while they were silent again, then Julia said softly:

"After all, nothing matters as long as we love each other!"

"No, no! You're right, Julie," he agreed seriously. "That's the only thing that counts. And you do love me, don't you?"

"Love you!" Julia said, with a shaky laugh.

"I get crazy notions. I nearly go mad, sometimes," Jim confessed. "I get to brooding—I know how rotten it is!" He fell silent, staring into the fire. "Happy?" he asked presently, glancing down at her as she rested quietly in his arms.

"Oh, *happy*!" Julia said, a break in her voice. "I wish I could die here, Jim. I wish I could go to sleep here and never wake up!"

"Like me as much as that baby, eh?" he asked, in a peculiar tone.

Julia sat up to face him, her cheeks bright under loosening films of hair, her eyes starry in the firelight.

"Jimmy, you couldn't be jealous of your own baby?"

"Oh, couldn't I? I can be jealous of anything and everything, sometimes." He fixed troubled eyes on the fire. "I've been unhappy, Julie," he confessed.

"Unhappy? I've just been *sick* about it," Julia said. "I can't believe that we're talking about it, and it's all over!" She sighed luxuriously. "There's no use of *my* doing anything when you're this way, Jim—I can't even remember that you love me," she went on after a silence. "Everything seems changed and queer. Sometimes I think you hate me, sometimes you give me such cold looks—oh, you *do*, Jimmy!—they just make me feel sick and queer all over, if you know what I mean! And oh," she sank back again with her head on his shoulder, "oh, if *only* then I could dare just come down to you here like this, and make you take me in your arms, and talk to me this way!"

"Don't!" Jim said briefly, kissing the top of her hair.

"It just seems to *smoulder* in my heart!" Julia said. "I can't bear it!';

"Don't!" he said again.

"Ah, but what makes you do it, Jim?" she asked, sitting erect to rest both wrists on his shoulders, and bring her blue eyes very near his own. Jim's glance did not meet hers, he looked sombrely past her at the fire. Suddenly she felt his arms tighten about her with a force that almost hurt her.

"Oh, it's this!" he said harshly, "I love you—you're mine! You're the thing I live for, the thing I'm proudest of! I can't bear to think there was a time when I didn't know you, my little innocent girl! I can't bear—my God!—to think that you cared for some one else—!"

And with swift force he got to his feet, and put her in his chair. Julia sat motionless while he took a restless brief turn about the room. He snatched a little jade god from the table, examined it closely, and put it down again, to come and stand with his back to the fire, one arm flung across the mantel, and his gloomy eyes fixed on her. Julia met the rushing, engulfing wave of her own emotion bravely.

"Jim," she said bravely, "does it mean nothing to you that there were other women in *your* life before you knew me?"

"Dearest," he answered seriously and quickly, "God knows that I would cut my hand off to be able to blot that all out of my boyhood. Those things mean nothing to a man, Ju, and they meant less to me than to most men. Women can't understand that, but if you knew how men regard it, you would realize that very few can bring their wives as clean a record as mine!"

He had said this much before, never anything more. Julia, looking at him now with all the tragic sorrow of her life in her magnificent eyes, felt the utter impossibility of convincing him that this accusation on her part, and bravely boyish and honest confession on his, had any logical or possible connection with the momentous conversation that they were having to-night. Her heart recoiled in sick terror from any word that would hurt or estrange him now, but she might have found that word, and might have said it, could she have hoped that it would convey her meaning to him. But Jim's standard of morals, for himself, was, like that of most men, still the college standard. It was too bad to have clouded the bright mirror, but it was inevitable, given youth and red blood. And it was admirable to regret it all now. Any fresh attempt on Julia's part to bring to his realization the parallel in their situations, would have elicited from him only fresh, youthful acknowledgments, until that second when anger and astonishment at her bold effort to reduce the two distinct codes to one would end this talk—like so many others!—with new coldnesses and silences. Julia abandoned this line of argument once and for all.

"I never cared for any one but you in my life, Jim," she said, with dry lips.

"I know," he muttered, brushing his hair back with an impatient hand. A second later he came to kneel penitently before her. "I'm sorry, sweetheart," he said pleadingly. "You're a little angel of forgiveness to me—I don't deserve it! I know how I make you suffer!"

"Jim," she said, feeling old, and tired, and cold to her heart's core, "do you think you do?"

"I know how *I* suffer!" he answered bitterly.

"Jim, suppose it was something you had done long ago that *I* couldn't forgive?"

"It isn't a question of forgiveness," he answered quickly. "Forgiveness—when you are the sweetest and best wife a man ever had! No, darling," he caught both her hands in his own, "you must never think that, it's never that! It's only my mad, crazy jealousy. I tell you I'm ashamed of it, and I *am*! Just be patient with me, Julia!"

Julia stared at him a few moments silently, her hands locked about his neck.

"Ah, but you *worry* me so when you're like this, Jim," she said presently, in the gentle, troubled tone a mother might use. "There seems to be nothing I can do. I can only worry and wait!"

"I know, I know," he said hastily. "Don't remind me of it! My father was like that, you know. My father shot at a man once because he was rude to my mother when he was drunk—shot him right through the shoulder! It raised the very deuce of a scandal down there in Honolulu! He took Mother to Europe to get away from the fuss, and paid the man the Lord knows what to quiet the thing!"

"Yes, but life isn't like that, Jim," Julia protested. "Life isn't so simple! Shooting at somebody, and buying his silence, and rushing off to Europe! Why can't you just say to yourself reasonably—"

"'Reasonably,' dearest!" he echoed cheerfully, with a kiss. "When was a jealous man ever reasonable!"

"But think how wonderfully happy we are, Jim," she persisted wistfully. "Suppose there *is* one part trouble, one part of your life that you don't like, why can't you be happy because ninety-nine parts of it are perfect?"

"I don't know; talking with you here, I can't understand it," he said. "But I get thinking—I get thinking, and my heart begins to hammer, and I lie awake nights, and I'd like to get up and strangle someone—"

His vehemence died into abashed silence before her grave eyes.

"I ought to be the one to stamp and rave over this," Julia said. "I ought to remind you that you knew my history when you married me; and you know life, too—you were ten years older than I, and how much more experienced! All I knew was learned at the settlement house, or from books. And the reason I *don't* rave and stamp, Jim," she went on, "is because I am different from you. I realize that that doesn't help matters. We must make the best of it now, we must help each other! You see I have no pride about it. I know I am better than many—than most—of these society women all about us, but I don't force you to admit that. They break every other commandment of God, yes, and that one, too, and they commit every one of the deadly sins! It seems to me sometimes as if 'gluttony, envy, and sloth' were the very foundation on which the lives of some of these people rest, and as for pride and anger and lust, why, we take them for granted! Yet, whoever thinks seriously of saying so?"

"You make me ashamed, Julie," Jim said, after a pause, during which his eyes had not moved from her face. "I can only say I'm sorry. I'm very sorry! Sometimes I think you're a good deal bigger man than I am; but I can't help it. However, I'm going to try. From to-night on I'm going to try."

"We'll both try," Julia said, and they kissed each other.

CHAPTER V

Miss Toland, who had accepted Julia's invitation for Thanksgiving, arrived unexpectedly on the afternoon before the holiday, to spend the night with the Studdifords. It was a wild, wet day, settling down to heavy rain as the early darkness closed in, and the Pacific Avenue house presented a gloomy if magnificent aspect to the guest as she came in. But Ellie beamingly directed her to the nursery, and here she found enough brightness to flood the house.

Caroline, it appeared, had gone to her own family for the afternoon, and Julia, looking like a child in her short white dress and buckled slippers, was sitting in a low chair with little Anna in her arms. The room was bright with firelight and the soft light from the subdued nursery lamps, and warm russet curtains shut out the dull and dying afternoon. Dolls and blocks were scattered on the hearth rug, and Julia sat her daughter down among them, and jumped up with a radiant face to greet the newcomer.

"Aunt Sanna—you darling! And you're going to spend the night?" Julia cried out joyfully, with her first kisses. "What a dear thing for you to do! But you're wet?"

"No, I dropped everything in my room," Miss Toland said. "Things were very quiet at The Alexander—that new woman isn't going to do at all, by the way, too fussy—so I suddenly thought of coming into town!"

"Oh, I'm *so* glad you did!" Julia exulted. Miss Toland rested firm hands on her shoulders, and looked at her keenly.

"How goes it?"

"Oh, splendidly!" The younger woman's bright eyes shone.

"No more blues, eh?"

"Oh, *no*!"

"Ah, well, that's a good thing!" Miss Toland sat down by the fire, and stretched sturdy shoes to the blaze. "Hello, Beautiful!" she said to the baby.

Julia dropped to the rug, and smothered the soft whiteness and fragrance of little Anna in a wild hug.

"She has her good days and her bad days," said Julia, biting ecstatic little kisses from the top of the downy little head, "and to-day she has simply been an *angel*! Wait—see if she'll do it! See, Bunny," Julia caught up a white woolly doll. "Oh, see poor dolly—Mother's going to put her in the fire!"

"Da!" said Anna agitatedly, and Julia tumbled her in another mad embrace.

"Isn't that *darling*, not six months old yet?" demanded the mother. "Here, take her, Aunt Sanna, and see if you ever got hold of anything nicer than that! Come, baby, give Aunt Sanna a little butterfly kiss!" And Julia swept the soft little face and unresponsive mouth across the older woman's face before she deposited the baby in her lap.

"She's like you, Julie," Miss Toland said, extending a ringed finger for her namesake's amusement.

"Yes, I think she is; every one says so. You see her hair's coming to be the same ashy yaller as mine. And see the fat sweet little knees, and don't miss our new slippers with wosettes on 'em!"

"She's really exquisite," Miss Toland said, kissing the tawny little crown as Julia had done, and watching the deep-lashed blue eyes that were so much absorbed by the rings. "Watching her, Ju, we'll see just what sort of a little girl you were."

"Oh, heavens, Aunt Sanna," Julia protested, with a rather sad little smile, "I was an awful little person with stringy hair, and colds in my nose, and no hankies! I never had baths, and never had regular meal hours, or regular diet, for that matter! Anna'll be very different from what I was."

"Your mother was to blame, Ju," Miss Toland said, gravely shaking her head.

"Oh, I don't know, perhaps *her* mother was," Julia suggested. "Yet my Grandmother Cox is a sweet little old woman," she went on, smiling, "always afraid we're hungry, and anxious to feed us, tremendously loyal to us all. I went out there to-day, to take Mama some special little things for Thanksgiving, and see if their turkey had gotten there, and so on, and my heart quite ached for Grandma—Mama's very exacting now, and the girls—my aunt, Mrs. Torney's girls—seemed so apathetic and dull. The house was very dirty, as it always is, and the halls icy, and the kitchen hot—I just wanted to pitch in and *clean*! Mama was cross at me for not bringing Anna, in this rain, and staying to dinner to-morrow; but Grandmother was so pleased to have the things, and she got to telling me of old times, poor thing, and how she had to work and scheme to get up a Thanksgiving dinner, and how my grandfather would worry her by promising that he'd only have one drink, and then disappearing for hours—"

"Does it ever occur to you that you are an unusual woman, Julia?" Miss Toland asked, holding her watch to the baby's ear. Julia flushed and laughed.

"Well, no, I don't believe it ever did!"

"Not so much in climbing up in the world as you have," pursued the older woman, "but in not despising the people you left behind you! That's very fine, Julie. I can't tell you how fine it seems to me!"

"There's nothing fine about it," Julia said simply. "It's just that I like that sort of people as well as I do—Jim's sort. I used to think that to work my way into a world where everything was fine and fragrant and costly would mean to be happy, but of course it doesn't, and I've come more and more to feel that I like the class where joys are real, and sorrows are real, and the goodness means more, and there's more excuse for the badness!"

"Did you ever think of writing, Julia?" Miss Toland asked. "Stories, I mean?"

"Everybody does nowadays, I suppose," Julia laughed. "Sometimes I think what good material The Alexander stuff would be, Aunt Sanna. But the truth is, Jim doesn't like the idea."

"Doesn't? Bless us all, why not?"

"Oh!" Julia dimpled demurely. "The great Mrs. Studdiford writing, like a mere ordinary person?" she asked.

"Oh, that's it? Where is Jim, by the way?"

"Sacramento. But the operation was on Sunday, so he should have been here yesterday, at latest," Julia said. "However, he'll rush in to-night or to-morrow; he knows you're all going to be here. Give her to me, Aunt Sanna, she's getting hungry, bless her little old heart! Ah, here's Ellie with something for Mother's girl!"

"And tea for you in the library," Ellie said in an aside, receiving the baby into her arms with a rapturous look.

"Tea, doesn't tea sound good!" Julia caught Miss Toland by the hand. "Come and have some tea, Aunt Sanna!" said she. "I'm starving!"

They were loitering over their teacups half an hour later when Lizzie came into the library with a special delivery letter.

"For me?" Julia smiled, reaching for it. "It's Jimmy!" she added ruefully, for Miss Toland's benefit, as she took it. "This means he can't get here!"

"Drat the lad!" his aunt said mildly. "What has he got to say?"

Julia pulled out a hairpin to open the letter, her face a little puzzled. She unfolded three pages of large paper closely written.

"Why, I don't understand this," said she. "Jimmy writes such short letters!"

And immediately fear, like cold iron, entered her heart, and she felt a chill of distaste for the letter; she did not want to read it, she wished she might fling it on the ere, and rid her hands of the horrible thing.

"It *is* Jim, isn't it?" Miss Toland said, with a sharp look. "Is he coming?"

"I don't know," Julia said, hardly above a whisper.

"Anything wrong?" Miss Toland asked, instantly alert.

"No, I don't suppose so!" Julia said, trying to laugh. "But—but I hate him to just send a letter when I expected *him*!" she added childishly.

She picked it up, and began slowly to read it. Miss Toland, watching her, saw the muscles of her face harden, and her eyes turn to steel. The blood rushed to her face, and then receded quickly. She read to the last word, and then looked up to meet the other woman's eyes.

"What *is* it?" Miss Toland demanded, aghast at Julia's look.

"It's Jim," said Julia. Her face was blazing again, and she seemed to be choking. "He's going to Europe," she went on, in a bewildered tone, "he's not coming back."

"*What*!" said Miss Toland sharply. "D'you mean to tell me he's simply walked off—"

Julia's colour was ghastly; her eyes looked sick and heavy.

"No, no, he can't mean that!" she said quickly. She crushed the pages of the letter together convulsively. "I can't—" she began, and stopped. Suddenly she rose to her feet, muttered something about coming back, and was gone.

She ran up to her room, and alone there, it seemed for a few moments as if she must suffocate. She put the letter on her desk, where its folded sheets instantly looked hideously familiar. She went into the bathroom, and found herself holding her fingers under the hot-water tap, vaguely waiting for hot water. Like a hunted creature she went through the luxurious rooms, the mortal wound in her heart widening every instant; finally she came back to her desk, and sat down, and read the letter again.

"Dear Julia," wrote Jim, "I have been thinking and thinking about this affair, and I cannot stand it. I am going away. Atkins is going to Berlin for a three months' course under Hofner and Braun, and I am going with him. I only made up my mind to-night, but I have thought of something like this a long, long time. I cannot bear it any longer. I think and think about things—that another man loved you and you loved him—and I nearly go mad. Even when people meet me and ask how you are, I am reminded of it; for weeks now I haven't thought of anything else; it just seems to rise up wherever I go.

"I think it will be better when I don't see you.

"I have been sitting here with my head in my hands, wondering if there is any way in which I can spare you the pain of reading this letter, but it's no use, it's impossible to go back and bluff about it.

"Collins spoke to me about the change in me; he said he thought it was that touch of the sun in September. I wish to God it was!

"I will take the course with Atkins, and then let you know. He wants to go to Benares for some reason or another, and perhaps I will go with him, or perhaps come home to you. But I don't think I will come back under a year.

"You hear of men all your life who do this, but I feel as if it was killing me, and you, too. I wish there was some other way.

"I have written Harry at the Crocker; my account there is to be transferred to your name. I don't know exactly what it is, but the money from the San Mateo lots went in there, and so there is plenty. For God's sake spend it, don't hesitate about getting anything you want. Why shouldn't you keep the house, until April anyway; some one would stay with you, and then you could go to San Rafael.

"I'm not going to try to tell you how I feel about all this, because you know. It all seems to me a bad dream. Every little while I try to make myself think that after a while it will all come right, but it seemed to me all dead and buried after that time on the steamer, and of course it wasn't!

"Tell people what you please, I leave all that to you.

"Chadwick will sell the car, and send you the bill of sale and the money. He knows what I want sent; he'll do all that.

"I've written and rewritten this ten times; my head is splitting. It seems strange to think it is you and me.

"God bless you always, and our little girl.

"*Jim.*"

Julia finished it with a little grinding sound, like a groan, heard herself make a dramatic exclamation, an "Ah!" of agonized unbelief. She sat down, got up again to take a few irresolute steps toward her desk, and finally went to her bedside telephone, and took down the receiver.

There was a delay; Julia rapped an impatient slipper on the floor, and rattled the hook.

"Western Union, please," she said, a moment later; "I want to send a telegram."

An interval of silence followed. Julia sat staring blankly at the wall. Then she rattled the hook again.

"No matter about that number, Central; I've changed my mind," she said. She walked irresolutely into the middle of the room, stood there a moment frowning, and then turned, to go back and fling herself on her bed, staring up into the dark, the letter crackling as it dropped beside her.

After a while she began to say, "Oh, oh, oh!" quietly and quickly under her breath. The cry grew too much for her, she twisted on her face to stifle it, and after a few moments it stopped. Then she turned on her back again, and said something sharply to herself in a whisper once or twice, and after that the moaning "Oh, oh, oh!" began again.

So Miss Toland found her, when she came into the room without knocking, a little later.

"Julia," Miss Toland said sharply, sitting down on the edge of the bed and possessing herself of one of Julia's limp, cold hands, "Ellie told me you—she came to the door and heard you! My child, this won't do! You mustn't make mountains out of molehills. If Jim Studdiford has had the senseless cruelty to go off to Europe in this fashion, why, he ought to be horsewhipped, that's all! But I don't believe he'll get any farther than New York, myself; I don't believe he'll get that far!" She paused, but Julia was silent. After a moment the older woman spoke again. "What does he say in the letter?" she asked. "One would really like to know just how this delightful piece of work is explained."

"Aunt Sanna!" Julia said, in a difficult half whisper. She took Miss Toland's hand and pressed it against her heart. Her lips were shut tight, and against the white pillow there was a little negative movement of her head.

"Well, of course you don't want to talk about it," Miss Toland said soothingly. "But was there a quarrel?"

"Oh, no—no!" Julia said quickly, briefly, with another convulsive pressure of Miss Toland's hand, and another jerk of her head. "It was something—that distressed Jim—something I couldn't change," she added with difficulty.

"H'm!" said the other, and the evidence for both sides was in, as far as Miss Toland was concerned, and the case closed. She sat beside Julia in the dark for a long time, patting her hand without speaking. After a while Ellie brought a glass of hot milk, and Julia docilely drank it, and submitted to being put to bed, raising a face as sweet as a child's for Miss Toland's goodnight kiss, and promising to sleep well.

The pleasant winter sunlight was streaming into the older woman's room when Julia came in the next morning, although all San Francisco echoed to the sombre constant call of the foghorn, and the air was cool enough to make Miss Toland's fire delightful. Julia had Anna with her, a delightful little armful in her tumbled nightwear, and she smiled at the picture of Miss Toland, comfortably enjoying her breakfast in bed. But it was evident that she had not slept: deep shadows lay under her blue eyes, and she was very pale. She put the baby down on the bed with a silver buttonhook and a bracelet, and sat down.

"Sleep any?" Miss Toland asked.

"Yes, I think I did!" Julia said, with an effort at brightness. She seemed nervous and restless, but showed no tendency to break down. "I've just been talking to Caroline," she went on. "I told her that Doctor Studdiford had been called away, and implied that there would be changes. Then I spoke to Foo Ting at breakfast—Mrs. Pope is crazy to get him—so that will be all right—"

"Julia—of course I've not read Jim's letter," Miss Toland said earnestly, "but aren't you taking this too much to heart—aren't you acting rather quickly?"

Julia looked down at her laced fingers for a few moments without speaking.

"Jim isn't coming back," she said soberly.

"But what makes you *say* so, dear? How do you know?"

"Well, I just know it," Julia said, raising heavy-lidded eyes. They looked at each other.

"But you aren't telling me seriously, my child, that you two—the most devoted couple I ever *saw*—why, Julia, show a little courage, child! Jim must be brought to his senses, that's all. We must think what's wisest to do, and do it. But, my dear, there'd be no marriages left in the world if people flew off the handle—"

"I *have* been thinking, all night," Julia said patiently, "and this is what I thought. I want"—she glanced restlessly about the room—"I want to get away from here! That'll take some little while."

"Go away by all means, dear, if you want to, but don't dismantle your house—don't make it impossible for the whole thing to blow over——"

"He won't come back," Julia repeated quietly.

"You don't think so?" Miss Toland said uncomfortably. "H'm!"

"No one must know, not even Doctor and Mother," pursued Julia. "No newspapers, *nobody*!"

"Well, in any case, that's wise!" the older woman assented. "And where will you go—to Sally?"

"No!" Julia said with a quick shudder. "Not anywhere near here! No, I should rather like to give the impression that I will be with Jim, or near Jim," she added slowly.

"Following him abroad with the baby, that's quite natural!" Miss Toland approved. "But why not stay a week or two in Sausalito, just to keep them from guessing?"

"Oh, I couldn't!" Julia said, in a quick breath.

"And where'll you go—New York?"

"Oh, no!" Julia leaned back and shut her eyes. The muscles of her throat worked. "We were so happy in New York," she said, with a sudden quivering of her lips. But a moment's struggle brought back her composure. "I thought—some little French village, or England," she hazarded.

"England," Miss Toland said promptly. "This is no time of the year to take a child to France; besides, you get better milk in England, and if Anna was sick, there's London, full of doctors who speak your own language."

"So long as it's quiet," Julia said, "and we see nobody—that's all I care about. Then if Jim should—But I couldn't wait here, with everybody asking, and inviting me places, and spying on me!"

"We'll take some sort of little place in Oxfordshire," Miss Toland said, "and then we can run up to London—"

"'We?'" Julia echoed. She gazed bewilderedly at the other woman for a moment, then put her hands over her face and burst into tears.

A month like a nightmare followed. Julia had never grown to care for the Pacific Avenue house; now it came to have an absolute horror for her. She seemed to see it through a veil of darkness; she seemed to move under the burden of an intolerable weight. Sometimes she found herself panting as if for air, as she went from silent room to silent room, and sometimes a memory unbearably poignant and dear smote her as with physical violence, and her face worked for a few moments, and she fought with tears.

There were other times, when life seemed less sad than dull. Julia grew sick of loneliness, sick of silence; she stared at her face in the mirror, when she was slowly dressing in the morning; stared at herself again at night—as if marvelling at this woman who was a wife, and a mother, and deserted in her young bloom. Deserted—her husband had gone away from her, and she knew no way to bring him back. A weary flatness of spirit descended upon her; it seemed a part of the howling winter storms, the dark and heavy weather.

For the servants other positions were quickly found, the furniture was stored, the motor car sold. On the last day on which the last was at her disposal, Julia, with Ellie and the baby, drove about downtown, and disposed of several odds and ends of business. She left the keys of the Pacific Avenue house at the agent's office, not without an agonized memory of the day she had first called for them, more than two years ago. She went to the bank, and was instantly invited into the manager's office and given a luxurious chair.

"Well, Mrs. Studdiford," said Mr. Perry pleasantly, "what brings you out in this dreadful weather?"

"Good-byes," Julia said, flinging back her veil, and laying her muff aside. "Miss Toland and I will probably leave for New York on the seventh, and sail as soon as we can after we get there. I want to take a letter of credit, and I want to know just how I stand here."

Mr. Perry touched a button, the letter of credit was duly made out, a clerk came in with a little slip, which he handed to Mr. Perry.

"Ah, yes, yes, indeed! And where is Doctor Studdiford now? In Berlin? Lovely city. You'll like Berlin," said Mr. Perry. He glanced at the slip. "Thirty-seven thousand, two hundred and twenty dollars, Mrs. Studdiford," said he. "Transferred to your name a month ago.

"I had no idea it was so much!" Julia said, her heart turning to lead. Why had he given her so much?

Mr. Perry, bowing her out, laughed that that was a fault on the right side, and Julia left the bank, with its brightly lighted warm atmosphere tinged with the odour of ink and polished wood and rubber flooring, and its windows streaming with rain. She got into the motor car again, and took little Anna on her lap.

"Now I think we'll drop you at the hotel, Ellie," said she, "and I'll take the baby out to say good-bye to my mother."

"Oh, Mrs. Studdiford, it's raining something terrible!" protested the maid.

"Yes, I know," Julia agreed, looking a little vaguely out of the blurred window. "But you see to-morrow may be just as bad, and we've got her all dressed and out now. So you go home and pack, and I'll just fly out there and fly back. Day after to-morrow I've promised to take her to Sausalito, and the day after that we start!"

The city streets looked dark and gloomy under the steady onslaught of the rain, as the car rolled along. Julia stared sombrely through the drenched glass, now and then kissing the perfumed top of the little silk cap that covered the drowsy head on her breast. It was a long trip to Shotwell Street; for all her family's peculiarities, it was rather a sad trip to-day. She let her thoughts drift on to the coming changes in her life. She thought of New York, of the great unknown ocean, of London—London to Julia meant fog, hansom cabs, and crossings that must be swept. It was not, she felt, with a certain baffled resentment, what she wanted to do. London was full of Miss Toland's friends, and Julia was too sick in spirit to wish to meet them now. To be alone—to be alone—to be alone—some gasping inner spirit prayed continually. They would go to Oxfordshire, of course. But Miss Toland would be miserable in the country, she was always miserable in the country.

They were passing Eighteenth Street, passing St. Charles's shabby little church. Julia stopped the motor. She got out and carried the baby up the stairs, and went up the echoing aisle to a front pew, where Anna could sit and stare about her. Julia, panting, dropped on her knees. The big edifice was empty, and smelled of damp plaster, rain rattled the high windows. The afternoon was so dark that the sanctuary light sent a little pool of quivering red to the floor below.

After a while a very plain young woman came out of the vestry, and walking up the steps to the main altar, carried away one of the great candlesticks. She was presently joined by a little nun; the two whispered unsmilingly together, came and went fifty times with flowers, with candles, with fresh altar linen.

Julia could not pray. Her thoughts would not settle themselves; they drifted back and forth like rippling breezes over grass. She felt that if she might kneel here an hour she could begin to pray. Now a thousand little things distracted her: the odour of the church, the crisping feet of some one entering the church far behind her, the odour of the damp glove upon which she rested her cheek.

Life troubled her; she was afraid. She had thought it lay plain and straight before her; now all her guide posts were gone, and all her pathways led into deeper and deeper uncertainty. The utter confusion into which she had been thrown made even her own identity indefinite to her; she suffered less for this bewilderment. If by the mere raising of her hand she might have brought Jim back to her, she would not have raised that hand; not now, not until some rule that would adjust their relationship was found. Her marriage seemed a dream, their love as strange and remote as their separation.

Only Anna seemed real, and as much a sorrow as a joy just now. To what heritage would the beautiful, mysterious little personality unfold? What of the swiftly coming time when she would ask questions?

Julia turned to the little white-capped, white-coated figure. Anna had chewed a bonnet string to damp limpness; now she was saying "Da!" in an alluring and provocative tone to a lady praying nearby. The lady regarded her with an unmoved eye, however, and Julia gathered her small daughter in her arms and went down to the motor car.

At her mother's door she dismissed Chadwick for an hour or two of warmth and shelter, and, sighing, went into the unaired dark hallway that smelled to-day of wet woollens and of a smoky kerosene wick, and retained as well its old faint odour of carbolic acid.

CHAPTER VI

Julia found the family as usual in the kitchen, and the kitchen as usual dirty and close. Her old grandmother, a little bent figure in a loose calico wrapper, was rocking in a chair by the stove. Julia's mother was helpless in a great wheeled chair, with blankets and pillows carelessly disposed about her, and her eager eyes bright in a face chiselled by pain. Sitting at the table was a heavy, sad-faced woman, with several front teeth missing, in whom Julia recognized her aunt, Mrs. Torney. A girl of thirteen, with her somewhat colourless hair in untidy braids, and a flannel bandage high about her throat, came downstairs at the sound of Julia's entrance. This was Regina Torney.

"Well, it's Julia!" Mrs. Cox said. "And the darlin' sweetie—you oughtn't to bring her out such weather, Julie! How's them little hands?"

She took the baby, and Julia kissed her mother and aunt, expecting to draw from the former the usual long complaints when she said:

"How are you, dear? How does the chair go?"

But Mrs. Page surprised her by some new quality in her look and tone, something poignantly touching and admirable. She was a thin little shadow of her former self now, the skin drawn tight and shining over her cheek bones, her almost useless hands resting on a pillow in her lap. She wore a soiled dark wrapper, her dark hair, still without a touch of gray, was in disorder, and her blankets and pillows were not clean. She smiled at her daughter.

"I declare, Ju, you do seem to bring the good fresh air in with you whenever you come! Don't her cheeks look pretty, Regina? Why, I'm just about the same, Ju. To-day's a real bad day, on account of the rain, but I had a good night."

"She's had an awful week, Julia. She don't seem to get no better," Mrs. Torney said heavily. "I was just saying that it almost seems like she isn't going to get well; it just seems like it had got hold of her!"

Julia sat down next to her mother, and laid her own warm young hand over the hand on the pillow.

"What does the doctor say?" she asked, looking from one discouraging face to another.

"Oh, I don't know!" Mrs. Page said, sighing, and old Mrs. Cox cackled out a shrill "Doctors don't know nothing, anyway!"

"Emeline sent for me," Mrs. Torney said in a sad, droning voice. "Mamma just couldn't manage it, Julia; she's getting on; she can't do everything. So me and Regina gave up the Oakland house, and we've been here three weeks. We didn't want to do it, Julia, but you couldn't blame us if you'd read your Mamma's letter. Regina's going to work as soon as she can, and help out!"

Julia understood a certain deprecatory and apologetic note in her aunt's voice to refer to the fact that the Shotwell Street house was largely supported by Jim's generous monthly cheque, and that in establishing herself and her youngest daughter there she more or less avowedly added one more burden to Julia's shoulders.

"I'm glad you did, Auntie," she answered cheerfully. "How's Muriel? And where's Geraldine?"

"Geraldine's at school," Mrs. Torney said mournfully. "But Regina's not going to start in here. She done awfully well in school, too, Julia, but, as I say, she feels she ought to get to work now. She's got an awful sore throat, too. Muriel's started the nursing course, but I don't believe she can go on with it, it's something fierce. All my children have weak stomachs; she says the smell in the hospital makes her awfully sick. I don't feel real well myself; every time I stand up—my God! I feel as if my back was going to split in two, and yet with poor Em this way I felt as if I had ter come. Not that I can do anything for Emeline, but I was losing money on my boarders. I wish't you'd come out Sunday, Julia, I cooked a real good dinner, didn't I, Ma?"

Mrs. Cox did not hear, and Julia turned to her mother.

"Made up your mind really to go, Ju?" Mrs. Page asked.

"Oh, really! We leave on the seventh."

"I've always wanted to go somewheres on a ship," Emeline said. "Didn't care so much what it was when I got there, but wanted to go!"

"So have I," contributed Mrs. Torney. "I was real like you at your age, Julia, and I used to think I'd do this and that when the children was big. Well, some of us are lucky and some of us aren't—ain't that it, Ma? I was talking to a priest about it once," she pursued, "and he said, 'Well, Mrs. Torney, if there was no sorrow and suffering in the world, there wouldn't be no saints!' 'Oh, Father,' I says, 'there isn't much of the saint in me! But,' I says, 'I've been a faithful wife and mother, if I say it; seven children I've raised and two I've buried; I've worked my hands to the bone,' I says, 'and the Lord has sent me nothing but trouble!'"

"Ma, ain't you going to put your clothes on and go to the store?" Regina said.

"I was going to," Mrs. Torney said, sighing, "but I think maybe now I'll wait, and let Geraldine go—she'll have her things on."

"I suppose you haven't got any milk?" Mrs. Page said. "I declare I get to feeling awfully gone about this time!"

"We haven't a drop, Em," Mrs. Torney said, after investigating a small back porch, from which Julia got a strong whiff of wet ashes and decaying cabbage leaves.

"How much milk do you get regularly?" Julia asked, looking worried.

"Oh, my dear," Mrs. Torney said, from the sink, where she was attacking a greasy frying pan with cold water and a gray rag worn into holes, "you forget we ain't rich people here. We don't have him leave milk, but if we want it we put a bottle out on the back steps."

"You ought to have plenty of milk, Mama, taking those strong, depressing medicines!" Julia said.

"Well, I ain't got much appetite, Julie," her mother answered, with that new and touching smile. "Now, last night the girls had cabbage and corn beef cooking—I used to be real fond of that dinner, but it almost made me sick, just smelling it! So Geraldine fried me an egg, yet that didn't taste good, either! Gettin' old and fussy, I guess!"

Julia felt the tears press suddenly behind her eyes as she answered the patient smile. "Mama, I think you are terribly patient!" said she.

"I guess you can get used to anything!" Emeline said.

Regina coughed, and huddled herself in her chair.

"But I thought since we had the air-tight stove put in the other room you were going to use it more?" said Julia, as Mrs. Torney shook down the cooking stove with a violence that filled the air with the acrid taste of ashes.

"Well, we do sometimes. I meant to clean it to-day and get it started again," her aunt said. "I'm sure I don't know what we're going to do for dinner, Ma," she added. "Here it is getting round to five, and Geraldine hasn't come in. I don't know what on earth she does with herself—weather like this!"

Mrs. Cox made no response; she was nodding in the twilight over the little relaxed figure of the baby; a fat little white-clad leg rolled on her knee as she rocked. A moment later Geraldine, a heavy, highly coloured girl, much what her sister Marguerite had been ten years before, burst in, cold, wet, and tired, with a strapful of wet books which she flung on the table.

"My Lord, what do you keep this place so dark for, Ma!" said Geraldine. "It's something awful! Hello, Julia!" She kissed her cousin, picked Julia's big muff from a chair, and pressed the soft sables for a moment to her face. "Well, the little old darling, she's asleep, isn't she?" she murmured over the baby. "Say, Mamma," she went on more briskly, "I've got company coming to-night—"

"*You*!" said Julia, smiling, and laying an affectionate hand on her young cousin's shoulder, as she stood beside her. "Why, how old are you, child?"

"I'm sixteen—nearly," Geraldine said stoutly. "Didn't you have beaus when you were sixteen?"

"I suppose I did!" Julia admitted, smiling. "But you seem awfully young!"

"I thought—maybe you'd go to the store for me," said Mrs. Torney. Geraldine glared at her.

"Oh, my God! haven't the things come?" she demanded, in shrill disgust. "I can't, Mamma, I'm sopping wet, and I've got to clean the parlour. It's all over ashes, and mud, and the Lord knows what!"

"Well, I couldn't get out to-day, that's all there is to that," Mrs. Torney defended herself sharply. "My back's been like it was on fire. I've jest been resting all day. And when you go upstairs you won't find a thing straightened, so don't get mad about that—I haven't been able to do one thing! Regina's been real sick, too; she may have made the beds—she was upstairs a while—"

"She didn't!" supplied Regina herself, speaking over her shoulder as she lighted the gas. They all blinked in the harsh sudden light.

"Oh, Lord!" Geraldine was beginning, when Julia interrupted soothingly:

"See here, I have the car here; Chadwick was to come back at five. Let me send him for the things! What do we want?"

"Well, we don't want to keep you, lovey," her mother began. But Julia was already writing a list.

"Indeed I'm going to stay and have some with you, Mrs. Page," she said cheerfully. "Chops for the family—aren't those quickest? And a quart of oysters for Mama, and cake and cheese and jam and eggs—tell me anything you think of, Aunt May, because he might as well do it thoroughly!

"Mama and Regina are going to have oyster soup and toast because they are the invalids!" she announced cheerfully, coming back from the door a little later, "You like oysters, don't you, Mama?"

"Oh, Julia, I like 'em *so* much!" Mrs. Page said, with grateful fervour.

"You can have other things, too, you know, Madam," Julia assured her playfully. "And why don't you let me push you, so—" She wheeled the chair across the kitchen as she spoke. "Over here, you see, you're out of the crowd," she said. She presently put a coaxing arm about Regina. "Do go up and brush your hair and change, dear, you'll feel so much better," she urged.

"I feel rotten," Regina said, dragging herself stairward nevertheless.

Poor Mrs. Page cried when the moment for parting came. It was still early in the evening when Julia bundled up the sleeping Anna, and sent her to the motor car by Chester, a gentle gray-haired man, who had been extremely appreciative of a good dinner, and who had been sitting with his wet socks in the oven, and his stupid kindly eyes contentedly fixed upon Julia and her mother.

"I may not see you again, Julie," Mrs. Page said with trembling lips. "Mama ain't strong like she once was, dear. And I declare I don't know what I *shall* do, when day after day goes by and you don't come in—always so sweet!" The tears began to flow, and she twisted her head, and slowly and painfully raised her handkerchief in a crippled hand to dry her eyes. Julia knelt down to kiss her, her young face very sober.

"Listen, Mama—don't cry! Please don't cry!" said she. "Listen! I'll *promise* you to see you again before I go!"

Her mother brightened visibly at this, and Julia kissed her again, and ran out in the dripping rain to her car. She took the baby into her arms, and settled back in the darkness for the long trip to her hotel. And for the first time in many months her thoughts were not of her own troubles.

She thought of the Shotwell Street house, and wondered what had attracted her grandfather and grandmother to it, forty years ago. She tried to see her mother there, a slender, dark-haired child; tried to imagine her aunt as young and fresh and hopeful. Had the rooms been dark and dirty even then? Julia feared so; in none of her mother's reminiscences was there ever any tenderness or affection for early memories of Shotwell Street. Four young people had gone out from that house, nearly thirty years ago, how badly equipped to meet life!

Julia's own earliest recollections centred in it. She remembered herself as an elaborately dressed little child, shaking out her little flounces for her grandmother's admiration, and having large hats tied over her flushed sticky face and tumbled curls. She remembered that, instead of the row of cheap two-story flats that now faced it, there had been a vacant lot across the street then, where horses sometimes galloped. She remembered the Chester of those days, a pimply, constantly smoking youth, who gave her little pictures of actresses from his cigarette boxes, and other little pictures that, being held to a strong light, developed additional figures and lettering. He called her "Miss O'Farrell of Page Street" sometimes, and liked to poke her plump little person until she giggled herself almost into hysterics.

Still dreaming of the old times, she reached her hotel, and while Ellie settled the baby into her waiting crib, Julia sat down before a fire, her slippered feet to the comfortable coals, her loose mandarin robe deliciously warm and restful after the tiring day.

"You want the lights, Mrs. Studdiford?" asked Ellie, tiptoeing in from the next room.

"Oh, no, thank you!" Julia said. "I'll just sit here for a while, and then go to bed."

Ellie went softly out; the clock struck nine—ten—eleven. Against the closely curtained windows the rain still fell with a softened hiss, the coals broke, flamed up, died down to a rosy glow. Still Julia sat, sunk in her deep chair, musing.

She saw the Shotwell Street house changed, and made, for the first time in its years of tenancy, into a home. There must be paint outside, clean paint, there must be a garden, with a brick path and rose bushes, where a little girl might take her first stumbling steps, and where spring would make a brave showing in green and white for the eyes of tired homegoers.

Indoors there should be a cool little orderly dining-room, with blue china on its shelves, and a blue rug under the round table, and there should be a drawing-room papered in clean tans and curtained in cream colour, with an upright piano and comfortable chairs. The ugly old storeroom off the kitchen must be her mother's; it must have new windows cut, and nothing but what was new and pretty must go in there. And the kitchen should have blue-and-white linoleum, with curtains and shining tinware; there must be the gleam of scrubbed white woodwork, the shine of polished metal. It was a big kitchen, the invalid might still like to have her chair there.

The basement's big, unused front room must be finished in durable burlaps and grass matting for Uncle Chester; there must be a bath upstairs; two rooms for Aunt May and the girls, one for Grandma, one for Julia and little Anna.

So much for externals. But what of changing the tenants to suit the house? Would time and patience ever transform Mrs. Torney into a busy, useful woman? Would Geraldine and Regina develop into hopeless incompetents like Marguerite, or pay Julia for all her trouble by becoming happy and helpful and contented?

Time must show. Only the days and the years would answer the question that Julia asked of the fire. There must be patience, there must be endless effort, there would be times of bitterest discouragement and depression. And in the end?

In the end there would only be, at best, one family, out of millions of other families, saved from unnecessary suffering. There would be only one household lifted from the weight of incompetence and wretchedness that burdened the world. There would be no miracle, no appreciation, no gratitude.

"But—who knows?" mused Julia. "It may save Geraldine and Regina from lives like Rita's, and bitterness like Muriel's and Evelyn's. It may save them from clouding their lives as I did mine. Rita's children, too, who knows what a clean and sweet ideal—held before them, may do for them? And poor Chess, who has been wronged all his life, and my poor little grandmother, and Mama—"

It was the thought of her mother that turned the scale. Julia thought of the dirty blankets and the soggy pillow that furnished the invalid's chair, of the treat that a simple bowl of oyster soup seemed to the failing appetite.

"And I can do it!" she said to herself. "It will be hard for months and months, and it will be hard now to make Aunt Sanna see that I am right; but I can do it!" She looked about the luxurious room, and smiled a little sadly. "No more of this!" she thought. And then longing for her husband came with a sick rush. "Oh, Jimmy!" she whispered, with filling eyes. "If it was only you and me, my darling! If we were going *anywhere* together, to the poorest neighbourhood and the meanest cabin in the world—how blessed I would be! How we could work and laugh and plan together, for Anna and the others!" But presently the tears dried on her cheeks. "Never mind, it will keep me from thinking too hard," she thought. "I shall be needed, I shall be busy, and nothing else matters much!"

She got up, and went to one of the great windows that looked down across the city. The rain was over, dark masses of cloud were breaking and stirring overhead; through their rifts she caught the silver glimmer of the troubled moon. Across the shadowy band that was the bay a ferryboat, pricked with hundreds of tiny lights, was moving toward the glittering chain of Oakland. There was a light on Alcatraz, and other nearer lights scattered through the dark masts and dim hulks of the vessels in the harbour below her.

"It will be bright to-morrow!" Julia thought, resting her forehead against the glass. She was weary and spent; a measureless exhaustion seemed to enfold her. Yet under it all there glowed some new spark of warm reassurance and certainty. "Thank God, I see my way clear at last!" she said softly.

CHAPTER VII

The kitchen in the old Cox house formed a sort of one-story annex behind the building, and had windows on three sides, so that on a certain exquisite morning in March, four years later, sunlight flooded the two eastern windows and fell in clear squares of brightness on the checkered blue-and-white linoleum on the floor. There were thin muslin sash curtains at these windows, and white shades had been drawn down to meet them. Some trailing English ivy made a delicate tracery in dark green beside one window, and two or three potted begonias on the sill lifted transparent trembling blooms to the sun. The rest of the large room was in keeping with this cheerful bit of detail. There was a shining gas stove beside the shining coal range, and a picturesque bit of colour in the blue kettles and copper casseroles that stood in a row on the shelves above the range. A pine cupboard had been painted white, and held orderly rows of blue plates and cups; there were several white-painted chairs, and two tables. One of these was pushed against the west wall, and was of pine wood white from scrubbing; the other stood on a blue rag rug by the eastern windows, and was covered by a fringed tablecloth in white and blue. Near the outer door, with a window above it, was a white-enamelled sink in a bright frame of hanging small utensils.

The sunlight twinkled here and there on a polished surface, and flung a trembling bright reflection on the ceiling from the brass faucets of the sink. A clock on the wall struck seven.

As the last stroke sounded, Julia Studdiford quietly opened the hall door and stepped into the kitchen. She softly closed the door behind her, and went to another door, at which she paused for a few seconds with her head bent as if listening. Evidently satisfied that no one stirred in the bedroom beyond the door, she set briskly if noiselessly about her preparations for breakfast.

These involved the tying on of a crisp checked apron, and various negotiations with a large enamelled coffee pot, an egg, and the dark grounds that sent a heartening odour of coffee through the room. Bread was sliced and trimmed for toast with delightful evenness and swiftness, a double boiler of oatmeal was lifted from the fireless cooker, and the ice box made to furnish more eggs and a jar of damp, firm butter.

It was while making a little journey to the back porch for milk and cream that the housekeeper first wavered in her swift routine. Below the back steps lay a little city garden, so lovely in the strengthening March sunlight that she must set her bottles down on the step, and run down for a whiff of the fragrance of climbing roses, just beginning to bloom, of bridal-wreath and white lilac. Cobwebs, caught from bush to wet bush, sparkled with jewels; a band of brown sparrows flew away from a dripping faucet, and a black cat, crouching on the crosspieces of the low fence, rose, yawned, and vanished silently. The wall was almost entirely hidden by vines, principally rose vines, which flung long arms in the air. Presently a woman in the next yard parted these vines, to look over and say pleasantly:

"Good-mornin', Mis' Studdiford! I's just looking over an' *dee*-spairin' of ever gettin' my backyard to look like yours! It does smell like one big bo'quet mornin's like this!"

"Oh, well, there are so many of us to fuss with it," said the young woman addressed, cheerfully. "My aunt and my cousins are nearly as crazy about flowers as I am, and the other day—that warm day, you know, when we had my mother out here—she was just as absorbed as the rest of us!" She put a friendly head over the wall. "But I don't see what you've got to complain of, Mrs. Calhoun," said she, "especially as you're just beginning! I see your geraniums all took hold!"

"Every one but the white Lady Washington," the woman said. "How is your mother?" she added.

"Pretty comfortable, thank you!" said the other. "I imagine she may have had a restless night, for both she and my aunt seem to be asleep, so I'm getting breakfast for my cousins and uncle myself! And I'm not supposed to be out here at all!" she added, with a farewell laugh and nod, as she turned back to the steps. "But I just couldn't resist the garden!"

She picked up the milk bottles and reentered the kitchen just as a trimly dressed young woman came into it from the hall. The newcomer was tall, and if not quite pretty was at least a fresh-looking, pleasant-faced girl. She wore a tailor-made skirt and white shirt waist, and a round hat covered with flowers, and laid her jacket over the back of a chair.

"Julie, where's Ma?" said she, in surprise. "Have you been doing everything?"

"Not everything!" Julia smiled. "But Aunt May must have overslept herself; there hasn't been a sound from their room this morning. Your suit looks lovely," she added admiringly.

"Oh, do you think so?" asked the younger woman eagerly. She interrupted her task of putting plates and cups on the table, to come close and turn toward Julia the back of her head for inspection. "Like it?" asked she.

Julia seriously inspected the rhinestone comb that glittered there.

"Why, I don't utterly dislike it," she said, in her pleasant voice.

"But you don't think it's in good taste, Julie?"

"Well no, not exactly. Not for the office, anyway."

"All right, then—that settles it!" the young woman assured her. "I'll run upstairs after breakfast and change. We had a glorious time last night!" she went on, putting her head on one side to give the table a critical glance. "I'll tell you about it. This has boiled up, hasn't it—it can be settled?"

"Yes, settle it." said Julia, buttering toast, "and tell me!"

But at this moment the hall door opened again, and a little girl of four and a half appeared in the doorway. She was so lovely a vision, with her trailing wrapper and white nightgown bunched up to be out of her way, curls tumbled about her face, and eyes big with reproach, that both women laughed with pleasure at the sight of her.

"Mother," said she, with that lingering on the last consonant that marks the hurt pride of a child, "why diddunt you wake me?"

"Because you were sleeping so nicely, Pussy!" Julia laughed, on her knees by this time, with both arms about the little figure. "Give me a thousand kisses and say 'I love my mother!'"

"I love my mother!" said Anna, her eyes roving the room over her mother's shoulder. "I guess you don't know how hard you're squeezing me, Mother!" she added. "Can I come out here in my wrapper, and have breakfast with Regina?"

"Yes, let her, Julia!" Regina urged. "Come on, darling! Bring your bowl up here to my end. Do sit down and eat something yourself, Julia."

"This is the way to enjoy breakfast; not twenty feet from the stove!" Julia said, pouring the cream into her coffee. "Was Geraldine stirring when you got up, Regina?"

"Not a stir!" Regina said cheerfully. "She and Morgan were talking last night until two—I looked at the clock when she came upstairs! What they have to talk about gets me!"

"Oh, my dear, engaged people could talk forever," Julia said leniently. "They were househunting yesterday, there's always so much to talk about!"

"It seems to me that the people who don't marry have the most fun," Regina said. "Look at Muriel and Evvy, the money they make! Evvy going

East for the firm every year, and Muriel getting her little twenty-five a week. And then look at Rita, with four children to slave for—"

"Ah, well, Rita's husband doesn't work steadily, and she hates housework—she admits it!" Julia protested swiftly. "Rita could do a good deal, if she would."

"Rita gives me a great big pain," said her younger sister absently.

"A boy named Willis had a sword, and he hit a little boy with it, and Mrs. Calhoun said it was a wonder he wasn't killed!" contributed Anna suddenly, her eyes luminous from some thrilling recollection.

"Fancy!" Julia said. "Eat your oatmeal, Baby, and run upstairs and get some clothes on!" she added briskly. "You'll catch cold!"

But there was no severity in the glance she turned upon her daughter. Indeed, it would have been a stern heart that little Anna Studdiford's first friendly glance did not melt. She had been exquisite from her babyhood, she was so lovely now, as she emerged from irresponsible infancy to thoughtful little girlhood, that Julia sometimes wondered how she could preserve so much charm and beauty unspoiled. Anna had her mother's ash-gold hair, but where Julia's rose firm and winglike from her forehead, and was held in place by its own smooth, thick braids, the little girl's fell in rich, shining waves, sprayed in fine mist across her eyes, glittered, a golden mop in the sunlight, and even in the shade threw out an occasional gleam of gold. Anna's eyes were blue, with curled thick lashes like her mother's, but in the firm little mouth and the poise of her head, in the quick smile and quicker frown, Julia saw her father a hundred times a day. Her skin had the transparent porcelain beauty of babyhood, there was a suggestion of violet shadow about her eyes, and on her cheeks there glowed the warm colour of a ripe apricot. Even the gingham aprons and sturdy little shoes which she customarily wore did not disguise Anna's beauty. Julia trusted more to the child's wise little head than to the faint hope that her own precautions could ward off flattery and adulation. The two had been constant companions for more than four years: Anna's little bed close to her mother's at night, Anna's bright head never out of Julia's sight by day. If Anna showed any interest in what her mother was reading, Julia gave her a grave review of the story; if Julia went to market, Anna trotted beside her, deeply concerned as to cuts of meat and choices among vegetables; and when baking was afoot, Anna had a tiny moulding board on a chair, and cut cookies or scalloped tarts with the deep enjoyment of the born cook.

Once or twice the child had asked for her father, accepting quietly enough the explanation that he was in Germany, and very busy.

"Aren't we going to see him some time, Mother?"

"Not while Grandma needs Mother so much, dear!" Julia would answer easily.

Easily, because the busy months with their pain and joy, their problems and their successes, had seemed to seal away in a deep crypt her memories of her husband. Julia had been afraid to think of him at first; she could not make herself think of him now; his image drifted vaguely away from her, as unreal as a dream. He was as much a name as if she had never seen him, never loved him, never suffered those exquisite agonies of grief and shame with which the first year of their separation was full. Jim's child had taken his place; the purity and sweetness of the child's love filled Julia's heart; she wanted only Anna, and Anna was her interpreter for all the relationships of life. Anna first made her draw close to her own mother; Anna was at once her spur and her reward during the first hard years at Shotwell Street.

Anna had gone upstairs, and Regina was finishing her breakfast when Chester came downstairs, followed by the still sleepy yet shining-eyed Geraldine. Geraldine was to be married in a few weeks now, and had given up her position in an office, to devote all her time to house-furnishing and sewing.

"I'm awfully sorry to be so late," smiled Geraldine, "but we talked until I don't know when last night!" She poured herself a cup of coffee; the meal went cheerfully on. Presently the bedroom door opened, and a stout, handsome, middle-aged woman came into the kitchen.

Julia was used, by now, to the transformation that had come to house and garden, that had affected every member of her mother's family in the past four years. But to the change in her aunt, Mrs. Torney, she never became quite accustomed. It had been slow in coming; it had come all at once. There had been weeks when Julia felt that nothing would ever silence the whining voice, or make useful the idle hands. There had been a wretched time when the young woman had warned the older that matters could not continue as they were. There had been agitated decisions on Mrs. Torney's part to go away, with Regina, to starve and struggle again; there had been a scene when Regina coolly refused to leave the new comforts of Julia's rule.

And then, suddenly, there was a new woman in the family, in Aunt May's place. Julia always dated the change from a certain Thanksgiving Day, when Mrs. Torney, who was an excellent cook, had prepared a really fine dinner. Julia and the girls put the dining-room in order, a wood fire roared in the air-tight stove, another in the sitting-room grate. Julia dressed prettily; she put a late rose in her mother's hair, draped the invalid's prettiest shawl about the thin shoulders, arrayed the toddling baby in her daintiest finery. She coaxed her aunt to go upstairs to make herself fresh and neat just before dinner, and during the whole evening Mrs. Torney's sons and daughters, Julia and Evelyn, Chester and Mrs. Page and little old Mrs. Cox united to praise the dinner and the cook.

It was as if poor Aunt May had come into her own, had been given at last the role to which she had always been suited. Handsome in her fresh shirt waist and black skirt, with her gray hair coiled above a shining face, she beamed over turkey dressing and cranberry sauce; she laughed until she cried, when Elmer, who had come from Oakland for the feast, solemnly prefaced a request for more mince pie with a reckless: "Come on, Lloyd, let's die together; it's worth it!"

From that day hers was the happy part of the bustling housewife. No New England matron ever took more pride in cup cakes or apple pies, no kitchen in the world gave forth more savoury odours of roast meats and new-baked bread. Mrs. Torney's heavy tread on the kitchen floor was usually the first thing Julia heard in the morning, and late at night the infatuated housekeeper would slip out to the warm, clean, fragrant place for a last peep at rising dough or simmering soup. Aunt May read the magazines now only to seek out new combinations of meats and vegetables. Julia would smile, to glance across the dining-room to her aunt's chair beneath the lamp, and see the big, kindly face pucker over some startling discovery.

"Em!" Mrs. Torney would remove her glasses, she would address her sister in shocked tones. "Here they've got a sour-cream salad dressing. Did you ever hear of such a thing!"

"For heaven's sake!" Mrs. Page would look up from her absorbed watching of Chester's solitaire, drop her emaciated little head back against the waiting pillow.

"Try it some time, Aunt May, you could make anything taste good!" Julia might suggest. But Mrs. Torney would shake a doubtful head and, with a muttered "Sour cream!" resume her glasses and her magazine.

Now she was tying a crisp apron over her blue cotton dress, and ready with a smiling explanation for Julia.

"I declare, Ju, I don't know what's got into my alarm. I never woke up at all until quarter to eight o'clock! Don't start those dishes, lovey, there's no hurry!"

"I was afraid that Mama'd had a bad night," Julia said, smiling a good-morning from the sink. "Sit. down, Aunt May, I'll bring you your coffee!"

"No, Emeline had a real good night. She was reading a while, about three, but she's sound asleep now."

"I lighted a fire in the dining-room," said Chester, "just to take the chill off, if Em wants to go in there!"

"Then I'll bring my sewing down, after the beds are made," Geraldine said. "You go to market if you want to, Julie; I'll do your room."

"Well," Julia agreed, "perhaps I can get back before Mama wakes. I'll go up and see what Anna is doing."

Regina and Chester presently went off to their work, Mrs. Torney and Geraldine fell upon the breakfast dishes, and Julia went upstairs. She found the little Anna dreaming by a sunny window, one stocking on, one leg still bare, and her little petticoat hanging unbuttoned.

"Come, Infant, this won't do!" Julia's practised hands made quick work of the small girl's dressing. A stiff blue gingham garment went on over Anna's head, the tumbled curls were subjugated by a blue ribbon. When it was left to Anna merely to lace her shoes, Julia began to go about the room, humming as she busied herself with bureau and bed. She presently paused at the mirror to pin on a wide hat, and her eye fell upon the oval-framed picture of Jim that she had carried away with her from the Pacific Avenue house. It had been taken by some clever amateur; had always been a favourite with her. She studied it dispassionately for a moment.

Jim had been taken in tennis clothes; his racket was still in his hand, his thin shirt opened to show the splendid line of throat and chin. His thick hair was rumpled, the sunlight struck across his smiling face. Julia's memory could supply the twinkle in his eye; she could hear him call to Alan Gregory: "For the Lord's sake, cut this short, Greg! It's roasting out here!"

Beside this picture hung another, smaller, and also a snapshot. This was of a man, too, a tall, thin, ungainly man, sitting on a roadside rock, with a battered old hat in his hand. Behind him rose a sharp spur of rough mountainside, and so sharply did the ground fall away at his feet that far below him was a glimpse of the level surface of the Pacific. Julia smiled at this picture, and the picture smiled back.

"Come, Mouse!" said she, rousing herself from a reverie a moment later. "Get on your hat! You and I have to go to market!"

The morning wore on; it was like a thousand other happy mornings. Julia and Anna loitered in the cool odorous fish stalls at the market, welcomed asparagus back to its place in the pleasant cycle of the year's events, inspected glowing oranges and damp crisp heads of lettuce; stopped at the hardware store for Aunt May's new meat chopper, stopped at the stationer's for Anna's St. Nicholas, stopped at the florist's to breathe deep breaths of the damp fragrant air, and to get some buttercups for Grandma.

Julia's mother was in the kitchen when she and Anna got home, her dark hair still damp from brushing, her thin wrists no whiter than her snowy ruffles. Presently they all moved into the dining-room, where Geraldine's sewing machine was temporarily established, and where Anna's blocks had a corner to themselves. The invalid, between intervals of knitting, watched them all with her luminous and sympathetic smile.

"A letter for you, Julie, and four for me," said the bride-elect, coming back from the door after the postman's ring.

"*Four* for you—Gerry! You lucky thing!"

"Well—two are from Morgan," admitted Geraldine, smiling, and there was a laugh as Julia opened her own letter.

"It's from Dr. Richard Toland," she announced a moment later. "He says Mill Valley is too beautiful for words just now. How'd you like to go over and see Uncle Richie to-morrow, Anna?"

"I'd love it," said Anna unhesitatingly.

"We've not been for weeks," Julia said, "I'd love it, too, if my Marmer doesn't mind?" She turned her bright smile to her mother. "Regina says she has an engagement with the O'Briens for Sunday," said she, "and if Gerry goes off with Morgan, will that leave things too quiet?"

"Indeed it won't!" said Mrs. Torney, looking up from the tissue-paper pattern over which she had hung in profound bewilderment for almost half an hour. "Rita may bring some of the children in, or Lloyd and Elmer may come over. Go along with you!"

Richie, much stronger in these days, and without his crutch, though still limping a little, met Julia and the dancing Anna on the following afternoon, and the three crossed the ferry together. It was a day bursting with summer's promise, the air was pure and warm, and the sky cloudless. Getting out of the train at Mill Valley, Julia drew an ecstatic breath.

"Oh, Richie, what heavenly freshness! Doesn't it just smooth your forehead down like a cool hand!"

There was a poignant sweetness to the mountain air, washed clear by the late rains, and warmed and invigorated by the sunshine of the lengthening March day. The country roads were dark and muddy and churned by wheel tracks, but fringed with emerald grass. Even at four o'clock the little valley was plunged in early shadow, but sunshine lay still upon the hills that framed it, and long lines of light threw the grim heights of Tamalpais into bold relief. The watching tiers of the redwoods looked refreshed, their spreading dark fans were tipped with the jade-green sprays of the year's new growth. The first pale smoke of wild lilac bloom lay over the hills.

"It makes you think of delicious words," said Julia, as Richie's rusty white mare plodded up and up the mountain road. "Ozone—and aromatic—and exhilarating! In town it was a little oppressive to-day—Anna and I were quite wilted!"

"You don't look wilted!" Richie smiled at his goddaughter, who was in her mother's arms. "Look, Ju—there's columbine! Loads of it up near my place!" "And the wild currant, with that delicious pungent smell!" sighed Julia blissfully. "What's new with you, Richie?" she asked presently.

"Oh, nothing much! Cable from Bab yesterday, but you must have had one, too?"

"Yes, I did. A third boy!" Julia laughed. "Poor Bab—when she wanted a girl so badly!"

"I suppose she did," grinned Richard.

"Oh, of course she did! Who wouldn't?" Julia hugged her own girl. "And isn't it glorious about Keith?" she added, with sudden enthusiasm.

"Is it? I suppose it is," Richie said. "But then those old guys in Germany called him a genius long before New York did, and you girls didn't make so much fuss!"

"Oh, but Richie, there's so much money in this American tour; three concerts in New York alone, think of it!" Julia protested eagerly. "And Sally's letter sounded so gay; they were having a perfectly glorious time. I hope they come to San Francisco!"

"Well, she deserves it," Richie observed, flicking the rusty mare with a whip she superbly ignored. "Sally's had a pretty rotten time of it for seven or eight years—paying his lesson bills when she didn't have enough to eat or shoes to wear—and losing the baby——"

"I don't believe all that meant as much to Sally as you think," Julia said sagely. "Her entire heart was set upon Keith's success, and that has come along pretty steadily. Her letter to me about the baby wasn't the sort I should have written; indeed, I couldn't have written at all! And then that was four years ago, Richie, and four years is a long time!"

"It is!" Richie agreed. "Keith's about all the baby she'll ever want; those fellows take an awful lot of spoiling. But I get more pleasure from Mother's and Dad's pleasure than for Sally herself," he added. "Mother saves up newspaper accounts, and has this translated from the German and that from the French—it's sort of pathetic to see! Dad and Janey are in New

York now; something was said last night about their going over to see Bab."

"Ted and your mother are alone, then? How's Ted?"

"Oh, driving Mother crazy, as usual. She'd flirt with the Portuguese milkman if she had a chance. She can't seem to understand that because she wants to be free she *isn't* free! Talks about 'if I marry again,' and so on. Of course Carleton's marrying again has made her wild."

"But, good heavens, Richie, Ted ought to have some *sense*!"

"Well, she hasn't. She stretched a point to marry him, d'you see? Carleton had been baptized as a child, and his first wife hadn't, and they were married by a Justice of the Peace, or something of that sort. So Ted claimed that in the eyes of the Church he hadn't been married at all, and she married him. Then——"

"But if she loved him, Richie—and Ted was so young!"

"All true, of course, only if you're going to push things to the point of taking advantage of a quibble like that, your chance of happiness is more or less slim! So three years ago Carleton proved that he hadn't cared a whoop about the legal or religious aspects of the case, and left Ted. And now Ted can't see herself, at twenty-seven, tied to another woman's husband!"

"She has her boy," Julia said severely.

"Yep, but that doesn't seem to count."

"Well, it's funny, Richie, take us all in all, what a mess we've made of marrying!" Julia mused. "Ned gives me the impression, every time I see him, of being a sulky martyr in his own home; Sally's managed to drag happiness out of a most hopeless situation; Ted, of course, will never be happy again, like Jim and me; and Connie, although she made an exemplary marriage, either has to leave her husband or bring her baby up in Manila, which she says positively isn't safe! Bab is the only shining success among us all!"

"Oh, I don't know," Richie said, stopping the horse, and flinging the reins to the Portuguese who came out of a small barn to meet them. "Here we are, Ju—take your time! I've always considered you rather successful," he resumed.

"Oh, me!" Julia laughed as she jumped down like a girl. She followed Anna across a little hollow filled with buttercups and long grasses, and they mounted the little rise to Richie's tiny cabin. The little house had Mount Tamalpais for a background, and its wide unroofed porch faced across the valley, and commanded a view of the wooded ridges, and the marshes, and the distant bay, and of San Francisco twelve miles away. Scrub oaks and bay trees grew in a tangle all about it, even a few young redwoods and an occasional bronze and white madrona tree. Wild roses and field flowers crowded against its very walls, and under the trees there were iris and brown lilies, and a dense undergrowth of manzanita and hazelnut bushes, wild currant and wild lilac trees.

The big room that Julia entered first was dim with pleasant twilight, and full of the sweet odours of a dying wood fire. It had nothing of distinction in it: a few shabby chairs, an old square piano, an unpainted floor crossed here and there by rugs, books in cases and out of them, candlesticks along the brick mantel, a green-shaded student's lamp on a long table, and several wide windows, dim and opaque now in the fast-gathering darkness, but usually framing each a picture of matchless mountain scenery.

A door at one side of the fireplace led into a tiny kitchen whose windows looked out into oak branches; and another door, on the other side, gave access to a little cement-floored bathroom with a shower, and two small bedrooms, each with two beds built in tiers like bunks. This was Richie's whole domain, and whether it was really saturated with the care-free atmosphere of childhood, and fragrant with the good breath of the countryside all about it, or whether Julia only imagined it to be so, she found it perfect, and was never so happy in these days as when she and Anna were there. She was always busy, and satisfied in her work, but there were needs of heart and mind that her own people could not meet, and when these rose strong within her she found no company as bracing and as welcome as Richard's.

"No Aunt Sanna?" said she cheerfully, when she had taken off her hat and the small girl's, and was in her favourite chair by the fire.

"No, darn it!" said Richie, struggling with a refractory lamp wick.

"Oh, don't be so blue, Rich! She'll be here on the seven."

"No, she won't—she said the four—I expected to find her here," Richie said, settling the glass chimney into place, as the light crept round the wick. A little odour of hot kerosene floated on the air, and was lost in other odours from the kitchen, where a Chinese boy was padding about in the poor light of one lamp. He began to come and go, setting the table, the ecstatic Anna at his heels. Whenever the outer door was opened, a cool rush of sweet country air came in. Richie began to stamp back and forth with great logs for the fireplace.

"Wonderful what millions of miles away from every one we seem, Rich!" Julia said contentedly. "Was there ever anything like the quiet of this mountain?"

"I'm terribly sorry about Aunt Sanna," Richie said. "I feel like an ass—getting you way up here!"

"Why, my dear boy, it's not *your* fault!" Julia said, round eyed.

"She said she would positively be here," Richie pursued. "I suppose there's no earthly reason—" he added uncomfortably.

"Why you and I shouldn't stay here alone? I should hope not!" Julia reassured him roundly. "And she may come on the seven, anyway!"

"These are the times I wish I had a telephone," said Richie.

"Aw leddy," contributed the Chinese boy. They took their places at the table, and dinner was eaten by the light of the lamp. But after dinner, when Julia had tucked Anna into bed, she came back and put out the lamp. She lighted two candles on the mantelpiece that sent a brave flicker over the dull walls and up to the ceiling.

"There!" said she, with an energetic stirring of the fire, as she took her chair again, "that's the way I like this room to look!"

Richard disposed of his awkward length in an opposite chair, his big bony hands interlocked. In the fire and candlelight Julia looked very young, her loosened hair glimmering against the back of her chair, her thin white skirts spreading in a soft circle above her slipper buckles. The man noticed the serene rise and fall of her breast under her thin blouse, the content in her half-shut blue eyes. He let his thoughts play for a moment with the perilous dream that she belonged here at his hearth, that her sweetness, her demure happiness, her earnest interest in everything that concerned him, were all his by right.

"I don't quite know what to do about this!" he said gruffly.

"What—our being here?" Julia looked surprised. "Why, Richie, what can we do? Do you think it matters, one night? After all, we're brother and sister-in-law!"

"Almost," said Richie, with a laugh.

"Why, Rich, I would never give it one moment's thought; not if I stayed here a month!" Julia assured him. "And neither would any one else. Don't be so silly!"

"It's not me; but it isn't fair to you!" Richard said.

Julia had grown a little red. Now she stared into the fire.

"This sort of fuss isn't like you, Rich," she said presently, with an uncomfortable laugh. "You—you don't usually talk about such things!"

"No, I know I don't," Richard admitted, untouched by her reproach. "I could go up to Porter's and try to get Aunt Sanna by telephone!" he muttered.

Julia was displeased, and made no answer, and presently he got up and went out. She sat there listening to the rattle of dishes in the kitchen, until a splash announced the dishpan emptied under the oak trees, and the Chinese through with his work for the night. After a while she went to the doorway, and stared out at the starry sky and the dark on darkness that marked masses of trees and long spurs of the mountain. The air was sweet and chilly, frogs were peeping, from somewhere near came the steady rush of a swollen creek.

While Julia stood on the porch a livery hack from the village creaked up, and stopped ten feet away. The horses were blowing on the steep grade, and a strong odour from the animals and their sweated harness smote the pure night air. The carriage lanterns sent a wavering brightness across the muddy road, the grass looked artificial in the yellow light. Miss Toland, vociferating apology and explanation, emerged from the carriage.

When Richard came back from his fruitless errand he found both women enjoying the fire, Miss Toland's skirt folded over her knees, her veil pushed up on her forehead. In his enormous relief, Richie felt that he could have danced and sung. He busied himself brewing a hot drink for the older woman.

"Richie," said Julia, with a pleasant childish note of triumphant reproach in her voice, "was worried to *death* because I was here alone with Anna! Don't you think he's crazy, Aunt Sanna?"

"Why, you two have been here alone?" Miss Toland asked, stirring her chocolate.

"No, we haven't!" Julia answered cheerfully. "I never thought of it before; but this dear old maid either has you here, or Janey, or Doctor Brice's Mary from the village—isn't he queer?"

"It isn't as if you weren't practically brother and sister, Richie," Miss Toland said moderately. "Not too much butter, dear!" she interpolated, in reference to the toast her nephew was making, adding a moment later, "Still, I don't know—a pretty woman in your position can't be too careful, Julia!"

"Oh, Lord, you're an appreciative pair!" Richard said disgustedly, going out to the kitchen for more bread.

Presently Miss Toland complained of fatigue, and left them to the fire. And sitting there, almost silent, Julia thought that she had never found her host so charming before. His rambling discourse amused her, touched her; she loved his occasional shy introduction of a line of poetry, his eager snatching of a book now and then to illuminate some point with half a page of prose.

"Pleasant, isn't this, Rich?" she asked lazily, in a quiet interval.

"Oh, *pleasant*!" He cleared his throat. "Yes—it's very pleasant!"

"And why couldn't you and I have done this just as well without Aunt Sanna?" Julia asked triumphantly.

Richard gave her a look full of all-dignified endurance, a look that wondered a little that she could like to give him pain.

"No reason at all," said he. And a sudden suspicion flamed in Julia's heart with all the surety of an inspiration.

The revelation came in absolute completeness; she had never even suspected Richie's little tragedy before. For a few moments Julia sat stunned, then she said seriously:

"I always feel myself so much Jim's wife, Rich; I suppose it's a sort of protection to me. It never occurs to me that any one could think me less bound than I think myself."

"Sure you do!" Richard said, struggling with the back log. "But other people might not! And it would be rotten to have him come back and hear anything."

"I suppose he'll come back," Julia said, dreamily, almost in a whisper. "I don't think of it much, now! I used to think of it a good deal at first; I used to cry all night long sometimes, and write him long letters that I never sent. It seemed as if the longing for him was burning me up, like a fire!"

"Damn him!" Richard muttered.

"Oh, no, Richie, don't say that!" Julia protested. Richard, still on one knee, with the poker in his hand, turned to her almost roughly.

"For God's sake, Julie, don't defend him! I'll hold my tongue about him, I suppose, as I always have done, but don't pretend he has any excuse for treating you this way! You—the best and sweetest and bravest woman that ever lived, bringing happiness and decency wherever you go—"

"Richie, Richie, stop!" Julia protested, between laughter and tears. "Don't talk so! I *will* defend Jim," she added gravely, "and he *did* have an excuse. It seems unfair to me that he should have all the blame." She held her hand out, fingers spread to the reviving flame, rosy and transparent in the glow.

"Rich, no one knows this but Jim and me; not Aunt Sanna, not my own mother," she presently resumed. "But it makes what he did a little clearer, and I'm going to tell you."

"Don't tell me anything," said Richard gruffly, eyes on the fire.

"Yes, I want to," Julia answered. But she was silent for a while, a look of infinite sadness on her musing face. "I made a serious mistake when I was a girl, Rich," she went on, after an interval. "I had no reason for it—not great love, or great need. I had no excuse. Or, yes, I did have this excuse: I had been spoiled; I had been told that I was unusual, independent, responsible to nobody. I knew that this thing existed all about me, and if I thought of it at all, I suppose I thought that there could be nothing so very dreadful about what men did as a matter of course! Perhaps that's the best explanation; my mind was like a young boy's. I didn't particularly seek out this thing, or want this thing; but I was curious, and it came my way—

"Don't misunderstand me, Richie. I wasn't 'betrayed.' I'd had, I suppose, as little good instruction, as little example, and watching and guarding as any girl in the world. But I knew better! Just as every boy knows better, and is taken, sooner or later, unawares. Of course, if I'd been a boy—all this would be only a memory now, hardly shameful or regrettable even, dim and far away! Especially as it lasted only a few weeks, before I was sixteen!

"And, of course, people would say that I haven't paid the full penalty, being a girl instead of a boy! Look at poor Tess, and Trilby, and Hetty in 'Adam Bede!' I never let any one know it; even your aunt never would have overlooked *that*, whatever she might say now. No; even Jim protected me—and yet," Julia put her head back, shut her eyes, "and yet I've paid a thousand times!" said she.

There was a long silence, and then Richard said:

"I've thought sometimes this might be it, Ju. Being alone so much, and reading and thinking—I've worked it out in my own mind. Aunt Sanna saw Jim in Berlin two years ago, you know, and gave him a horrible raking over the coals, and just from what she quoted, it seemed as if there was some secret about it, and that it lay with you. Then, of course," Richie eased his lame leg by stretching it at full length before him, sinking down in his chair, finger tips meeting, "of course I knew Jim," he resumed. "Jim's pride is his weak point. He's like a boy in that: he wants everything or nothing. He's like all my mother's children," said Richie, comfortably analytical, "undisciplined. Chill penury never repressed our noble rages; we never knew the sweet uses of adversity. I did, of course, but here I am, a childless getting on in years, not apt to leave a deep impression on the coming generation. It's a funny world, Julie! It's a strange sort of civilization to pose under the name of Christ. Christ had no double standard of morals; Christ forgave. Law is all very well, society has its uses, I have no doubt, but there are higher standards than either!" "Well, that has come to me forcibly during the past few years," Julia said thoughtfully. "I wasn't a praying small girl; how could I be? But after I went to The Alexander, being physically clean and respectable made me long to be clean all over, I suppose, and I began to go to church, and after a while I went to confession, Rich, and I felt made over, as if all the stain of it had slipped away! And then Jim came, and I told him all about it—"

"Before you were married?"

"Oh, Richie, of course!"

"Well, then, what—if he knew—"

"Oh, Richie, that's the terrible part. For I thought it was all dead and gone, and it *was* all dead and gone as far as I was concerned! But we couldn't forget it—it suddenly seemed a live issue all over again; it just rose and stood between us, and I felt so helpless, and poor Jim, I think he was helpless, too!"

Richard made no comment, and there was a silence.

"You know Jim wasn't a—wasn't exactly a saint, Ju," Richard said awkwardly after a while.

"I know," she answered with a quick nod.

"I believe he was an exceptionally decent fellow, as fellows go," pursued Richie. "But, of course, it is the accepted thing. On Jim's first vacation, after he entered college, he told me he didn't care much for that sort of thing— we had a long talk about it. But a year or two later there was a young woman—he used to call her 'the little girl'—I don't know exactly—Anyway, Dad went East, there was some sort of a fuss, and I know Jim treated her awfully well—there never was any question of that—she never felt anything but gratitude to him, whatever grievances she had about any one else—"

His voice dropped.

"But it's not the same thing," Julia said with a sigh.

"No, I suppose not," Richard agreed.

"Life has been too violent and too swift with me," Julia resumed, after a while. "If I had the past fifteen years to live over again, I would live them very differently. I made an idol of Jim; he could do no wrong. He wanted more bracing treatment than that; he should have been boldly faced down. If I had been wiser, I would have treated all my marriage differently. If I had been very wise, I should not have married at all, should have kept my own secret. Perhaps, marrying, I should not have told him the truth; I don't know. Anyway, I have mixed things up hopelessly, given other people and myself an enormous amount of pain, and wrecked my life and Jim's. And now, when I am thirty, I feel as if I could begin to see light, begin to live—as if now, when nothing on earth seems really important, I knew how to meet life!"

"Well, that's been my attitude for some years," Richie said, shifting his lame leg again. "Of course I started in handicapped, which is a great advantage—"

"Advantage? Oh, Richie!" Julia protested.

"Yes, it is, from one point of view," he insisted whimsically. "'Who loses his life,' you know. Most boys and girls start off into life like kites in a high wind without tails. There's a glorious dipping and plunging and sailing for a little while, and then down they come in a tangle of string and paper and broken wood. I had a tail to start with, some humiliating deficiency to keep me balanced. No football and tennis for me, no flirting and dancing and private theatricals. When Bab and Ned were in one whirl of good times, I was working out chess problems to make myself forget my hip, and reading Carlyle and Thoreau and Emerson. Nobody is born content, Ju, and nobody has it thrust upon him; just a few achieve it. I worked over the secret of happiness as if it was the multiplication table. Happiness is the best thing in the world. It's only a habit, and I've got it."

"*Is* happiness the best thing in the world, Rich?" Julia asked wistfully.

"I think it is; real happiness, which doesn't necessarily mean a box at the Metropolitan and a touring car," Richie said, smiling. "It seems to me, to have a little house up here on the mountain, and to have people here like me, and let me take care of them—"

"For nothing?" interposed Julia.

"Don't you believe it! I didn't write a cheque last month! Anyway, it suits me. I have books, and letters, and a fire, and now and then a friend or two—and now and then Julia and Anna to amuse me!"

"I'm happy, too," Julia said thoughtfully. "I realized it some time ago—oh, a year ago! I feel just as you might feel, Rich, if you had left some critical operation unfinished, or done in a wrong way, and then gone back to do it over. I feel as if, in going back to first principles, and doing what I could for my own people, I had 'trued' a part of my life, if you can understand that! I had gone climbing and blundering on, and reached a point where I couldn't help myself, but they were just where they started, and I *could* help them!"

"It was probably the best thing you could have done for yourself, at the same time," Richard interpolated, with a swift glance.

"Oh, absolutely!" Julia laughed a little sadly. "I was like an animal that goes out and eats a weed: I had a wild instinct that if I rushed into my grandmother's house, and bullied everybody there, and simply shrieked and stamped on the dirt and laziness and complaining, on the whole wretched system that I grew up under, in short, that it would be a heavenly relief! My dear Richie," and Julia laughed again, and more naturally, "I wonder they didn't tar and feather me, and throw me out of the house! I scoured and burned and scolded and bossed them all like a madwoman. I told them that we had enough money to keep the house decently, and always had had, but, my dear! I never dreamed the whole crowd would fall in line so soon!"

"But, my Lord, Julie, what else could they do? You were paying all the expenses, I suppose?"

"No, indeed I wasn't! Chester has a pretty fair salary now, and my aunt's boys are awfully good about helping out. And then Muriel has a position, and Evelyn is in a fair way to be a rich woman. Besides, the mere question of where money is coming from never worried my people! They managed as well with almost nothing at all, as with a really adequate amount—which is to say that they don't know in the least what the word manage means! Jim left me an immense sum, Rich, but I've never touched anything but the interest. When we shingled or carpeted or gardened out there, we paid for it by degrees, and it cost, I must admit, only about one third of what it would have been on the other side of town. I look back now at those first months, more than four years ago," went on Julia, smiling as she leaned forward in her low chair, her hands locked about her knees, her thoughtful eyes on the flickering logs, "and I wonder we didn't all rise up in the night and kill each other. I was like a person with a death wound, struggling madly through the little time left me, absolutely indifferent to what any one thought. I simply wanted to die fighting, to register one furious protest against all the things I'd hated, and suffered, too! I remember reporters coming, at first, wild with curiosity to know what took Doctor Studdiford abroad, and why Mrs. Studdiford was living in a labourer's house in the Mission. What impression they got I haven't the faintest idea. Once or twice women called, just curious of course, Mrs. Hunter and Miss Saunders—but that soon stopped. I was better hidden on Shotwell Street than I would have been in the heart of India! Miss Saunders came in, and met Mama and Grandma; we were having the kitchen calcimined, the place was pretty well upset, I remember.

Dear me, how little what they thought or did or said seemed to count, when my whole life was one blazing, agonizing cry for Jim!"

"That got better?" Richard asked huskily, after a pause.

"Rich, I think the past two, well, three years, have been the happiest in my life," Julia said soberly. "My feet have been on solid ground. I not only seem to understand my life better as it is, but all the past seems clearer, too. I thought Jim was like myself, Richie, but he wasn't; his whole viewpoint was different; perhaps that's why we loved each other so!"

"And suppose he comes back?" Richard asked.

Julia frowned thoughtfully.

"Oh, Richie, how do I know! It's all so mixed up. Everybody, even Aunt Sanna, thinks that he will! Everybody thinks I am a patient, much-enduring wife, waiting for the end of an inexplicable situation. Aunt Sanna thinks it's temporary aberration. Your father thinks there's another woman in it. Your mother confided to Aunt Sanna that it is her opinion that Bab refused Jim, and Jim married from pique."

"That sounds like Mother!" Richie said with a dry laugh.

"Doesn't it?" Julia smiled. "But the truth is," she added, "Jim has no preconcerted plan. He's made a very close man friend or two in Germany, belongs to a doctors' club. I know him so well! He lets the days, and the weeks, and the years go by, forgetting me and everything that concerns me as much as he can, and getting into a slow, dull rage whenever he remembers that fate hit him, of all men in the world, such a blow!"

"And the baby?" said Richie. "Don't you suppose she counts? Oh, Lord, to have a kid of one's own," he added slowly, with the half-smiling sigh Julia knew so well.

"I imagine she would count if he had seen her lately," Julia suggested. "But she was such a tiny scrap! And Jim, as men go, isn't a lover of children."

"You wouldn't divorce him, Julie?" Richard asked, after a silence.

"Oh, never!" she answered quickly. "No, I won't do that." She smiled. "Yet, Rich," she added presently, "it's a strange thing to me that really my one dread is that he will come back. I *think* he means nothing to me, yet, if I saw him—I don't know! Sometimes I worry for fear that he might want Anna, and of course I wouldn't give her up if it meant a dozen divorces."

Richard sat staring into the fire for a few moments; then he roused himself to ask smilingly:

"How'd we get started on this little heart to heart, anyway?"

"Well, I don't know," Julia said, smiling, too. "I couldn't talk of it for a long while. I can't now, to any one but you. But it all means less to me than it did. Jim never could hurt me now as he did then." She straightened up in her chair. "It's been a wonderful talk!" she said, with shining eyes. "And you're a friend in a million, Richie, dear! And now," very practically, "where are you going to sleep, my dear? Aunt Sanna has your room."

"This couch out here is made up!" Richard said, with a backward jerk of his head toward the room behind him.

"Ah, then you're all right!" Julia rose, and stopped behind his chair for a moment, to lay a light kiss on his hair. "Good-night, Little Brother!" she said affectionately.

Instantly one of the bony hands shot out, and Julia felt her wrist caught as in a vise. Richard swiftly twisted about and got on his own feet, and for a minute their eyes glittered not many inches apart. Julia tried to laugh, but she was breathing fast.

"*Richard!*" she said in a sharp whisper. "What is it?"

"Julia!" he choked, breathing hard.

For a long moment they remained motionless, staring at each other. Then Richard's grip on her wrists relaxed, and he sank into his deep chair, dropped his elbows on his knees, and put his hands over his face. Julia stood watching him for a second.

"Good-night, Richie!" she said then, almost inaudibly.

"Good-night!" he whispered through his shut fingers. Julia slipped softly away, closing the door of her bedroom noiselessly behind her.

Anna was asleep in the upper bed, lying flat on her back, with her lovely hair falling loosely about her flushed little face. The little cabin bedroom was as sweet as the surrounding woodland, wide-open windows admitted the fragrant coolness of the spring night. There was no moon, but the sky that arched high above the little valley was thickly spattered with stars. Richie's cat, a shadow among paler shadows, leaped swiftly over the new grass. Julia got the milky odour of buttercups, the breath of the little Persian lilac that flanked one end of the porch.

Her heart was beating thickly and excitedly, she did not want to think why. Through her brain swept a confusion of thoughts, thoughts disconnected and chaotic. She tried to remember just what words on her part—on Richard's—had led to that strange mad moment of revelation, but the memory of the moment itself overleaped all those preceding it. Julia knelt, her elbows on the window sill, and felt merely that she never wanted to move again. She wanted just to kneel here, hugging to her heart the thrilling emotion of the moment, realizing afresh that life was not dead in her; youth and love were not dead in her; she could still tremble and laugh and cry in the exquisite joy of being beloved.

And it was Richie, so weak in body, so powerful in spirit; so humble in little things, so bold and sure in the things that are great; not rich in money, but rich in wisdom and goodness; Richie, who knew all her pitiful history now, and had long suspected it, who loved her! Julia knew even now that it was an ill-fated love; she knew that deep under this first strangely thrilling current of pride and joy ran the cold waters of renunciation. But cool reason had little to do with this mood; she was as mad as any girl whose senses are suddenly, blindly, set free by a lover's first kiss.

After a while she began mechanically to undress, brushed her hair, moved about softly in the uncertain candlelight. And as she did so she became more and more unable to resist the temptation to say "Good-night" to Richie again. Neither brain nor heart was deeply involved in this desire, but some influence, stronger than either, urged her irresistibly toward its fulfilment.

She would not do it, of course! Not that there was harm in it; what possible harm could there be in her putting her head into the sitting-room and simply saying "Good-night?" Still, she would not do it.

A glance at herself in the dimly lighted mirror set her pulses to leaping again. Surely candlelight had never fallen on a more exquisite face, framed in so shining and soft an aureole of bright hair. The long loose braid fell over her shoulder, a fine ruffle of thin linen lay at the round firm base of her throat. She was still young—still beautiful—

Anna stirred, sighed in her sleep. And instantly Julia had extinguished the candle, and was bending tenderly over the child.

"It's only Mother, Sweet! Are you warm enough, dear? You *feel* beautifully warm! Let Mother turn you over—so!"

"Is it morning, Mother?" murmured Anna.

"No, my heart! Mother's just going to bed." And ten minutes later Julia was asleep, her face as serene as the child's own.

The morning brought her only a shamed memory of the night before and its moods, and as Richie was quite his natural self, Julia determined to dismiss the matter as a passing moment of misinterpreted sentiment on both their parts. To-day was a Sunday, so perfect that they had breakfast on the porch, and in the afternoon took a long climb on the mountainside, across patches of blossoming manzanita, and through meadows sweet with the liquid note of rising larks. They came back in the twilight: Anna limp and drowsy on Richard's shoulders, Miss Toland admitting to fatigue, but all three ready to agree with Julia's estimate that it had been a wonderful Sunday.

But night brought to two of them new and strange self-consciousness that each had been secretly dreading all day. Julia fought it as she might have fought the oncoming of a physical ill, yet inexorably it arrived. Supper was an ordeal, she found speech difficult, she could hardly raise her eyes.

"Julie, you're as rosy as a little gipsy," said Miss Toland approvingly. "Doesn't colour become her, Rich?"

"She looks fine," Richard muttered, almost inarticulately. Julia looked up only long enough to give Miss Toland a pained and fluttering smile. She was glad of an excuse to disappear with Anna, when the little girl's bedtime arrived, and lingered so long in the bedroom that Miss Toland came and rapped on the door.

"Julia! What *are* you doing?" called the older woman impatiently. Julia came to the door.

"Why, I'm so tired, Aunt Sanna," she began smilingly.

"Tired, nonsense!" Miss Toland said roundly. "Come sit on the porch with Richie and me. It's like summer out of doors, and there'll be a moon!"

So Julia went to take her place on the porch steps, with a great curved branch of the white rose arching over her head, and the fragrant stretch of the grassy hilltop sloping away, at her feet, to the valley far below. Miss Toland dozed, and the younger people talked a little, and were silent for long spaces between the little casual sentences that to-night seemed so full of meaning.

The next day Julia went home, to Miss Toland's disgust and to little Anna's sorrow. Richie drove Julia and the little girl to the train; there was no explanation needed between them; at parting they looked straight into each other's eyes.

"Ask us to come again some day," Julia said. "Not too soon, but as soon as you can. And don't let us ever feel that we've done anything that will hurt or distress you, Richie."

"You and Anna are both angels," Richard answered. "Only tell me that you forgive me, Julie; that things after this will be just as they were before?"

Julia smiled, and bit a thoughtful under lip.

"This is March," she said. "We'll come and see you, let me see—in July, and everything shall be just as it was before! Perhaps I am really getting old," she said to herself, half laughing and half sad, when she was in her own kitchen an hour or two later. "But, while home is not exciting, somehow I'd rather be here than philandering on the mountain in the moonlight with Richie!"

"What you smiling about, Julie?" her mother asked, from the peaceful east side of the kitchen where her chair frequently stood while Julia and Mrs. Torney were busy in that cheerful apartment.

"Just thinking it was nice to be home again, Mama!"

"I don't hold much with visiting, myself," said Mrs. Torney, who was becoming something of a philosopher as she went into old age. "But you can't get that through a young one's skull!" she added, trimming the dangling pastry from a pie with masterly strokes of her knife. "Either you have such a good time that your own home is spoiled for you, for dear knows how long, or else you set around wondering why on earth you ever come. And then you've got to have the folks back to visit you, and wear yourself all out talking like all possessed while you cook for 'em and make their beds. I don't never feel clean when I've washed my face away from home anyway, and I like my own bed under me. You couldn't get me to visit anywheres now, if it was the Queen of Spain ast me!"

Julia laughed out merrily, and agreed with her aunt, glad to have left the episode with Richie behind her. But it haunted her for many days, nevertheless, rising like a disturbing mist between her and her calm self-confidence, and shaking her contented conviction that the renunciations necessary to her peace of mind had all been made. She found fresh reason to gird herself in circumspection and silence, and brooded, a little in discouragement, upon the incessantly recurring problems of her life.

She went to visit the cabin on Tamalpais earlier even than she had promised, however, for in June Barbara came home for a visit, bringing two splendid little boys, with whom Anna fell instantly in love, and a tiny baby in the care of a nurse. Julia spent a good deal of her time in Sausalito during the visit, and more than once she and Barbara took the four children to Mill Valley, and spent a few days with Richie, quite as happy as the boys and Anna were in the free country life.

Five years of marriage had somewhat changed Barbara; she was thinner, and freckled rather than rosy, and she wore her thick dark hair in a fashion Julia did not very much admire. Also she seemed to care less for dress than she once had done, even though what she wore was always the handsomest of its kind. But she was an eagerly admiring and most devoted wife, calmly assuming that the bronzed and silent "Francis" could do no wrong, and Julia thought she had never seen a more charming and conscientious mother. Barbara, whose husband's uncle was a lord, who had been presented at the English court, and whose mail was peppered with coats-of-arms, nursed her infant proudly and publicly, and was heard to mention to old friends—not always women either—social events that had occurred "just before Geordie came" or "when I was expecting Arthur." Her rather thin face would brighten to its old beauty when Geordie and Arthur, stamping in, bare kneed and glowing, recounted to her the joys of Sausalito, and in evening dress she was quite magnificent, and somehow seemed more at ease than American women ever do. Her efficiency left even the capable Julia gasping and outdistanced. Barbara was equal to every claim husband, children, family, and friends could make. She came down to an eight o'clock breakfast, a chattering little son on each side of her, announcing briskly that the tiny Malcolm had already had his bath. She started the little people on the day's orderly round of work and play while opening letters and chatting with her father; earned the housemaid's eternal affection by personally dusting the big drawing-room and replacing the flowers; answered the telephone in her pleasantly modulated voice; faced her husband during his ten o'clock breakfast, and discussed the foreign news with him in a manner Julia thought extraordinarily clever; and at eleven came with the baby into her mother's sunny morning-room for a little feminine gossip over Malcolm's second breakfast. Barbara never left a note unanswered, no old friend was neglected; tea hour always found the shady side porch full of callers, children strayed from the candy on the centre table to the cakes near the teapot, the doctor's collie lay panting in the doorway. Barbara's rich soft laugh, the new tones that her voice had gained in the past years, somehow dominated everything. Julia felt a vague new restlessness and discontent assail her at this contact with Barbara's full and happy life. Perhaps Barbara suspected it, for her generous inclusion of Julia, when plans of any sort were afoot, knew no limit. She won Anna's little heart with a thousand affectionate advances; loved to have the glowing beauty of the little girl as a foil for her own dark-haired boys.

"You're so busy—and necessary—and unself-conscious, Barbara," Julia said, "you make other women seem such fools!"

It was a heavenly July afternoon, and the two were following Richie and the children down one of the mountain roads above Mill Valley. Barbara, who had acquired an Englishwoman's love of nursery picnics, had lured her husband to join them to-day, and Julia had been pleasantly surprised to see how fatherly the Captain was with his small boys, how willing to go for water and tie dragging little shoe laces. But presently the soldier grew restless, stared about him for a few moments, and finally decided to leave the ladies and children to Richie's escort, and walk to the summit of the mountain and back, as a means of working off some excess of energy and gaining an appetite for dinner. He apparently did not hear Barbara's warning not to be late, and her entreaty to be careful, merely giving her a stolid glance in answer to these eager suggestions, and remarking to the boys, who begged to accompany him a little way: "Naow, naow, I tell you you carn't, so don't make little arsses of yourselves blabbering abaout it!"

This, however, was taken in good part by his family; there was much waving of hands and many shouted good wishes as he walked rapidly out of hearing.

"Poor Francis, I hope he's going to enjoy his walk," Barbara said, as they started homeward. "He gets so bored out here in California!"

"I wonder why?" Julia said, hiding a Californian's resentment.

"Oh, well, it *is* different, Ju—you can't deny it! One wants to be loyal, and all that," Barbara said, "but in England there's a *purpose*—there's a recognized order to life! They're not eternally experimenting; they don't want to be idle and ignorant like our women—they've got better things to do. There's a finish and a pleasantness about life in London; men have more leisure to take an interest in women's work; why, you've no idea how many interesting, clever, charming men I know in London! How many does one know here? And as for the *women*—"

It was then Julia said:

"Ah, well, you're different from other women. You're so busy—and necessary—and unself-conscious, Barbara. You make other women seem such fools!"

"Not necessarily," said Barbara, smiling. "And don't think I'm horribly conceited, Julia, talking this way. It's only to you!" They walked a little way without speaking, and then Barbara sat down on a low bank, some quarter of a mile above Richie's cabin, and added: "Do sit down, Ju. You and I are never alone, and I want to talk to you. Julie, don't be angry—it's about Jim."

Julia's eyes immediately widened, her lips met firmly, she grew a little pale.

"Go ahead," she said steadily. "Have you seen him?"

Barbara answered the question with another.

"You knew he was in London?"

"No," said Julia, "I didn't know it."

She had remained standing, and now Barbara urged her again to sit down. But Julia would not, pleading that she would rather walk, and in the end Barbara got up, and they began slowly to walk down the road together.

"Tell me," Julia commanded then.

"Now, dearest girl," Barbara pleaded, "*Please* don't get excited over nothing. Jim's been in London nearly a year; in fact, he's settled there. He's associated with one of the biggest consulting surgeons we have, old Sir Peveril McCann. They met in Berlin. I didn't know it until this spring—March it was. We'd just come up from the country to meet Francis, home on a year's leave; it was just before Malcolm arrived. Somebody spoke of this Doctor Studdiford, and I said at once that it must be my foster brother. I explained as well as I could that since Francis and I had been travelling so much, Jim and I had fallen out of touch, and so on."

"Who told you about him?" Julia asked.

"A Mrs. Chancellor. She's quite a character," Barbara said. "Some people like her; some don't. I don't—much. She's rich, and a widow; she studies art, and she loves to get hold of interesting people."

Julia winced at the vision of a plump, forty-year-old siren sending coquettish side glances at an admiring Jim. Anger stirred dully within her.

"Pretty?" she asked, in as nonchalant a voice as she could command.

"Ivy Chancellor? No—she's really plain," Barbara said, "a sandy, excitable little chatterbox, that's what *she* is! She's Lady Violet Dray's daughter; Lady Violet's quite lovely. How much Jim admires Ivy I can't say; she took him about with her everywhere; he was always at the house."

This was too much. Julia felt the friendly earth sway under her, a dry salty taste was in her mouth, a very hurricane of resentment shook her heart.

"Oh, Barbara, do you see how he *can*?" she asked, in a stricken voice.

"No, I don't!" Barbara answered, with a concerned glance at Julia's white face. "Well, as I know him, I can't believe it's the same Jim!"

"I wish you had seen him," Julia said, after an interval of thought. Barbara said nothing for a few moments, then she confessed suddenly:

"I *did* see him, Julie."

"You did? Oh, Bab, and you never told me all this time!"

"Well, Mother and Aunt Sanna begged me not to, Ju, and Francis was most emphatic about it," Barbara pleaded.

"Aunt Sanna—and Francis! But—" Julia's keen eyes read Barbara's face like an open page. "Then there was more to it!" she declared. "For they couldn't have minded my knowing just this!"

"I wish I had never mentioned Jim," Barbara said heartily. "It's none of my business, anyway, only—only—it makes me so unhappy I just can't bear it! I simply can't bear it!" And to Julia's astonishment, Barbara, who rarely showed emotion, fumbled for her handkerchief and began to cry. "I love Jim," pursued Barbara, with that refreshed vehemence that follows a brief interval of tears. "And you're just as dear to me as my own sisters—dearer! And I can't *bear* to have you and that *darling* baby here alone, and Jim off in trailing around after a little *fool* like Ivy Chancellor! I can't bear it," said Barbara, drying her eyes, which threatened to overflow again. "It's monstrous! You're—you're wonderful, of course, Julie, but you can't make me think you're happy! And Jim is *wretched*. I've known him since I was a baby, and he can't fool *me*! He can bluff about his work and his club and all that as long as he pleases! But he can't fool *me*; I know he's utterly miserable."

"And you saw him?" Julia asked.

They were in a little strip of woods just above Richard's cabin now, and Julia seated herself on the low-hanging branch of an oak. Her face, as she turned to Barbara, was full of resolute command.

"Sit down, Bab," she said, indicating a thick fallen log a few feet away. "Tell me all about it."

"Francis would strangle me," Barbara murmured, seating herself nevertheless. "And there isn't very much to it, anyway," she added, with a bright air of candour. "I wrote Jim a line, and he came to our house in Ludbroke Road, and we had a little talk. He's fatter. He was awfully interested in some knee-cap operation—"

"Babbie!" Julia reproached her.

"And we talked about everything," Barbara hastened to say.

"Me?" Julia asked flatly.

"A little," Barbara admitted. "I had nurse bring the boys in—"

"Oh, Barbara, for God's sake tell me!" Julia said, in an agonized burst.

"Oh, Julie—if only I'm doing the right thing!" Barbara answered in distress.

"This *is* the right thing," Julia assured her. "This is my affair."

"Francis and Mother—" Barbara began again, hesitatingly. But immediately she dismissed the doubts with a shake of her head, and suddenly assuming a confident air, she began: "I'll tell you exactly what happened, Ju. Jim came one afternoon; I was all alone, and we had tea. He's very much changed, Ju. He's harder, in some way, and—well, changed. Jim never used to be able to conceal his feelings, you know, but now—why, one feels that he's dissembling all the time! He was so friendly, and cheerful, and interested—and yet—There was something all wrong. He didn't exactly *evade* the subject of you and Anna, but he just said 'Yes?' or 'No?' when I talked of you—"

"I know exactly how," Julia said, wincing at some memory.

"I touched him on the quick finally," Barbara pursued; "something I said about you made him colour up, that brick-red colour of his—"

"I know!" Julia said quickly again.

"But, Julia," Barbara added earnestly, "you've no *idea* how hard it was! I told him how grieved and troubled we all were by this silence between you, and I went and got that snapshot Rich took of Anna, you know, the one with the collies. Well, way in the back of that picture you were snapped, too, the tiniest little figure, for you were way down by the road, and Anna close to the porch. But, my dear, he hardly glanced at Anna; he said in a quick, hushed sort of voice, 'What's she in black for?' Then I saw your picture for the first time, and said, 'Why, that must be Julia!' 'Certainly, it's Julia,' he said. I told him your grandmother had died, and he said, 'But she's still needed there, is she?' That was the first sign of *anything* like naturalness. And, oh, Ju, if only it had happened that Francis didn't come in then! But he did, starving for his tea, and wondering who on earth the man that I was sitting in the dark with was—it was so unfortunate! You know Francis thinks we've all spoiled Jim, always, and he looked right over him. I said, 'Francis, you remember my brother?' and Francis said, with a really insulting accent, 'Perfectly!' Jim said something about liking London and hoping to settle there, and Francis said, 'Studdiford, I'm glad you've come to see my wife, and I hope the affection you two have felt for years won't be hurt by what I say. But I admire your own wife very deeply, and you've put her in a most equivocal and humiliating position. I can't pretend that I hope you'll settle here; you've caused the people who love you sufficient distress as it is. I don't see that your staying here is going to make anything any easier, while things are as they are in California!' My dear," said Barbara with a sigh, "Francis gets that way sometimes; English people do—there seems to be a sort of moral obligation upon them to say what's true, no matter how outrageously rude it sounds!"

"I had no idea Captain Fox felt that way," Julia said, touched.

"Oh, my dear! He's one of your warmest admirers. Well," Barbara went on, "of course Jim ruffled up like a turkey cock. I didn't dare say anything, and Francis, having done his worst, was really pretty fair. Luckily, some other people came in, and later I went with Jim to the nursery. Then he said to me, 'Do you think Julia's position is equivocal, Bab?' And I said, 'Jim, I never knew any one to care so little for public opinion as Julia. But all the rumour and gossip, the unexplained mystery of it, are very, very hard for her.' I said, 'Jim, aren't you going back?' and he said, 'Never.' Then he said, 'I think Francis is right. This way is neither one thing nor the other. It ought to be settled. Not,' he said, 'that I want to marry again!' I said, 'Jim, you *couldn't* marry again, don't talk that way!' He said something about my clinging to old ideas, and I said, 'Jim, don't tell me you have given up your faith?' He said, very airily, 'I'm not telling you anything, my dear girl, but if the law will set me free, perhaps that's the best way of silencing Francis's remarks about Julia's equivocal position!'"

Julia was silent for a while, staring beyond Barbara, her eyes like those of a sick person, her face ashen. Barbara began to feel frightened.

"So that's it," Julia said finally, in a tired, cold voice.

"Ju—it's too dreadful to hurt you this way!" Barbara said. "But that's not all. The only reason I told you all this was because Jim may be coming home; he may come on in October, and want to see you. Francis thinks— But it seems too cruel to let him come on and take you by surprise!"

"Oh, my God!" said Julia, in a low, tense tone, "what utter wreck I have made of my life! Why is it," she said, springing up and beginning to walk again, "why is it that I am so helpless, why must I sit still and let the soul be torn out of my body! My child must grow up fatherless—under a cloud—"

"Julie! Julie!" Barbara begged, wild with anxiety, as she kept pace beside Julia on the dry brown grass. "Dearest, don't, or you'll make me feel terribly for having told you!"

"Oh, no—no," Julia said, suddenly calm and weary. "You had to tell me!" The two walked slowly on for a moment, in silence, then Julia added passionately: "Oh, what a wretched, miserable business! Oh, Bab, why do I simply have to go from one agony to another? I'm so tired of being unhappy; I'm so wretched!" Her voice fell, the fire went out of her tone. "I'm tired," she said, in a voice that seemed to Barbara curiously in keeping with the flat, toneless summer twilight, the dull brown hills, the darkening sky, the dry slippery grass over which a cool swift breeze was beginning to wander. "If Anna and I could only run away from it all!" said Julia sombrely.

"Julie, just one thing." Barbara hesitated. "Shall you see Jim?"

Julia paused, and their eyes met in the gloom. Barbara thought she had never seen anything more marked than the tragic intensity of the other woman's face. Julia might have been a young priestess, the problems of the world on her shoulders.

"That I can't say, Bab," she answered thoughtfully. And a moment later they reached the cabin, and were welcomed by Richie and the children.

CHAPTER VIII

It was in late September that the mail brought her a note from Jim. Julia's heart felt a second of paralyzing cramp as she put her hand on the letter; she read its dozen lines in a haze of dancing light; the letters seemed to swim together.

Jim wrote that he was at home for a few days, and was most anxious to see her, and to have a talk that would be of advantage to them both. For obvious reasons, her home was not suitable; would she suggest a time and place? He was always hers faithfully, James Studdiford.

Anna, glowing and delicious, was leaning against Julia's shoulder as Julia read and reread the little document. The mother looked down obliquely at the little rose-leaf face, the blue, blue eyes, the fresh, firm, baby mouth.

"When I am a grown-up girl," Anna said, with her sweet, mysterious smile, "I shall have letters, and I will write answers, and write the envelopes, too! And I'll write you letters, Mother, when you go 'way and leave me with Grandma!"

"Will you?" asked Julia, rubbing the child's soft cheek with her own.

"Every day!" Anna said. "Who's writing you with that cunning little owl on the paper, Mother?"

"That's the Bohemian Club owl," Julia evaded, giving Anna only one fair look at him before she closed the letter. She went to her desk, and swiftly, unhesitatingly, wrote her reply. Jim must excuse her, she could not see the advantage of their meeting, she would much prefer not to see him. Briskly rubbing her blotter over the flap of the sealed envelope, she had a vision of him, interrupting his evening of talk with old friends to scratch off the note to her, and felt that she detested him.

An unhappy week followed, in which Julia had time to feel that almost any consequences would have been easier to bear than the unassailable wall of silence and misgiving and doubt that hemmed her in. Constant nervous terrors weakened her spiritually and bodily, and she could not bear to have Anna for one moment out of her sight. Mrs. Page and Mrs. Torney saw notice in the papers of Jim's return, and suspected the cause of this new agitation in Julia, but neither dared attempt to force her confidence.

"Men are the limit!" said Mrs. Torney to her sister, one day when they were sitting together in the kitchen. "As I've said before, it's a great pity there ain't nothing else to do but marry, and nothing to marry but men! It's awful to think of the hundreds of women who spend their happiest hours going about doing the housework, and planning just what they'd do if their husbands was to be taken off suddenly! Some girls can set around until they're blue moulded, and never a feller to ask 'em, and others the boys'll fret and pleg until they're fit to be tied, with nerves! Evvy you couldn't marry off if she was Cleopatra on the Nile, and poor Julia could hang smallpox flags all over her, and every man in the place'd want her jest the same! He wants her back, you see if he doesn't!"

"I don't know that he does," said Emeline, knitting needles flashing slowly in her crippled fingers. "Maybe that's the trouble."

"What'd he come on for, then?" demanded Mrs. Torney. "Jest showing off, is he? Or is it another woman? The only difference between men reely seems to be that some wear baggy pants and own up to being sultans, and others don't!" She spread her fingers inside the stocking she was darning, and eyed it severely. "The idea of a man with a five-year-old girl sashaying round the country this way is ridiculous, to begin with," said she indignantly.

"Has Ju seen him?" asked Mrs. Page.

"No, I'm pretty sure she hasn't," Mrs. Torney answered. "She acks more like she was afraid to, than like she ackshally had. She'd be real relieved to start fighting, but just now she's like a hen that gets its chickens under its wings, and looks up and round and about, and don't know whether it's a hawk or a fox or a man with a knife that's after her!"

"I don't believe Julie hates him," said her mother. "I think she'd go back to him, if only for Anna's sake—if it seemed best for Anna."

"For that matter, she'd go keep house for the gorilla at the Chutes if it seemed best for Anna!" Mrs. Torney concluded sagely.

It was only a day or two later that the telephone rang, and Julia, answering it, as she always did now, with chill foreboding in her heart, heard Barbara's voice.

"Julie, dear, is it you? Darling, we want you right away. It's Dad, Julie—he's terribly ill!" Barbara's voice broke. "He's terribly ill!"

"What is it?" Julia asked, tense and pale.

"Oh, we don't know!" Barbara gasped. "Julie—we—and Mother's quite wonderful! Con's coming right away, Janey's here, and we've wired Ted."

"Barbara, is it as bad as that?"

"I'm afraid so!" And again tears choked Barbara. "Of course we don't know. He fell, right here in the garden. Think if he'd been on the road, Julie, or in the street. That was the first thing Mother said. Mother's too wonderful! Richie was here, they carried him in. And he wrote Con's and Ted's and your name on a piece of paper. We saw he was trying to say something, and gave him the paper, and that's what he wrote! And Aunt Sanna in New York!"

Stricken, and beginning to realize for the first time what an empty place would be left in the Sausalito group when the kindly old doctor was gone, Julia hastily dressed herself for the hurried trip. She must see Jim now; there was a sort of dramatic satisfaction in the thought that he must know the accident of their meeting at last to be none of her contriving. And she would see Richie, too; her heart fluttered at the thought. She sat on the boat, dreamily watching the gray water rush by, dreamily ready for whatever might come. The day was dull and soft; boat whistles droned all about them on the bay; from Alcatraz, shouldering through an enveloping fog, came the steady ringing of a brass gong.

Long drifts of fog had crept under the trees in the Toland garden, the rose bushes were beaded with fine mist, the eaves dripped steadily. Julia began to be shaken with nervous anticipation of the moment when she must meet Jim. Would he meet her at the door, or would they deliberately arrange—these loyal brothers and sisters—that the dreaded moment should not come until they were all about her? She gave a quick nervous glance about the big hallway when a tearful maid admitted her. But it was only Barbara who came forward, and Barbara's first word was that Jim and Richie were not there; Dad had sent both on errands. "His mind is absolutely clear," said Barbara shakenly. She herself was waiting for an important telephone call, and occasionally pressing a folded handkerchief to her eyes. The two women kissed, with sudden tears on both sides, before Julia went noiselessly upstairs. Constance and Theodora were in their mother's room, Mrs. Toland with them. The mother had been crying, and was now only trying to muster sufficient self-control to reenter the sickroom without giving the beloved patient alarm. Julia's entrance was the signal for fresh tears; but they all presently brightened a little, too, and Julia persuaded Mrs. Toland to drink a cup of hot soup, "the very first thing she's touched all day!" said all the girls fondly.

Only Janey was with the invalid when Julia went into the sickroom, a silent, white-faced Janey, who stared at Julia with sombre eyes. The doctor lay high in pillows, looking oddly boyish in his white nightgown in spite of his gray hair. A fire flickered in the old-fashioned polished iron grate; outside the window twilight and the fog were mingling. The room had some unfamiliar quality of ordered emptiness already, as if life's highway must be cleared for the coming of the great Destroyer.

Julia knelt down by the bed and laid her hand over the old man's hand. To her surprise he opened his eyes. They moved from her face to the clock on the mantel, as if he had lost count of time, and had not expected her so soon.

"How are you, Dad?" she said, with infinite tenderness.

"He's better," Janey answered. "Aren't you, darling? You *look* better!"

The doctor's look, with its old benevolent twinkle, went from one girl's face to the other.

"Know—too—much!" he said, with difficulty, in his eyes the innocent triumph of the child who will not be deceived. Quite unexpectedly, Julia felt her lip tremble, tears brimmed her eyes. The invalid saw them, felt one drop hot on his hand.

"No—no—no!" he said, with pitying gentleness. And, with great effort, he added, "Seen—Jimmy?"

"Not yet," stammered Julia, shaken to her very soul.

The doctor shut his eyes, his fingers still clinging to Julia's. After perhaps two full minutes of silence, he whispered:

"Be good to Jimmy, Julia! Be good to him."

Julia could not answer. Barbara found her, in her own room, half an hour later, crying bitterly. It was then quite dark. The two had a long talk, ended only when Constance came flying in. Dad seemed better, much brighter, was asking for Richie, wanted to know if Ned had come.

Constance and Barbara went back to the sickroom, and Julia went downstairs to find them. She entered the almost dark library, where Richie and Ned were sitting before the fire. There was some one with them; Julia knew in an instant who it was. Her heart began to hammer, her breath failed her. A murmur of friendly low voices ended with her entrance; the three dim forms rose in the gloom.

"Con?" asked Richie. Julia touched a wall switch, and the great lamp on the centre table bloomed into sudden light.

"No, it's Julia—they want you, Rich," she said, "and you, too, Ned. Con says he's much brighter. He asked for you both."

"Hello, dear, I didn't know you were here," Richie said affectionately, kindly eyes on her face. "But you mustn't cry, Ju!" he added gently.

"I—I saw him," Julia said, mingled emotions making speech almost impossible. "Isn't there *any* hope, Richie?"

"None at all," Jim said, leaving the fireplace to quietly join Julia and Richie at the centre table.

The unforgotten voice! Every fibre in Julia's body thrilled to mortal shock. She rallied her courage and endurance sternly; she must not betray herself. Anger helped her, for she knew him well enough to know that the situation for him was not devoid of a certain artistic enjoyment.

"Yes, it may come to-night, it may come to-morrow," Richie assented sorrowfully. "But it's the end, I'm afraid!"

Julia clung to his arm; never had Richie seemed so dear and good to her.

"Your mother will die of it, Rich," she said, to say something. The room seemed to her shouting with Jim's presence; she kept her eyes on Richie's face. Ned, never more than an overgrown boy, put his face in his hands and began to sob.

"Sh—h!" Jim warned them. Mrs. Toland came in.

"He's better—he wants to see you boys!" she said, tremulously happy. Her eyes went from face to face. "Why, what's the matter?" she demanded. "You don't think it's—do you, Richie? Do you, Jim?"

Richie merely flung up his head and set his lips. Jim put one arm around her.

"He's pretty ill, dear," he said gently, and Julia found his smooth tenderness infinitely less bearable than Richie's bluntness.

"Why, but what are you talking about—what do you mean—I don't know what you mean!" Mrs. Toland said bewilderedly. "Doctor Barr has gone home, Richie; he said he wouldn't come back unless we sent for him!" No one answered her, and as her pitiful look went from Julia's grave face to Richard's sorrowful one, from Ned's despairing figure by the fire to Jim's troubled look, terror seemed to seize her. Her pretty middle-aged face wrinkled; she began to cry bitterly.

Julia put her in a deep chair, knelt before her, trying rather to calm than to comfort her, and after a while so far succeeded that she could take the poor shaken old lady upstairs. She did not glance again at Jim, although he opened the door for them, and tried his best to catch her eye.

Between five and six o'clock he was summoned to the sickroom. They were all there: the girls on their knees, Richard kneeling by his father, his fingers on the failing pulse. Mrs. Toland was seated, Julia kneeling beside her, holding both her cold hands. A sound of subdued sobbing filled the air; no sound came from the dying man except when a fluttering breath raised his chest. His eyes were shut; he appeared to be sleeping.

The clock on the mantel struck six, and as if roused, Doctor Toland stirred a little, and whispered, "Janey!" Poor Janey's head went down against the white counterpane; she never dreamed that the little-girl aunt, dead fifty years ago, with apple cheeks under a slatted sun-bonnet, and more apples in her lunch bag, had come in a vision of old orchard and sun-bathed river, to put her warm little hand in her brother's again, and lead him home. And before the clock struck again, Robert Toland, with not even a twitch of his kind old face, went smiling away from earth in a dream of childhood, and Richie, with a finger on the silent pulse, and Jim, with a hand on the silent heart, had said together: "Gone!"

An hour later Jim, standing thoughtful at an upper window, looked down to see Richie bring the runabout to the front door. Down the steps came Barbara, bare headed, and Julia, in her wide black hat and flying veil. The three talked for a few moments together, the light from the open hall door falling on their faces; then Julia got into the car. She leaned out to say some last word to Barbara, her face composed and sweetly grave, then turned to Richie, and they were gone.

Jim would have found it difficult to analyze his own emotion. Something in that look toward Barbara, so brave and quiet, so bright with some inward serenity, stirred his heart. He went downstairs to meet Barbara in the hall.

"Where's Rich?" asked Jim, in the hushed voice that had supplanted all the usual noise and gayety of the house.

"He'll be right back," Barbara said apathetically. "He's driving Julie to the boat."

For some reason Jim's heart sank. He had supposed them as performing only some village errand, at the florist's, the drug store, or the post office. A certain blank fell upon his spirits; Julia had her grievance, of course, but she seemed singularly indifferent to the—well, the appearances of things!

But Julia, alone on the boat, could have laughed in the joy of escape, in the new sense of freedom on which she seemed to float. Above all her sympathy for the family she so deeply loved, and above the sorrow of her own very real personal loss, rose the intoxicating conviction that Jim's sway over heart and soul was gone; he was no longer godlike; no longer mysteriously powerful to hurt or to enchant her; he was just a handsome man nearing forty, not particularly interesting, not noticeably magnetic, not remarkable in any way.

She caught the welcoming Anna to her heart when she reached the Shotwell Street house, telling her sad news to the others over the child's little shoulder. But the kisses she gave her daughter were inspired by joy instead of sorrow, and Julia lay down to sleep that night with a new content, and slept as she had not slept for months. With a confidence amounting almost to indifference she faced Jim on the day of the old doctor's funeral, her beauty absolutely startling in its setting of demure black veil and trailing sombre garments.

Jim watched her, some curious emotion that was compounded of resentment and jealousy and astonishment darkening his face. So dignified, so poised, so strangely, hauntingly lovely she seemed, so much in demand and so quietly equal to all demands. Jim flattered his vanity for a while with the assurance that she was trying to impress as well as evade him, but could not long preserve the illusion; there was no acting there.

"Julia," he said, when they were all at home again after the funeral, "I want to see you alone for a few moments, if I may?"

Julia was in the dining-room, busy with a great sheaf of letters. She gave a quick glance at the chair which Barbara had filled only a moment ago, as if realizing for the first time that she had been left alone.

"What is it?" she asked, dryly and unencouragingly.

Jim sat down, leaned back, folded his arms, and looked at her steadily, in a manner that might have been confusing. But Julia went on serenely opening, reading, and listing her letters.

"I want to ask how you are getting on, Julie," said Jim at last, in a hurt tone. "I want to know if there is anything in the world I can do for you?"

"Nothing, thank you!" Julia said pleasantly. "Financially, I am very comfortable. You left me I don't know how many thousands in the Crocker. I've never had one second's worry on that score, even though I've never touched the capital—as you can easily find out."

"My dear girl, do you think for one second I doubt you!" Jim said uncomfortably. "You've been perfectly wonderful to do it, only you must have scrimped yourself! But it wasn't about that. Surely, Julia, you and I have things more important to say to each other," he added reproachfully.

"I don't know what's more important than money," she assured him whimsically. "Of course I didn't want to use it at all; I should have preferred to be self-supporting at any cost," she went on. "But there was Anna and Mama to consider. And more than that, there was your name, Jim; I didn't want to start every one talking of the straits to which your wife had been reduced."

"Oh, for God's sake!" Jim growled. "Don't let's talk of money." "That was all I meant to say," Julia said politely. "Is Mother lying down?" she added naturally. Jim jerked his whole body impatiently.

"I think she is!" he snapped. Julia opened a letter.

"Isn't that a pretty hand?" she asked. "English—it's Mrs. Lawrence, the Consul's wife. What pretty hands English people write!"

"You've changed very much," Jim observed, after a sulphurous silence.

"I have?" Julia asked naively. "In what way?"

"Why didn't you want to see me?"

"Oh—" Julia laid the letter down, and for the first time gave him her full attention. "I've changed my mind about that, Jim," she said frankly. "I thought at first that it was an unwise thing, but I feel differently now. Of course you know," continued Julia, with pretty childish gravity, "that for me there can be no consideration of divorce; I shall never be any other man's wife, and never be free. But if, as Bab says, you have come to feel that you want something different, and if you have drifted so far from your religion as to feel that a legal document can undo what was solemnly done in the name of God, why then I shan't oppose it. You can call it desertion or incompatibility, I don't care."

"Who said I wanted a divorce?" Jim demanded, in his ugliest tone. His face was a dull, heavy red, and veins swelled on his forehead.

"My life is full and happy," Julia pursued contentedly, paying no attention to his question. "I'm not very exacting, as you know. Mama needs me, and I have everything I want."

"You talk very easily of divorce," Jim said, in an injured tone, after a pause. "But is it fair to have it all arranged before I say a word?"

Julia's answer was only a look—a full, clear, level look that scorched him like a flame; her cheeks above the black of her gown burned scarlet; she was growing angry.

Jim played with an empty envelope for a few minutes, fitting a ringer tip to each corner and lifting it stiffly. Presently he dropped it, folded his arms, and rested them on the table.

"This is a serious matter," he said gravely. "And we must think about it. But you must forgive me for saying that it is a great shock to come home and find you talking that way, Julie. I—God knows I'm bad enough, but I *don't* think I deserve quite this!" added Jim gently.

A long interval of silence, for Julia a busy interval, followed.

"When am I going to see Anna?" Jim asked, ending it.

"Whenever you want to," Julia said pleasantly. "I've familiarized her with your picture; she'll be friendly at once; she always is. Some day, when you are going to be here, I'll send her over for the day. She loves Sausalito, and I really believe she'd do poor Mother good."

"And when shall I come and see you—to talk about things?" Jim asked humbly.

"My dear Jim," Julia answered briskly, "I cannot see the need of our meeting again; I think it is most unwise—just a nervous strain on both sides. What have we to discuss? I tell you that I am perfectly willing to let you have your way. It's too bad, it's a thing I detest—divorce; but the whole situation is unfortunate, and we must make the best of it!"

Jim's stunned amazement showed in a return of his sullen colour and the fixed glassy look in his eyes.

"What will people think of this, Ju? Every one will have to know it—it will make a deuce of a lot of talk!" he said, trying to scare her.

Julia shook her head, with just a suggestion of a smile.

"Much less than you think, Jim," she answered sensibly. "Society long ago suspected that something was wrong; the announcement of a divorce will only confirm it."

"We'll have the whole crowd of them buzzing about our heads," Jim said, determined to touch her serenity by one phase or another.

"Oh, no, we won't!" Julia returned placidly. "The only circumstances under which there would have been buzzing would have been if I had tried to keep my place in society. I dropped out, and they let me go without a murmur. No buzzing from San Francisco society ever reaches Shotwell Street, and as for you, you'll be in London."

"How do you know I'll be in London?" Jim growled, utterly nonplussed.

Julia gave him a bright look over a letter, but did not answer, and the man fell to worrying an envelope again. Moments passed, the autumn twilight fell, Julia began to stack her letters in neat piles.

Presently she quietly rose, and quietly left the room, without a word, without a backward glance. Jim sat on in the dusk, staring moodily ahead of him, his eyes half shut, the fingers of one big hand drumming gently on the table.

A few days later he went out to Shotwell Street to see her. Julia met him very quietly, and presented the little Anna with the solicitous interest in the child's manner that she would have shown had Jim been any casual friend. Anna, who was lovely in a pale pink cotton garment a little too small for her, looked seriously at her father, submitted to his kisses, her wondering eyes never moving from his face, and wriggled out of his arms as soon as she could.

"My God! She's beautiful, isn't she?" said Jim, under his breath.

"She looks very nice when she's clean and good," Julia agreed practically, kissing Anna herself.

"'My God's' a bad word," Anna said gravely to her father, "isn't it, Mother?"

"I wouldn't like to hear you say it," Julia answered. "Now trot out to Aunt Regina, dear, and ask her to give you your lunch. Mother'll be there immediately."

"She's exquisite," Jim said, when the child was gone. "You all over again, Ju!"

"She's smarter than I was." Julia smiled dispassionately. "I've taught her to read—simple things, of course; she writes a little, and does wonders with her numerical chart. She's very cunning, she has an unusual little mind, and occasionally says something that proves she thinks!"

A silence followed. Sunshine was streaming into the sitting-room; nasturtiums bloomed in Julia's window boxes; the net curtains fanned softly to and fro in the soft autumn air. In the city, a hundred whistles shrilled for noon.

"I hardly knew the place," Jim said, searching for something to say. "You've made it over—the whole block looks better!"

"Gardens have come into fashion," Julia explained; "the Mission is a wonderful place for gardens. And the change in my mother is more marked," she went on, with perfunctory pleasantness; "you would hardly know her. She is much thinner, of course, but so bright and contented, and so brave!"

"I am going to meet her, I hope?" Jim suggested. Julia looked troubled.

"I hardly see how," she said regretfully. "As things are I can't exactly ask you to lunch, Jim. It would be most unnatural, and they—they look to me for a certain principle," she went on. "They know what these four years have meant for me; I couldn't begin now to treat the whole thing casually and cheerfully."

"I don't expect you to," Jim said quickly. "I'm not taking this lightly. I only want to think the thing well over before any step is taken that we might regret."

Again Julia answered him with only a tolerant, bright look. She stood up and busied herself with the potted fern that stood on the centre table, breaking off dead leaves and gathering them into the palm of her hand. Jim, feeling clumsy and helpless, stood up, too. And as he watched her, a sudden agony of admiration broke out in his heart. Her head was bent a little to one side, as if the weight of the glorious braids bowed it; her thick lashes hid her eyes; her sweet, firm mouth moved a little as she broke and straightened the fern. Where the wide collar of her checked gown was turned back at her throat, a triangle of her soft skin showed, as white and pure as the white of daisy petals; her firm young breast moved regularly under the fresh crisp gingham; the folds of her skirt were short enough to show her slender ankles and square-toed sensible low shoes tied with wide bows.

"You used not to be so cold, Julie," Jim said, baffled and uncomfortable.

"I am not cold," she answered mildly. "I never was a very demonstrative—never a very emotional person, I think. Three years ago—two years ago, even—I would have gone on my knees to you, Jim, begged you to come back, for Anna's sake as well as my own. But that time has gone by. This life, I've come to see, is far better for Anna than any child in our old set leads, and for me—well, I'm happy. I never was so happy, or busy, or necessary, in my life, as I am now."

"Do you mean that there's *no* chance of a reconciliation?" Jim asked huskily. Julia gave him a glance of honest surprise.

"Jim," she asked crisply, "do you mean that you came on with the hope of a reconciliation? I thought you told Barbara something very different from that!"

"I don't know what I came on for. I wish Barbara would mind her own business," said Jim, feeling himself at a disadvantage.

"My dear Jim," Julia said with motherly kindness, "I know you so well! You came on here determined to get a divorce, you want to be free, you may already have in mind some other woman! But I've hurt your feelings by making it all easy for you—by coming over to your side. You wanted a fuss, tears, protests, a convulsion among your old friends. And you find, instead, that all San Francisco takes the situation for granted, and that I do, too. I've made my own life, I have Anna, and more than enough money to live on; you have your freedom; every one's satisfied."

"That's nonsense and you know it!" Jim exclaimed angrily. "There's not one word of truth in it!" He began to pull on his gloves, a handsome figure in his irreproachable trim black sack suit with low oxfords showing a glimpse of gray hose, and an opal winking in his gray silk scarf. "There's absolutely no reason in the world why you should consider yourself as more or less than my wife," he said. "There's no object in this sort of reckless talk. We've been separated for a few years; it's no one's business but our own to know why!"

"Oh, Jim—Jim!" Julia said, shaking her head.

"Don't talk that way to me!" he said fiercely. "I tell you I'm serious! It's all nonsense—this talk of divorce! Why," he came so near, and spoke in so menacing a tone, that Julia perforce lifted her eyes to his, "this situation isn't all of my making," he said. "I've not been ungenerous to you! Can't you be generous in your turn, and talk the whole thing over reasonably?"

"I can't see the advantage of *talking*!" Julia answered in faint impatience.

"No, because you want it your own way," said Jim. "You expect me to give up my child completely, you refuse me even a hearing, you won't discuss it!"

"But what do you want to discuss?" protested Julia. "The whole situation is perfectly clear—we shall only quarrel!"

How well she knew the look he gave her, the hurt look of one whose sentiment is dashed by cool reason! He suddenly caught her by the shoulders.

"Look here, Julia!"

"Ah, Jim, please don't!" She twisted in a vain attempt to escape his grip.

"Please don't what?"

"Don't—touch me!"

Jim dropped his hands at once, stepped back, with a look of one mortally hurt.

"Certainly not—I beg your pardon!" he said punctiliously. He took up his hat. "When do I see you again, Julia? Will you dine with me to-morrow? Then we can talk."

"No, I don't think so," Julia said, after reflection.

"Have you another engagement?"

"Certainly not!" There was almost a flash of amusement in her face; her glance toward the kitchen spoke volumes for the nature of her engagements.

"Why do you say no, then?" asked Jim.

"Because I prefer not to do so," Julia answered, with sudden spirit. "We look at this thing very differently, Jim," she added roundly. "To me it is a tragedy—the saddest thing that ever happened in my life; that you and I should have loved each other, and should be less than nothing to each other now! It's like a sorrow, something shameful, to hide and to forget. For years I was haunted by the horror of a divorce, Jim; I never wrote to you, I never begged you to come back, just because I was afraid of it! I used to say to myself in the first awful weeks in this house: 'Never mind—it isn't as if we were divorced; we may be separated, we may be estranged, but we are still man and wife!'" Tears came to Julia's eyes, she shook her head as if to shake them away. "I've hungered for you, Jim, until it seemed as if I must go mad!" she went on, looking far beyond him now, and speaking in a low, rapt voice as if to herself. "I've felt," she said, "as if I'd die for just one more kiss from you, die just to have you take my big coat off once more, and catch me in your arms, as you used to do when we came back from dinner or the theatre! But one can't go on suffering that way," said Julia, giving him a swift, uncertain smile, "and gradually the pain goes, and the fever dies away, and nothing is left but the cold, white scar!"

Jim had been staring at her like a man in a trance. Now he took a step toward her, lightly caught her in one big arm.

"Ah, but Julia, wouldn't the love come back?" he asked tenderly, his face close to her own. "Couldn't it all be forgotten and forgiven? You've suffered, dear, but I've suffered, too. Can't we comfort each other?"

"Please don't do that," Julia said coldly, wrenching herself free. "This is no whim with me; I'm not following a certain line of conduct because it's most effective. I've changed. I don't want to analyze and dissect and discuss it; as I say, it seems to me too sacred, too sad, to enjoy talking about!"

"You've not changed!" Jim asserted. "Women don't change that way."

"Then I'm not like other women," Julia said hotly. "Do believe me, Jim. It's all just gone out of my life. You don't seem like the man I loved, who was so sweet and generous to me. I've not forgotten that old wonderful time; I just don't connect you with it. You could kiss me a thousand times now, and it would only seem like—well, like any one else! I look at you as one might look on some old school friend, and wonder if I ever really loved you!"

She stopped, looking at him almost in appeal. Jim stood quite still, staring fixedly at her; they remained so for a long minute.

"I see," he said then, very quietly. "I'm sorry."

And without another word he turned to the hall door and was gone. Julia stood still in the hall for a few minutes, curiously numb. All this was very terrible, very far reaching in its results, very important, but she could not feel it now. She did feel very tired, exhausted in every fibre of her body, confused and weary in mind. She put her head in the kitchen door only long enough to say that she was not hungry, and went upstairs to fling herself on her bed, grateful for silence and solitude at last.

To Jim the world was turned upside down. He could hardly credit his senses. His was not a quick brain; processes of thought with him were slow and ruminative; he liked to be alone while he was thinking. When he left Julia he went down to his club, found a chair by a library window, and brooded over this unexpected and unwelcome turn of events, viewing from all angles this new blow to his pride. He did not believe her protestations of a change of heart, nothing in his life tended to make such a belief easy. But her coldness and stubbornness hurt him and upset the plans he had been allowing to form of late in his mind.

All his life he had been following, with sunny adaptability, the line of the least resistance. Thrown out of his groove by the jealousy and resentment of the dark time in his married life, Jim had realized himself as fairly cornered by Fate, and had run away from the whole situation rather than own himself beaten. Rather than admit that he must patiently accept what was so galling to his pride, he had seized upon any alternative, paid any price.

And Germany had not been at all unpleasant. There was novelty in every phase of his home and public life; there was his work; and, for at least the first year, there was the balm for his conscience that he would soon be going home to Julia. He had allowed himself the luxury of moods, was angry with her, was scornful, was forgiving. He showed new friends her beautiful pictures—told them that she was prettier than that, no picture could do justice to her colour.

Among the new friends there had been two sweet plain Englishwomen: the widowed Lady Eileen Hungerford, and her sister, the Honourable Phyllis. These had found the rich young American doctor charming, and without a definite word or look had managed to convey to him the assurance of their warmest sympathy. They could only guess at his domestic troubles, but a hundred little half allusions and significant looks lent spice to the friendship, and Jim became a great favourite in the delightful circle the Englishwomen had drawn about them.

The midsummer vacation was spent, with another doctor, in Norway, and in September Jim went for a week or two to London, where Eileen and Phyllis, delicately considerate of the possible claims of the unknown wife, nevertheless persuaded him that he would be mad to decline the offer of the big German hospital. So back to Berlin he went, and in this second winter met old Professor Sturmer, and Senta, his wife.

Senta was a Russian, the tiniest of women, wild, beautiful, nineteen. She was a most dramatic and appealing little figure, and she knew it well. She smoked and drank just as the young men of her set did, she danced like a madwoman, she sang and rode and skated with the fury of a witch. She was like a child, over-dressed, overjewelled, her black hair fantastically arranged; always talking, always unhappy, a perfect type of the young female egotist. She liked to use reckless expressions, to curl herself up on a couch, in a room dimly lighted, and scented with burning pastilles, and discuss her marriage, her age, her appearance, her effect upon other women. Senta's was an almost pathetic and very obvious desire to be considered daring, pantherine, seductive, dangerous.

Jim, fancying he understood her perfectly, played into her hand. He would not flirt with her, but he took her at her own valuation, and they saw a good deal of each other. Senta confessed to him, read him love letters, wrote him dashing, penitent little notes, and Jim scolded her in a brotherly way, laughed at her, and sometimes delighted her by forbidding her to do this or that, or by masterfully flinging some cherished note or photograph of hers into the fire. He loved to hear her scold her maid in Russian; it seemed to him very cunning when this stately gipsy of a child took her seat in her box at the opera, or flung herself into the carriage, later, all the more a madcap because of three hours of playing the lady. He exchanged smiling looks over her little dark head with her husband, when he dined at the Sturmers'; the good professor was far more observing than was usually supposed; he knew more of Jim's character, it is probable, than Jim did himself; he knew that Senta was quite safe with the young American, and he liked him. But Senta, who was quite unscrupulous, was slow to realize it. She found this brotherly petting and scolding very well for a time, but months went by, a whole year went by, and there was no change in their relationship. Senta was only precocious, she was neither clever nor well educated; she based her campaign on the trashy novels she read, and deliberately set herself to shake Jim from his calm pleasure in her society.

Then, suddenly, Jim was bored. Charm dropped from her like a rich, enveloping cloak, and left only the pitiful little nude personality, a bundle of childish egotisms and shallow pretences. Once he had been proud to escort her everywhere, now her complacent assumption that he should do so annoyed him; once he had laughed out heartily at her constant interruption of the old professor, her naive contention that she was never to be for one second ignored; now she only worried him, and made him impatient. Her invitations poured upon him, her affectedly deep voice, reproachful or alluring, haunted his telephone. She challenged him daringly, wickedly, across dinner tables, or from the centre of a tea-table group, to say "why he didn't like her any more?"

Jim went to Italy, and Senta, chaperoned by her sister-in-law, a gaunt woman of sixty, went, too, turning up at his hotels with the naughty grace of a spoiled child, sure to be welcome. She eyed him obliquely, while telling him that "people were beginning to talk." She laughed, with a delight that Jim found maddening, when they chanced to meet some friends from Berlin in a quiet side street in Rome. Jim cut his vacation short, and went back to work.

This angered Senta for the first time, and perhaps began to enlighten her. She came sulkily back to Berlin, and began to spread abroad elaborate accounts of a quarrel between Jim and herself. Jim so dreaded meeting her that he quite gave up everything but men's society, but he could not quite escape from the knowledge that the affair was discussed and criticised.

And at this most untimely moment old Professor Stunner died, leaving a somewhat smaller fortune to his little widow than she had expected, and naming his esteemed young friend, Herr Doctor Studdiford, as her guardian and his executor. This again gave Senta the prominence and picturesqueness she loved; to Jim it was a most deplorable mischance; it was with difficulty that he acquitted himself of his bare duty in the matter, his distaste for his young ward growing stronger every moment. For weeks there was no hour in which he was not made exquisitely uncomfortable by her attitude of chastened devotion; eventually the hour came in which he had to stab her pride, and stab deep. It was an ugly, humiliating, exasperating business, and when at last it was over, Jim found himself sick of Berlin, and yet sullenly unready to go home to California, as if he had failed, as if he were under even so faint a cloud.

Just then came a letter from Eileen, another from Phyllis. Wasn't he ever coming to London any more? London was waiting to welcome him. They had opened their little house in Prince's Gate, the season was beginning, it was really extraordinarily jolly. Did he know anything of the surgeon, Sir Peveril McCann? He had said such charming things of Doctor Studdiford. He had said—but no, one wasn't going to tell him anything that might, untold, make him curious enough to come!

Jim went to London, revelling in clear English speech after years of Teutonic gutturals, and rejoicing in the clean, clear-cut personalities with which he came in contact. He loved the wonderful London drawing-rooms, the well-ordered lives, the atmosphere of the smart clubs and hotels, the plays and pictures and books that were discussed and analyzed so inexhaustibly.

He found Eileen and Phyllis more charming than ever; and he very much admired their aunt, stately Lady Violet Dray, and their bright, clever, friendly cousin Ivy, who was as fresh and breezy as the winds that blew over her native heather. Ivy was slender and vivacious; her face was thin and a little freckled, and covered with a fine blond down, which merged on her forehead into the straight rise of her carrot-coloured hair. Her eyes were sharply blue, set in thick, short, tawny lashes. She was an enthusiastic sportswoman, well informed on all topics of the day, assured of her position and sure of herself, equally at home in her riding tweeds and mud-splashed derby, and the trailing satin evening gowns that left her bony little shoulders bare, and were embellished by matchless diamonds or pearls. There was no sentiment in her, her best friends were of both sexes and all ages, but she attached Jim to her train, patronized and bullied him, and they became good friends.

Mrs. Chancellor talked well, and talked a great deal, and she stimulated Jim to talk, too. Never in his life had so constant a demand been made upon his conversational powers; and every hour with her increased his admiration for Ivy and lessened his valuation of his own wisdom. She was a thorough Englishwoman, considering everything in life desirable only inasmuch as it was British. Toward America her attitude was one of generous laughter touched with impatience. She never for one moment considered seriously anything American. Mrs. Chancellor thought all of it really too funny-"rarely too fenny," as she pronounced it. Only one thing made her more angry than the defence of anything American, and that was dispraise of anything British. The history of England was sacred to her: London was the crown and flower of the world's civilization; English children, English servants, English law, were all alike perfect, and she also had her country's reverence for English slang, quoting and repeating it with fondest appreciation and laughter. Nothing pleased her more than to find Jim unfamiliar with some bit of slang that had been used in England for twenty years; her laughter was fresh and genuine as she explained it, and for days afterward she would tell her friends of his unfamiliarity with what was an accepted part of their language.

She took him to picture galleries, bewildering him with her swift decisions. Jim might come to a stand before a portrait by Sargent.

"Isn't this wonderful, Ivy Green?" It was his own name for her, and she liked it.

"That?" A sweeping glance would appraise it. "Yes, of course, it's quite too extraordinary," she would concede briskly. "An impossible creature, of course; one feels that he was laughing at her all the time—it's not his best work, rarely!" And she would drag Jim past forty interesting canvases to pounce upon some obscure, small painting in a dark corner. "There!" she would say triumphantly, "isn't that astonishing! So kyawiously frank, if you know what I mean? It's most amazing—his sense of depth, if you know what I mean? Rarely, to splash things on in that way, and to grasp it." A clawed little hand would illustrate grasping. "It's astonishing!"

Jim, staring at a picture of some sky, some beach, and a face of rock, would murmur a somewhat bewildered appreciation, looking out of the corner of his eye, at the same time, at the attractive gondolier singing to his pretty lady passengers, on the right, or the nice young peasant nursing her baby in a sunny window while her mother peeled apples, on the left.

"Of course, it's the only thing here, this year, absolutely the only one," Mrs. Chancellor would conclude. "The rest is just one huge joke. I know Artie Holloway—Sir Arthur, he is—quite well, and I told him so! He's a director."

"But I don't see how you know so much about it!" Jim would say admiringly.

"One must know about such things, my dear boy," she always answered serenely. "One isn't an oyster, after all!"

It was this dashing lady and not Barbara who first brought Jim's mind to a sense of his own injustice to Julia, or rather to a realization that the situation, as it stood, was fair to neither Julia nor himself. Not that he ever mentioned Julia to Ivy; but she knew, of course, of Julia's existence, and being a shrewd and experienced woman she drew her own conclusions. One day she expressed herself very frankly on the subject.

"You've taken the rooms above Sir Peveril's, eh?" she asked him.

"Well, yes," Jim answered, after a second's pause. "They're bully rooms!"

"Oh, rather—they're quite the nicest in town," she stated. "But, I say, my dear boy, wasn't the rent rather steep?"

"Not terrible." He mentioned it. "And I've taken 'em for five years," he added.

"For—eh?" She brought her sandy lashes together and studied him through them. "You're rarely going to stay then, you nice child?"

"Yes, Grandmother dear. Sir Peveril wants me. I've taken his hospital work; people are really extraordinarily kind to me!" Jim summarized.

"Oh, you've been vetted, there's no question of that," she agreed thoughtfully. They were at tea in her own drawing-room, which was crowded with articles handsome and hideous, Victorian lace tidies holding their own with really fine old furniture, and exquisite bits of oil or water colour sharing the walls with old steel engravings in cumbersome frames. Now Ivy leaned back in her chair, and stirred her tea, not speaking for a few minutes.

"There's just one thing," she said presently. "Before you come here to stay, put your house in order. Don't leave everything at haome in a narsty mess that'll have to be straightened aout later, if you know what I mean? Get that all straight, and have it understood, d'ye see?"

The colour came into Jim's face at so unexpected an attack, yet speech was a relief, too.

"I don't know whether I *can* straighten it out," he confessed, with a nervous laugh.

"It's not a divorce, eh?"

"No—not exactly."

"The gell's gone home to her people?"

"Yes." Jim cleared his throat. "Yes, she has."

"And there's a kiddie?"

"Anna—yes."

"Well, now." Mrs. Chancellor straightened in her chair, set her cup down on a nearby table. "I take it the gell was the injured one, eh?" said she.

Jim was a little surprised to find himself enjoying this cross-examination immensely.

"Well—no. She had no definite cause to feel injured," he said. "We quarrelled, and I came away in a hurry—"

"What, after a first quarrel?"

"No—o. It had been going on a long time."

"Is the cause of it still existing?" Mrs. Chancellor asked in a businesslike way, after a pause.

"Well—yes."

"Can't be removed, eh? It's not religion?"

"It's an old love affair of hers," Jim admitted. The lady's eyes twinkled.

"And you're jealous?" she smiled. But immediately her face grew sober. "I see—she still cares for him, or imagines she does," she said.

Jim felt it safest to let this guess stand.

"Of course, if she won't she won't," pursued Mrs. Chancellor comfortably. "But the best thing you could do would be to bring her on here!"

Jim shook his head sullenly and set his jaw.

"She won't, eh?" asked the lady, watching him thoughtfully.

"I don't want to do that," Jim persisted stubbornly.

"*You* don't want to?" She meditated this. "Yet she's young, and beautiful, and presentable?" she asked, nodding her own head slowly as he nodded affirmatives. "Yes, of course. Well, it's too bad. One would have liked to meet her, take her about a bit. And it would help you more than any one thing, my dear boy. Oh, don't shake your head! Indeed it would. However, you must be definite, one way or the other. You must either admit outright that you're divorced, or you must tell an acceptable story. As it is—one doesn't know what to say—whether she's impossible in some way—just what the matter is, if you know what I mean?"

"I see," Jim said heavily.

"Go have a talk with her," commanded Mrs. Chancellor brightly. "Finish it up, one way or another. You're doing her an injustice, as it is, and you're not just to yourself. One can't shut a marriage up in a box, you know, and forget it. There's always leakage somewhere—much better make a clean breast of the whole thing! You're not the first person who's made an unfortunate early marriage, you know!"

"I loved my wife," said Jim, in vague, resentful self-defence. "I'm naturally a domestic man. I loved my little girl—"

"Certainly you did," Mrs. Chancellor interrupted crisply. "And perhaps she did, too! The details are all the same, you know. Some people make a success of the thing, some people fail. I've been married. I'm a little older than you are in years, and ages older in experience—I know all about it. In every marriage there are the elements of success, and in every one the makings of a perfectly justifiable divorce. Some women couldn't live with a saint who was a king and a Rothschild into the bargain; others marry scamps and are perfectly happy whether they're being totally ignored or being pulled around by the hair! But if you've made a failure, admit it. Don't sulk. You'll find that doing something definite about it is like cleaning the poison out of a wound; you'll feel better! There, now, you've had your scolding, and you've taken it very nicely. Ring for some hot water, and we'll talk of something else!"

On just this casual, kindly advice Jim really did go home, prepared to be very dignified with Julia; and to make the separation definite and final, if not legal, or to bring her back, however formally, as his wife, exactly as he saw fit.

And then came the meeting in the Toland library, when in one stunning flash he saw her as she was: beautiful, dignified, and charming, a woman to whom all eyes turned naturally and admiringly, grave, sweet, and wise in a world full of pretence and ignorance, selfishness and shallowness.

She spoke, and her voice went through him like a sword, a mist rose before his eyes. He tried to remember that bitter resentment upon which his pride had fed for more than four long years; he battled with a mad desire to catch her in his arms, and to cry to her and to all the world, "After all, you are still mine!"

He watched her, her beauty as fresh to him as if he had never seen it before. Had those serious eyes, turned to Richie with such sisterly concern, and so exquisitely blue in the soft lamplight, ever met his with love and laughter brightening them? Had the kindly arms that went so quickly about his mother, in her trouble, ever answered the pressure of his own? She could look at him dispassionately, entirely forgetful of herself in the presence of death, but in the very sickroom his eyes could not leave her little kneeling figure; whenever she spoke, he felt his heart contract with a spasm of pain. It seemed to him that if he could kneel before her, and feel the light pressure of her linked hands about his neck, and have her lay that soft, sweet cheek of hers against his, in heavenly token of forgiveness, he would be ready to die of joy.

How far Julia was from this mood he was soon to learn, and no phase of their courtship eight years ago had roused in him such agonies of jealousy and longing as beset him now, when Julia, quiet of pulse and level eyed, convinced him that she could very contentedly exist without him.

All these things went confusedly through Jim's mind, as he sat at his club window, staring blankly down at the dreary summer twilight in the street. The club was a temporary wooden building, roomy and comfortable enough, but facing on all four sides the devastation of the great earthquake. Here and there a small brick building stood in the ashy waste, and on the top of Nob Hill the outline of the big Fairmont Hotel rose boldly against the gloom. But, for the most part, the rising hills showed only one ruined brick foundation after another, broken flights of stone steps leading down to broken sidewalks, twisted, discoloured railings smothered in rank, dry grass. Through this wreckage cable cars moved, brightly lighted, and loaded with passengers, and to-night, in the dusk, a steady wind was blowing, raising clouds of fine, blinding dust.

Jim stared at it all heavily, his mind strangely attuned to the dreary prospect. He felt puzzled and confused; he wanted to see Julia again, to have her forgive and comfort him. When he thought of the old times, of the devotion and tenderness he had taken so much for granted, a sort of sickness seized him; he could have groaned aloud. Only one thought was intolerable: that she would not forgive him, and let him make up to her for the lost years, and show her how deeply he loved her still!

He mused upon the exactions she might make, the advantages that would appeal to her. Not jewels—she must have more jewels now than she would ever wear, safely stored away somewhere. He remembered giving her a certain chain of pearls, with a blinding vision of the white young throat they encircled, and the kiss he had set there with the gift. No, jewels were for such as Senta, not for grave, stately Julia.

Nor would position tempt her. She was too wise to long for it; the glory of a London season meant nothing to her; position was only a word. She was happier in the Shotwell Street house, clipping roses on a foggy morning; she was happier far when she scrambled over the rough trails of the mountain with Richie than ever London could make her. Position and wealth might have their value for Ivy, but Julia cared as little as a bird for either.

And now it came to him that she was infinitely more fine, more beautiful, and more clever than Senta, and that her pure and fragrant freshness, her simple directness, her candid likes and dislikes, would make Ivy seem no more than a jaded sophist, a quoter of mere words, a worshipper of empty form.

To have Julia in London! To take her about, her bright face dimpling in the shadow of a flowered hat, or framed in furs, or to see her at the tea table, a shining slipper showing under the flowing lines of her gown, the lovely child beside her, at once enhancing and rivalling the mother's beauty—Jim's heart ached with the pain and rapture of the dream.

He was roused by Richie, who came limping into the club library, and over whose tired face came a bright smile at the sight of Jim.

"Hello!" said Richie, taking an opposite chair. His expression grew solicitous at the sight of Jim's haggard face. "Headache, old boy?" he asked sympathetically.

Jim shook his head. The big room was almost dark now, and they had it quite to themselves.

"Thinking what a rotten mess I've made of everything, Rich," Jim said desperately.

Richie took out a handkerchief and wiped the palms of his hands, but did not answer.

"She'll never forgive me, I know that," Jim presently said. And as Richie was again silent, he added: "Do you think she ever will?"

"I don't know," poor Richie said hesitatingly. "She's awfully kind—Julia."

"She's an angel!" Jim agreed fervently. He sat with his head in his hands for a few moments. Then he cleared his throat and said huskily: "Look here, you know, Rich, I'm not such an utter damn fool as I seem in this whole business. I can't explain, and, looking back now, it all seems different; but I had a grievance, or thought I had—God knows it wasn't awfully pleasant for me to go away. But I *had* a reason."

"It wasn't anything you didn't know about before you were married, I suppose?" asked Richie, with what Jim thought unearthly prescience.

"No," Jim answered, with a startled look.

"Nor anything you'd particularly care to have the world know or suspect?" pursued Richie. "Not anything Julia could change?"

"No," Jim said again. Richard leaned back in his chair.

"Some scrap with her people, or some old friends she wanted to hang on to," he mused. Jim did not speak. "Well," said Richie, "there would be plenty of people glad to be near Julia on any terms."

"Oh, I know that," Jim said. And after a moment he burst out again: "Richie, am I all wrong? Is it *all* on my side?"

"Lord, don't ask me," Richie said hastily. "The older I grow the less I think I know about anything."

There was a silence. Richard clamped the arms of his chair with big bony fingers and frowned thoughtfully at the floor.

"I wish to God I did know what to advise you, Jim," he said presently. "I'd die for her—she knows that. But she's rare, Julia; it's like trying to deal with some delicate frail little lady out of Cranford, like trying to guess what

Emily Bronte might like, or Eugenie de Guerin! Julia's got life sized up, she likes it—I don't know whether this conveys anything to you or not!—but she likes it as much as if it was part of a play. You don't matter to her any more; I don't; she sees things too big. She's quite extraordinary; the most extraordinary person I ever knew, I think. There's a completeness, a *finish* about her. She's not waiting for any self-defence from you, Jim. It won't do you any good to tell her why you did this or that. You thought this was justified, you thought that was—certainly, she isn't disputing it. You did what you did; now she's going to abide by it. You never dreamed thus and so—very well, the worse for you! You want to hark back to something that's long dead and gone; all right, only abide by your decision. And afterward, when you realize that she's a thousand times finer than the women you compare her to, and try to make her like, then don't come crying to *her*!"

A long silence, then Jim stood up.

"Well, I've made an utter mess of it, as I began by saying!" he said, with a grim laugh. "Going to dine here, Rich? Let's eat together. Here"—one big clever hand gave Richard just the help he needed—"let me help you, old boy!"

"I thought I'd go home to Mill Valley," Richard said. "I can't catch anything before the six-forty, but the horse is in the village, and my boy will scare me up some soup and a salad. I'd rather go. I like to wake in my own place."

"I wish you'd let me go with you, Rich," Jim said, with a gentleness new to him. "I'm so sick of everything. I can't think of anything I'd like so well."

"Sure, come along," Richard said, touched. "Everything's pretty simple, you know, but I'll telephone Bruce and have him—"

"Cut out the telephoning," Jim interrupted. "Bread and coffee'll do. And a fire, huh?"

"Sure," Richard said again, "there's always a fire."

"Great!" Jim approved. "We can smoke, and talk about—"

"About Ju," Richie supplied, with a gruff little laugh, as he paused.

"About Ju," Jim repeated, with a long sigh.

Two days later he went to see her, to beg her to be his wife again. He asked her to forget and forgive the past, to trust him once more, to give him another chance to make her happy. He spoke of the Harley Street house, of the new friends she would find, of Barbara's nearness with the boys that Julia loved so well. He spoke of Anna; for Anna's sake they must be together; their little girl must not be sacrificed. Anna should have the prettiest nursery in London, and in summer they would go down to Barbara, and the cousins should play together.

Julia listened attentively, her head a little on one side, her eyes following the movements of Anna herself, who was digging about under the rose bushes in the backyard. Julia and Jim sat on the steps that ran down from the kitchen porch. It was a soft, hazy afternoon, with filmy streaks of white crossing the pale blue sky, and sunshine, thin and golden, lying like a spell over Julia's garden.

"I was a fool," said Jim. "There—I can't say more than that, Ju. And I've paid for my folly. And, dearest, I'm so bitterly sorry! I can't explain it. I don't understand it myself—I only know that I'd give ten years off the end of my life to have the past five to live over again. Forgive me, Ju. It's all gone out of my heart now, all that old misery, and I never could hurt you again on that score. It *doesn't exist*, any more, for me. Say that you'll forgive me, and let me be the happiest and proudest man in the world—how happy and proud—taking my wife and baby to England!"

The hint of a frown wrinkled Julia's forehead, her eyes were sombre with her own thoughts.

"Think what it would mean to Mother, and to Bab, and to all of us," Jim pursued, as she did not speak. "They've been so worried about it—they care so much!"

"Yes, I know!" Julia said quickly, and fell silent again.

"Is it your own mother's need of you?" the man asked after a pause.

"No." Julia gave a cautious glance at the kitchen door behind her. "No—Aunt May is wonderful with her. Muriel's at home a good deal, and Geraldine very near," she said. "And more than that, this separation between you and me worries Mother terribly; she doesn't understand it. She's very different in these days, Jim, so gentle and good and brave—I never saw such a change! No, she'd love to have me go if it was the best thing to do—it's not that—"

Her voice dropped on a note of fatigue. Her eyes continued to dwell on the child in the garden.

"I've done all I can do," Jim said. "Don't punish me any more!"

Julia laughed in a worried fashion, not meeting his eyes.

"There you are," she said, faintly impatient, "assuming that I am aggrieved about it, assuming that I am sitting back, sulking, and waiting for you to humiliate yourself! My dear Jim, I'm not doing anything of the kind.

I don't hold you as wholly responsible for all this—how could I? I know too well that I myself am—or was—to blame. All these years, when people have been blaming you and pitying me, I've longed to burst out with the truth, to tell them what you were too chivalrous to tell! For your sake and Anna's I couldn't do it, of course, but you may imagine that it's made me a silent champion of yours, just the same! But our marriage was a mistake, Jim," she went on slowly and thoughtfully. "It was all very well for me to try to make myself over; I couldn't make you! I never should have tried. Theoretically, I had made a clean breast of it, and was forgiven; but actually, the law was too strong. It's hard and strange that it should be so, isn't it? I don't understand it; I never shall. For still it seems as if the punishment followed, not so much the fact, as the fact's being made known. If I had robbed some one fifteen years ago, or taken the name of the Lord in vain, I wonder if it would have been the same? As for keeping holy the seventh day, and honouring your father and mother, and not coveting your neighbour's goods, how little they seem to count! Even the most virtuous and rigid people would forgive and forget fast enough in *those* cases. It's all a puzzle." Julia's voice and look, which had grown dreamy, now brightened suddenly. "And so the best thing to do about it," she went on, "seems to me to make your own conscience your moral law, and feel that what you have repented truly, is truly forgiven. So much for me." She met his eyes. "But, my dear Jim, I never could take it for granted again that *you* felt so about it!"

"Then you do me an injustice," said Jim, "for I swear—"

"Oh, don't swear!" she interrupted. "I know you believe that now, as you did once before. But I know you better than you do yourself, Jim. Your attitude to me is always generous, but it's always conventional, too. You never would remind me of all this, I know that very well, but always, in your own heart, the reservation would be there, the regret and the pity! I know that I am a better woman and a stronger woman for all this thinking and suffering; you never will believe that. Let us suppose that we began again. Don't you know that the day would come when my opinion would clash with that of some other woman in society, and you, knowing what you know of me, would feel that I was not qualified to judge in these things as other women are? Let us suppose that I wanted to befriend a maid who had got herself into trouble, or to take some wayward girl into my house for a trial; how patient would you be with me, under the circumstances?"

"Of course, you can always think up perfectly hypothetical circumstances!" Jim said impatiently.

"Marriage is difficult enough," Julia pursued. "But marriage with a handicap is impossible! To feel that there is something you can't change, that never will change, and that stands eternally between you! No, marriage isn't for us, Jim, and we can only make the best of it, having made the original mistake!"

"Don't ever say that again—it's not true!" Jim said, with a sort of masterful anger. "Now, listen a moment. That isn't true, and you don't believe it. I've told you what I think of myself. I was blind, I was a fool. But that's past. Give me another chance. I'll make you the happiest woman in the world, Julia. I love you. I'll be so proud of you! You can have a dozen girls under your wing all the time; you can answer the Queen back, and I'll never have even a *thought* but what you're the finest and sweetest woman in the world!"

The preposterous picture brought a shaky smile to Julia's lips and a hint of tears to her eyes. She suddenly rose from her seat and went down to the garden.

"Our talking it over does no good, Jim," she said, as he followed her, and stood looking at her and at Anna. "It's all too fresh—it's been too terrible for me—getting adjusted! I stand firm here, I feel the ground under my feet. I don't want to go back to feeling all wrong, all out of key, helpless to straighten matters!"

"But we were happy!" he said, a passionate regret in his voice. "Think of our day in Chicago, Ju, and the day we took a hansom cab through Central Park—and were afraid the driver wasn't sober! And do you remember the blue hat that *would* catch on the electric light, and the day the elevator stuck?"

"I think of it all so often, Jim," Julia answered, with a smile as sad as tears could have been, and in the tender voice she might have used in speaking of the dead. "Sometimes I fit whole days together, just thinking of those old times. 'Then what did we do after that lunch?' I think, or 'Where were we going that night that we were in such a hurry?' and then by degrees it all comes back." Julia drew a rose toward her on a tall bush, studied its leaves critically. "That was the happiest time, wasn't it, Jim?" she asked, with her April smile.

Jim felt as if a weight of inevitable sorrow were weighing him to the ground. Julia's quiet assurance, her regretful firmness, seemed to be breaking his heart. She was in white to-day, and in the thin September sunlight, among the blossoming roses, she somehow suggested the calm placidity of a nun who looks back at her days in the world with a tender, smiling pity. The child had left her play, and stood close to her mother's side, one of Julia's hands caught in both her own.

"Anna," Jim said desperately, "won't you ask Mother to come to London with Dad?"

Anna regarded him gravely. She did not understand the situation, but she answered, with a child's curious instinct for the obvious excuse:

"But Grandmother needs her!"

"I never asked you to give her up, Julie," Jim said, as if trying to remind her that he had not been so merciless as she. Julia's eyes widened with a quick alarm, her breast rose, but she answered composedly:

"That I would have fought."

"And you have always had as much money—" Jim began again, trying to rally the arguments with which he had felt sure to overwhelm her.

"I spent that as much for your sake as for mine," Julia said soberly. "She is a Studdiford. I wanted to be fair to Anna. But I could do without it now, Jim; there are a thousand things—"

"Yes, I know!" he said in quick shame.

A silence fell, there seemed nothing else to be said. A great space widened between them. Jim felt at the mercy of lonely and desolate winds; he felt as if all colour had faded out of the world, leaving it gray and cold. With the sickness of utter defeat he dropped on one knee and kissed the wondering child, and then turned to go.

"You won't—change your mind, Ju?" he asked huskily.

Julia was conscious of a strange weakening and loosening of bonds throughout her entire system. Vague chills shook her, she felt that tears were near, she had a hideous misgiving as to her power to keep from fainting.

"I will let you know, Jim," she heard her own voice answer, very low.

A moment later she and Anna were alone in the garden.

"What *is* it, Mother?" Anna asked curiously, a dozen times. Julia stood staring at the child blindly. One hand was about Anna's neck, the loose curls falling soft and warm upon it, the other Julia had pressed tight above her heart. She stood still as if listening.

"What *is* it, Mother?" asked the little girl again.

"Nothing!" Julia said then, in a sort of shallow whisper, with a caught breath.

A second later she kissed the child hastily, and went quietly out of the green gate which had so lately closed upon Jim. She went as unquestioningly as an automaton moved by some irresistible power; not only was all doubt gone from her mind, but all responsibility seemed also shed.

The street was almost deserted, but Julia saw Jim instantly, a full block away, and walking resolutely, if slowly. She drifted silently after him, not knowing why she followed, nor what she would say when they met, but conscious that she must follow and that they would meet.

Jim walked to Eighteenth Street, turned north, and Julia, reaching the corner, was in time to see him entering the shabby old church where they had been married eight years ago. And instantly a blinding vertigo, a suffocating rush of blood to her heart, made her feel weak and cold with the sudden revelation that the hour of change had come.

She climbed the dreary, well-remembered stairs slowly, and slipped into one of the last pews, in the shadow of a gallery pillar.

Jim was kneeling, far up toward the altar, his head in his hands. In all the big church, which was bleak and bare in the cold afternoon light, there was no one else. The red altar light flickered in its hanging glass cup; a dozen lighted candles, in a great frame that held sockets for five times as many, guttered and flared at the rail.

Minutes slipped by, and still the man knelt there motionless, and still the woman sat watching him, her eyes brilliant and tender, her heart flooded with a poignant happiness that carried before it all the bitterness of the years. Julia felt born again. Like a person long deaf, upon whose unsealed ears the roar of life bursts suddenly again, she shrank away from the rush of emotion that shook her. It was overpowering—dizzying—exhausting.

When Jim presently passed her she shrank into the shadow of her pillar, but his face was sadder and more grave than Julia had ever seen it, and he did not raise his eyes. She listened until his echoing footsteps died away on the stairs; then the smile on her face faded, and she sank on her knees and burst into tears.

But they were not tears of sorrow; instead, they seemed to Julia infinitely soothing and refreshing. They seemed to carry her along with the restful sweep of a river. She cried, hardly knowing that she cried, and with no effort to stop the steady current of tears.

And when she presently sat back and dried her eyes, a delicious ease and relaxation permeated her whole body. Like a convalescent, weak and trembling, she drew great breaths of air, rejoicing that the devastating fever and the burning illusions were gone, and only the quiet weeks of getting well lay before her.

She sat in the church a long time, staring dreamily before her. Odd thoughts and memories drifted through her mind now: she was again a little girl of eight, slipping into the delicatessen store in O'Farrell Street for pickles and pork sausage; now she was a bride, with Jim in New York, moving through the dappled spring sunlight of Fifth Avenue, on the top of a rocking omnibus. She thought of the settlement house: winter rain streaming down its windows, and she and Miss Toland dining on chops and apple pie, each deep in a book as she ate; and she remembered Mark, poor Mark, who had crossed her life only to bring himself bitter unhappiness, and to leave her the sorrow of an ineffaceable stain!

Only thirty, yet what a long, long road already lay behind her, how much sorrow, how much joy! What mistakes and cross purposes had been tangled into her life and Jim's, Mark's and Richie's, Barbara's and Sally's and Ted's—into all their lives!

"Perhaps that *is* life," mused Julia, kneeling down to say one more little prayer before she went away. "Perhaps my ideal of a clean-swept, austere little cottage, and a few books, and a few friends, and sunrises and sunsets—isn't life! It's all a tangle and a struggle, ingratitude and poverty and dispute all mixed in with love and joy and growth, and every one of us has to take his share! I have one sort of trouble to bear, and Mother another, and Jim, I suppose, a third; we can't choose them for ourselves any more than we could choose the colour of our eyes! But loving each other— loving each other, as I love Anna, makes everything easy; it's the cure for it all—it makes everything easier to bear!" And in a whisper, with a new appreciation of their meaning, she repeated the familiar words, "Love fulfils the law!"

The next evening, just as the autumn twilight was giving way to dusk, Julia opened the lower green gate of the Tolands' garden in Sausalito, and went quietly up the steep path. Roses made dim spots of colour here and there; under the trees it was almost dark, though a soft light still lingered on the surface of the bay just below. From the drawing-room windows pale lamplight fell in clear bars across the gravel, but the hall was unlighted, the door wide open.

Julia stepped softly inside, her heart beating fast. She had got no farther than this minute, in her hastily made plans; now she did not quite know what to do. She knew that Barbara and the boys had gone back to Richie in Mill Valley. Captain Fox was duck shooting in Novato, and Constance had returned to her own home. But Ted and her little son should be here, Janey, Jim, and the widowed mother.

Presently she found Mrs. Toland in the study, seated alone before a dying fire. Julia kissed the shrivelled soft old cheek, catching as she did so the faint odour of perfumed powder and fresh crepe.

"Where are the girls, darling, that you're here all alone?" she asked affectionately.

"Oh, Julie dear! Isn't it nice to see you," Mrs. Toland said, "and so fresh and rosy, like a breath of fresh air! Where are the girls? Bab's with Richie, you know, and she took her boys and Ted's Georgie with her, and Connie had to go home again. I think Ted and Janey went out for a little walk before dinner."

"And haven't you been out, dear?"

Ready tears came to poor Mrs. Toland's eyes at the tender tone. She began to beat lightly on Julia's hand with her own.

"I don't seem to want to, dearie," she said with difficulty; "the girls keep telling me to, but—I don't know! I don't seem to want to. Papa and I used to like to walk up and down in the garden—"

Speech became too difficult, and she stopped abruptly.

"I know," Julia said sorrowfully.

"It would have been thirty-five years this November," Mrs. Toland presently said. "We were engaged in August and married in November. Marriage is a wonderful thing, Julia—it's a wonderful thing! Papa was very much smarter than I am—I always knew that! But after a while people come to love each other partly for just that—the differences between them! And you look back so differently on the mistakes you have made. I've always been too easy on the girls, and Ned, too, and Papa knew it, but he never reproached me!" She wiped her eyes quietly. "You must have had a sensible mother, Julie," she added, after a moment; "you're such a wise little thing!"

"I don't believe she was very wise," Julia said, smiling, "any more than I am! I may not make the mistakes with Anna that Mama made with me, but I'll make others! It's a sort of miracle to see her now, so brave and good and contented, after all the storms I remember."

Mrs. Toland did not speak for a few moments, then she said:

"Julie, Jim's like a son of my own to me. You'll forgive a fussy old woman, who loves her children, if she talks frankly to you? Don't throw away all the future, dear. Not to-day—not to-morrow, perhaps, but some time, when you can, forgive him! He's changed; he's not what he used to be—"

Tears were in Julia's eyes now; she slipped to her knees beside Mrs. Toland's chair, and they cried a little together.

"I came to see him," whispered Julia. "Where is he?"

"He came in about fifteen minutes ago. He's packing. You know his room—"

Julia mounted the stairs slowly, noiselessly. It was quite dark now throughout the airy, fragrant big halls, but a crack of light came from under Jim's door.

She stood outside for a few long minutes, thrilling like a bride with the realization that she had the right to enter here; where Jim was, was her sanctuary against the world and its storms.

She knocked, and Jim shouted "Come in!" Julia opened the door and faced him across a room full of the disorder of packing. Jim was in his shirt sleeves, his hair rumpled and wild. She slipped inside the door, and shut it behind her, a most appealing figure in her black gown, with her uncovered bright hair loosened and softly framing her April face.

"Jim," she said, her heart choking her, "will you take Anna and me with you? I love you—"

There was time for no more. They were in each other's arms, laughing, crying, murmuring now and then an incoherent word. Julia clung to her husband like a storm-driven bird; it seemed to her that her heart would burst in its ecstasy of content; if the big arms about her had crushed breath from her body she would have died uncaring.

Jim kissed her wet cheeks, her tumbled hair, her red lips that so willingly met his own. And when at last the tears were dry, and they could speak and could look at each other, there was no need for words. Jim sat on the couch, and Julia sat on his knee, with one arm laid loosely about his neck in a fashion they had loved years ago, and what they said depended chiefly upon their eyes and the tones of their voice.

"Oh, Jim—Jim!" Julia rested her cheek against his, "I have needed you so!"

Jim tightened an arm about her.

"I adore you," he said simply, unashamed of his wet eyes. "Do you love me?" To this Julia made no answer but a long sigh of utter content.

"Do you?" repeated Jim, after an interval.

"Does this *look* as if I did?" Julia murmured, not moving.

Silence again, and then Jim said, with a great sigh:

"Oh, Petty, what a long, long time!"

"Thank God it's over!" said Julia softly.

"What made you do it, dear?" Jim asked presently, in the course of a long rambling talk. At that Julia did straighten up, so that her eyes might meet his.

"Just seeing you—pray about it, Jim," she said, her eyes filling again, although her lips were smiling. "I thought that, this time, we would both pray, and that—even if there are troubles, Jim—we'd remember that hour in St. Charles's, and think how we longed for each other!"

And resting her cheek against his, Julia began to cry with joy, and Jim clung to her, his own eyes brimming, and they were very happy.

CHAPTER IX

September daylight, watery and uncertain, and very different from the golden purity of California's September sunshine, fell in pale oblongs upon the polished floor of a certain London drawing-room, and battled with the dancing radiance of a coal fire that sent cheering gleams and flashes of gold into the duskiest corners of the room.

It was a beautiful room, and a part of a beautiful house, for the American doctor and his wife, deciding to make the English capital their home, had searched and waited patiently until in Camden Hill Road they had discovered a house possessed of just the irresistible combination of bigness and coziness, beauty and simplicity, for which they had hoped. In the soft tones of the rugs, the plain and comfortable chairs, the warm glow of a lamp shade, or the gleam of a leather-bound book, there was at once a suggestion of discrimination and of informal ease. And informal yet strangely exhilarating the friends of Doctor and Mrs. Studdiford found it. Very famous folk liked to sit in these deep chairs, and talk on and on beside this friendly fire, while London slept, and the big clock in the hall turned night into morning. No hosts in London were more popular than the big, genial doctor, and his clever, silent, and most beautiful wife. Mrs. Studdiford was an essentially genuine person; the flowers in her drawing-room, like the fruit on her table, were sure to be sensibly in season; her clothes and her children's clothes were extraordinarily simple, and her new English friends, simple and domestic as they were, whatever their rank, found her to be one of themselves in these things, and took her to their hearts.

Julia herself was sitting before the fire now, one slippered foot to the blaze. Four years in London life had left her as lovely as ever; perhaps there was even an increase of beauty in the lines of her closed lips, a certain accentuation of the old spiritual sweetness in her look. Her bright hair was still wound about her head in loose braids, and her severely simple gown of Quaker gray was relieved at the wrists and throat by transparent frills of white. In her arms lay a baby less than a year old, a splendid boy, whose eyes, through half-closed lids, were lazily studying the fire. His little smocked white frock showed sturdy bare knees, and the fine web of his yellow hair blew like a gold mist against his mother's breast.

The room's only other occupant, a tall, handsome woman, in a tan cloth suit, with rich furs, presently turned from the deep curtained arch of a window. This was Barbara Fox, Lady Curriel now, still thin, and still with a hint of sharpness and fatigue in her browned face, yet with rare content and satisfaction written there, too. Barbara's life was full, and every hour brought its demand on her time, but she was a very happy woman, devoted to her husband and her three small sons, and idolizing her baby daughter. Her winters were devoted to the social and political interests that played so large a part in her husband's life and her own, but Julia knew that she was far more happy in the summers, when her brood ran wild over the old manor house at High Darmley, and every cottager stopped to salute the donkey cart and the shouting heirs of "the big family."

"Not a sign of them!" said Barbara now, coming from the window to the fire, and loosening her furs as she sat down opposite Julia. "Is he asleep?" she added in a cautious undertone.

"Not he!" answered Julia, with a kiss for her son. "He's just lying here and finking 'bout fings! I don't know where the others can be," she went on, in evident reference to Barbara's vigil at the window. "Jim said lunch, and it's nearly one o'clock now! Take your things off, Babbie, and lunch with us?"

"Positively I mustn't, dear. I must be at home. I've to see the paperers at two o'clock, and to-morrow morning early, you know, we go back to the kiddies at the seaside."

"And they're all well?"

"Oh, splendid. Even Mary's out of doors all day, and digging in the sand! We think Jim's right about Geordie's throat, by the way; it ought to be done, I suppose, but it doesn't seem to trouble him at all, and it can wait! Julie dear, why *don't* you and the boy and Anna come down, if only for four or five days? Bring nurse, and some old cottons, and a parasol, and we'll have a lovely, comfy time!"

"But we're just home!" Julia protested laughingly. "I've hardly got straightened out yet! However, I'll speak to Jim," she went on. "This gentleman thinks he would like it, and Anna is frantic to see the boys."

"And we must talk!" Barbara added coaxingly. "Is California lovely?"

"Oh—" Julia raised her brows, with her grave smile. "Home is home, Bab."

"And Mother looks well?"

"Your mother looks *very* well. But when she and Janey come on in January you'll see for yourself. Janey's so pretty; I wish she'd marry, but she never sees any one but Rich! Rich is simply adorable; he had Con and her husband and little girl with him this summer. Con's getting very fat—she's great fun! And Ted's very much improved, Bab, very much more gentle and sweet. She told me about Bob Carleton's death, poor fellow! She went to see him and took George, and do you know, I don't think Ted will marry again, although she's handsomer than ever!"

"And Sally's the perfect celebrity's wife?" Barbara asked, with a smile.

"Sally? But I wrote you that," Julia laughed. "Yes, Keith was giving a concert in Philadelphia when we went through at Easter. So Jim and I made a special trip down to hear it, and, my dear! The hall was packed, the women went simply crazy over him, and he's really quite poetical looking, long hair and all that. And Sally—I saw her at the hotel the next morning, and such a manner! Protecting the privacy of the genius, don't you know, and seeing reporters, and answering requests for autographs, and declining invitations, here, there, and everywhere! I think she has more fun than Keith does! He's quite helpless without her; won't see a manager or answer a note, or even order a luncheon! 'Sally,' he says, handing her a card, 'what do I like? Tell them not to ask me!' He worships her, and, of course, she worships him; she even said to me that it was lucky there were no children—Keith hated children!"

"Funny life!" Barbara mused, half laughing. "And your people are well, Ju?" "Splendidly," Julia smiled. "Mama looks just the same; she was simply wild about our Georgie—saw him nearly every day, for if I couldn't go I sent nurse with him. My cousin Marguerite is dead, you know, and her husband is really a very clever fellow, a tailor, making lots of money. He and the three children have come to live with Aunt May; Regina manages the whole crowd; it's really the happiest sort of a home! Anna had beautiful times there; she remembered it all, and Aunt May and Mama nearly spoiled her!"

"You couldn't spoil her," Barbara said affectionately. "She is really the dearest and most precious! Are you going to let La Franz paint her?"

"No." Julia's motherly pride showed only in a sudden brightness in her blue eyes. "And I hope no one will tell her that he asked! Even at ten, Bab, they are quite sufficiently aware of admiration. She had on a sort of greeny-yallery velvet gown the day we met him, and really she was quite toothsome, if you ask an unprejudiced observer. But Jim and I were wondering if it's wise to make her *quite* so picturesque!"

"You can't help it," Barbara said. "She's just as lovely in a Holland pinny, or a nightie, or a bathing suit! I declare she was too lovely on the sands last year, with her straw-coloured hair, and a straw-coloured hat, and her pink cheeks matching a pink apron! She's going to be prettier than you are, Ju!"

"Well, at that she won't set the Thames afire!" Julia smiled.

"I don't know! You ought to be an absolutely happy woman, Julie."

Julia settled the baby's head more comfortably against her arm, and raised earnest eyes.

"Is any one, Bab? Are you?"

"Well, yes, I think I am!" Lady Curriel said thoughtfully. "Of course those months before Francis's uncle died were awfully hard on us all, and then before Mary came I was wretched; but now—there's really nothing, except that we do *not* live within our income when we're in the town house, and that frets Francis a good deal. Of course I try to economize in summer, and we catch up, but it's an ever-present worry! And then our Geordie's throat, you know, and being so far from Mother and Rich and the girls, of course! But those things really don't count, Ju. And in the main I'm absolutely happy and satisfied. I'm pleased with the way my life has gone!"

"Pleased is mild," Julia agreed. "I'd be an utter ingrate to be anything but pleased, looking back. Jim is exceptional, of course, and Anna and this young person seem to me pretty nice in their little ways! And when we went home this year it was really pleasant and touching, I thought; all San Francisco was gracious; we could have had five times as long a visit and not worn our welcome out!"

"So much for having been presented," laughed Barbara.

"Well, I suppose so. Mama was wild with interest about it; she has my photograph, in the gown I wore to the drawing-room, framed on the wall. But Aunt May was dubious, isn't at all sure that she admires the British royal family. She's a most delightful person!" Julia laughed out gayly. "If ever I happen to speak of the Duchess of This or Lady That, Mama's eyes fairly dance, but Aunt May isn't going to be hoodwinked by any title. 'Ha!' she says. 'Do you think they're one bit better in the sight of God than I am?' And I like nothing better than to regale her on their silliness, tell her how one has forty wigs, and another is so afraid of losing her diamonds she has a man sit and watch them every night. Long afterward I hear her exclaiming to herself, 'Wigs, indeed!' or 'Diamonds! Well, did you ever!'"

"When you come to think of it, Ju, *isn't* it odd to think of your own people doing their own work, 'way out there on the very edge of the western world, and you here, in a fair way to become a London f'yvourite!"

"Doing their own work, indeed!" laughed Julia. "My good lady, you forget Carrie. Carrie comes in every night to do the dishes, and because she's coloured, my Aunt May has always felt that she stole sugar and tea. However, we all laughed at Aunt May this year, when it came to suspecting Carrie of stealing Regina's face powder! No, but you're quite right, Bab," she went on more seriously. "It's all very strange and dramatic. Saturday, when the Duchess came in to welcome us, and flowers came from all sides, and the Penniscots came to carry us off to dinner, I really felt, 'Lawk a mussy on me, this can't be I!'"

"Well, then, where *is* the pill in the jelly?" asked Barbara solicitously.

Julia had flung back her head and was listening intently. Footsteps and voices were unmistakably coming up the hall stairs.

"No pills—all jelly!" she had time to say smilingly, before the door opened and three persons came into the room: Doctor Studdiford, handsomer and more boyishly radiant than ever; Miss Toland, quite gray, but erect and vigorous still; and little Anna, a splendid, glowing ten-year-old, in the blue serge sailor suit and round straw hat made popular by the little English princess.

Babel followed. Every one must kiss Barbara; little George must come in for his full share of attention. Presently the beaming Ellie was summoned, and the children went away with her; Barbara carried off her aunt for a makeshift luncheon in the dismantled Curriel mansion, and the Studdifords were left alone.

"We picked Aunt Sanna up at the corner," said Jim, one arm about his wife as they stood in the window looking down at the departing visitors, "and of course Anna must drag her along with us to see the baby lion! I stopped at Lord Essels's, by the way, and it's a perfect knit—can't tell where one bone stops and the other begins!"

"Oh, Jimmy, you old miracle worker! Aren't you pleased?"

"Well, rath-*er*! And young Lady Essels wants to call on you, Ju; says you were the loveliest thing at the New Year's ball last year! Remember when we rushed home to feed Georgie, and rushed back again?"

"Oh, perfectly. I hope she will come; she looked sweet. And every one's coming to our Tuesday dinner, Jim, except Ivy; notes from them all. Ivy says Lady Violet is so ill that she can't promise, but Phyllis is coming with the new husband. She wrote such a cunning note! And—I'll see Ivy this afternoon, and I think I'll tell her that I'm going to leave her place open; if she can't come, why we'll just have to have a man over, that's all! It won't be awfully formal anyway, Jimmy, at this time of the year!"

"Whatever you say, old lady!" Jim was thinking of something else. "How do you feel about leaving the kids and going off for a little run with the Parkes to-morrow night?" he asked. "He's found some new place in which he wants us to dine and sleep. Home the next morning."

"Well, I could do that," Julia said thoughtfully.

"You're terribly decent about leaving 'em," said Jim, who knew how Julia hated to be away from Anna and George at night, "but, really, I think this'll be fun—cards, you know, and a good dinner."

"That's to-morrow?"

"To-morrow." Jim hesitated. "I know you're not crazy about them," he said.

"I don't *dislike* them," Julia said brightly. "She's really lots of fun, but of course he's the Honourable and he's a little spoiled. But I'm really glad to go. Was Anna nice this morning?"

"Oh, she was lovely—held her little head up and trotted along, asking *intelligent* questions, don't you know—not like a chattering kid. She pitched right into me on the governess question; she's all for Miss Percival's school, won't hear of a governess for a minute!"

"And the stern parent compromised on Miss Percival?" smiled Julia.

"Well, I only promised for a year," Jim said, shamefaced. "And you were against the governess proposition, too," he added accusingly.

"Absolutely," she assured him soothingly. "I love to have Anna with me in the afternoons, and when Bab's in town we can send her over there—she's no trouble!" Julia turned her face up for a kiss. "Run and wash your hands, Doctor dear!" said she.

"Yes—and what are you going to do?" Jim asked jealously.

"I'm going to wait for you right here, and we'll go down together," she said pacifically. Jim took another kiss.

"Happy?" he asked.

Just as he had asked her a thousand times in the past four years. And always she had answered him, as she did now:

"Happiest woman in the world, Jim!"

The happiest woman in the world! Julia, left alone, still stood dreaming in the curtained window, her eyes idly following the quiet life of the sunny street below. A hansom clattered by, an open carriage in which an old, old couple were taking an airing. Half a square away she could see the Park, with gray-clad nurses chatting over their racing charges or the tops of perambulators.

But Julia's thoughts were not with these. A little frown shaded her eyes, and her mouth was curved by a smile more sad than sweet. The happiest woman in the world! Yet, as she stood there, she felt an utter disenchantment with life seize upon her; she felt an overwhelming weariness in the battle that was not yet over. For Julia knew now that life to her must be a battle; whatever the years to come might hold for her, they could not hold more than an occasional heavenly interval of peace. Peace for Jim, peace for her mother, peace for her children and for all those whom she loved; but for herself there must be times of an increasing burden, an increasing weariness, and the gnawing of an undying fight with utter discouragement. Her secret must never be anything but a secret; and yet, to Julia, it sometimes seemed that her only happiness in life would be to shout it to the whole world.

Not always, for there were, of course, serene long stretches of happiness, confident times in which she was really what she seemed to be, only beautiful, young, exceptionally fortunate and beloved. But it was into these very placid intervals that the word or look would enter, to bring her house of cards crashing about her head once more.

Sometimes, not often, it was a mere casual acquaintance whose chance remark set the old, old wound to throbbing; or sometimes it was Barbara's or Miss Toland's praise: "You're so sweet and fine, Ju—if only we'd all done with our opportunities as you have!" Oftener it was Jim's voice that consciously or unconsciously on his part stabbed Julia to the very soul. For him, the sting was gone, because, at the first prick, Julia was there to take it and bear it. No need to conceal from her now the bitterness of his moods; she would meet him halfway. He was worrying about that old affair? Ah, he mustn't do that—here were Julia's arms about him, her lovely face close to his, her sweet and earnest sympathy ready to probe bravely into his darkest thought, and find him some balm. Still gowned from a ball, perhaps, jewelled, perfumed, dragging her satin train after her, she would come straight into his arms, with: "Something's worrying you, dearest, tell me what it is? I *love* you so—"

No resentment on Jim's part could live for a moment in this atmosphere. He only wanted to tell her about it, to be soothed like a small boy, to catch his beautiful wife in his arms, and win from her lips again and again the assurance that she loved him and him alone. What these scenes cost Julia's own fine sense of delicacy and dignity, only Julia knew. They left her with a vague feeling of shame, a consciousness of compromise. For a day or two after such an episode a new hesitancy would mark her manner, a certain lack of confidence lend pathos to the sweetness of her voice.

But no outside influence ever could bring home to her the realization of the shadow on her life as forcibly as did her own inner musings, the testimony of her own soul. If she had but been innocent, how easy to bear

Jim's scorn, or the scorn of the whole world! It was the bitter knowledge that she had taken her life in her own hands nearly twenty years ago, and wrecked it more surely than if she had torn out her own eyes, that made her heart sick within her now. She, who loved dignity, who loved purity, who loved strength, must carry to her grave the knowledge of her own detestable weakness! She must instruct her daughter, guarding the blue eyes and the active mind from even the knowledge of life's ugly side, she must hold the highest standard of purity before her son, knowing, as she knew, that far back at her life's beginning, were those few hideous weeks that, in the eyes of the world, could utterly undo the work of twenty strong and steadfast years! She must be silent when she longed to cry aloud, she must train herself to cry aloud at the thing that she had been. And she must silently endure the terrible fact that her husband knew, and that he would never forget. Over and over again her spirit shrank at some new evidence of the fact that, with all his love for her, his admiration, his loyalty, there was a reservation in her husband's heart, a conviction—of which he was perhaps not conscious himself—that Julia was not quite as other women. Her criticism of others must be more gentle, her opinion less confidently offered. Others might find in her exceptional charms, rare strength, and rare wisdom—not Jim. For him she was always the exquisite penitent, who had so royally earned a perpetually renewed forgiveness, the little crippled playfellow whom it was his delight to carry in his arms. His judgment for what concerned his children was the wiser, and for her, too, when she longed to throw herself into this work of reform or that—to expose herself, in other words, to the very element from which a kind Providence had seen fit to remove her. Obviously, on certain subjects there must not be two opinions, in any house, and, whatever the usual custom, obviously he was the person to decide in his own.

"Rich says you were not a saint yourself when you were in college, Jim!" she had burst out once, long years ago, before their separation. But only once. After all, the laws were not of Jim's making; whatever he had done, he was a respecter of convention, a keeper of the law of man. Julia had broken God's law, had repented, and had been forgiven. But she had also broken the law of man, for which no woman ever is forgiven. And though this exquisite and finished woman, with her well-stored brain and ripened mind, her position and her charm, was not the little Julia Page of the old O'Farrell Street days, she must pay the price of that other Julia's childish pride and ignorance still.

She must go on, listening, with her wise, wistful smile, to the chatter of other women, wincing at a thousand little pricks that even her husband could not see, winning him from his ugly moods with that mixture of the child and the woman that his love never could resist.

His love! After all he did love her and his children, and she loved the three with every fibre of heart and soul. Julia ended her reverie, as she always ended her reveries, with a new glow of hope in her heart and a half smile on her lips. Their love would save them all—love fulfilled the law.

"Julia!" said Jim, at the door, "where are you?"

She turned in her window recess.

"Not escaped, O Sultan!"

"Well"—he had his arm about her, his air was that of a humoured child—"I didn't suppose you had! But I hate you to go down without me!"

"Well, the poor abused boy!" Julia laughed. "Come, we'll go down together!"

"What were you thinking of, standing there all that time?" he asked.

"You principally, Doctor Studdiford!" Julia gave him a quick sidewise glance.

"Glad I came out to the Mission to fix the Daley kid's arm?" Jim asked.

"Glad!" said Julia softly, with a great sigh that belied her smile. They took each other's hands, like children, and went down the broad stairway together.

THE END

Milton Keynes UK
Ingram Content Group UK Ltd.
UKHW031924221024
2303UKWH00004B/340